Asian Religions, Technology and Science

Over the past five decades, the field of religion-and-science scholarship has experienced a considerable expansion. This volume explores the historical and contemporary perspectives of the relationship between religion, technology and science with a focus on South and East Asia. These three areas are not seen as monolithic entities, but as discursive fields embedded in dynamic processes of cultural exchange and transformation. Bridging these arenas of knowledge and practice traditionally seen as distinct and disconnected, *Asian Religions, Technology and Science* reflects on the ways of exploring the various dimensions of their interconnection.

Through its various chapters, the collection provides an examination of the use of modern scientific concepts in the theologies of new religious organizations, and challenges the traditional notions of space by Western scientific conceptions in the nineteenth century. It looks at the synthesis of ritual elements and medical treatment in China and India, and at new funeral practices in Japan. It discusses the intersections between contemporary Western Buddhism, modern technology, and global culture, and goes on to look at women's rights in contemporary Pakistani media. Using case studies grounded in carefully delineated temporal and regional frameworks, chapters are divided into two parts: Part I on religion and science, and Part II on religion and technology.

Illustrating the manifold perspectives and the potential for further research and discussion, this book is an important contribution to the studies of Asian Religion, Science and Technology, and Religion and Philosophy.

István Keul is Professor in the Study of Religions at the University of Bergen, Norway. His areas of research include various aspects of the history and sociology of South Asian religions. He is the author of a monograph on the Hindu deity Hanuman and has edited volumes on tantra, Yoginis and Banaras.

Routledge Studies in Asian Religion and Philosophy

1 **Deconstruction and the Ethical in Asian Thought**
Edited by Youru Wang

2 **An Introduction to Daoist Thought**
Action, language, and ethics in Zhuangzi
Eske Møllgaard

3 **Religious Commodifications in Asia**
Marketing gods
Edited by Pattana Kitiarsa

4 **Christianity and the State in Asia**
Complicity and conflict
Edited by Julius Bautista and Francis Khek Gee Lim

5 **Christianity in Contemporary China**
Socio-cultural perspectives
Edited by Francis Khek Gee Lim

6 **The Buddha and Religious Diversity**
J. Abraham Velez de Cea

7 **Japanese Religions and Globalization**
Ugo Dessi

8 **Religion and the Subtle Body in Asia and the West**
Between mind and body
Geoffrey Samuel and Jay Johnston

9 **'Yogini' in South Asia**
Interdisciplinary approaches
Edited by István Keul

10 **The Confucian Philosophy of Harmony**
Chenyang Li

11 **Postcolonial Resistance and Asian Theology**
Simon Shui-Man Kwa

12 **Asian Perspectives on Animal Ethics**
Edited by Neil Dalal and Chloe Taylor

13 **Objects of Worship in South Asian Religions**
Forms, practices and meanings
Edited by Knut A. Jacobsen, Mikael Aktor and Kristina Myrvold

14 **Disease, Religion and Healing in Asia**
Collaborations and collisions
Ivette Vargas-O'Bryan and Zhou Xun

15 **Asian Religions, Technology and Science**
Edited by István Keul

Asian Religions, Technology and Science

Edited by
István Keul

Routledge
Taylor & Francis Group
LONDON AND NEW YORK

First published 2015 by Routledge

2 Park Square, Milton Park, Abingdon, Oxfordshire OX14 4RN
711 Third Avenue, New York, NY 10017

Routledge is an imprint of the Taylor & Francis Group, an informa business

First issued in paperback 2018

Copyright © 2015 István Keul

The right of the editor to be identified as the author of the editorial
material, and of the authors for their individual chapters, has been asserted
in accordance with sections 77 and 78 of the Copyright, Designs and
Patents Act 1988.

All rights reserved. No part of this book may be reprinted or reproduced or
utilised in any form or by any electronic, mechanical, or other means, now
known or hereafter invented, including photocopying and recording, or in
any information storage or retrieval system, without permission in writing
from the publishers.

Notice:
Product or corporate names may be trademarks or registered trademarks,
and are used only for identification and explanation without intent to infringe.

British Library Cataloguing in Publication Data
A catalogue record for this book is available from the British Library

Library of Congress Cataloging in Publication Data
Asian religions, technology and science / edited by István Keul.
   pages cm. -- (Routledge Studies in Asian Religion and Philosophy ; 15)
Includes bibliographical references and index.
1. Religion and science--South Asia. 2. Religion and science--East Asia.
I. Keul, István, editor.
   BL240.3.A87 2015
   201'.65095--dc23
      2014029404

ISBN: 978-1-138-77966-2 (hbk)
ISBN: 978-1-138-31928-8 (pbk)

Typeset in Times New Roman
by Taylor & Francis Books

Contents

List of figures	vii
Contributors	viii
Acknowledgements	xi

Introduction: Asian religions, technology and science ISTVÁN KEUL	1

Part I
Asian religions and science   9

1	"True facts of the world": media of scientific space and the transformations of cosmo-geography in nineteenth-century Buddhist-Christian encounters ADRIAN HERMANN	11
2	An illusion of conciliation: religion and science in Debendranath and Rabindranath Tagore C. MACKENZIE BROWN	31
3	Vedic science, modern science and reason ANNA S. KING	54
4	Is the Earth round? Traditional cosmography and modern science in Jainism KNUT AUKLAND	74
5	On 'science' in 'The Science of Happiness': the Japanese new religious movement *Kōfuku no kagaku*, occult 'science' and 'spiritual technology' FRANZ WINTER	102

vi *Contents*

6 The synthesis of religious and medical healing rituals in the Song   122
PHILIP S. CHO

7 Medical treatments described in the ritual texts of Kerala:
interaction between religion and science   137
S. A. S. SARMA

Part II
Asian religions and technology   151

8 New technology and change in the Hindu tradition:
the Internet in historical perspective   153
HEINZ SCHEIFINGER

9 Japanese new religions and social networks: toward a
2.0 interactive religious discourse?   169
DANILO GIAMBRA

10 #Hashtag meditation, cyborg Buddhas, and enlightenment as
an epic win: Buddhism, technology, and the new social media   186
ANN GLEIG

11 The technology of tradition: Javed Ahmad Ghamidi and the
contemporary Pakistani media's participatory construction of
women's *shari'a*   204
DAVID A. DOSS

12 New technologies and new funeral practices in
contemporary Japan   227
FABIENNE DUTEIL-OGATA

13 Producing deities? Ritual as technology   245
ISTVÁN KEUL

Index   255

List of figures

4.1	The three Jain constructions in Hastinapur	82
4.2	*Jambūdvīpa* and Mount Meru	84
4.3	*Jambūdvīpa* boating	86
4.4	*Tīn lok racnā*	87
4.5	Southern part of *Jambūdvīpa*	88
9.1	Religious communication and the interaction between offline and online	170
9.2	Digital space semiotic triangulation	172
12.1	A memorial diamond displayed in the LifeGem Japan branch company, Tokyo	233
12.2	An Eternal Plate displayed in the Eternal Japan Company, Tokyo	235
12.3	Grave-computer in the Kôtoku Buddhist temple, Tokyo	238

Contributors

Knut Aukland studied Indian religions at the Universities of Oslo and Heidelberg, and Hindi and Indian history at Oxford University. His MPhil thesis on a possession cult in Jainism was awarded Best Norwegian Master's Thesis 2010 by *The Network for Asian Studies* in Oslo. Aukland received the Norway Scholarship in 2010 to complete a MSt on Indian colonial history at the University of Oxford, Wadham College. His ongoing PhD project at the University of Bergen is on the interface between pilgrimage and tourism practices in North India.

C. Mackenzie Brown is Professor of South Asian Religions and Religion and Science at Trinity University, San Antonio, Texas, USA. He is author of *Hindu Perspectives on Evolution: Darwin, Dharma, and Design* (2012). Recent articles include 'The Design Argument in Classical Hindu Thought,' *International Journal of Hindu Studies* 12:2 (2008); 'Vivekananda and the Scientific Legitimation of Advaita Vedānta,' in *Handbook on Religion and the Authority of Science*, edited by James R. Lewis and Olav Hammer (2011); 'Origins: The Hindu Case,' in *The Routledge Companion Reader to Religion and Science*, edited by James Haag *et al.* (2012).

Philip S. Cho is an Assistant Professor at Yonsei University, Underwood International College, Seoul. He draws on a background in cognitive neuroscience from the Massachusetts Institute of Technology and history and sociology of science from the University of Pennsylvania. His work spans historical, ethnographic, and scientific research on the role of cognition in Chinese science and popular religion. He is currently working on a book manuscript, *Cognition and Culture in Chinese Science, Technology, and Medicine.*

David A. Doss, a DAAD Scholar and a Fulbright Scholar, researched in Germany, Russia, and Morocco on the intersections of biopolitics, public health, and Abrahamic religious/ethical concepts. Since his MA, his research is expanding into international development and work related to facilitating peace and cooperation between religious communities in Asia and the Middle East.

Fabienne Duteil-Ogata is a researcher associated with the Institute of Interdisciplinary of Contemporary Anthropology at CNRS/EHESS in Paris. She obtained a Master's Degree in Japanese Language and Civilization from Paris VII University and a PhD in Anthropology from Paris X University in 2002. Her doctoral thesis focused on the impact of social changes in Japanese religious practices. Fabienne Duteil-Ogata was awarded the Shibusawa-Claudel Prize in 2004.

Danilo Giambra is a senior doctoral candidate at the University of Otago, New Zealand. His main fields of interest include the mediation and mediatization of religion through the Internet, the study of religious persona and charismatic leaders, and the analysis of the development of official religious communicative strategies by religious organizations. He has taught papers on New Religious Movements, and Religion and the Internet, and he is presently completing his dissertation on Japanese New Religions Online Communication, focusing on the religious organizations Tenrikyō and Seichō no Ie as case studies.

Ann Gleig is an Assistant Professor of Religious and Cultural Studies at the University of Central Florida, Orlando, USA. Her main research areas are Buddhism and Hinduism in the West, and religion and psychology. She has published on topics such as the dialogue between Buddhism and psychotherapy, Queer Buddhists, and integrating insider and outsider perspectives in the academic study of religion. She has a co-edited collection called *Homegrown Gurus: From Hinduism in America to American Hinduism* (SUNY Press, 2013) and is currently working on a monograph on the American assimilation of Asian enlightenment discourses.

Adrian Hermann received a doctorate in the Scientific Study of Religion from the University of Basel in 2011 with a dissertation on the globalization of the category of 'religion'. In 2014/15 he is a Visiting Scholar in the Department of Philosophy and Religious Studies, Utrecht University, and the Department of Anthropology, Stanford University, USA. His research interests include Method and Theory in the Study of Religion, Buddhist Modernism, Non-Western Christianity, and Religion and Documentary Film.

István Keul is Professor in the Study of Religions at the University of Bergen, Norway. His areas of research include various aspects of the history and the sociology of South Asian religions. He is presently engaged in the study of complex rituals and in comparative work on modern religious movements in South and East Asia.

Anna S. King is a Reader in Theology and Religious Studies at the University of Winchester, and is attached to the Winchester University Centre of Religions for Reconciliation and Peace. She trained as a social anthropologist at the Institute of Social and Cultural Anthropology, Oxford. She x *Contributors*

is Convenor of the annual Spalding Symposium on Indian Religions, and founder and joint editor of *Religions of South Asia* (*RoSA*). Her research interests initially focused on patterns of pilgrimage in North India and the Kumbha Mela, and she has a long-standing interest in ISKCON. Her recent articles include studies of death and dying, animal theology and *prasadam*.

S.A.S. Sarma has been a researcher at the Pondicherry Centre of the Ecole française d'Extrême-Orient (EFEO) since 1989. After completing his post-graduate in Sanskrit from the University of Kerala, he joined the Adyar Library and Research Centre as a research scholar where he worked under Professor K. Kunjunni Raja and Professor K.V. Sarma on various indological projects. He did his PhD at the University of Calicut under the guidance of Professor N.V.P. Unithiri. He is presently engaged in various projects at the EFEO, some of which concentrate on the edition of Shaiva texts.

Heinz Scheifinger was a Post-doctoral Fellow at the University of Aberdeen, Scotland, and at the Asia Research Institute, National University of Singapore. He is currently a Lecturer in Sociology-Anthropology at the University of Brunei Darussalam. He researches digital religion (especially regarding religious traditions originating in the Indian sub-continent) and has spent time (2012–13) as a Visiting Scholar at the Singapore Internet Research Centre at Nanyang Technological University.

Franz Winter received PhDs in Classical Studies (1999) and Religious Studies (2005) from the University of Vienna, and a Habilitation in Religious Studies (2010) from the same university. He is currently Dozent at the Institute for Religious Studies in Vienna and works as a research associate at the Austrian *Bundesstelle für Sektenfragen*. Among his major areas of interest are the history of contact between Europe and Asia from antiquity to modern times, new religious movements in East and West, and the history of Buddhism.

Acknowledgements

Even though the present collection is not, strictly speaking, a conference volume, it originated in an International Association for the History of Religions (IAHR) special conference entitled 'Religion, Science and Technology in Cultural Contexts: Dynamics of Change', organized by the Department of Archaeology and Religious Studies at the Norwegian University of Science and Technology (NTNU, Trondheim) in March 2012. I would like to thank the Department and NTNU's Faculty of Humanities for generously financing the event. My colleagues in the organizing committee, Ulrika Mårtensson and Filip Ivanovic, agreed to have the contributions on South and East Asia published separately. The chapters by Anna King, S.A.S. Sarma, Danilo Giambra and myself are extended versions of the conference presentations. Adrian Hermann and David Doss, who had previously sent in abstracts but were eventually not able to participate in the conference also submitted chapters. As the papers presented by Donald Lopez, John Schultz, Erica Baffelli, and Frank Neubert could not be included in this volume for various reasons, other specialists were invited to contribute. The inclusion of essays by Knut Aukland, C. Mackenzie Brown, Philip Cho, Fabienne Duteil-Ogata, Anne Gleig, Heinz Scheifinger, and Franz Winter are the result of this invitation. I thank all the scholars mentioned above for their cooperation in the different stages of this project. I am also grateful to the two anonymous reviewers for their comments and to Rebecca Lawrence and Sabrina Lacey at Routledge for their support and patience during the publication process.

Introduction

Asian religions, technology and science

István Keul

Over the past five decades,[1] the field of religion-and-science scholarship has experienced a considerable expansion, generating a vast amount of literature. Major historical developments and central themes of past and current debates have been mapped and addressed, for example, in *The Oxford Handbook of Religion and Science* (Clayton 2006), *The Cambridge Companion to Religion and Science* (Harrison 2010) and, most recently, in *The Routledge Companion to Religion and Science* (Haag *et al.* 2014).[2] The many well-written chapters of these works illustrate at the same time the difficulties in the treatment of topics that engage with areas as vast as religion and science, with truth claims and norms that have universal scope. Focusing on scientific, theological, ethical questions and contents, the contributions often do not seem to pay sufficient attention to cultural contexts.[3] In addition, the majority of chapters are written about or from within Western religious and philosophical discourses, with the *Routledge Companion* including a number of essays that engage more thoroughly with non-Christian traditions and perspectives.[4] The present volume intends to contribute to these perspectives by focusing on South Asia and East Asia-related, culturally contextualized religion-and-science as well as religion-and-technology topics.[5]

The range of themes explored in the volume is necessarily limited and selective, with case studies grounded in carefully delineated temporal and regional frameworks. For the sake of convenience, the contributions are divided into two Parts, Part I on religion and science, and Part II on religion and technology, even though in some cases all three areas are linked. Part I is a collection of chapters that focus on the relationship between scientific and religious world models, on the concept of science in a new religious movement, and on religion and medicine. The cases discussed in these chapters will contribute to a further rethinking and refining of the taxonomy of religion-and-science relations, as well as material and methodological issues.[6] Part II comprises case studies that add to the existing literature on those new forms of religious mediation/mediatization, communication platforms, and strategies of representation that are part of the so-called 'media turn' in the study of religions. One of the remaining chapters looks at the ways in which modern technologies transform funeral practices in Japan (Chapter 12), while

2 *István Keul*

Chapter 13 reconceptualizes a ritual consecration of a Hindu temple image as a sociotechnical event.

A number of chapters in the present volume include reflections on scientific and religious cosmologies in Buddhism, Jainism, and Hinduism. The study of cultural cosmologies, their history and transformations includes instances in which the juxtaposition of differing world models flagged as scientific or religious generate complex dynamics with considerable repercussions. The modalities of encounter between such models range from dialogue to confrontation and conflict, and the consequences from the rejection of scientific models to the replacing of traditional notions. A possible outcome is the formation of hybrid knowledge, as in one of the cases discussed in Adrian Hermann's contribution (Chapter 1), that looks at the ways in which Buddhist elites in Siam react to the transfer of scientific knowledge ("true facts of the world") by repositioning core elements of the tradition within modern scientific contexts. Here, and in other encounters, the Christian missionaries' strategy of delegitimizing Buddhism and winning new adepts is crowned by little success: Even though the Mount Meru cosmology is recognized as untenable when confronted with the evidence of Western geography and astronomy, the Buddha's sermon to his mother in the Davadungsa heaven may still have taken place on one of the planets of the new system. The claim that science and Buddhism are compatible to a certain extent becomes thus one of the leitmotifs of Buddhist modernist thought in the nineteenth century. In another exchange between monks and missionaries, this time in Ceylon, the Buddhist side argues for the existence of Mount Meru (Mahameru) and questions the validity of Newtonian science and the accuracy of globes, maps and astronomical models. Hermann analyzes the role of such devices ("the media of scientific space") in the processes of knowledge transfer and transformation in nineteenth-century Buddhist Asia. In the discussion, the author draws on Bruno Latour's concept of the 'immutable mobile' and his claim that a successful knowledge transfer is dependent both on these visual representations and on extended networks that ensure the transmission and circulation of scientific facts.

The context of C. Mackenzie Brown's article (Chapter 2) is the religion-and-science discourse in colonial India, and the cosmological writings of the Nobel Laureate writer Rabindranath Tagore and of his father, Debendranath Tagore, who was active in the reformist movement, Brahmo Samaj. Both Tagores authored poetic cosmologies, in an apparent attempt to reconcile religious ideas with certain elements of scientific knowledge. Debendranath Tagore uses cosmogonic motifs from the Upanishads, with allusions to biblical themes, and combines them with nineteenth-century geological theories on melting and cooling, vapour condensation, and the beginning of vegetation, arguing for the existence of a providential creator. Reinterpreting the classical Upanishadic conceptions of higher and lower knowledge, Debendranath establishes a hierarchy of the lower (natural) sciences and the science he views as the highest, "namely the knowledge of God from all these sciences". Rabindranath's approach, on the other hand, is described as a teleological or

Introduction 3

creative evolutionism, with the postulation of an inherent vital, creative impulse that combines Henry Bergson's *élan vital* with the Upanishadic notion of 'life-force' (*prāṇa*). As Mackenzie Brown shows, Rabindranath Tagore's evolutionist model is not only orthogenetic-vitalistic, but also theistic, with a consciousness-endowed creative force. Contrary to the results of earlier analyses, Rabindranath's approach is described not as a conciliation of religion and science, but as one of the anti-Darwinian evolutionary speculations of the early 1900s. The world-views of both Tagores, Brown argues, have to be seen in the context of Western philosophical developments, to which they are indebted.

Knut Aukland's contribution (Chapter 4) on the engagement of Jainism with science includes a description of the North Indian Digambar pilgrimage site Jambudweep where, in addition to academic and ritual activities, recreation plays a major role. Models depicting elements of traditional Jain cosmography serve both educational and entertainment purposes. Believers can learn about their tradition, but also enjoy themselves by climbing to the top of the *axis mundi* of the Jain cosmos, or ride on a boat around it. They can also circumambulate the island Jambudvipa on an elephant, or take an elevator to Siddhasila, the realm of the siddhas, the liberated souls located on top of the Jain universe. Even though the models at the site include a modern-day depiction of the continents, the founder and other officials at the site stress the authority of the Jain scriptures. Aukland argues that Jainism's present-day engagement with academia and modern science has its effects and generates different strategies. Those who view the Jain teachings as correct search for their confirmation, resorting to modern scientific knowledge. Others base their inquiries on the correctness of the scientific model and interpret elements in the teachings as compatible with modern science. In both cases, traditional cosmography is situated in new contexts. In Jambudweep, the religious teachings are presented as superior to modern science. At the same time, the site also proclaims itself a research institute that – through lectures and seminars – investigates traditional Jain cosmography academically.

While the Jain debate over modern science and religion appears to be plurivocal to a certain extent, the religious organization discussed by Anna S. King in Chapter 3, ISKCON, classifies its teachings as unequivocally scientific, asserting at the same time that true scientific knowledge can only be based on religion. The first stage in the organization's engagement with modern science was shaped by the teachings of ISKCON's founder, Prabhupada, who considered Vedic civilization far superior to modernity and classified all Vedic knowledge as 'science'. In a second stage, aiming at decolonizing knowledge of what they see as Western, Jewish-Christian influences, 'ISKCON scientists' challenged and dismissed the results of archaeological, paleontological and historical research. Today, ISKCON cosmology and science continue to be promoted on websites with articles on a wide range of topics and with numerous links to the works of the founder and of the 'Vedic scientists'. As King remarks, ISKCON's cause is aided by the spread of Creationism and

4   *István Keul*

the Intelligent Design Movement, with occasional collaborations of devotee academics with proponents of Intelligent Design. Among the most prominent and vehement critiques of Vedic Science are Meera Nanda and Martha Nussbaum, who argue that it promotes and legitimates a Hindu nationalist ideology.

The volume's contributions relate and explore the fields of religion and science in various ways. Franz Winter's article (Chapter 5) on the Japanese new religious movement *Kōfuku no kagaku* (literally: 'The Science of Happiness', founded in 1986) looks at the background and the specific use of the concept of 'science' in the movement's teachings. Influences and connections can be traced back to the 'spiritualist' ideas and movements that became popular in Japan from the end of the nineteenth century onwards, as well as to the reception of theosophical thought. Another aspect that plays a role for the use of 'science' in the movement's designation was the initial idea of forming an institute instead of a religious organization. Even after being officially registered in 1991 as a 'religious corporation', the group has used an academic terminology in its educational activities. However, in the course of some major shifts in the development of the movement, the study aspect decreased in importance. In newer publications, and in the members' perception, the 'science of happiness' refers to the basic teachings of the movement called the four 'principles of happiness' (love, wisdom, self-reflection, and progress), presented as a modified version of the Buddhist four noble truths. Winter points to a number of other 'scientific' elements in the movement's publications and films, such as the founder's interest in the history of mankind, as well as the concept of 'spiritual technology', meaning the ability to design technical devices through which one can communicate with the 'spirit world'. Some of the other aspects that are relevant for the very specific connections to 'science' and 'research' are the theories about 'lost continents' and 'ancient astronauts' that often appear in the movement's publications.

The two remaining chapters in Part I deal with religion (Daoism and Hinduism) and medicine. In Chapter 6, Philip S. Cho discusses the measures taken by the Song government in the twelfth century to standardize popular religion in the empire, assimilate local deities into a new cosmological and ritual order, and synthesize ritual healing techniques and medical healing. One way of introducing popular religious healing techniques into classical medicine was by reinterpreting the concept of *zhuyou* from a ritual prayer against illness into a complex of incantations and movements meant to transform the circulation of *qi* in the body. Healing rituals and exorcism were thus incorporated into the medical system by a somatization of possession. S.A.S. Sarma's contribution (Chapter 7) begins by pointing to the importance given by the religious texts of various Vedic traditions to health and the treatment of illness. On the other hand, medical texts of the Āyurveda include prescriptions regarding the use of mantras and rituals in treatments. Looking primarily at ritual literature, the author discusses early Śaiva tantric texts in which ritual healing was often complemented by medicinal cures. Some of the manuals were subdivided into one part to deal with mantras, and another with medicine. A number of ritual texts produced in Kerala deal extensively with medical treatments, illustrated by examples of prescriptions in connection with snakebite and poisoning. The treatment of infertility, fever and childhood diseases are further topics in these texts.

The three first chapters in Part II deal with the significance and use of the Internet in various religious contexts. In Chapter 8 on the impact of the Internet on Hinduism, Heinz Scheifinger looks from a historical perspective at the ways in which the use of new communication technologies has brought about processes of transformation on different levels. Among the developments generated by the successive introduction of the printing press, chromolithographic technology, film and television, were homogenization, omnipraxy, the formation of transnational guru organizations, but also standardization and the disembedding of local deities and religious figures. According to the author, the Internet amplifies the effects of earlier new technologies, adding new implications. Among the most important examples are the altering of worship forms (standardized online worship), the status change of religious figures due to online mediatization, as well as the propagation of nationalist ideas.

Danilo Giambra discusses in Chapter 9 the increasing use of online social platforms by new religions in Japan. Communication in social networks occurs on various levels: on an individual, group and organization level. This three-tiered communication can be observed also in the religious movements studied, Tenrikyō and Seichō no Ie. Among the various social networks used by these movements, the global platform Facebook is described as the one that suits the needs of organizations with an international outreach, while regional networks such as the Japanese social platform Mixi and the religious social network PostingJoy offer a framework that is culturally more homogenous. The chapter concludes that Japanese new religions using social networks will continue to establish their presence via multiple social platforms, increasing in this way their visibility, communicating with members in various locations, and adapting their communicative strategies according to their immediate needs.

In her contribution on the Buddhist Geeks network, Chapter 10, Ann Gleig focuses on an online media community from Boulder, Colorado, launched in 2007 initially as a podcast with the aim of exploring how contemporary Buddhism is transformed through new social media. Earlier studies on Buddhism and the new technologies, on the various types of e-mail discussion lists, 'cybersanghas', and other online Buddhist resources reveal different attitudes, which the author describes as ranging from "suspicious reservation to an enthusiastic embrace", with the Buddhist Geeks network "firmly situated in the celebratory camp". Continuing a tradition that began in the nineteenth century and that presents Buddhism as a religion compatible with science, this community updates this scientific lineage by using technological concepts in connection with central elements of the Buddhist doctrine

6 *István Keul*

(*vipassana* meditation is described as form of 'mind-hacking'). Gleig explores the ways in which the Buddhist Geeks community seeks to refashion the use of social media through the application of Buddhist principles into a contemplative activity ('#hashtag meditation'), as well as how – in addition to promoting classical Buddhist practices – the community experiments with innovative forms and devices.

Writing about the Pakistani public Islamic theologian Javed Ahmad Ghamidi and his use of modern media and social networks, in Chapter 11, David Doss points out that Ghamidi's strategy of combining ideology with technology is based on "a unified vision fusing the informative with the performative". The informative aspect is characterized as having the function of preserving religious networks through the transmission of information, while the performative expresses and transforms religious information. In Ghamidi's approach, the Islamic religious tradition is combined with a distinct methodology based on analysis and interpretation ('a double hermeneutic') of Quranic texts, as well as with the application of media and social network technology. Initiator of a foundation for Islamic research and education and organizer of seminars and courses on Islam, Ghamidi is a regular guest on various television channels. He also creates online lectures and publications, websites and social network pages, reaching a large audience of middle-class, educated men and women, and lay Islamic intellectuals in Pakistan and worldwide. Doss shows how Ghamidi applies this encompassing strategy (described as non-political, and media- and education-based) while addressing his audience on the relationship between *shari'a* ethics and womens' rights issues.

In Chapter 12, on the role of new technologies in funeral practices in Japan, Fabienne Duteil-Ogata outlines a historical overview of traditional Japanese practices, before looking at two 'technological revolutions' that are closely connected. The first of these new technologies is the high-temperature cremation, introduced at the end of the 1980s, in the course of which the whole body is pulverized, offering thus the possibility of creating new types of funerary objects. The author discusses two types of such objects: memorial diamonds, made exclusively of the deceased's ashes in a lengthy and complex technological process, and so-called hybrid cinerary objects, that are less expensive and involve mixing the ashes with metal-based substances and creating ceramic plates and pendants. The second new technology with regard to new funeral practices in Japan is based on the disappearance of all DNA in the high-temperature cremation process and the 'recreation' of the deceased's identity through 'grave-computers' and 'online graves'. Duteil-Ogata shows how these technologies contribute significantly to changing religious practices by shifting the focus from family units and rules of affiliation to an individualization of the relationship between the living and the dead. Through the orientation of memorial practices towards the living, ancestor rituals recede into the background. The new funeral, cinerary, and memorial procedures offer viable alternatives and challenge traditional religious frameworks.

Introduction 7

In the final chapter of the collection, I propose to reconceptualize ritual combining theoretical approaches from ritual studies and the anthropology of technology, using one ethnographical instance of ritual – a consecration of an image of the Hindu deity Hanumān in the North Indian city of Vārāṇasī – and attempting to 'translate' it as a 'sociotechnical event'. The chapter begins with a more general inquiry into the connections between technology and ritual, and the associations between these two areas in some classical works of anthropology. It then looks at the complex issue of ritual efficacy and discusses briefly some of the more important Sanskrit analogues to 'ritual'. After an outline of the sociotechnical system concept, various sequences of the event are succinctly described, followed by a brief assessment of the consecration as a sociotechnical event.

Notes

1 *Zygon: Journal of Religion and Science* was founded in 1966, and in the same year Ian Barbour published *Issues in Science and Religion* (Englewood Cliffs, NJ: Prentice Hall, 1966).
2 Another recent publication is Dixon, Cantor and Pumfrey (2010), with contributions, among other themes, on categories (Harisson, Golinski) and historical perspectives and patterns (Numbers, Efron).
3 As Willem Drees, the current editor of *Zygon*, points out:

> Theology, ethics and science have universal ambitions; their truth claims and norms seek to be valid for people of all walks of life and all cultures. While their ambitions are lofty, religion and science are human, contexts and assumptions shape the questions asked, the criteria used, the content proposed.
>
> (2010: 1)

4 See the articles by Larson, Raman, Goodman, Payne, Kaplan, Chapple, Mackenzie Brown, Findly, and Gold, in *The Routledge Companion to Religion and Science* (Haag *et al.* 2014).
5 For an excellent discussion of central issues and recent developments in religion-and-technology, see Stolow (2013: 1–22), who also points out the problems posed by the "assumed normativity – if not universality – of the Western Christian experience … for the integration of studies dealing with the conceptualization, reception, and use of technologies in non-Western and non-Christian religious contexts" (ibid.: 19). An example of a more recent publication on the relationship between technology and religion in an Asian context is Lim (2009). However, the collection's essays deal primarily with Southeast Asia.
6 The four general types proposed by Ian Barbour (1990) conflict, independence, dialogue, and integration, have been complemented and diversified in later years, among others, by Stenmark (2004) and Russell (2008). See Shults (2014: 7–9).

References

Barbour, I. (1966) *Issues in Science and Religion*. Englewood Cliffs, NJ: Prentice Hall.
Barbour, I. (1990) *Religion in an Age of Science*. San Francisco, CA: HarperCollins.

8 *István Keul*

Clayton, P. (ed.) (2006) *The Oxford Handbook of Religion and Science*. Oxford: Oxford University Press.

Dixon, T., Cantor, G. and Pumfrey, S. (eds) (2010) *Science and Religion: New Historical Perspectives*. Cambridge: Cambridge University Press.

Drees, W.B. (2010) *Religion and Science in Context: A Guide to the Debates*. London: Routledge.

Haag, J.W., Peterson, G.R. and Spezio, M.L. (eds) (2014) *The Routledge Companion to Religion and Science*. London: Routledge.

Harrison, P. (ed.) (2010) *The Cambridge Companion to Religion and Science*. Cambridge: Cambridge University Press.

Lim, F.K.G. (2009) *Mediating Piety: Technology and Religion in Contemporary Asia*. Leiden: Brill.

Russell, R.J. (2008) *Cosmology: From Alpha to Omega*. Minneapolis, MN: Fortress Press.

Shults, F.L. (2014) 'Religion and Science in Christian Theology', in J.W. Haag, G.R. Peterson, and M.L. Spezio (eds) *The Routledge Companion to Religion and Science*. London: Routledge, pp. 3–12.

Stenmark, M. (2004) *How to Relate Science and Religion: A Multidimensional Model*. Grand Rapids, MI: Eerdmans.

Stolow, J. (ed.) (2013) *Deus in Machina: Religion, Technology, and the Things in Between*. New York: Fordham University Press.

Part I
Asian religions and science

1 "True facts of the world"

Media of scientific space and the transformations of cosmo-geography in nineteenth-century Buddhist-Christian encounters*

Adrian Hermann

Introduction

In a letter to John Bowring, the Governor of Hong Kong, written in 1855, the Siamese King Rama IV (Mongkut) critically commented on a report which a seventeenth-century Siamese diplomatic mission to the king of France had brought back from its journey. This report, according to Mongkut, is "very exaggerated from the facts of truth, and opposed to geographical knowledges [*sic*] which we know now to be true facts of the world" (quoted in Bowring 1857: 445). The letter, which goes on to request "a book relating the detail of the visit of Siamese Ambashy [*sic*] to France" to supplement the Siamese report, provides an insight into the mentality of Siamese elite in the middle of the nineteenth century, many of whom had accepted Western geographical learning as a form of knowledge no longer to be challenged by indigenous knowledge traditions. Western notions of geographical and astronomic space had, at least among the elite, replaced traditional Buddhist cosmo-geography and a conception of the universe centered on Mount Meru.

It is the aim of this chapter to analyze the role of what I will call 'media of scientific space' in this transformation of the cosmo-geographical imagination in nineteenth-century Theravada-Buddhist Modernism. Christian missionaries used these instruments and devices – maps, globes, compasses, and astronomical models – in their debates with Buddhists all over Asia and deemed them essential to their challenge to traditional notions of space. In exploring the missionaries' fascination with these devices and in order to analyze their impact on nineteenth-century Buddhist Asia, I start with the premise that concepts of space are always intimately linked to the media through which they are conveyed. While this is valid for all cosmo-geographical notions, the focus of this chapter will be on devices that lay claim to being illustrative of *scientific* conceptions of space. In trying to characterize these further, I will draw on Bruno Latour's concept of the *immutable mobile* to explore the way in which the 'true facts' of modern geography and astronomy traveled to Siam and Ceylon in the nineteenth century.

12 *Adrian Hermann*

In what follows, I will first present the theoretical perspective of this chapter in a more detailed fashion while discussing an early example of the encounter between Buddhists and Christians in Ceylon in the 1820s. Then I will illustrate the importance of the media of scientific space in the context of Buddhist Modernism in nineteenth-century Siam, while the third section will present a Latourian perspective on a later stage of the Buddhist-Christian encounter in Ceylon, namely, the public debates culminating at Panadura in the 1870s.

Transformations of cosmo-geographical space in nineteenth-century Theravada-Buddhist Modernism and the early Buddhist-Christian encounter in Ceylon

In classical Indian and Buddhist cosmo-geography, in which the world-system is imagined as a flat disk, Mount Meru is considered to be the center of the world, encircled by seven concentric rings of mountains and oceans. These are surrounded by an additional saltwater ocean in which four continents are located in the four cardinal directions, and which is circumscribed by an outer ring of iron mountains. The southern continent Jambudvipa is populated by humans (and animals). The different hells, inhabited by ghosts (*peta*), anti-gods (*asura*) and hell beings (*naraka*), are located below these four continents. Along the slopes of Mount Meru and above it, the six heavenly realms in which the gods (*devas*) dwell are situated. These 11 realms (of hell beings, anti-gods, ghosts, animals, humans, gods) make up the world of the senses (*kamadhatu*), beyond which the 16 realms of form (*rupadhatu*) and the four formless realms (*arupadhatu*) can be found. Measurements and distances in this cosmology are given in *yojana*, which the secondary literature interprets in various ways (7 km following Sadakata 1997: 25). Meru rises 80,000 *yojanas*, that is 560,000 km, above the water. The diameter of the entire world-disk is given as 1,203,450 *yojanas* (ibid.: 25–30). The Sun and the Moon circle around Mount Meru inside of a ring of wind, which is located exactly in the middle between the surface of the ocean and the top of the mountain and which also contains the stars (ibid.: 38–9).

In his study of Pali-Buddhist concepts of nirvana, Steven Collins (1998) considers this cosmo-geography a central part of what he calls the 'Pali-Imaginaire'. In his view, this extraordinarily stable "mental universe created by and within Pali texts" (ibid.: 41) was held together by the common language as well as the world contained within the Pali texts, giving rise to a relatively stable world-view in the different regions of the Pali-Buddhist ecumene (ibid.: 51, 63–4). Dividing Pali-Buddhist history into three periods, he describes early Buddhism as the period between the Buddha's time and the reign of Asoka (268–39 BCE), traditional Buddhism as lasting from the third century BCE to the end of the eighteenth century, and the modern period as beginning in the nineteenth century. The latter is mainly characterized by the fact that Pali has ceased to be the central linguistic and textual medium for Buddhism.

Additionally, however, he describes it as follows: "[O]ne might say it is the period of modernist Buddhism, in which the self-definition of the tradition has come to include, as an intrinsic component, the reaction to western colonialism and science" (ibid.: 54). Drawing on the example of Buddhist Modernism in nineteenth-century Thailand, Collins claims that as a result of these encounters, "something very definite has changed" (ibid.: 63), especially in regard to the "cosmo-geography" (ibid.: 301) centered on Mount Meru. These transformations as an important aspect of Buddhist Modernism and a central part of the "discourse of scientific Buddhism" (McMahan 2004) are the topic of this chapter.

In 1826, the Church Missionary Society's *The Missionary Register* printed a letter written by the Methodist missionary Benjamin Clough (1791–1853) in Colombo (Ceylon) on November 5th, 1825, to which it gave the heading 'The Faith of a Buddhist Priest Shaken'.[1] In this letter Clough relates a discussion with a learned Buddhist abbot lasting several hours. When asked if the Buddha should be considered omniscient and therefore "all which he has said and caused to be recorded" should be regarded as infallible, the monk answers in the positive. Clough questions this omniscience:

> Then, may I ask how it happened that your god should, in the course of his orations and religious revelations, have given to the world so erroneous a view of the geography of the world? – a system, which was not only false at the very time that it was delivered by him, but one that has kept his adherents in error to the present day.

The abbot answers that this is impossible, which leads Clough to claim that he can prove the Buddhist geography to be false. The monk protests and tells him that no mortal can dispute the word of a deity. Clough responds: "[I]f a divinity, or pretended divinity, makes a revelation that contradicts my experience and daily matter of fact, have I not just cause to call in question such a revelation?" When the monk acknowledges this, Clough tells him that he can prove that "the orations and revelations of Buddhu, as given in the Jatakas" are not to be trusted. The rest of Clough's report is as follows:

> I produced some maps, a globe, a quadrant, and a compass; and proceeded to give him as correct an outline of our geography, navigation, &c., as I could: and showed him, by a variety of experiments, which he readily understood, how we must, in the nature of things, understand this matter. "And now," said I, "not a day passes but we make fresh discoveries that Buddhu mistook. He represents the world as a vast plane. Now," said I, "on this principle, if a ship leave a port, and for two years together continue to sail at such a rate in a direct westerly course, then at the end of that two years she must be so many thousand miles from the place she left." "Certainly," said he. "But," said I, "our ships have often tried this; and, at the end of two years, instead of finding themselves many thousand

14   *Adrian Hermann*

miles from the place they left, they have found themselves in the port from which they sailed." Having a globe before me, I now explained the matter, and he immediately apprehended it. "Besides," said I, "here is this quadrant, and this compass, by which instruments we find our way to every part of the world. And I can assure you, that Buddhu has referred to oceans, to continents, to islands, and empires, and people, which never had an existence! Besides," I added, "he pretends to have described the whole world." And here I handed him a list of all the places mentioned in their books, as well known by him; and, showing him a map of the world, said, "This list of yours does not include one quarter of the world." By this time the Priest was in a pitiable state: his face, though a native, turned pale – his lips quivered – and his whole frame was agitated. When he recovered, he excused himself, and apologised for his agitations, and said, "Sir, I have heard with amazement these things. I see the truth of what you state on these points; but how are we situated in other respects?" "Well," said I, "your astronomy, your history, and in fact, the whole system of your theology, are precisely in the same state. It is all error!" With great emotion he now rose, took me by the hand, shook it in the most hearty manner, and said he never could have expected such discoveries to be made to him; thanked me much for the time that I had spent with him, and begged me to become his spiritual instructor.

It might be fruitless to try to read this account written by a Methodist missionary in nineteenth-century Ceylon as an accurate report on if and how this meeting took place and which positions the Buddhist monk actually defended in the conversation. Nevertheless, the letter illustrates two important aspects of nineteenth-century Christian-Buddhist encounters: on the one hand it reveals much about the aspirations of Christian missionaries in the nineteenth century and their attitude towards the scientific knowledge of the time, especially in the areas of astronomy and geography. In that respect, this report relates – as we will see – a typical example of a widespread nineteenth-century missionary strategy, which was based on the conviction that the whole Buddhist system would fall apart as soon as its cosmological basis were shattered. This collapse of the Buddhist world-view was also seen as the necessary first step for a later acceptance of Christianity. The use of scientific knowledge in an attempt at a de-legitimation of Buddhist ideas and as a preparation for conversion was highly popular and played an important role in the controversies between Christians and Buddhists in Ceylon and elsewhere (Young and Somaratna 1996: 69–70; Lopez 2008: 53–7). On the other hand, and intimately linked with this first aspect, the text indicates the central importance of controversial debates about spatial concepts and ideas linked to traditional Buddhist cosmology. As can be gleaned from Clough's letter, Western actors often relied on the argumentative evidence of modern media of space such as the map and the globe in their challenging of traditional Buddhist cosmo-geography.

The term 'media of space' is used here with reference to the work of Hermann Doetsch (2004), Tristan Thielmann (2007, 2010) and Jörg Dünne (2008, 2011). It refers to the idea that spatiality and mediality are intimately linked, and "that every mediatic dispositive produces a specifically structured space. Stages in the history of space are therefore also stages in the history of media" (Doetsch 2004: 73).[2] This idea makes it possible to ask "which spaces can possibly be constituted through which media at a particular historical point in time?" (Dünne 2008: 49).[3] While any medium – e.g. a text or an image – can thus be understood as a medium of space, this chapter will focus on a specific range of *scientific* media of space, which claim to be conveying scientific knowledge as well as to be faithfully representing geographical, physical spatial conditions. Such scientific media of space – like the modern map, for example – are understood as the historical condition of possibility for distinctly modern notions of space (Dünne 2008, 2011).

By focusing on the fundamental aspect of mediality in the constitution of spatial notions, space can be conceptualized in a perspective that is neither purely social constructivist nor geo-deterministic. Instead, the varying relationships between notions of space and different media can be taken into account and the conditions of possibility linked to specific media of space such as, for example, modern cartography can be analyzed. On the one hand, through the establishment of a relationship between mediatic representations and concrete locations, such media of space play an important role in naturalizing specific understandings of space. On the other hand, they make diverse spaces of possibility imaginable (Dünne 2011: 44) and can therefore be understood as 'matrixes of imagination' (Dünne 2008).

However, rather than being understood purely as a mental capacity or as being grounded in 'the imaginary' in a Lacanian sense, imagination as understood from the perspective of media theory "only realizes itself in a mediatically based semioticity and thus stands between a purely mental interiority and the technicity of external images" (Dünne 2011: 52).[4] The geographical imagination (Gregory 1994) linked to different media of space points to those notions of space which are imaginable in the context of a certain order of knowledge at a specific point in time (Dünne 2008: 50). Far from reducing imagination to a mediatic *a priori*, it is the articulation of notions of space in specific media of space that make them available for analysis. Notions of space therefore emerge in an interplay between media of space and the imagination, both of which not only contribute to their various transformations, but make their emergence possible in the first place (Dünne 2011: 47).

In regard to cosmo-geographical notions of space, media of space can be considered even more important, since this space is never experienced directly through sensory perception, but always only conveyed and imagined through media, be they traditional or scientific. Therefore, novel and modern media of space like the modern map and the globe unsurprisingly played a decisive role in challenging the traditional Buddhist cosmo-geography centered around Mount Meru not only in Ceylon, but also in other Buddhist contexts.

16 *Adrian Hermann*

Maps and globes: Buddhist Modernism in nineteenth-century Siam and the media of scientific space

Beginning in the 1830s, Siam experienced a transformation of notions of cosmo-geographical space that was mostly the result of contacts that different members of the political and monastic elites established with representatives of Western powers and especially the Protestant missionaries who had newly arrived in the country (Terwiel 1986; Aphornsuvan 2009). In this process, the engagement with the claims of a new geographical knowledge and the confrontation with modern media of scientific space turned out to be crucial. Moreover, as Thongchai Winichakul (1994) has shown in an influential study, Siam's national territory was constituted as the 'geo-body of a nation' over the course of the nineteenth century, not least with the help of Western geography and modern technologies of mapping. At the same time, a large number of scientific devices found a highly interested audience among the monks and local elites and contributed to new understandings of cosmo-geographical space.

Until the middle of the nineteenth century, spatial notions in Siam were dominated by the Mount Meru cosmology sketched above. After 1830, these were challenged not only by the representatives of Western powers and Christian missionaries, but by the Siamese political and monastic elites themselves. The monk and future King Mongkut (1804–68, r. 1851–68) emerged as the leader of a small group of Buddhist intellectuals who engaged closely with Western knowledge and technical inventions. Mongkut – who early on was close to the Catholic missionary Jean-Baptiste Pallegoix (1805–62) as well as the Protestants Jesse Caswell (1809–48) and Dan Beach Bradley (1804–73) – also founded the Thammayut Nikaya, a modernist reform order in Siamese Buddhism, and was one of the central actors in this reception of Western learning and its media by the Siamese elite.

Karl Gützlaff (1803–51), one of the first Protestant missionaries in the country, met Mongkut, who already spoke English, in 1831 and refers to him as a "decided friend of European sciences" (Gützlaff 2001: 67). The missionary J.T. Jones (1802–51) writes in 1836: "[H]e has an eighteen inch celestial globe, respecting which I had previously given him considerable information. He seems tolerably well to understand the Copernican system of astronomy as to its most important facts, and to believe it" (Jones 1836: 233). Jones also expects that this interest in Western knowledge "must affect his religious beliefs". In the same letter he writes about Mongkut's fascination with European maps:

> He received me kindly, and after a few inquiries, called for his maps (European), and asked many questions regarding various countries, and especially in reference to the different length of days and nights occasioned by the perihelion and aphelion and the obliquity of the earth's axis; particularly, in what regions the sun withdraws his beams for six months of the year.
>
> (ibid.: 233)

In this way, in Siam, as in other Buddhist countries, the interest in Western maps and globes shown by Mongkut and other members of the Siamese elite contributed to the emergence of Buddhist Modernism. At first glance, these developments seem to confirm the expectations of the missionaries. When taking a closer look, however, it quickly becomes apparent that their hope that this change would also lead to conversions to Christianity was not fulfilled. Rather, such an acceptance of the foreign religion was explicitly rejected by most members of the elite (Keyes 1993; Drover 2012: 26–36). The new geographic knowledge provided by Western maps and globes, however, was readily received and accepted. How can the novelty of these media of scientific space be described and their role in the transformation of notions of space be analyzed? In what ways do they differ from other media of space and earlier mapping practices?

With respect to the development of Western geography and cartography, the fifteenth century should be regarded as the period of the most crucial advances (Woodward 1991). While maps had certainly existed in Europe for a long time, available maps were mostly either medieval *mappae mundi* based on the T-O scheme or local topographical depictions produced for specific occasions. Acting mainly as memory devices, these early maps can be understood as 'spatial stories' (Kitchin *et al.* 2011: 2) that did not lay claim to the conveyance of exact geographical knowledge. Additionally, so-called Portolan maps had emerged in the thirteenth century. These were mainly nautical charts of the Mediterranean, even if they sometimes also depicted a bigger portion of space up to the boundaries of the known world. However, it took another 150 years until the Latin translation of the writings of Claudius Ptolemy led to the establishment of an abstract, geometrical and homogeneous space as the basis of the cartographical imagination (Woodward 1991: 84). The rediscovery of Ptolemy laid the foundation for modern methods of projection, and in 1569 Mercator's isogonal cylindrical projection showed that a depiction of geographic coordinates and straight compass routes could be combined in a single map. A grid of longitudes and latitudes now spanned the whole world and every reachable point in the world was thus located in this surveyed space. The "objectivistic vision of the world" (Siegert 2005: 6) brought about by this homogeneous space now stood in competition with alternative topographies. At the same time, notions of space changed "from the circumscribed cage of the known inhabited world to the notion of the finite whole earth" (Woodward 1991: 85).

At the same time, it would be wrong to think that substantial records of geographical knowledge only developed in Europe and were introduced to non-Western contexts only in the modern era (cf. e.g. Harley and Woodward 1994 for an overview of the history of cartography in East and Southeast Asia). In Siam, for example, a plurality of local conceptions of space existed well before the nineteenth century. While in most instances these were linked to religious notions of space, there were also a number of other topographical records resulting in cartographic depictions. In contrast to the primarily

18 *Adrian Hermann*

Buddhist and cosmographic representations, these maps represented segments of the Earth's surface. A manuscript from 1776, for example, contains a number of drawings which portray the paths of rivers and also show Ceylon. Another extant map depicts, albeit with considerable divergences from modern maps, the coastlines from Korea to Arabia (Winichakul 1994: 28–9). Additionally, a strategic map dating back to the time of Rama I shows today's northeastern Thailand and was probably used for military purposes in the 1827 war against Vientiane. This map also does not include any cosmological aspects (ibid.: 30–1). It would therefore be misguided to understand indigenous notions of space as generally cosmological and imaginary and contrast them with the scientific knowledge of Western mapping. Rather, the indigenous maps already point to complex combinations of different notions of cosmological and geographical space, represented in the medium of the map.

Nevertheless, as Joseph E. Schwartzberg concludes in his study on the history of Southeast Asian cartography, there are no surviving globes or non-cosmological world maps from pre-modern Southeast Asia, and only a single map which depicts a territory of roughly continental size (Schwartzberg 1994: 839). The surviving maps from Siam differ from modern maps primarily through the fact that they do not include any information on how the topography depicted on them relates to the totality of the Earth's surface. Winichakul notes in regard to one of the maps studied by him: "[T]here is no reference to the larger earth's surface, such as latitude and longitude lines, or the relation of this territory to nearby kingdoms in terms of boundaries" (1994: 31).

While at first glance it therefore appears to make sense to differentiate clearly between indigenous and Western topographical depictions, the theoretical perspective presented above has highlighted the close relationship between mediality and notions of space and thus makes a different assessment possible: Rather than being distinguished, on the one hand, by conveying imaginary geographies and, on the other, by objective geographical knowledge, the spaces being constituted by pre-modern as well as modern scientific maps emerge in an interplay of perception, imagination and the media of space that co-produce them.

Moreover, the central role of the imagination in the constitution of scientific notions of geographical space can be made clear by considering the mediatic characteristics of the Western map. Based on a geometric projection, the modern map is an 'a-perspectivical medium': its depiction of space is significantly *not* seen from a perspective. The Earth can never be *seen* as it is depicted on a map which is ruled by a mapping grid (Stockhammer 2007: 27). On the contrary, the spatiality constituted by the map as a medium of space is only available through a form of cartographic imagination enabled by the map itself.

The differences between notions of space which are at issue in the controversies between Buddhist monks and Christian missionaries in the encounter with Western geographical knowledge and its forms of dissemination should therefore not be regarded as lying in the different status of the imaginary spaces they induce. On the contrary, both kinds of spaces are only constituted in the interplay of media of space, perception and imaginary constructions of space. These media of space thus can be understood as the condition of possibility for alternative practices of imagining space and as the point of departure for imaginative spaces, independent of their claim to topographical representation. This is as much the case for the map as it is for the globe, which can only be observed in parts – even from a bird's-eye-view. At the same time, however, the globe is a central medium of the bounded and homogeneous space of modernity. As Denis Cosgrove writes: "[O]n the globe the 'ends of the earth' cannot be ignored" (2001: 13).

Therefore, while Western maps and globes do not in themselves represent superior knowledge, they nevertheless lay claim to a different space than local maps. They point to the homogeneous and singular space of which they are only a small part; their claim to universality stands in stark contrast to the plurality of local geographic traditions. In this way the issue of the scientific character of cartographic representations is linked to the homogenization and universalization of space in modernity. Subsequently, any notion of cosmo-geographical space therefore enters into a competitive relationship to any knowledge flagged as scientific (Winichakul 1994: 21–2). At the same time, the idea that modern scientific maps present an objective representation of the Earth's surface and can therefore be used to delegitimize other, competing depictions and notions of space met with the missionaries' persuasion that the Christian religion would most successfully be spread in the wake of scientific knowledge in geography and astronomy. In this vein, the missionary Jesse Caswell wrote to the American Board of the Commissioners of Foreign Missions on January 2nd, 1846:

> A little money expended in purchasing a few articles of apparatus illustrative of scientific truth may probably obtain that for the cause of Christ which is greatly needed, and cannot be obtained from any other quarter, while at the same time it contributes to enlarge the minds of those who render the service and qualify them the better to operate on the minds of their fellow countrymen.
>
> (Caswell, quoted in Bradley 1966: 40)

This belief in the effectiveness of scientific media of space and their role in transforming cosmo-geographical notions in Siam can, however, as indicated by King Mongkut's letter quoted at the beginning of this chapter, not only be found in missionary writings, but was also shared by various members of the Siamese elite. Mongkut's letter exhibits this persuasion that modern scientific geography was to be awarded the status of "true facts of the world" (quoted in Bowring 1857: 445) and was not to be questioned.

The impact of these transformations of cosmo-geographical space resulting from the encounters of the first half of the nineteenth century can best be understood by looking at a book printed in 1867. *Nangsue Sadaeng Kitchanukit* [A Book on Various Things], written by Chaophraya Thipakorawong

20   *Adrian Hermann*

(Kham Bunnag), who held the post of *Phra Klang* (similar to a minister of foreign affairs) for a number of years, can be regarded as a central text of early Buddhist modernism. It represents the early culmination of the encounters and hybrid processes of knowledge transfer in which the Siamese elite was involved over the course of the nineteenth century.[5]

Thiphakorawong's perspective is based on the assumption that Western-scientific astronomy and its model of the Earth as a sphere is superior and convincing knowledge which should replace traditional notions of cosmo-geographical space. As an argument for this conviction, he presents the discovery of the New World by Columbus as well as a number of other observable phenomena which can only be accounted for by this Western knowledge (Winichakul 1994: 41). Regarding the question of whether this contradicts the omniscience of the Buddha, he argues that not only the Siamese but also the traditional cosmological conceptions of all other religions differ from the modern world-view: "[T]he ancients, whether Brahmins or Arabs, or Jews or Chinese, or Europeans, had much the same idea of cosmography, and their present ideas on the subject are the work of scientific men in modern times" (quoted in Alabaster 1871: 14).

Therefore, while Western scientific notions contradict the traditional cosmo-geography, Thiphakorawong points out that the Buddha himself never taught this false cosmology:

> Those who have studied Pali know that the Lord ... never discoursed about cosmography ... For if he had taught that the world was a revolving globe, contrary to the traditions of the people, who believed it to be flat, they would not have believed him.
>
> (quoted in Alabaster 1871: 15)

This argument makes it possible to retain the doctrine of the omniscience of the Buddha, who "by refraining from a subject which men of science were certain eventually to ascertain the truth of ... showed his omniscience" (ibid.: 16).

Conceding the scientific untenability of the Mount Meru cosmology does not, however, lead to a rejection of Buddhism as a whole. It also does not mean that all Buddhist stories connected to this cosmology are rejected:

> I have explained about this matter of Meru, and the other mountains, as an old tradition. But with respect to the Lord preaching on Davadungsa as an act of grace to his mother, I believe it to be true, and that one of the many stars or planets is the Davadungsa world.
>
> (ibid.: 17)

In an instance of hybrid knowledge formation, the traditional story of the Buddha preaching to his mother in the Davadungsa heaven is relocated as having taken place on one of the many planets of the new western cosmo-geographical space.

The example of the *Kitchanukit* shows that, on the one hand, the confrontation with the scientific cosmo-geography had profound consequences for the Siamese Buddhist elite. On the other hand, it did not lead to an abandoning of Buddhism, as had been expected by the missionaries. Rather, in Siam, as in many other Buddhist contexts, the encounter between the new scientific knowledge and ancient Buddhist ideas was used to purge the 'true doctrine of the Buddha' from later accretions and claim the compatibility of Buddhism and science, which became a central strategy of Buddhist modernism in the nineteenth century. In Thipakorawong's case, the fact that the other religions had proposed a flat Earth even led him to the following claim: "One who thinks that the earth is flat is a follower of those who believe in God the Creator. For one who believes that the earth is spherical is following the Buddha's words about what is natural" (quoted in Winichakul 1994: 41). The strategy the missionaries were using to de-legitimize Buddhism was thus redirected at them, not only in Siam but also in Ceylon, where the claim to possess the true understanding of cosmo-geography was not given up so easily, as will be seen below.

Media of scientific space as immutable mobiles: the circulation of scientific facts and the nineteenth-century Buddhist-Christian debates in Ceylon

The exemplary examination of Buddhist-Christian encounters in nineteenth-century Siam has illustrated the interest in Western maps and scientific devices shown by local elites, and detailed the importance of these new media of scientific space in the transformation of notions of cosmo-geographical space. Likewise, the encounter between Rev. Clough and the monk served as an illustration of the epistemological fissures which open up in the encounter of geography, cosmology and the confrontation with Christian missions. At the same time, it was left undetermined how these media of space actually work, from where they draw their effectiveness that makes them so useful in challenging traditional conceptions of space, and how they differ from pre-modern media of space. How can the power of scientific knowledge and its media be described without resorting to a history of scientific progress which in retrospect can only consider these media to be conveying a naturally superior, objective, and scientifically correct geography and astronomy? How can the superior rhetorical power of the 'objective facts' of scientific knowledge in these encounters be analyzed? How can a situation be described, in which the possibilities of reaction and the forms of knowledge formation were much more hybrid, varied and plural than was expected by the missionaries, and in which the result of a displacement of traditional notions of space was all but to be expected with certainty?

22   Adrian Hermann

These questions become even more urgent if we consider the fact that such instruments and devices had already been in high demand in Siam since the early contacts between European powers and the Siamese court. In the seventeenth century, representatives of the V.O.C. presented King Narai (r. 1656–88) with numerous gifts, and obtained for him a large number of technical objects. Among these were watches and telescopes as well as military devices. At the end of his reign Narai possessed "a model of the solar system constructed of silver and gold, various watches, and many other pieces of scientific equipment" (Hodges 1998: 88). A diplomatic mission sent to France, which in 1685 was granted an audience with Louis XIV in Versailles, also visited the Paris Observatory. As a result of this visit to France, Louis XIV sent "globes of the heavens and earth" to Siam, as well as a mechanical model which displayed the movements of the sun, the moon and the planets (ibid.: 89). However, according to Ian Hodges, Narai's interest in European knowledge and technology in the seventeenth century did not have a lasting influence on the spatial and cosmological ideas in Siam (ibid.: 90).

This pre-history of the Siamese interest in Western maps and technical devices illustrates that the mere availability of scientific instruments was not sufficient to initiate a transformation of spatial conceptions. Drawing on the work of Bruno Latour, this can be understood as a failure to extend the network in which scientific facts are constituted and enabled to travel. Therefore the technological instruments which reached Siam in the seventeenth century remained isolated and the scientific facts did not travel with them (Latour 1987: 167, 250).

Following Latour, media of scientific space like the maps and globes described in this chapter can be understood as 'immutable mobiles' (ibid.; in regard to maps, cf. Cosgrove 2008: 167–8). Latour developed this concept not least in his engagement with early modern cartography in his study *Science in Action* (1987). His is a perspective in which "any single distinction between prescientific and scientific cultures, minds, methods or societies" (Latour 1986: 2) is replaced by the reconstruction of incremental changes which take the place of such a basic and general dichotomy and which can explain the later establishment of drastic differences without having to essentialize them.

Latour attempts to explain the special power of scientific knowledge and its technological-material representations as an effect of the combination of a consistent repertoire of cultural techniques and thus to describe the media-technological superiority of the West in a way that makes the assumption of a 'great divide' unnecessary (cf. Schüttpelz 2009: 69). He focuses on practices of inscriptions that are connected to paper media like the printing press, the linear perspective, geometrical projections and cartographic advances, as well as statistics, tables and diagrams. While each of these inventions is of central importance in of itself, Latour treats these cultural techniques and their products mainly as elements whose power lies in their being *immutable* as well as *mobile*. The superiority of scientific knowledge therefore cannot be attributed to the mental superiority of Western actors or a basic difference in the quality of knowledge. Rather, the power of scientific knowledge lies in the combination of a multitude of observations and parts of knowledge in and with the help of immutable mobiles. This 'drawing together' takes place in 'centers of calculation' in a process in which the combination of inscriptions of immutable mobiles produces new immutable mobiles of a higher order (Latour 1987: 232–47).

Taking as an example the expedition to the Pacific by La Pérouse, Latour shows how, with the help of the data gathered and brought back to Europe, it is possible that the navigator of the subsequent fleet will on his arrival be able to see the characteristics of the islands already for the second time, after he had studied the maps produced from the writings of La Pérouse at home. The establishment of this asymmetry of knowledge thus depends on "the possibility for some traces of the travel to go back to the place that sent the expedition away" (ibid.: 218). With the concept of the immutable mobile, therefore, Latour answers his own question regarding the power of the media of scientific knowledge:

> [H]ow to act at a distance on unfamiliar events, places and people? Answer: by somehow bringing home these events, places and people. How can this be achieved, since they are distant? By inventing means that (a) render them mobile so that they can be brought back; (b) keep them stable so that they can be moved back and forth without additional distortion, corruption or decay, and (c) are combinable so that whatever stuff they are made of, they can be cumulated, aggregated, or shuffled like a pack of cards.
>
> (ibid.: 233)

At the same time this indicates that, according to Latour, the existence of scientific knowledge is not independent of the immutable mobiles and the actor-networks constituted through them: "There is no outside of science but there are long, narrow networks that make possible the circulation of scientific facts" (Latour 1983: 167). The persuasion of another of the knowledge transported through the immutable mobiles is the same thing as the expansion of a network linking actors and things with the centers of calculation in which this knowledge was produced. Latour writes: "[E]very time you hear about a successful application of a science, look for the progressive extension of a network. Every time you hear about a failure of science, look for what part of which network has been punctured. I bet you will always find it" (1987: 249).

The scientific facts which play a role in the constitution of new notions of cosmo-geographic space in the nineteenth-century Buddhist-Christian encounter could not arrive in Bangkok or Colombo independent of the devices used to transport them: "Facts and machines have no inertia of their own; like kings or armies they cannot travel without their retinues or impedimenta" (ibid.: 250). Only on the basis of this mobility can their power be secured from a distance and a stable connection between center and periphery be established.

24   *Adrian Hermann*

The modern map is a prime example of an immutable mobile as a material device which is used as a medium of scientific knowledge and its claims to truth. It combines information collected in many different places, which has been collected and combined in a center of calculation and then, in an immutable mobile of a higher order, has been put into circulation again (Cosgrove 2008: 167–8). Even if from the perspective of a post-structuralist geography and cartography it is rightly emphasized that in the modern map as an immutable mobile, the status of an 'objective representation' can never be realized, this is exactly the claim which goes along with mapping and which characterized Western geography: "The entire history of cartography can be told as a history of struggle to realize such a status for the map" (ibid.: 168).

From this Latourian perspective it becomes possible to see the events in pre-modern and in nineteenth-century Siam in a new light. The devices and instruments obtained by King Narai in the seventeenth century did not function as media of scientific facts, because they did not form part of an actor-network in which these facts could have been transported. King Mongkut and the other members of the Siamese elite since the 1830s, however, had become integrated into such a network, among other things through the work of such devices, which in that case could function as media for the transportation of facts. In this way, a map of the world or a globe can function as a medium of 'objective scientific factual knowledge'. Its plausibility, however, depends on whether it becomes possible to extend the network of actors through it.

If the scientific actor-network is successfully extended through the immutable mobiles, the scientific facts can effect their power. The monk in the first example, just like the members of the Siamese elite, are then recruited as allies in a network. As Latour stresses, however, such a network (in which scientific facts are constituted and transported) is only expandable and stable if the scientific controversies which are at issue are resolved. This can be illustrated by a last example from Ceylon, which at the same time draws attention to the possibility of hybrid notions of space and therefore complicates the idea of a simple replacement of indigenous knowledge with scientific knowledge in these processes of knowledge transfer.

In a famous public controversy between missionaries and monks on Ceylon in the 1870s, scientific devices and especially a Western globe stood once again at the center of attention. It is reported that in the most famous of these debates, at Panadura in 1873, the Rev. David de Silva challenged the Mount Meru cosmo-geography in the following way:

> Where, then, is this great mountain … situated? How is it possible that it could not be seen to the eyes of men? This globe represents the earth. (Here the globe was shown.) In this the shape of the earth, its dimensions, the great rivers and seas, and the positions of the countries, etc., are all represented. Now, the circumference of the earth is 25,000 miles. This is

admitted by all the civilized nations of the world. This fact is proved by every day's experience. Therefore, a mountain with such dimensions could not exist on this earth. Wherever it existed it must be seen, as this globe which now stands on this little inkstand must be seen by all who are on the four sides of it ... Men at no period ever saw such a mountain, nor have they known by science that there could be such a mountain. One who had said that there was such a mountain cannot be supposed to have been a wise man, nor one who spoke the truth ... Is this person to be believed who speaks that which could esily [*sic*] be proved as false, and declares a thing not existing as if it existed? Certainly not. Besides, everything that is stated in Buddhism is connected with Mahameru.[6] ... Mahameru ... must be placed on the earth; if not, Buddhism must be rejected at once.

(quoted from Abhayasundara 1990: 140–3)

Once more, the status of the Buddhist cosmo-geography was at the center of the controversy. Geographical knowledge and new notions of space were presented with the help of devices like the globe used by Rev. Silva. His argumentation can be read as an attempt to extend the actor network of the scientific knowledge connected to this immutable mobile and to enforce an alternative understanding of cosmo-geographic space. At the same time, this debate at Panadura has become famous because, in the opinion of many observers, it was not the missionaries but the monks who emerged victorious from the debate.

The Buddhist debater, Rev. Migettuwatte, responded by conceding that the scriptures quoted by Silva show that the Buddha had proposed the existence of the Mount Meru. However, instead of abandoning the traditional cosmo-geography and, like the Siamese exponents of Buddhist Modernism, distinguishing a true Buddhism from later accretions, Migettuwatte defends the existence of Mahameru and questions the basis on which Silva made his claims:

The Rev. Gentleman no doubt alluded to Sir Isaac Newton's theory when he made that remark, according to which day and night were caused by the earth revolving round its axis, and not by the sun being hidden behind Mahameru. The little globe which the Rev. Gentleman produced was one made on Newton's principle ...

(quoted in ibid.: 153)

This principle, however, as the report of Migettuwatte's response in the debate continues, is not uncontroversial:

[E]ven amongst Englishmen there were serious doubts and differences of opinion as to whether Newton's theory was correct or not. Among others, Mr. Morrison, a learned gentleman, had published a book refuting Newton's arguments, and he would be happy to allow the Christian

26 *Adrian Hermann*

party a sight of this book, which was in his possession. (Here he produced and handed around the 'New principia' by R.J. Morrison, F.A.S.L., published in London.) How unjust, then, to attempt to demolish the great Buddha's sayings by quoting as authority an immature system of astronomy, the correctness of which is not yet accepted.

(quoted from ibid.: 153–4)

Moreover, Migettuwatte not only questions the persuasive power of Newtonian science and the globe based on it. He also tries to prove the existence of Mahameru and in order to do so calls upon the authority of another scientific device:

The mariner's compass was the best proof he could give them of the existence of Mahameru. Keep it where you may, the attraction of the magnetic needle is always towards the North. This demonstrated that there was a huge mass in that direction which attracted the needle towards it, and according to the Buddhist books, Mahameru, the grandest and most stupendous rock on the face of the earth, was situated in the North ... The mariner's compass was the most conclusive argument for the existence of the famed Mahameru.

(ibid.: 153–6)

Not only is Migettuwatte unwilling to accept the argument for the non-existence of the Mount Mahameru. Rather, the globe used by Silva as an argument is itself questioned in its status as a medium of scientific space. Instead of a device that represents 'natural facts', it is turned into the object of a scientific controversy.

In analyzing such instances of conflict between 'scientific' and 'religious' knowledge, it is especially important to take a non-deterministic position. Latour's third rule of method is helpful here, which claims that decisions about 'nature' are only the result of the end of a controversy and therefore cannot be used to explain how the decisions in the controversy were taken:

Nature is the final cause of the settlement of all controversies, *once controversies are settled* ... When studying controversy – as we have so far – we cannot be *less* relativist than the very scientists and engineers we accompany; they do not *use* Nature as the external referee, and we have no reason to imagine that we are more clever than they are. ... [S]ince the settlement of a controversy is *the cause* of Nature's representation not the consequence, we *can never use the outcome – Nature – to explain how and why a controversy has been settled.*

(Latour 1987: 99)

While the missionary Silva regards the controversy around the spherical form of the Earth as a closed issue and the globe as a medium of this secure

"True facts of the world" 27

knowledge, the monk uses the book by R. J. Morrison,[7] a proponent of a geo-centric world-view in nineteenth century England, to question the status of the globe as a medium of secure knowledge and thus opens up the controversy once more (ibid.: 97–8). By referring to this book, the monk now tries to recruit Morrison as an ally in a network against the missionary Rev. Silva, a network which now suddenly spans the great distance between London and Colombo and turns both into actors in a newly flared up scientific controversy.

Conclusion

The developments discussed in this chapter can be understood as a reaction to a situation in which the authoritative claims of science are directed towards no longer allowing multiple descriptions of the world – at least on the level of scientific knowledge. Buddhist elites in Ceylon and Siam react with a reformulation of Buddhist cosmology, which retains central pieces of the Buddhist cosmological tradition as possibly true – and literally true – but at the same time locates them in the context of modern science as a new system of world description with new aspirations. In this way, these transformations tell us something about the location of religious knowledge in modernity, which cannot escape being positioned in relation to scientific knowledge. This distinction between religion and science is articulated in controversies around notions of cosmo-geographical space and scientific claims to the universalization of a singular and universal global geographical space.

The media of space, the maps and globes of the examples discussed in this chapter, appear in the transformations of Buddhist notions of space simultaneously as manifestations as well as agents of change. In constructing religious and scientific knowledge as two different kinds of knowledge and in referring to the claims of a universal scientific geography, they deny alternative Buddhist notions of space their veracity. In reaction to these claims, exponents of Buddhist modernism either appropriated this universalism and began to treat the classical Mount Meru cosmology as pre-scientific and un-Buddhist (while alternative ways of locating traditional stories remained possible), or went on to confront the challenge on the level of science itself (and, for example, questioned the scientific basis of Newtonian physics). All this was going on in a world in which all actors were acting as 'conscripts of modernity' (Asad 1992) in a territory that had already been fundamentally transformed by the universalistic claims of modern science.

Notes

* A longer version of this chapter is published in German in A. Wilke and L. Traut (eds) (2015) *Religion – Imagination – Ästhetik. Vorstellungs- und Sinneswelten in Religion und Kultur*. Göttingen: Vandenhoeck & Ruprecht.

1 In what follows, this letter, also printed in other missionary publications as well as a later history of the Methodist Church in Ceylon, is quoted from *The Missionary Register* for 1826: 610–11. Typographical errors in the original have been corrected.

28 *Adrian Hermann*

2 "Dass jedes mediale Gefüge einen spezifisch strukturierten Raum produziert. Etappen in der Geschichte des Raumes stellen deshalb auch Etappen in der Mediengeschichte dar." (Translations from the German here and in the following by the author, A.H.)
3 "Welche Räume sich über welche Medien zu einem gegebenen historischen Zeitpunkt konstituieren können."
4 "Sich immer nur in medial gestützter Zeichenhaftigkeit äußert und so zwischen rein mentaler Interiorität und der Technizität äußerer Bilder steht."
5 See Reynolds (1976), Winichakul (1994: 37–61), and Hermann (2011). The *Kitchanukit* was partly published in an English translation in London in 1871 as the first part of the book *The Wheel of the Law* by Henry Alabaster. All quotations are taken from this translation.
6 Mount Meru is often also referred to as *Mahameru* [Great Meru].
7 Richard James Morrison published the first edition of his book *The New Principia; or, True System of Astronomy. In which the Earth is Proved to be the Stationary Centre of the Solar System, and the Sun is Shewn to be Only 365,006.5 Miles from the Earth, and the Moon Only 32,828.5 Distant; While the Sun Travels Yearly in an Ellipse around the Earth, the Other Planets Moving about the Sun in Ellipses Also* in 1868. The book was at least successful enough to warrant a second edition in 1872. See Lopez (2008: 56).

References

Abhayasundara, P. (ed.) (1990) *Controversy at Panadura or Pānadura Vādaya.* Colombo, Sri Lanka: State Printing Corporation.

Alabaster, H. (1871) *The Wheel of the Law: Buddhism Illustrated from Siamese Sources.* London: Trübner & Co.

Aphornsuvan, T. (2009) 'The West and Siam's Quest for Modernity: Siamese Responses to Nineteenth Century American Missionaries,' *South East Asia Research*, 17(3): 401–31.

Asad, T. (1992) 'Conscripts of Western Civilization,' in C.W. Gailey (ed.) *Dialectical Anthropology: Essays in Honor of Stanley Diamond.* Vol. 1: *Civilization in Crisis: Anthropological Perspectives.* Gainesville, FL: University of Florida Press, pp. 333–51.

Bowring, J. (1857) *The Kingdom and People of Siam: A Narrative of the Mission to That Country in 1855.* London: John W. Parker and Son.

Bradley, W.L. (1966) 'Prince Mongkut and Jesse Caswell,' *The Journal of the Siam Society*, 54(1): 29–41.

Collins, S. (1998) *Nirvana and Other Buddhist Felicities: Utopias of the Pali Imaginaire.* Cambridge: Cambridge University Press.

Cosgrove, D. (2001) *Apollo's Eye: A Cartographic Genealogy of the Earth in the Western Imagination.* Baltimore, MD: The Johns Hopkins University Press.

Cosgrove, D. (2008) *Geography and Vision. Seeing, Imagining and Representing the World.* London: I.B. Tauris.

Doetsch, H. (2004) 'Einleitung. (II) Räumlichkeit und Schriftkultur,' in J. Dünne *et al.* (eds) *Von Pilgerwegen, Schriftspuren und Blickpunkten. Raumpraktiken in medienhistorischer Perspektive.* Würzburg: Königshauses & Neumann, pp. 73–7.

Drover, L. (2012) *Christen in Thailand. Am Beispiel der Karen und der Akha.* Frankfurt am Main: Peter Lang.

Dünne, J. (2008) 'Die Karte als Operations- und Imaginationsmatrix. Zur Geschichte eines Raummediums,' in J. Döring and T. Thielmann (eds) *Spatial Turn. Das*

Raumparadigma in den Kultur- und Sozialwissenschaften. Bielefeld: Transcript, pp. 49–70.

Dünne, J. (2011) *Die kartographische Imagination. Erinnern, Erzählen und Fingieren in der Frühen Neuzeit*. München: Fink.

Gregory, D. (1994) *Geographical Imaginations*. Oxford: Blackwell.

Gützlaff, K. (2001) 'Journal of Three Voyages along the Coast of China,' in A. Farrington (ed.) *Early Missionaries in Bangkok: The Journals of Tomlin, Gutzlaff and Abeel, 1828–1832*. Bangkok: White Lotus Press, pp. 65–90.

Harley, B.J. and Woodward, D. (eds) (1994) *The History of Cartography*, Vol. 2, *Cartography in the Traditional East and Southeast Asian Societies*. Chicago, IL: The University of Chicago Press.

Hermann, A. (2011) 'Buddhist Modernism in 19th Century Siam and the Discourse of Scientific Buddhism: Towards a Global History of "Religion",' *Journal of the South and Southeast Asian Association for the Study of Culture and Religion*, 5: 37–57.

Hodges, I. (1998) 'Western Science in Siam: A Tale of Two Kings,' *Osiris*, 13: 80–95.

Jones, J.T. (1836) 'Extracts from the Journal of Mr. Jones,' *The Baptist Missionary Magazine*, 16(10): 233–7.

Keyes, C.F. (1993) 'Why the Thai Are Not Christian. Buddhist and Christian Conversion in Thailand,' in R. Hefner (ed.) *Conversion to Christianity: Historical and Anthropological Perspectives on a Great Transformation*. Berkeley, CA: University of California Press, pp. 259–83.

Kitchin, R., Dodge, M. and Perkins, C. (2011) 'Introductory Essay: Conceptualising Mapping,' in M. Dodge, R. Kitchin, and C. Perkins (eds) *The Map Reader: Theories of Mapping Practice and Cartographic Representation*. Oxford: Wiley-Blackwell, pp. 1–8.

Latour, B. (1983) 'Give Me a Laboratory and I Will Raise the World,' in K. Knorr-Cetina and M. Mulkay (eds) *Science Observed: Perspectives on the Social Study of Science*. London: Sage, pp. 141–70.

Latour, B. (1986) 'Visualisation and Cognition: Thinking with Eyes and Hands,' *Knowledge and Society: Studies in the Sociology of Culture and Present*, 6: 1–40.

Latour, B. (1987) *Science in Action: How to Follow Scientists and Engineers through Society*. Cambridge, MA: Harvard University Press.

Lopez, D.S. Jr. (2008) *Buddhism and Science: A Guide for the Perplexed*. Chicago, IL: University of Chicago Press.

McMahan, D.L. (2004) 'Modernity and the Early Discourse of Scientific Buddhism,' *Journal of the American Academy of Religion*, 72(4): 897–933.

Reynolds, C.J. (1976) 'Buddhist Cosmography in Thai History, with Special Reference to Nineteenth-Century Culture Change,' *The Journal of Asian Studies*, 35(2): 203–20.

Sadakata, A. (1997) *Buddhist Cosmology: Philosophy and Origins*, trans. G. Sekimori. Tokyo: Kosei Publishing.

Schüttpelz, E. (2009) 'Die medientechnische Überlegenheit des Westens. Zur Geschichte und Geographie der *immutable mobiles* Bruno Latours,' in J. Döring and T. Thielmann (eds) *Mediengeographie: Theorie – Analyse – Diskussion*. Bielefeld: Transcript, pp. 67–110.

Schwartzberg, J.E. (1994) 'Conclusion to Southeast Asian Cartography,' in J.B. Harley and D. Woodward (eds) *The History of Cartography*. Vol. 2, *Cartography in the Traditional East and Southeast Asian Societies*. Chicago, IL: University of Chicago Press, pp. 839–42.

30 *Adrian Hermann*

Siegert, B. (2005) 'Repräsentationen diskursiver Räume. Einleitung,' in H. Böhme (ed.) *Topographien der Literatur. Deutsche Literatur im transnationalen Kontext.* Stuttgart: Metzler, pp. 3–11.

Stockhammer, R. (2007) *Kartierung der Erde: Macht und Lust in Karten und Literatur.* München: Fink.

Terwiel, B.J. (1986) 'Mu'ang Thai and the World. Changing Perspectives during the Third Reign,' paper presented at the seminar on "Asia: A Sense of Place," Australian National University, Canberra.

Thielmann, T. (2007) '"You Have Reached Your Destination!" Position, Positioning and Superpositioning of Space Through Car Navigation Systems,' *Social Geography*, 2(1): 63–75.

Thielmann, T. (2010) 'Locative Media and Mediated Localities: An Introduction to Media Geography,' *Aether: The Journal of Media Geography*, 5: 1–17.

Wilke, A. and Traut, L. (2015) *Religion – Imagination – Ästhetik. Vorstellungs- und Sinneswelten in Religion und Kultur.* Göttingen: Vandenhoeck & Ruprecht.

Winichakul, T. (1994) *Siam Mapped: A History of the Geo-Body of a Nation.* Honolulu, HI: University of Hawaii Press.

Woodward, D. (1991) 'Maps and the Rationalization of Geographic Space,' in D. Woodward, *Circa 1492: Art in the Age of Exploration.* New Haven, CT: Yale University Press for the National Gallery of Art, pp. 83–7.

Young, R.F. and Somaratna, G.P.V. (1996) *Vain Debates: The Buddhist-Christian Controversies of Nineteenth-Century Ceylon.* Vienna: Sammlung de Nobili.

2 An illusion of conciliation

Religion and science in Debendranath and Rabindranath Tagore

C. Mackenzie Brown

Introduction

Rabindranath Tagore (1861–1941), the famous Nobel Laureate in literature, and his somewhat less well-known father, Debendranath Tagore (1817–1905), a key figure in the early history of the Brahmo Samaj, grappled with various issues of reconciling tradition with modernity. Both were intrigued by the discoveries of modern science, and each had a desire to taste the flavor (*rasa*) of science, even though neither was a scientist. As Rabindranath stated in one of his last works, *Visva Parichay* (1937), written when he was 76, urging the young to undertake the study of science:[1]

> It is needless to say that I am not a scientist, but from childhood my strong desire to enjoy the *rasa* [flavor, elegant beauty] of science knew no bounds ... My mind was exercised only with astronomy and life science. That cannot be called proper knowledge, in other words, it does not have the sound foundation of scholarship. But constant reading created a natural scientific temper in my mind.
>
> (trans. and quoted in Ghose 2010: 48)

Much of his *rasa* for science and the "natural scientific temper" of his mind the son imbibed from his father. When he was still a boy, for instance, he was taken by his father on a journey to the Himalayas during which, as Rabindranath recalls in his *My Reminiscences*:

> Every time we got down at the end of a stage, my father had chairs placed for us outside the bungalow and there we sat. As dusk came on, the stars blazed out wonderfully through the clear mountain atmosphere, and my father showed me the constellations or treated me to an astronomical discourse.
>
> (Tagore 1917: 93)

It is not surprising, then, to find that both father and son produced poetic, romanticized cosmologies in which, among other things, they attempted to

32 C. Mackenzie Brown

synthesize and harmonize certain aspects of the science of their times with their religious ideals—these latter derived in large part from their readings of the Vedāntic texts, the Upanishads. To effect this Vedānta-based harmony, Debendranath had recourse to the natural theology typical of the late eighteenth and early nineteenth centuries in Europe and America. Rabindranath attempted to integrate science and religion by assimilating and elaborating upon various non-Darwinian evolutionary theories popular in the late nineteenth and early twentieth centuries. In this chapter, I shall examine these cosmological narratives and underlying teleological and epistemological assumptions of the two Tagores to illuminate facets of the interaction of religion and science in colonial India that resulted in a highly spiritualized hermeneutic of science. This hermeneutic, based on a hierarchical model of two knowledges or sciences, raises questions about the alleged Tagorean reconciliation of modern science and their Upanishadic ideals.

Debendranath's natural theology

Debendranath presents his chief cosmological rhapsody in a sermon entitled, 'God, the Creator.'[2] This was one of a series of extempore sermons given in Kolkata upon his return home in 1858 after several months' wandering in the Himalayan foothills seeking spiritual renewal. During the 1840s and 1850s, he had been engaged in re-establishing, reforming, and overseeing the Brahmo Samaj, founded by Rammohan Roy in the late 1820s. In 1848, in a three-hour session inspired by what he felt was the grace of God, he had composed the theological principles of the Brahmo religion, based on the spiritual teachings of the Upanishads, later published as the *Brahmo Dharma*. In the *Brahmo Dharma*, Debendranath emphasized God's creative power and benevolence, themes elaborated upon in his later sermons.

Following personal, familial, and business crises that distracted him from his spiritual pursuits, and alienated him from members of his family and from certain factions in the Brahmo Samaj, he had decided in 1856 to follow the example of the ancient rishis and, renouncing the world, left for the Himalayas in search of God, intending never to return. There he experienced the glorious splendors of nature in her various seasons, seeing in her grandeur the manifestations of the God of the Upanishads. The beauty of the valleys and waterfalls, the forests and flowers, he saw as proof of the creator's artistic skill and providential concern for all creatures. Then, hearing a divine call to broadcast to the world the truths he had discovered in nature, he abandoned his wanderings and returned home, "a regenerated Soul, full of ardour and enthusiasm to propagate the holy religion he had embraced," in the words of his son Satyendranath (S. Tagore 1994: v).

The opening of the sermon, 'God, the Creator,' reverberates with cosmogonic motifs drawn from the Upanishads: "In the beginning, there was naught. Before this universe came into being, O Beloved, there existed *Sat* [Being], the only reality, one without a second" (D. Tagore 1994: 127).[3] Debendranath then refers to the all-pervading darkness that existed prior to the beginning, but there was also He who simply is, who is "the light of darkness." Debendranath alludes to the various Upanishadic statements regarding this supreme light, identified as the Supreme Spirit, the Essence or Sat, that exists beyond or behind the sun, stars, and planets, enduring even when those lights are extinguished. Then, he says, the Lord willed all things into being, first creating the sun to dispel the darkness, thereby bringing about the first wondrous morning. God next created our world, which "commenced to rotate round the sun" (ibid.: 128). Debendranath then asks:

> Who could have known that this world which was then covered with hot, molten metallic substances, like live coal, and filled with gaseous vapours, with its atmosphere enveloped in masses of clouds—that such a world should eventually be adorned most wonderfully with life and joy, light and beauty, and be filled with numberless living creatures, and innumerable spacies [sic] of plant life?
>
> (ibid.)

Following a brief query and exposition on the nature of the creative power behind the developing Earth, to which we shall return, Debendranath supplies further details of the world-forming process, now with occasional allusions to biblical rather than Upanishadic themes:[4]

> In the course of time the earth cooled, and became the dwelling place of many living creatures, and the home of many pleasures. The vapours condensed into clouds, and poured down as cool water, wherein fishes and reptiles and other kinds of aquatic animals lived and moved and had their being. Mountains rose up from amidst the water, and lifting their heads towards the sun, proclaimed the glory of the Lord. The earth came to have two divisions, land and water, and many plants and trees and animals were born therein.
>
> (ibid.)

The idea of a molten but cooling Earth with surrounding vapors, an important nineteenth-century theory long before the development of plate tectonics, was put forward especially by the American geologist James Dwight Dana (1813–95). Dana provides a terrestrial history similar to Debendranath's, including such details as the once molten surface of the Earth, the gradual condensation of vapors to form the rains that filled the oceans, the emergence of dry land and the rising of the mountains, and the beginning of vegetation in preparation for animal life (Dana 1856: 113–16).

Debendranath, of course, was not a geologist and was far more interested in the theological implications of any scientific account of the history of the Earth than in the science *per se*. Thus, regarding the nature of the creative

34 C. Mackenzie Brown

power behind the universe, Debendranath first poses a series of questions beginning with "Who?" He asks:

> Who was it that sowed in this world the seeds of all these things? Who created it as the store-house of an infinite variety of mineral wealth, grains, flowers and fruits? There shines the sun millions of miles away from us, here rolls the earth in its orbit, and on its surface are all these animals and plants! But yet from that far-off sun comes the light which illumines the world, and makes the stream of life flow, and dispels our blindness. Who is it that has established such relationship between the earth and the sun?
>
> (D. Tagore 1994: 128)

He now wonders, quite rhetorically, whether some blind force might not be responsible for creating such a pleasant, comfortable, even luxurious, and orderly world: "[I]s it the work of an insensate power? This life, this vitality, this wealth of various possessions, this happiness which we enjoy—are all these showered on us by a blind power?" (ibid.). The answer is predictable:

> No, it is by the will of that Being who is All-wise and All-good, that all this that is, has come into being. God meditated, and then implanted in it those diverse and wonderful forces that gradually rendered the once hot, lifeless and desolate world a home and a place of comfort such as it is now.
>
> (ibid.)

Debendranath goes on to list a number of other specific benefits bestowed on us by the merciful creator: "teeth to masticate our food," and before we had teeth, "milk [poured] into our mother's breast for us to drink;" he also lists "medicines to cure and relieve [our] maladies;" and finally, sounding a rather Christian note, "repentance," sent to save us from sin (ibid.: 128–9).

Clearly emphasized in Debendranath's sermon are the aspects of the world that are beneficial to human well-being. The underlying teleological assumption that the world was created by a supernatural being as a suitable habitat for human life was also shared by, and inspired the work of, many of the European natural philosophers or scientists of the eighteenth and nineteenth centuries. Like Debendranath, even if they were more directly involved in doing science, they evinced an equal interest in the theological implications of the latest scientific findings. For instance, the so-called father of geology, James Hutton (1726–97), saw the world in its general form, its constitution, and particular parts as "evidently calculated for the purpose of this earth as a habitable world," concluding:

> That there is not any particular, respecting either the qualities of the material, or the construction of the machine, more obvious to our

perception, than are the presence and efficacy of design and intelligence in the power that conducts the work.

(Hutton 1795: Chap. I, Sec. I)

Hutton further noted that by seeing the interdependence of all the parts of the world machine, we shall "be led to acknowledge an order, not unworthy of Divine wisdom, in a subject which, in another view, has appeared as the work of chance" (ibid.). And the American geologist Dana propounded his Cooling-Earth Theory in an essay, 'The Bible and Science,' in which he attempted to reconcile scripture with science. He concluded, in typical teleological fashion, that nature, under the direction of the wisdom and power of God, during the early period of creation as recorded in Genesis:

[was] preparing his [humankind's] earthly abode, arranging every ridge, and plain, and sea, and living thing, for his moral and intellectual advancement, and with so much beneficence that man, when he came to take possession of the domain, found everywhere lessons of love and adoration, and read in his own exaltation a hope, though a trembling hope, of immortality.

(Dana 1856: 129)

Debendranath's sermon invokes the same sort of sentiments expressed in this piously poetic passage of one of the great geologists of his day.

In winding down his sermon, Debendranath, as most natural theologians attempt to do somewhere along the way, offers a very brief explanation of the suffering in the world: "adversity, like a preceptor, teaches us noble lessons and leads us unto Him, and then adversity becomes to us the highest prosperity" (D. Tagore 1994: 129).

While the romantic cosmology of the sermon, 'God, the Creator,' frequently appeals to classical design arguments—usually of the aesthetic and providential, rather than of the mechanical sort—for the existence of a superintending and provident Lord, Debendranath had years earlier come to distrust the rationalistic underpinnings of such arguments. Such reliance on reason, he felt, could all too readily lead to a lifeless Deism. It was inner conviction, confirmed by his Himalayan adventures, rather than logical deduction that led him to reject the idea of a universe created through processes of blind chance. He thus came to subordinate reason (as well as Vedic revelation) to personal intuition and the inner realization of the all-pervading presence of God in the universe and within one's inner self, as one's inner guide. As he states in a subsequent sermon: "[T]his Supreme Spirit cannot be known by fine speech, nor by keen intellect, nor by much learning" (ibid.: 134); and: "[T]his Antar-yamin, the inner guide, the immortal Being, is in close contact with our souls. He cannot be touched with the external hand, but we can feel him and realise His presence in our souls" (ibid.: 130).

36   *C. Mackenzie Brown*

His resolution of any possible tension between intuition and tradition, on one hand, and reason and modern science, on the other, is clearly spelled out in the *Brahmo Dharma*, where he elaborates upon the idea of two knowledges or sciences, building on and reinterpreting the classical Upanishadic notion of *para-* and *apara-vidya* (higher and lower knowledges).[5] Debendranath declares: "[T]he science by the study of which, that supremely desirable pearl of knowledge [God] can be attained is the true, the highest science, all other sciences are inferior" (D. Tagore 1928: 15). He concludes: "[A]stronomy, Geology, Medical Science, Psychology, Philosophy, Theology and all other sciences declare His infinite wisdom and goodness. One should attain the crown of all sciences, namely the knowledge of God from all these sciences" (ibid.: 33). This epistemological strategy of creating a hierarchical model of the relation between religion and science, or of the lower natural sciences and a higher spiritual science, based on a dichotomizing of reason and intuition has remained a hallmark of the Hinduism-science discourse to the present day. In effect, this hierarchical model allows for any scientific idea or theory that conflicts with higher spiritual ideals to be dismissed as only a partial or incomplete truth—a misinterpretation of the data.

Debendranath returned to Kolkata from his Himalayan wanderings in 1858, the year in which Charles Darwin's and Alfred Wallace's papers on evolution by natural selection were presented at the Linnaean Society in London. Debendranath was soon preoccupied with internal developments within the Brahmo Samaj, and in any case never addressed himself to the challenges posed by Darwinian evolutionary theory with its non-teleological view of nature. His son, Rabindranath, however, in the coming decades, could not avoid such challenges. Eventually the son availed himself of late nineteenth- and early twentieth-century teleological evolutionary views to argue for an inherent vitalistic drive akin to Bergson's *élan vital*, and promoting a Vedānticized, progressivist view of the cosmos.

Rabindranath's creative evolutionism

Rabindranath presents his rhapsodic Vedāntic cosmology in his book, *The Religion of Man*, given originally as the Hibbert Lectures in 1930 at Manchester College, England. Regarding this book, the Tagorean scholar William Radice notes two pervading tendencies, "the rational and the irrational" (2010: 106). For Radice, the rationalist tendency in the book manifests "Tagore's passionate interest in science" (ibid.: 107), in particular, his interest in "the life sciences, and particularly the theory of evolution" (ibid.: 108). Summarizing Rabindranath's engagement with evolutionary theory, Radice notes:

> Darwin is not mentioned by name, and I have not yet been able to confirm how well Tagore knew Darwin's works, but the attitude of mind that *The Religion of Man* displays seems to me very Darwinian, and prophetic

An illusion of conciliation 37

too of debates in our own age about 'emergence' and the mystery of how complexity and organization in life-forms evolve in apparent defiance of the second law of thermodynamics.

(ibid.: 108)

With this reference to the idea that the evolution of complex life-forms is "in apparent defiance of the second law of thermodynamics," a common notion put forth by Christian creationists as a challenge to Darwinian evolution, I begin to wonder how familiar Radice is with contemporary evolutionary science. In any case, Radice continues by observing that Rabindranath both accepts the continuity and connection of humans with the other animals, and stresses what distinguishes us from them, namely our endowment with "greater and greater freedom" (ibid.). Radice acknowledges that Rabindranath was a much more religious man than Darwin, citing the former's belief in a 'life god' ('Lord of my life' or *Jivan devata*),[6] but nonetheless finds that:

[their] two minds touched not just in their appreciation of the physical *Descent of Man* but in their awareness of how the same evolutionary processes were at work in the human mind, including the capacity for religion that is Tagore's main subject.

(ibid.: 109)

Radice concludes that reading Tagore and Darwin together is "an antidote to the strident warfare between 'evolutionists' and 'creationists' that has become tiresomely prominent in recent years" (ibid.: 111).

Let us now examine more closely the claims that Rabindranath and Darwin shared the same view of the "evolutionary processes ... at work in the human mind," and that Rabindranath can serve as "an antidote" to the evolution-creationism warfare. Before exploring the details of Rabindranath's evolutionary saga in *The Religion of Man*, I shall begin by asking what at first may seem like a largely extraneous question: why did the dinosaurs become extinct? Or more precisely, what were common explanations of dinosaur extinction in Rabindranath's day?

Darwin had attributed extinction of species in general to natural selection, but he offered no specific causes for any particular case beyond the broad notions that as some species increase in numbers, others inevitably decline to the point of extinction, and that the various and complex contingencies upon which a given species depends for its survival are constantly changing (1859: 109–10, 322). He recognized the profound ignorance of his own day regarding extinction, and cautioned others not to be so presumptuous as to "invoke cataclysms to desolate the world, or invent laws on the duration of the forms of life!" (ibid.: 73).

By Darwin's time, the idea of extinction was no longer widely held to contradict God's omniscient designing of life forms manifest in the Great Chain of Being—any missing link in the Chain once being seen as destructive

38   *C. Mackenzie Brown*

of the ordered universe and thus reflecting poorly on the Master Architect's planning abilities. But Darwin's summary explanation of extinction as due to natural selection seemed to make of life a random and ruthless process, and thus equally appalling in conventional theological terms. And it was viewed with suspicion by many scientists themselves.

Accordingly, in the late 1800s and early 1900s we find in Europe and America a number of speculative explanations of extinction being proposed, with the case of the dinosaurs often cited. Among these explanations was the theory of orthogenesis, an anti-Darwinian, evolutionary theory popularized by Theodor Eimer in his (1898) *On Orthogenesis and the Impotence of Natural Selection in Species-Formation*. Orthogenesis, according to Eimer, is the idea of "definitely directed evolution," that is, a universal law demonstrating that in the process of species-formation, "organisms develop in definite directions without the least regard for utility through purely physiological causes as the result of *organic growth*" (Eimer 1898: 2). Organic growth occurs in predetermined patterns or directed stages, and in the more extreme versions of orthogenesis, the history of a species (phylogeny) was regarded as analogous to the development of individual organisms (ontogeny), each going through the "inevitable stages of youth, maturity and old age" (Gould 2002: 366). And as the renowned historian of evolutionary theories, Peter Bowler, notes: "[T]he most powerful manifestation of this idea [of orthogenesis] was the theory of overdevelopment, according to which the evolutionary growth of certain once-useful organs would gain a 'momentum' that would eventually lead to excessive growth and finally, extinction" (1988: 101). The most hardline orthogenetic theorist, according to Stephen Jay Gould, was the American geologist, Alpheus Hyatt, whose 'old age theory' of racial senility of species represented "the most uncompromisingly recapitulatory of all 19th century views, the most committed of all proposed evolutionary mechanics to 'programmed' racial life cycles" (2002: 370). The theory of racial senility clearly disregarded Darwin's caution not to "invent laws on the duration of the forms of life!"

From this most rigid of orthogenetic perspectives, the ideas of overdevelopment, loss of youthful vitality, and species aging could readily be applied to the dinosaurs, whose "remarkable horns, frills, and spines of some late Cretaceous dinosaurs were occasionally cited as evidence for this racial senility" (Benton 1990: 376). Consequently, monstrous "dinosaurs could be viewed as primitive lumbering beasts that *had* to give way to the more advanced mammals" (ibid.). As F.B. Loomis wrote in 1905 of the stegosaurs with their huge, bony dorsal plates, "with such an excessive load of bony weight entailing a drain on vitality, it is little wonder that the family was short-lived" (quoted in Benton 1990: 379). C. Schuchert in 1924, in a geology textbook intended for universities as well as the general public, argued that "just as individuals may in old age develop senescent characters, so frequently do the races [species]" (1924: 11). He lists among the senescent characters "relative increase in size" and "spinescence, or the tendency to overdevelopment of once useful or

An illusion of conciliation 39

ornamental features, as spines, horns, or bodily armor" (ibid.). He concludes: "when races are senile, or overspecialized, or are the giants of their stocks, they are apt to disappear with the great physiographic and climatic changes that periodically appear in the history of the earth" (ibid.: 12; also quoted in Benton 1990: 379).

Another thinker, in 1930, commenting on the "ruthless competition" in the "material world ... of quantity," proclaimed:

> It appears that such scramble and fight for opportunities of living among numerous small combatants suggested at last an imperialism of big bulky flesh—a huge system of muscles and bones, thick and heavy coats of armour and enormous tails. The idea of such indecorous massiveness must have seemed natural to life's providence; for the victory in the world of quantity might reasonably appear to depend upon bigness of dimension. But such gigantic paraphernalia of defence and attack resulted in an utter defeat, the records of which every day are being dug up from the desert sands and ancient mud flats.[7] For the heavy weight which these creatures carried was mainly composed of bones, hides, shells, teeth and claws that were non-living, and therefore imposed its whole huge pressure upon life that needed freedom and growth for perfect expression of its own vital nature.
>
> (R. Tagore 1931: 25–6)

These are the words of Rabindranath in his *The Religion of Man*, appearing in the second chapter entitled 'The Creative Spirit.' Regarding this chapter, Radice comments:

> The story of man's evolution that he [Rabindranath] tells, especially in his marvelous second chapter, 'The Creative Spirit', connects all aspects of our bodies and minds with the rest of nature, yet sees everything that distinguishes us from other animals as Life's drive towards greater and greater freedom. It is a vision as thrilling and basically optimistic as Darwin's, because all setbacks, all failures, all imperfections are seen as a necessary process of learning, expansion and improvement.
>
> (2010: 108)

The dinosaur-extinction episode in *The Religion of Man* clearly reveals Rabindranath's indebtedness to Western theories of racial senility proclaimed by men like Loomis, and Schuchert. Yet Rabindranath could not have been entirely happy with the basic orthogenetic theories of scientists like Eimer, who found purely material, non-intelligent or non-conscious causes as sufficient to account for the internal push within organisms responsible for the creation of new organs and species. One French philosopher, in particular, came to Rabindranath's rescue at this point, Henri Bergson. In his (1907)

40   C. Mackenzie Brown

book, *L'Evolution créatrice* (English translation, *Creative Evolution*, [1911] 1944), Bergson wrote:

> Where we differ from Eimer is in his claim that combinations of physical and chemical causes are enough to secure the result. We have tried to prove, on the contrary, by the example of the eye, that if there is "orthogenesis" here, a psychological cause intervenes.
>
> ([1911] 1944: 96–7)

This psychological cause or spiritual force is Bergson's famous *élan vital*, the vital impulse "by means of which life fought against the restrictions of the matter in which it was clothed," but which had "no predetermined goal" (Bowler 1983: 116).

The idea of a creative vital impulse struggling against dead matter had immense appeal for Rabindranath. It resonated deeply with his Upanishadic world-view inspired by his father, and specifically with the Upanishadic idea of *prāṇa* or life-force.[8] As Brian Hatcher notes: "[O]ne of Rabindranath's favorite [Upanishadic] passages was a line in praise of *prāṇa* taken from the *Kaṭha Upaniṣad* (6.2): 'All that there is comes out of life [*prāṇa*] and vibrates in it'" (Hatcher 2011: 124).[9]

For Rabindranath in *The Religion of Man*, as for Bergson in *Creative Evolution*, the story of Life is an ongoing set of experiments with unpredictable outcomes, a "creative venture" (R. Tagore 1931: 24) that occurs in three principal acts. The first act covers the development of plant life, commencing with the initial victory of the vital impulse, what Rabindranath calls the "Spirit of Life," in her "fight against the giant Matter" (ibid.: 25). As he describes the first victory: "[T]he Spirit of Life began her chapter by introducing a simple living cell against the tremendously powerful challenge of the vast Inert" (ibid.: 24). Similarly, in Bergson, we find: "[T]he resistance of inert matter was the obstacle that had first to be overcome. Life seems to have succeeded in this by dint of humility, by making itself very small" ([1911] 1944: 109). Life next, according to Rabindranath, assembled multiple cells together, imparting to them a cooperative spirit, and culminating in the apex of the vegetable kingdom, the grand creation of the tree with "its inner harmony and inner movement of life in its beauty, its strength, its sublime dignity of endurance" (R. Tagore 1931: 24).

But this climax of the plant world, grand as it may have been, Rabindranath proclaims, was insufficient for the restless Spirit of Life. She thus ventured to introduce, in the second act, "another factor into her work, that of locomotion," thereby increasing the risks of living, but also providing new creative opportunities (ibid.: 25). Again, we find close parallels in Bergson, who stresses two divergent developments in life, that of "vegetables" and later of animals, a divergence manifest first "in the method of alimentation" ([1911] 1944: 118). While vegetables assimilate the necessary elements to support life directly from the soil, water, and air where it grows, animals must seek out

An illusion of conciliation 41

plants, and even other animals to eat. Thus, "the animal must be able to move" (ibid.: 120).

The second act of Life, the animal phase, witnessed the increasing competitive struggle among mobile beings that led to an emphasis on size, culminating in the dinosaurs. But as we have already noted for Rabindranath, such cumbersome burdens of dead matter in the form of the heavy protective plates or huge claws and teeth prevented these "megalomaniac monsters" from continuing along the path of "their true progress" (R. Tagore 1931: 26–7). Thus, in conformity with the idea of racial senility, these monsters became extinct, playing "a losing game [that] has now become obsolete" (ibid.: 27). Or as Bergson notes:

> [T]he more species became mobile, the more they became voracious and dangerous to one another. Hence a sudden arrest of the entire animal world in its progress toward higher and higher mobility; for the hard and calcareous skin of the echinoderm, the shell of the mollusk, the carapace of the crustacean, and the ganoid breast-plate of the ancient fishes probably all originated in a common effort of the animal species to protect themselves against hostile species.
>
> ([1911] 1944: 145)

Bergson goes on to detail Life's abandonment of ever-heavier weapons of defense and offense such as massive body armor, teeth and claws. The vital impulse, Bergson proclaims, now focused on the development of greater agility among various species, in particular the evolution of instinct in insects and of intelligence in vertebrates culminating in *Homo sapiens*. Rabindranath had much less interest in the finer points of these developments, leaping from the megalomaniac monsters, which he termed "the biggest failures in life's experiments," directly to a novel experiment in disarmament constituting the third act: the creative evolution of Man and Mind (R. Tagore 1931: 27). As Rabindranath explains:

> [T]he form of life that seeks the great privilege of movement must minimize its load of the dead and must realize that life's progress should be a perfect progress of the inner life itself and not of materials and machinery; the non-living must not continue outgrowing the living, the armour deadening the skin, the armament laming the arms.
>
> (ibid.: 32)

The Spirit of Life, Rabindranath continues, thus began increasing the sensory powers of animals, such as the eyesight of bees, but always bound by habit or instinct: "[F]or centuries the bee repeats its hive, the weaver-bird its nest, the spider its web; and instincts strongly attach themselves to some invariable tendencies of muscles and nerves never being allowed the privilege of making blunders" (ibid.: 34). And then Life fought against instinct,

42   *C. Mackenzie Brown*

entertaining "a dangerously explosive factor which she had cautiously introduced into her council—the element of Mind" (ibid.: 35). With this development, Life reached its true meaning in freedom and creativity. At the same time, certain aspects of the physical body of Man suffered increasing neglect, and his mechanical efficiency significantly dwindled, so that "[h]is own puny muscles cried out in despair, and he had to invent for himself in a novel manner and in a new spirit of evolution ... He began to create his further body, his outer organs" that were not part of his own body, such as the bow and arrow (ibid.: 37). And with hands not specialized like those of other animals, Man can handle not just bows and arrows, but also pens and lutes (ibid.: 38). While Man's less specialized hands have lost the particular efficiency of animal claws and paws, his additional "new limbs" (like bows and arrows), being detached, freed Man from the physical burden of inborn weapons, thus putting "minimal pressure of taxation upon the vital resources of his body" (ibid.: 38–9).

This third act of Rabindranath's, though not yet finished, again follows closely the mystical evolutionary scientism of Bergson himself. We have already noted Bergson's contrast of instinct with intelligence that is echoed in Rabindranath. And Bergson emphasized that the lack of specialization of vertebrate limbs "becomes complete in man, whose hand is capable of any kind of work" ([1911] 1944: 147). Animals possess tools, but "the instrument forms a part of the body that uses it; and corresponding to this instrument, there is an *instinct* that knows how to use it" (ibid.: 154). Bergson notes that such natural instruments have greater efficiency "for the satisfaction of immediate wants" than the artificial instruments created by man, but the latter are guided by intelligence rather than driven by instinct, creating new needs, and giving greater and greater freedom to their wielder (ibid.: 155–56).

Returning to Rabindranath's evolutionary account, we find that in the final phases of the third act Man is able to transcend the "[w]earisome subjection to the haphazard gropings of natural selection ... [through] the purposeful selection of opportunities with the help of his reasoning mind" (R. Tagore 1931: 39). Herein we see that the Spirit of Life has now given pre-eminence to the Spirit of Man: "[I]t is the consciousness in Man of his own creative personality which has ushered in this new regime in Life's kingdom" (ibid.: 40). This Spirit contains "a surplus far in excess of the requirements of the biological animal in Man" (ibid.: 41). Rabindranath adds some Vedāntic flavoring at this point by citing a verse from the *Atharva Veda* to the effect that all the great spiritual virtues, including righteousness, truth, and religion, "dwell in the surpassing strength of the surplus" (ibid.: 42). It is in this surplus that we realize "the final truth of man" that is, "the truth of human unity," to which love testifies (ibid.: 47). The Spirit of Love helps us transcend the "sole monarchy of hunger, of the growling voice, snarling teeth and tearing claws," as it "emancipates our consciousness from the illusory bond of the separateness of self" (ibid.: 47). In closing the chapter on 'The Creative Spirit' and again

An illusion of conciliation 43

Vedānticizing his evolutionary tale, he quotes from the *Śvetāśvatara Upanishad* 4.1:

> He who is one, above all colours, and who with his manifold power supplies the inherent needs of men of all colours, who is in the beginning and in the end of the world, is divine, and may he unite us in a relationship of good will.

> (ibid.: 48)

In not too dissimilar a vein, but without mention of love or the Vedāntic theistic elements, Bergson talks about "the life of the body" being "on the road that leads to the life of the spirit," ([1911] 1944: 293). He proceeds to speculate on the rising wave of consciousness whose destiny is not bound to the physical brain as "consciousness is essentially free; it is freedom itself" (ibid.: 293–4). We come, he proclaims, to a realization in which we "feel ourselves no longer isolated in humanity, humanity no longer seems isolated in the nature that it dominates" (ibid.: 295). Bergson concludes his own evolutionary narrative by summing up: "The animal takes its stand on the plant, man bestrides animality, and the whole of humanity … is one immense army galloping beside and before and behind each of us in an overwhelming charge able to beat down every resistance and clear the most formidable obstacles, perhaps even death" (ibid.: 295).

Bergson's suggestion here of humanity's transcending death is paralleled in Chapter 4, 'Spiritual Union,' in *The Religion of Man*. Inculcating Vedāntic notions of absolute unity (but not the more extreme Advaitic notion of absolute identity that promotes an illusory view of the world), Rabindranath asserts that Man's progression from concern with physical survival to spiritual inquiry into his own nature led to the realization of unity of his self with the 'infinite One' that is 'infinite Love' (*anandam*) manifest in the supreme 'Person' (*Purushah*) (R. Tagore 1931: 64–5). Rabindranath concludes by quoting from the final part of the *Katha Upanishad* verse cited earlier (6.2) dealing with *prāṇa*: "[T]hose who realize him [*prāṇa*, or the divine Person], transcend the limits of mortality" (ibid.: 67).

The details of Debendranath's vitalistic evolutionism propounded in *The Religion of Man* so closely parallel Bergson's orthogenetic vitalism that clearly the Indian Nobel laureate was either one of Bergson's many readers or had otherwise been introduced to the fundamental ideas of Bergson's *Creative Evolution*. It is interesting to note that Rabindranath was invited to Manchester College for the Hibbert lecture by Lawrence Pearsall Jacks, Principal of the College from 1915 until 1931 and editor of the *Hibbert Journal*—dealing with issues of religion and science—from 1902 until 1948. Jacks was intrigued by eastern religion, and also by Bergson's philosophy which he taught (Unitarian Universalist History and Heritage Society: 1999–2013).

With his final Upanishadic paean in the chapter on 'The Creative Spirit' and his frequent references elsewhere to the scripturally sanctioned ideal of

44   C. Mackenzie Brown

the divine 'Person,' Rabindranath clearly reveals the underlying theistic assumptions of his evolutionary romance. His vitalistic force, far from being an impersonal potency inherent in nature, is endowed with some sort of consciousness or cosmic personality. He asserts, for instance, that there must be some sort of guiding or enabling "will" behind nature, an intending and purposeful power that gives order to the universe. He rejects the idea that such order is simply the work of "some impersonal insanity that unaccountably always stumbled upon correct results" (R. Tagore 1931: 62). And he proclaims, with an anthropic-sounding tone:

> Somewhere in the arrangement of this world there seems to be a great concern about giving us delight, which shows that, in the universe, over and above the meaning of matter and forces, there is a message conveyed through the magic touch of personality.
>
> (ibid.: 102)

Rabindranath's theistic evolutionism, then, even in its more muted form as orthogenetic-vitalism, is simply not the evolutionary theory of Darwin's *Origin*. As Bowler points out, while adherents to orthogenesis largely avoided any explicit teleological notions, this evolutionary theory, as well as Lamarckism, was simply a new form of theistic evolutionism in "more superficially scientific" guise (1988: 96–7). Bowler adds:

> The theory of orthogenesis is the most extreme form of anti-Darwinism. It not only replaced common descent with parallel evolution in the explanation of organic affinities, but also repudiated the whole Darwinian emphasis on the power of adaptation to shape evolution.
>
> (ibid.: 102)

And regarding the Bergsonian vitalistic version of orthogenesis, Bowler comments:

> In contrast to the scientific supporters of orthogenesis, who tended to suggest a physicochemical factor controlling variation from within the organism, Bergson proclaimed the existence of what was, in effect, a spiritual force imposing a rational order on the development of life.
>
> (1983: 57)

Bowler concludes: "Bergson was widely read in the early part of the [twentieth] century, and his philosophy represented a parallel influence to that of Lamarckism, promoting a slightly different but equally anti-Darwinian view of evolution" (ibid.: 117). In light of Bowler's comments, I find it difficult to see how Rabindranath's Vedāntic evolutionary vitalism can serve in any way as Radice's prescribed antidote to the contemporary evolution-creationism warfare.

Radice further argues, quite dubiously in my mind, that:

> Tagore would have rejected "intelligent design" in Nature as an absurd idea, above all else in the case of man, who, as he wryly observes, pays a price for his free hands and horizon-encompassing "view", with a tendency to trip and fall, and a tailless back that is a "wide surface practically unguarded."
>
> (2010: 111)

Radice correctly points out here the frequent blindness to bad design on the part of Intelligent Design (ID) proponents. But he seems not to realize that the vulnerable bipedal design of the human body alluded to by Rabindranath is interpreted by the poet not in terms of Darwinian adaptation to the environment but as part of an underlying, purposeful, vitalistic propulsion tending upwards towards an evolutionary culmination in 'Man,' 'Mind,' or 'Spirit.' Rabindranath's interpretation is typical of the many teleological evolutionary schemes of the early twentieth century that are deeply antagonistic to Darwinian evolution.

While there are certainly important differences between creationism (including Intelligent Design creationism) and the emergent or vitalistic evolutionism of thinkers like Bergson and Rabindranath, the two perspectives are at one in their invocation—implicit or otherwise—of supernatural, spiritual, or non-material conscious agents to explain the history of life on Earth. In fact, it sometimes becomes difficult to tell the two perspectives apart. As one example, we may note the frequent appeal to such agents to explain—contra Darwin—the phenomenon of cell differentiation, that is, how all the cells of a developing organism, having originally all the same constitution (DNA, we would say today), know how to divide into different sorts of cells/tissues, such as stomach, skin, brain, or muscle.

This particular phenomenon is often cited by both Christian creationists and ID proponents as evidence against Darwinian evolution, as a quick Google search will confirm.[10] We also find various recent Vedic creationists and Vedāntic evolutionists claiming that modern biologists cannot explain cell-differentiation, and that some sort of supernatural or non-material intelligent cause is needed, whether it be Krishna's bija-seeds containing the body plan of an organism that reside mysteriously in every cell, as the Vedic creationist Michael Cremo of ISKCON proclaims (2003: 485–6), or the quantumcollapsing observation of Brahman, as the Neo-Advaitin Amit Goswami explains in his theory of quantum evolution (2006: 66–8), or the reflected light of the *ātman* upon the cells of the developing embryo, as the Vedāntic evolutionist N.C. Panda argues (2002: 542–3).[11] And almost 80 years ago Rabindranath, in his book, *Our Universe*, proposed an occult intelligence or consciousness or inner urge at work within the cell "that is capable of amalgamating, readjusting, innovating and manipulating machinery of great complexity" (R. Tagore [1937] 1969: 111). He marvels at the way in which the 'life-cells' of a developing

46   C. Mackenzie Brown

organism are capable of "assembling at their destined places in the live body," and opines:

> How through sheer inner urge this miraculous division of labor has taken place in the functioning of the body, one never knows. The cell of the stomach has its specific duty, while the cell in the brain has its work of an entirely different nature. And yet, the atoms in the life-cells are fundamentally the same.
>
> (ibid.)

From a Darwinian perspective, it makes little difference whether one invokes an unspecified (but in the final analysis divine) conscious agent as in ID, or the God of Genesis as in creation science, or the bija-seeds of Krishna as in ISKCON, or the quantum-collapsing observation of Brahman, or Rabindranath's occult inner urge. All of these, at best, are unnecessary hypotheses, and none does anything to advance our understanding of the biochemical processes involved.

While in *The Religion of Man* Rabindranath plays several evolutionary-sounding notes, his later book *Our Universe*, resounds with themes that are reminiscent of more traditional design arguments, as already suggested by his comments on cell-differentiation. For instance, in *Our Universe*, he also argues that the order and harmony of the planets cannot be due to "mere coincidence," recalling the same sort of intuitive feeling concerning a planetary designer that we find underlying the design arguments of Isaac Newton and William Paley, and of his own father, Debendranath. Even in *The Religion of Man*, Rabindranath's account of the evolution of Man, with his hands able to hold detached tools and his mind free to think all thoughts, resonates with the teleological sentiments expressed by Debendranath in his *Brahmo Dharma*: "He [God] has given us two hands, so we can catch hold of all things ... He has given us the organ of speech, so we become happy by giving expression to all the thoughts of our mind" (D. Tagore 1928: 81). The distinction between vitalistic evolutionism and divine design thus seems rather small, in contrast to the great gap between them and the thoroughly non-teleological view of nature that we find in any robust Darwinian explanation of the world.

The temptation to see 'Darwinism' in Rabindranath Tagore's romantic cosmology is not an improbable confusion on the part of those not particularly familiar with Darwin's writings. As Bowler has noted:

> Historians have become increasingly aware of how difficult it is to define what late-nineteenth-century 'Darwinism' really was, even in biology. All too often, the term was used as little more than a synonym for evolutionism by writers who had no real interest in what Darwin actually said.
>
> (1988: 73)

It seems that this tradition is still alive and well among those who claim that Rabindranath is somehow compatible or in harmony with Darwinism.

Father, son, and scientistic spirit

In many ways, as we have seen, Rabindranath provides a religious interpretation of nature closely allied in spirit with that of Debendranath. Despite outward differences between Debendranath's natural theology and Rabindranath's evolutionary speculations, the following deep similarities reflected in their romantic cosmologies are noteworthy: (1) both thinkers insist upon a purposive drive and will behind the manifest universe;[12] (2) both reject in the end a monistic (Advaita) ontology and illusory view of the world in favor of a Vedānticized monotheism; (3) both accept the authority of modern science and thus feel compelled to scientize their Vedāntaic theism; and (4) both insist upon the priority of intuitive knowledge over reason, thereby attempting to spiritualize science. It is especially this latter epistemological perspective, epitomized in Debendranath's notion of two sciences, which is critical to their attempted reconciliations of modern science and their traditional religious, Vedāntic world-views.

While not explicitly referring to the notion of two sciences, Rabindranath assumes the same sort of hierarchy between naturalistic-mechanistic science and the metaphysical science or knowledge of harmony and love expounded by his father. Rabindranath provides a striking metaphor expressive of this hierarchy in *The Religion of Man* (R. Tagore 1931: 104–5). He refers to two secret halls, a 'dark hall' and a 'hall of union.' The dark hall lies behind the locked and secret doors of Nature's 'workshop department' where "dwells the mechanic," apparently referring to the scientist who labors therein creating useful inventions. But by laboring in this dark hall, we "can never attain finality." This claim is reasonable enough, for as Massimo Pigliucci points out, "Science is not about final (ultimate) answers" (2002: 144). But then, revealing a rather limited view of what constitutes science, Rabindranath declares that in the dark hall one finds simply a "storehouse of innumerable facts … that have not the treasure of fulfillment in them." While science does not lead to any final 'Truth' or some sort of metaphysical fulfillment, science is more than just a storehouse of facts—a common misperception of what science is.[13] Again, as Pigliucci notes, "science is a method, not a body of results" (2002: 138). As a method, science is a means of understanding our world and our place within it, and can thereby bring a certain delight of its own.

Let us proceed now to Rabindranath's second hall, the hall of union. Here "dwells the Lover in the heart of existence" (R. Tagore 1931: 105). Rabindranath emphasizes the contrast between the two halls, one dealing with the external aspects of things, the other with the "inner soul" (ibid.). The dark hall concerns "mere information about facts, mere discovery of power," the hall of union attends to "gladness" which "is the one criterion of truth,"

48   *C. Mackenzie Brown*

for when we touch 'Truth,' we know it "by the music it gives, by the joy of greeting it sends forth to the truth in us" (ibid.). There is no recognition here of the possibly misleading nature of intuitively pleasing notions. Instead, Rabindranath invokes the Upanishadic notion that "the joy of his own soul" is sufficient warrant for truth as it sets aside "all doubts and fears" (ibid.: 106). Intuitive notions, I suggest, are pleasing because they readily align with natural and common-sense thinking, but these are often in opposition to scientific thinking. As the noted developmental biologist Lewis Wolpert argues in his *The Unnatural Nature of Science*, "[S]cientific ideas are, with rare exceptions, counter-intuitive: they cannot be acquired by simple inspection of phenomena and are often outside everyday experience ... [and] doing science requires a conscious awareness of the pitfalls of 'natural' thinking" (1992: xi–xii).

The metaphor of the two halls gives us considerable insight into the specific character of Rabindranath's "strong desire to enjoy the *rasa* [flavor or essence] of science" that had been inspired by his father. This *rasa*, for Rabindranath, seems to consist primarily of a nature mystic's delight in the harmonious, benign, and aesthetic qualities of our universe allegedly revealed by science and interpreted as a "stream of love which pours down from the blue sky and wells up from the bosom of the earth" (R. Tagore 1931: 104), and not in the actual, demanding scientific enterprise that focuses on distinctions, differences, and analysis of parts (as well as of wholes). Very telling in this regard is an incident of his youth that Rabindranath relates in *The Religion of Man* just prior to presenting his metaphor of the two halls:

> I still remember the shock of repulsion I received as a child when some medical student brought to me a piece of human windpipe and tried to excite my admiration for its structure. He tried to convince me that it was the source of the beautiful human voice. But I could not bear the artisan to occupy the throne that was for the artist who concealed the machinery and revealed the creation in its ineffable unity.
>
> (ibid.: 99)

While it is not entirely clear who the artisan is, I suggest that Rabindranath had in mind God in his role as a mechanic, designing the various parts of human anatomy, while the artist is God as lover of beauty and unity. In any case, Rabindranath immediately adds that God hides the inner workings of nature, such as found in 'geological inscriptions' as well as in human anatomy. But, our nature-mystic concludes, God "is proudly glad of the expression of beauty which he spreads on the green grass, in the flowers, in the play of the colours on the clouds, in the murmuring music of running water" (ibid.).[14] Clearly expressed here is Rabindranath's preference for an artist's or poet's perception of a grand organic unity, tinged with the flavor of "an all-pervading personality" (ibid.: 100), over against the impersonal methodology and concern with parts that characterize science. Let me again quote Wolpert:

An illusion of conciliation 49

"[A]ny philosophy that is at its core holistic must tend to be anti-science, because it precludes studying parts of a system separately" (1992: 138).

The relevance of Wolpert's observation in relation to Rabindranath is further confirmed by another account of the same windpipe episode. This other account, by Rabindranath in his *My Reminiscences*, provides new insights into his reactions to anatomical science. The medical student was his English tutor, Aghore Babu, who brought to one lesson a paper parcel containing the windpipe. Unwrapping the parcel, Aghore declared, "I'll show you to-day a wonderful piece of the work of the Creator" (R. Tagore 1917: 42). This seems to confirm, incidentally, the identity of the artisan mentioned above with God as the mechanic-designer. Rabindranath then explains:

> I can still call to mind the shock this gave me at the time. I had always thought the whole man spoke—had never even imagined that the act of speech could be viewed in this detached way. However wonderful the mechanism of a part may be, it is certainly less so than the whole man.
> (ibid.: 42–3)

When Aghore Babu later took Rabindranath and some of his brothers to the medical college where they saw an old woman's cadaver laid out on the dissecting table, our poet indicates that the sight was not particularly upsetting. But he also noticed an amputated leg lying nearby on the floor, a sight which haunted him for days, as the "unmeaning leg" evoked a disturbing and "fragmentary" vision of humankind.

Rabindranath's taste for science, the allegedly "natural scientific temper" of his mind, like that of his father, represents a scientistic temper or spirit. Rabindranath's approach to science is wholly tempered by his vision of an all-pervading and beneficent cosmic unity in line with his Vedāntic ideals and often at odds with the temper of scientific empiricism with its sober look at the cruelties of natural selection unmitigated by any vitalistic promises.

The illusory conciliation of science and religion in the Tagorean mode

The two-sciences solution of the Tagores to the problem of the relationship between modern science and traditional religion represents a common Hindu version of what Mikael Stenmark refers to as a reconciliation model. As Stenmark points out, there is a great variety of reconciliation models such as the reformative model, which attempts to reformulate aspects of religion on the basis of science or vice versa, and the supportive model, which uses science to confirm the truths of religion or vice versa (2010: 285). These reconciliation models stand in contrast to models of independence (Gould's famous NOMA principle) and of irreconcilable conflict. This latter, Stenmark argues, is not the same as a general warfare model, in that some warfare models may be compatible with a reconciliation model. Thus, Young-Earth creationists and Intelligent Design advocates, despite their conflict with

50   *C. Mackenzie Brown*

mainstream contemporary science, ultimately espouse a reconciliation model, inasmuch as they believe that once science reforms itself to embrace supernatural as well as natural causation and modifies its stance on evolution, then science and religion will be in harmony (ibid.).

I think Stenmark's insight here is an important one, because the prestige of science today is so great that no one wants to be thought of, or to think of him- or herself, as 'unscientific.' Accordingly, I find that just as so-called conflict models are often reconciliation models in the minds of the thinkers involved, so also the more obvious and apparent reconciliation models often mask an underlying and possibly irreconcilable conflict. And the basic reason for this is that unlike the independence model, reconciliation models presuppose or highlight areas of contact and overlap, and thus the potential for conflict is ever present. In such models religiously-inspired pronouncements are invariably made about how the physical world works that dismiss or flatly contradict scientific explanations of how the world works. The potential for conflict is readily apparent in the Tagorean mode of reconciliation via the two-sciences model, despite the attempt by father and son to use science to complement, evoke, and affirm the 'higher' truths of religion.

The irreconcilability of the two Tagorean 'sciences' or 'knowledges' arises from fundamental cognitive differences between science and religion. Religious cognition, in the words of the philosopher of science Robert N. McCauley, "is primarily dependent on the natural proclivities of human minds," while the scientific requires, among other things, "a mastery of … radically counter-intuitive conceptions" (2011: 236). Each type of cognitive disposition, further, rests on radically different assumptions regarding the "the way the world works." McCauley concludes: "[R]eligions presume that the most penetrating accounts of the world will always, ultimately, look to agent causality. Science does not" (ibid.). And as Wolpert observes, the natural proclivities of the human mind seem rooted in our early mental development as children. Citing Piaget, Wolpert notes "two aspects of children's theory of the world: animism, the tendency to regard objects as living and endowed with will, and artificialism, the idea that everything is made by someone for a special purpose" (1992: 13). The animistic predisposition leads one "to believe as if nature were charged with purpose and as if chance did not exist" (ibid.: 14). Neither Debendranath nor Rabindranath could accept that the order in the world was not charged with purpose.

In tracing the Tagorean trajectory from Debendranath's providential design to Rabindranath's vitalistic evolutionism, we see a clear parallel with and indebtedness to European and American theological and philosophical developments of the nineteenth and early twentieth centuries. Religiously-inspired appeals to any straightforward notions of design in the West gradually gave way under the onslaught of evolutionary ideas. But many of these new evolutionary notions were strenuously anti-Darwinian, preserving—sometimes surreptitiously—indirect notions of design. None of these anti-Darwinian evolutionary speculations, however, have stood the test of time. Mendelian genetics spelled the death of orthogenesis (Bowler 1988: 103). And recent developments in evolutionary biology, such as Evo-Devo, make it increasingly evident that all vitalistic evolutionary hypotheses invoking conscious purpose and/or some sort of supernatural or spiritual enabling power within or behind nature, in order to explain one or another aspect of terrestrial life, are unnecessary, if not simply wrong. The alleged Tagorean conciliation founders on the advances of science.

Notes

1 For a brief discussion of the *Visva-Parichay*, see Mohit Chakrabarti (1995: 22).
2 The text of the sermon may be found in R. Tagore (1994: 127–9).
3 This passage paraphrases and synthesizes *Bṛhadāraṇyaka Upaniṣad* 1.2.1 and *Chāndogya Upaniṣad* 6.2.1. Citations of Upanishadic texts are to P. Olivelle's (1998) *The Early Upaniṣads*, unless otherwise noted.
4 Debendranath's son, Satyendranath, who composed the Introduction to Debendranath's autobiography, asserted that his father never quoted the Bible and was opposed to the spirit of the Hebrew Scriptures (S. Tagore 1994: viii). Similarly, Amiya P. Sen (2010: 53) claims that Debendranath was the only Brahmo "not particularly enthused by the moral life of Jesus and he also probably joined this to an unfeigned dislike for the Bible". But as this passage from the sermon indicates, there were some teachings of the Bible that resonated with Debendranath's own world-view. Debendranath seems to have been selective not only in what he found useful in the Bible, but also in the Upanishads, rejecting or at least ignoring their more monistic passages.
5 See *Muṇḍaka Upaniṣad* 1.1.5 for the two knowledges. For the European influence on Debendranath's idealization of intuition, see Wilhelm Halbfass (1988: 396, 570 n).
6 See R. Tagore (1931: 95).
7 As Bowler notes, paleontologists were particularly attracted to the theory of orthogenesis, as they "were convinced that they could see nonadaptive trends in the fossil record" (1988: 101).
8 Regarding Rabindranath's embracing of the Upanishadic ideal of *prāṇa*, Brian Hatcher comments: "[A]nd how did Rabindranath come to this vital truth? From his father, of course. It was Debendranath who entrusted his own faith in the Upaniṣads to Rabindranath beginning when his son was just a boy" (2011: 124).
9 Interestingly, Sarvepalli Radhakrishnan (1953: 642), in commenting on this and the following verse of the *Kaṭha Upaniṣad* in his translation of the Upanishads argues: "[T]he source and sustaining power of the universe is *Brahman*. Evolution is not a mechanical process. It is controlled by *Brahman*, who is here represented as *prāṇa*, the life-giving power."
10 See, for instance, the following: (1) http://creation.com/images/pdfs/tj/j22_2/j22_2_6–8.pdf; (2) http://creation.com/multicellularity; (3) http://creation.com/serial-cell-differentiation-intricate-system-of-design; (4) www.calhunter.com/evidence_of_intelligent_design1.htm; and (5) www.evolutionnews.org/2007/01/cellular_zip_codes_wheres_the003087.html (all accessed 19 March 2013).
11 The explanations of Cremo, Goswami, and Panda are discussed in Brown (2012: 179–80, 189, 195–6).
12 For Rabindranath, see *The Religion of Man* (R. Tagore 1931: 62, 90, 93–5, 102).
13 As Lewis Wolpert (1992: xi) points out, one of the widely held misperceptions of scientists today is that they are "interested only in facts and yet more facts, the collection of which is the hallmark of the scientific enterprise".

52   C. Mackenzie Brown

14 Cf. what Rabindranath says in his *Visva Parichay*: "[T]he universe has hidden its micro-self or shelved it out of sight behind the curtain. It has dressed itself up and revealed itself to us in a form that man can perceive with the structure of his simple power" (trans. by and quoted in P. Ghose 2010: 48).

References

Benton, M.J. (1990) 'Scientific Methodologies in Collision: The History of the Study of the Extinction of the Dinosaurs,' *Evolutionary Biology*, 24: 371–400.

Bergson, H. ([1911] 1944) *Creative Evolution*. New York: Random House.

Bowler, P.J. (1983) *The Eclipse of Darwinism: Anti-Darwinian Evolution Theories in the Decades around 1900*. Baltimore, MD: Johns Hopkins University Press.

Bowler, P.J. (1988) *The Non-Darwinian Revolution: Reinterpreting a Historical Myth*. Baltimore, MD: Johns Hopkins University Press.

Brown, C.M. (2012) *Hindu Perspectives on Evolution: Darwin, Dharma, and Design*. London: Routledge.

Chakrabarti, M. (1995) *Rabindranath Tagore: A Quest*. New Delhi: Gyan Publishing House.

Cremo, M. (2003) *Human Devolution: A Vedic Alternative to Darwin's Theory*. Los Angeles, CA: Bhaktivedanta Book Publishing, Inc.

Dana, J.D. (1856) 'Science and the Bible: A Review of "The Six Days of Creation" of Prof. Tayler Lewis,' *Bibliotheca Sacra*, 13(49): 80–129.

Darwin, C.R. (1859) *On the Origin of Species by Means of Natural Selection, or the Preservation of Favoured Races in the Struggle for Life*. London: John Murray. Available at: http://darwin-online.org.uk/content/frameset?itemID=F373&viewtype=text&pageseq=1 (accessed 28 March 2013).

Eimer, T. (1898) *On Orthogenesis and the Impotence of Natural Selection in Species-Formation*, trans. T.J. McCormack. Chicago, IL: Open Court. Available at: https://play.google.com/books/reader?id=-wgRAAAAMAAJ&printsec=frontcover&output=reader& authuser=0&hl=en&pg=GBS.PP7 (accessed 15 March 2013).

Ghose, P. (2010) 'The Scientist in Tagore,' *India Perspectives*, 24(2): 46–9.

Goswami, A. (2006) *Science and Spirituality: A Quantum Integration*, 3rd edn. New Delhi: Centre for Studies in Civilization.

Gould, S.J. (2002) *The Structure of Evolutionary Theory*. Cambridge, MA: Harvard University Press.

Halbfass, W. (1988) *India and Europe: An Essay in Understanding*. Albany, NY: State University of New York Press.

Hatcher, B.A. (2011) 'Father, Son and Holy Text: Rabindranath Tagore and the Upaniṣads,' *Journal of Hindu Studies*, 4: 119–43.

Hutton, J. (1795) *Theory of the Earth: with Proofs and Illustrations*, vol. 1, Edinburgh. Available at: www.gutenberg.org/files/12861/12861-h/12861-h.htm (accessed 13 March 2013).

McCauley, R.N. (2011) *Why Religion Is Natural and Science Is Not*. Oxford: Oxford University Press.

Olivelle, P. (trans.) (1998) *The Early Upaniṣads: Annotated Text and Translation*. Oxford: Oxford University Press.

Panda, N.C. (2002) *Cyclic Universe: Cycles of the Creation, Evolution, Involution and Dissolution of the Universe*, 2 vols [continuous pagination]. New Delhi: D.K. Printworld.

An illusion of conciliation   53

Pigliucci, M. (2002) *Denying Evolution: Creationism, Scientism, and the Nature of Science*. Sunderland, MA: Sinauer Associates.

Radhakrishnan, S. (ed.) (1953) *The Principal Upaniṣads, Edited with Introduction, Text, Translation and Notes*, trans. S. Radhakrishnan. London: George Allen & Unwin.

Radice, W. (2010) 'Tagore's *Religion of Man*,' *Faith and Freedom*, 63(171): 99–116.

Schuchert, C. (1924) 'Historical Geology,' 2nd rev. edn. Part II, in L.V. Pirsson and C. Schuchert, *A Text-book of Geology, for Use in Universities, Colleges, Schools of Science, Etc. and for the General Reader*. New York: John Wiley & Sons.

Sen, A.B. (2010) *Explorations in Modern Bengal c. 1800–1900: Essays on Religion, History and Culture*. Delhi: Primus Books.

Stenmark, M. (2010) 'Ways of Relating Science and Religion,' in P. Harrison (ed.) *The Cambridge Companion to Science and Religion*. Cambridge: Cambridge University Press, pp. 278–95.

Tagore, D. (1928) *Brahmo Dharma of Maharshi Debendranath Tagore*, trans. H.C. Sarkar. Calcutta: H.C. Sarkar.

Tagore, D. (1994) *The Auto-Biography of Maharshi Devendranath Tagore*, trans. S. Tagore and I. Devi. Calcutta: S.C. Sarkar & Sons.

Tagore, R. (1917) *My Reminiscences*, trans. S. Tagore. New York: Macmillan.

Tagore, R. (1931) *The Religion of Man, Being the Hibbert Lectures for 1930*. New York: Macmillan.

Tagore, R. ([1937] 1969) *Our Universe*, trans. I. Dutt. Bombay: Jaico Publishing House.

Tagore, S. (1994) 'Introduction 1,' in *The Auto-Biography of Maharshi Devendranath Tagore*, trans. S. Tagore and I. Devi. Calcutta: S.C. Sarkar & Sons.

Unitarian Universalist History and Heritage Society (1999–2013) 'Lawrence Pearsall Jacks.' Available at: www25.uua.org/uuhs/duub/articles/lawrencepearsalljacks.html (accessed 19 March 2013).

Wolpert, L. (1992) *The Unnatural Nature of Science*. Cambridge, MA: Harvard University Press.

3 Vedic science, modern science and reason

Anna S. King

Introduction

In the latter half of the twentieth century, the Enlightenment project (commitment to universal values, science and rationality) was often disparaged by scholars and writers as a pretext for 'ethnocentrism', 'Euro-centrism', even 'racism', or at least for Western arrogance (Cliteur and Gordon 2009: 312). Radical Enlightenment was often conceived to involve a rejection of all supernatural agencies, magic, disembodied spirits, and divine providence (Israel 2006: 866), and multiculturalists held "the Enlightenment responsible for violating cultural traditions, advocating instead a kind of radical pluralism and cultural relativism" (Cliteur and Gordon 2009: 312). As disillusionment with the military-industrial complex grew in the West in the wake of the Vietnam War and civil rights struggles, many young people turned to the East in a spiritual quest. Swami Prabhupada, because of his personal piety, but also his 'alternative' lifestyle, attracted many disciples from the 1960s' counter-culture to the International Society for Krishna Consciousness (ISKCON). The acceptance of his teachings meant to some extent the acceptance of pre-modern ways of thinking, and a world-view grounded in the authority of scripture and the commentaries of *bona fide* gurus. (Western) science became understood as ideologically-driven and culturally imperialistic. Prabhupada's encouragement of dialogue between devotees and scientists was imaginative, even visionary. However, he, like his successors, saw it largely as 'preaching':

> This preaching to the scientists is the next phase. If we can make an impression in the mind of the scientists then it will be easy to spread Krishna consciousness throughout the world. The scientists are a bogus group. They gave no factual knowledge, but are claiming to be authorities. Perhaps this is the first attempt to minimise their authority. Besides me, no one dares to. I never cared for their rascaldom.
>
> (quoted in Goswami 1977)

Prabhupada reinstated metaphysics and theology as generating certainty, and science as speculative, arbitrary and ideologically coloured. ISKCON's public documents frequently offer impoverished and hostile understandings of the relation between a monolithic science and religion. They identify science with scientific fundamentalism – the view that absolute truth is obtainable through science and through science alone. Unlike the use of the scientific method as only one mode of reaching knowledge, scientism claims that science alone can render truth about the world and reality.

Introduction: Vedic science

One of ISKCON's greatest architectural achievements, the magnificent Vedic Planetarium in Mayapur, India, reveals very clearly the tensions and ambivalences surrounding the notion of 'Vedic science'. The Vedic Planetarium, due to be completed in 2016, will cost in excess of $60 million, and is inspired by the vision of ISKCON's spiritual master, A.C. Bhaktivedanta Prabhupada (henceforth Prabhupada). It is believed that this grand Mayapur temple was predicted five hundred years ago by Nityananda, the 'most intimate associate' of Chaitanya Mahaprabhu. Speaking to Jiva Goswami, Nityananda prophesied:

> When our Lord Chaitanya disappears, by His desire, the Ganges will swell. The Ganges water will almost cover Mayapur for a hundred years, and then the water will again recede. For some time only the place will remain, devoid of houses. Then again, by the Lord's desire, this place will again be manifest, and the devotees will build temples of the Lord. One exceedingly wonderful temple (adbhuta-mandira) will appear from which Gauranga's eternal service will be preached everywhere.
> (www.skyscrapercity.com/showthread.php?t=1435661)

Sri Mayapur Chandrodaya Mandir, the Temple of the Vedic Planetarium, is the world headquarters of the International Society for Krishna Consciousness and its global flagship. Described on ISKCON websites as "A Landmark Spiritual Project of Universal Significance", its aim is to make the "vast culture and philosophy of the timeless Vedic tradition accessible to everyone". The temple is designed "according to the sacred architecture that has facilitated spiritual self-realisation for millions of people throughout the ages". The Planetarium will feature a giant rotating model that demonstrates the movements of the planetary systems as described in the *Srimad-Bhagavatam* and other sacred texts. It will give information about the phenomenal universe and explain its source, purpose and 'subtle' laws. The Vedic Science Centre will house exhibits demonstrating various aspects of Vedic cosmology, mathematics, science and archeology, while information centres will inform visitors about the fallacy of the Arian Invasion Theory, the solid scientific basis underpinning concepts of Intelligent Design and Vedic social science and social organization (http://news.iskcon.com/node/4293#ixzz1u112ux1z).

If the Vedic Planetarium looks back to a Vedic golden age, it is also a very modernist project. At an ideological level the presentation of Vedic science is

56 *Anna S. King*

highly reactive to, and therefore dependent on, a particular construction of modern science (a back-handed compliment) since it is intended "to directly challenge the accepted modern version of the universe, and establish the legitimacy of the Vedic version, as well as using science to counteract the prevalence of modern atheism" (www.tovp.org/en/about-us/chairmans-message).

At a material level it incorporates many non-Vedic elements. In July 1976, during a visit to Washington, DC, Prabhupada instructed Yadubara Dasa and Visakha Dasi to take photographs of the domed Capitol building as a basis for the Temple's architectural plans. (www.skyscrapercity.com/showthread.php?t=1435661). Teams of engineers, architects and surveyors have laboured on the project using the latest technology. Ambarisa das, the American great-grandson of Henry Ford, the chairman of the project, is the principal donor, while ToVP's Director of Development, Vraja Vilasa Dasa, originally from South India, previously worked for major IT companies in India, and also lived in the USA, where he worked as a consultant on Google Products for American railroads. ISKCON's strong relationship with the Internet is demonstrated by numerous websites which provide full coverage of every stage of construction and offer facilities for online donations (http://tovp.org/en/donate/how-to-give-a-donation). This project in fact illustrates acutely the ambivalence with which ISKCON regards modern sciences, and the challenges of building a purely Vedic structure. While devotees regard Vedic science as ancient wisdom, a revealed universal science, critics regard it as a new creation, created to support the claims of *Hindu* majoritarianism. Thus the Planetarium is driven by several competing forces: on the one hand, the desire to associate Vedic scriptures with the prestige of modern science, on the other, the conviction that the spirit of modern science subverts truth.

In this chapter I explore how 'Vedic science' is understood within ISKCON by examining the authoritative teachings of Prabhupada, the writings of 'Vedic' scientists, and ISKCON's latest public discussions of science. I explore the perplexities, ambiguities and tensions to which the notion of 'Vedic science' gives rise. In describing Vedic culture and philosophy as a 'science', Prabhupada reflects his engagement with the world around him, and the all-absorbing debates thrown up by modern cosmology, physics and archeology. The Planetarium, for example, is not intended to show Vedic culture and science simply as part of the history of science or of Vedic religion. It is intended to impart 'true' knowledge and 'true' science (http://news.iskcon.com/node/4293#ixzz1u112ux1z).

Before beginning the chapter, it is important to examine ISKCON's use of the terms 'Vedic' and 'Vedic science'. The Vedas are in a strict sense the canonical texts, liturgical works, composed in the last two millennia BCE. However, ISKCON, like many other guru movements of the twentieth century, uses the term loosely to indicate all sacred writings that are important to their tradition. 'Vedic science' has an equally fluid definition, and context becomes all-important. The phrase may sometimes have a definite referent – Vedic cosmology, astrology, archeology, mathematics, *vastu*, or Vedic creationism, etc.

At other times its use encompasses universal divinely-authorized lifestyle, values and culture.[1] In the Vaishnava context, Vedic knowledge is considered to have been first proclaimed by Krishna to Brahma who passed this knowledge down to Narad Muni, Narad Muni to Vyasadev, and then in unbroken preceptorial succession to Prabhupada. Prabhupada envisioned a cultural conquest of the West – a peaceful conquest – in which Vedic culture would prevail (Rosen 2002: 60). Rosen writes: "Vedic culture is our birthright. This holds true not only for Hindus but for the rest of the world as well" (ibid.: 140).

In India and among Hindu-born, diasporic congregations where its backward gaze contributes to a sense of national pride, ISKCON is increasingly popular. ISKCON's aim is to increase awareness of Vedic science, culture and philosophy among the younger generation, and to inspire a sense of pride in their rich tradition and heritage. However, Prabhupada's original disciples were more often than not from non-Hindu backgrounds. These disciples were disenchanted with Christianity and organized religion, and had a degree of scepticism with regard to science and scientific reductionism. 'Turn on, tune in, drop out', a counter-culture phrase popularized by Timothy Leary sums up this mood. A positive valorization of modern (Western) science and rationalism was important to neither the early generation of disciples nor later to the 'Indian' Hindu congregations.

Stages in ISKCON's thinking about science

There are overlapping, but distinctive stages in ISKCON's engagement with modernity and in particular with the natural sciences. In the first phase, Prabhupada's views, particularly of the origins of the universe and life, shape the ways in which ISKCON constructs the notion of (Western) science. 'Science' and 'scientism' become inextricably muddled. In this phase ISKCON theological interest in modern science tends to focus on the implications of relativity and modern cosmology. Prabhupada's famous phrase, 'Life comes from life', becomes a banner of resistance.

Phase 1 The teachings of Prabhupada

Many 'neo-Hindu' gurus who came to the West were influenced by Vivekananda's depiction of the East as spiritual and the West as materialistic, and, like Vivekananda, focused on the remarkable synergy between Vedic science and modern science.[2] Prabhupada, like Vivekananda, taught that India had retained its spiritual values while the West had succumbed to godlessness and materialism. He too was also passionately engaged with science, both debunking its universalist pretensions and progress, but also claiming that some of its findings were actually Vedic. Sharing many of the beliefs of right-wing Hindu apologists and nationalists, he believed not only that all truth was in the Vedas, but also that the 'discoveries' of modern science were also contained

58   *Anna S. King*

within the Vedas. Vedic science is not merely an inner science; when interpreted correctly, it contains *all* knowledge.

Prabhupada was not scientifically illiterate. He was educated at Kolkata's prestigious Scottish Church College and later owned a small pharmaceutical business. However, though he accepts the instrumental uses of science (i.e. technology) in the service of Krishna, he adopts a deeply anti-science, anti-secular and anti-modern rhetoric. He makes fun of science and 'demoniac' scientists. Scientists are 'rascals', 'bluffers', 'fools', 'cheats', 'frauds', 'frogs in a well', 'thieves', 'asses', 'jugglers of words'. Prabhupada ([1979] 1981: 21) famously argues that humans never succeeded in going to the moon – to this day devotees speak of 'the moon hoax' – and many of his statements about science could be seen as profoundly embarrassing for those who in the future may wish to adopt an eirenic approach.[3]

Prabhupada seeks to return civilization to a Vedic style of life and culture, and proclaims the superiority of Vedic civilization over modernity. He attacks modern science's methodological naturalism, or the exclusion of the super-natural as an explanation of natural phenomena. Modern science is inferior because it fails to acknowledge divine instrumentality. God and divine action are seen as the causal force in nature. Krishna is the material and the efficient cause of all nature. Advances in modern science which contradict or negate elements of the sacred texts are rejected, but modern science can also be held to affirm Hindu cosmology and epistemology. Prabhupada classifies Vedic knowledge revealed in the texts as 'science'. Thus Vedic science today in ISKCON covers everything from Vedic astrology, Vedic mathematics, Vedic cosmology, Vedic creationism, Ayurveda, *karma-kand*, to urine therapy. In a word, it is everything that Vaishnavism teaches.

Prabhupada arrived in the USA in 1966, bringing missionary Vaishnavism. He had survived two heart attacks at sea, he spoke English with a strong accent, his dress was perceived as exotic – yet he had come to tell people to give up meat-eating, illicit sex, intoxication, and gambling, and to teach them to worship Krishna. As the founder of ISKCON, he emerged as a major figure in the Western counter-culture, writing more than 80 books on Vedantic philosophy, religion, literature, culture and science, and watching ISKCON grow to a confederation of more than 108 temples, various institutes and farm communities. Prabhupada's arrival in the United States at the age of 70 came at an opportune time. It coincided with the passing of new immigration laws allowing the migration of Asians into America, young people in Europe and America were turning to Indian spiritualities, and, for the first time, travel was within the means of many spiritual seekers. Indian gurus and holy men found economic as well as religious reasons to attract foreign devotees, and many revivalists believed that the West was spiritually bankrupt.

Prabhupada advocated a simple Vedic way of life, one that opposed exploitive consumerism and depended on organic farming and cows. He taught that the Western world was dominated by a mechanistic, materialistic, and essentially godless view of the universe. It had become an industrial-consumer civilization bent on exploiting and dominating matter. Prabhupada advocated a way of life in which spiritual values were central. He saw the ultimate well-being of humans as lying in a relation of submission and service to Krishna. Like many orthodox Hindu gurus of his time, he understood Western intellectual and scientific ways of comprehending the universe and humanity as abandoning the soul and the search for ultimate spiritual meaning, rejecting metaphysics and accepting a form of biological and physical determinism. Vaishnavism as the universal religion offered a radically different portrait of human nature and the nature of the universe, a portrait which stressed divine relationality and playful creativity. Prabhupada's spiritual understandings of personhood challenged purely materialistic explanations of human thoughts, beliefs and desires, his emphasis on the ethical component of religious belief challenged the view that scientific knowledge should be value-free, his stress on cosmic purpose attacked evolutionary theory, his emphasis on the sanctity of human and animal life would lead his disciples to challenge new reproductive technologies, stem cell research, the prospect of human cloning, etc. Prabhupada spoke dismissively of 'materialism' and 'atheism' as characteristic of much Western intellectual endeavour. Today his successors routinely use phrases such as 'positivism', 'materialism', 'reductionism' and 'scientific naturalism' to describe the diverse world of the sciences and social sciences. These phrases are shorthand ways of describing explanations of the universe or human history that leave out God.

ISKCON's public documents argue that while society assumes that scientific theories are 'facts' or pure knowledge, in truth, science is simply a system of belief like any religious tradition, but a system which increasingly dominates global cultural paradigms and empties them of spiritual and ethical content and meaning. Science not only leaves out the role of God, but renders irrelevant the knowledge and authority of scripture, and subjective and emotional experiences. It is paradigm-bound, while masquerading as universal.

'Life comes from life'

ISKCON views Prabhupada's greatest contribution to science as the central proposition that life is not generated from matter, but matter from life. Prabhupada challenges scientists over the origin of life, the 'materialist' view that the soul is a mythological concept, and the 'reductive' understanding that consciousness results from a series of interactions in the brain. Perhaps most importantly he challenged scientists over the notion of evolution. Prabhupada taught that humans have been present on the Earth since the beginning of time and that human history extends through vast cycles of cosmic time. The Vaishnava understanding of the immense age of humanity is that ordinary human beings have been born and reborn many millions of times before, and that souls evolve through successive lives.

60 *Anna S. King*

The universe: time, space and the Big Bang

Prabhupada holds fast to traditional Vaishnava notions of the universe as revealed in the sacred scriptures, especially the *Bhagavata Purana*, despite the fact that 'western' sciences are proving the facts to be quite other. He attacks modern cosmological findings about the origin of the universe and the creation of life, contradicting the physics of the Big Bang theory and the claims of palaeontology and biology. ISKCON scientists claim that the age of the universe according to Vedanta is an order of 10^4 times older than that predicted by the Big Bang. Creation and destruction (big crunch, *pralaya*) take place periodically and continue eternally (cf. Singh 2004/2005b: 37). And while the West on the whole understands history as a process of progress in which evolutionary ideas play a part, mainstream ISKCON, like traditional Hinduism, turns that model on its head. It refutes the theory of progressive evolution of civilization and talks of gradual degradation throughout the great cycles of four ages. History is therefore a process of deterioration of world order, of *dharma*. Krishna's appearance in the world and departure from it about five thousand years ago inaugurate the present age, the Kali Yuga, which is one of gradual decay and corruption. For Prabhupada, there is nothing mythical about the world of Krishna and the *gopis*, but it requires the power of true devotion to understand it as part of synchronic historical and eternal reality (van der Velde 2004: 127).

Phase 2 'ISKCON Scientists'

In the second phase, the Krishna Conscious agenda, with its missionary imperative, tends to reinforce the idea that 'Western' science and religion are in a state of continual warfare. 'ISKCON scientists' attack global science, in particular archaeology and palaeontology, as an all-embracing worldview, a carrier of Western atheistic values and as a secular reflection of the Jewish-Christian linear model of history. ISKCON scientists, like many Hindu nationalists, justify developing a science in accord with Vedic cosmology as an attempt to decolonize, or purify, knowledge of Western, Jewish-Christian influences. They take up the challenge of defeating scientists on their own ground, claiming to show that archaeologists, palaeontologists and historians are engaged in a vast cover-up. They query the reliance on the evidence of fossils to show the evolutionary stages through which many plants and animals have passed. They dismiss scientific research findings about the structure, embryonic development, chemistry and geographic distribution of organisms which point to the descent of widely differing species from common ancestors. They dispute the results of chemical and radioactive dating and other methods by which scientists estimate the first evidence of life on Earth (4,000 billion years) and the evolution of modern humans (*homo sapiens*) 200,000 years ago. They reject the idea that all living things are descended, from one or a few simple original forms – in particular that humans are like apes because they share a common (recent) ancestor.

Krishna devotees, Michael A. Cremo, and Richard L. Thompson are undoubtedly the best known of ISKCON scientists. They co-authored *Forbidden Archeology: The Hidden History of the Human Race* (Cremo and Thompson 1993). Michael Cremo also wrote *Forbidden Archeology's Impact* (1998) which documents the scientific community's responses to *Forbidden Archeology* with its extensive 'evidence' for extreme human antiquity. Cremo and Thompson state that, according to standard scientific views, humans emerged only within the past one hundred thousand years or so; in *Forbidden Archeology* they claim to document abundant evidence that actually supports the Vedic time scale that humans have existed for millions, even billions, of years on Earth. They invoke the notion of a 'knowledge filtration' by Western-trained scientists which protects the ruling paradigm and keeps out the evidence that supports Vedic cosmology. Kuhn's notion of paradigm has been used by ISKCON scientists to deny the entire idea of scientific progress. However, Kuhn himself refutes this view:

> Later scientific theories are better than earlier ones for solving puzzles in the often quite different environments to which they are applied. That is not a relativist's position, and it displays the sense in which I am a convinced believer in scientific progress.
>
> (Kuhn 1970: 206)

Outside ISKCON, Cremo and Thompson are often regarded as 'whacky conspiracy theorists'. Inside they are admired because they appear scholarly, carefully examining (suppressed) historical evidence. They claim to prove that bones and artefacts have been found which show that people existed on Earth millions of years ago, and that the prevailing paradigm of human evolution is wholly untenable. They accumulate evidence of advanced civilizations extending back millions of years into the past. To account for the lack of scientific interest in these claims, they posit a passive conspiracy to suppress a huge body of data that contradicts the prevailing paradigm. The scientific establishment has suppressed, ignored or forgotten these remarkable facts. Evolutionary prejudices, deeply held by powerful groups of scientists, have acted as a knowledge filter. The filtering, whether intentional or not, has left us with a radically incomplete set of facts for building our ideas about human origins. Cremo also argues that the modern human evolutionary account is a 'Judeo-Christian heterodoxy' which covertly retains the fundamental structures of Jewish-Christian cosmology, salvation history and eschatology while overtly dispensing with the scriptural account of divine intervention in the origin of species.

The Bhaktivedanta Institute and T.D. Singh (His Holiness Bhaktisvarupa Damodara Swami)

Conflicting impulses to engage scientists in dialogue, while disproving their theories, are evident throughout ISKCON's history. Prabhupada inspired his

62   *Anna S. King*

disciples to advance formal dialogue with scientists, and to promote the study of the relationship between science and Vedanta. He founded the Bhaktivedanta Institute in Vrindavan in 1974 with this express aim, appointing T.D. Singh as the Institute's director. Singh who was born in 1937 in the Himalayan Kingdom of Manipur, studied at the University of California, Irvine, where his doctoral research in physical organic chemistry was supervised by Robert W. Taft, the inventor of the Taft equations. While in the USA, Singh met Prabhupada, and eventually took *sannyas*, becoming a celibate renouncer. Under Singh's guidance, the Institute organized several world congresses for the synthesis of science and spirituality, and published several volumes of collected papers. At his death in 2006, many scientists including several Nobel Laureates – Charles H. Townes, Richard Ernst, Werner Arber, Ahmed H. Zewail and William D. Phillips among them—joined others in praising his contribution to the understanding of the relationship between science and religion (Bhaktivedanta Institute 2008).

Singh regarded science and religion as the two dominant forces of humanity, shaping humanity's search for the ultimate meaning of life and the universe. However, he was first and foremost a faithful disciple of Prabhupada. Despite personal friendship with many leading scientists, he publicly contextualizes the debate between science and religion in terms of a contest; atheists versus theists, scientific materialism versus 'spiritualism' or religious principles. He attacks 'scientific materialism', identified with atheism, as an empty and mechanistic world-view. He charges evolutionary scientists with adopting a reductionist framework, and, like Cremo and Thompson, critiques biologists and others for assuming that evolution is a fact rather than a theory. He argues that scientific culture has come to dominate human civilization, pushing it towards the complete erosion of moral and ethical values (Singh 2005a: 14). Singh cites approvingly the work of physicists like Einstein, Born, Planck, Schrödinger and others, whose research (he believes) led them to acknowledge the existence of God. He praises also (ibid.) the work of Michael J. Behe, a leading advocate of the Intelligent Design Movement (IDM). In dialogue with Behe (Singh 2005b), he argues that advances in science point to a fine-tuned universe purposefully designed by a Supreme Being or God.

Singh's vision of lasting world peace depends upon the cooperative dialogue between science and spirituality, which in turn is based upon the recognition that the Supreme Being is the foundation of reality. Spirituality or the pure form of religion should guide humanity in creating a just and meaningful society. Science should offer the means and skills to implement this vision (ibid.: 50). Science, unlike religion, is unable to deal with meaning. The explosive developments of science and technology, especially in the field of biotechnology and bioengineering, require ethical guidelines that must be based on 'age-old spiritual wisdom'. Biomedical issues like abortion and organ transplantation cannot be resolved without a spiritual understanding of life.[4]

Vedic science, modern science and reason 63

Phase 3 The present

The third phase begins at the end of the twentieth century when ISKCON starts to face complex issues of self-representation. While Christian theologians on the whole have come to reinterpret the Biblical account of creation as metaphorical and poetic, and even to see theistic accounts of the origin of the universe as compatible with modern physics,[5] for ISKCON, reformulating an ancient Indian religious tradition in this new scientific context is almost impossible. Scientific experimental findings are believed to conflict outright with spiritual truth. The notion of modern science as a source of universally valid and objective knowledge is itself regarded as a sign of Western secular imperialism and materialism.

The most comprehensive way today of examining ISKCON's public position on science and religion is to turn to the internet. Here we find extensive websites (e.g. http://krishnascience.com/) which engage very directly with the relationship between Vedic and modern science and challenge scientists from the perspective of Vedic physics, Vedic astrology or Vedic creationism. Most prominent, as one might expect, are links to the writings of Swami Prabhupada, 'ISKCON scientists', and increasingly to the theistic writings of the Intelligent Design Movement (IDM). ISKCON media of all kinds continue to focus on stories attacking evolutionism and Darwin, and critiquing modern scientific methodology. Krishna sites present uncritically the counter-arguments of 'Vedic scientists' like Danavir Goswami (Dr Dane Holtzman), Svarupa Damodara (T.D. Singh), Sadaputa Dasa (Richard L. Thompson), and HH Bhakti Madhava Puri (Dr. M.A. Marchetti). Indeed, many devotees believe that the mission of devotee scientists is precisely to promote ISKCON cosmology and science. Danavir Goswami, the author of *Vedic Cosmology*, argues that: "The job with which Vedic scientists are faced is to utilize their knowledge of the material world to provide to the materially-affected persons that what is stated in the shastras is perfect and unassailable, even by material calculations" (http://krishna.org/the-moon-sadaputas-is-the-bona-fide-iskcon-opinion/). Vedic scientists are also the driving force behind several modern ISKCON projects – the most ambitious being the Sri Mayapur Vedic Planetarium and Temple (www.tovp.org/en/vedic-science/vedic-planetarium).

Thus, the Vedic Science Research Center (http://vedicscience.eu/) has articles on the Anthropic principle, the Big Bang, the Antiquity of Vedic Culture, evidence for reincarnation, Krishna Creationism and the origin of the Human Species, the Life and Origin of the Universe, Consciousness: Irreducible Non-material Aspect of Reality, Forbidden Archeology, Vedic Ecology, Mechanistic and Non-Mechanistic Science, the Synthesis of Science and Spirituality, etc.

The rise of militant atheism today is inspiring ISKCON devotees to attack 'God-bashers' like Richard Dawkins, Christopher Hitchens, Sam Harris, Daniel Dennett, and Victor J. Stenger, while the current resurgence and spread of Creationism and the Intelligent Design Movement in America and

64   *Anna S. King*

elsewhere also aid ISKCON's cause. Lalitanatha Dasa, author of the (2010) BBT book, *Rethinking Darwin: A Vedic Study of Darwinism and Intelligent Design*, collaborates with some of Intelligent Design's leading proponents, Michael Behe, William Dembski, and Jonathan Wells, to point out the flaws in the Darwinian paradigm and examine the case for intelligent design.

ISKCON's Vedic scientists are not the only academics with degrees in science who are publishing books claiming that Vedic literature is actually a record of scientific information or discoveries. Nanda cites many academics working in the United States and Canada – notably Subhash Kak, David Frawley, N.S. Rajaram (now in India), Ram Mohan Roy, the Vedic creationists associated with the Ramakrishna Mission, the 'unified field physicists' associated with Maharishi Mahesh Yogi, and the monks of Ramakrishna Mission's Vedanta centres around the world (2004: 75).

Prophets facing backwards

Meera Nanda is the most articulate and fearless critique of 'Vedic science'. Her views are echoed by Martha Nussbaum in *The Clash Within: Democracy, Religious Violence, and India's Future* (2007). Nanda (2003b) argues that:

> The mixing up of the mythos of the Vedas with the logos of science must be of great concern not just to the scientific community, but also to the religious people, for it is a distortion of both science and spirituality … Any erosion of the dividing line between science and myth, between reasoned, evidence-based public knowledge and the spiritual knowledge accessible to yogic adepts, is bound to lead to a growth of obscurantism dressed up as science.

A central theme of *Prophets Facing Backward* is Nanda's description of the 'malignant' collusion of Western postmodernists, feminists, and anti-imperialists with reactionary Hindutva, a convergence between a supposedly emancipatory postmodernist deconstruction of science and the "clearly reactionary, chauvinistic doublespeak of Vedic science". Nanda (2004) traces the ancestry of Vedic Science to the 'so-called' Bengal Renaiss.ance, which was in turn influenced by Orientalist constructions of Vedic antiquity as the 'Golden Age'. Heavily influenced by German Idealism and British Romanticism, important Orientalists including H.T. Colebrooke, Max Müller and Paul Deussen tended to locate the central core of Hindu thought in the Vedas and Upanishads, as well as the Advaita tradition of Shankara. While apologists for Hinduism like Vivekananda, Aurobindo and Bankim Chandra Chatterjee appropriated modern scientific thought for their own purposes, Hindutva ideologues and postcolonial scholars denounce modern science and its reductionist methodology as serving colonial interests.

Thus, Nanda argues that Vedic Science is the legitimation of the Hindu nationalist world-view. She notes that Hindutva theoreticians and propagandists like to describe themselves as 'intellectual Kshatriyas' or "self-proclaimed

Vedic science, modern science and reason   65

guardians of 'Hindu India' having taken it upon themselves to defend Hindu culture, its core values, and its worldview from liberals and Marxists at home, and from Eurocentric stereotypes abroad" (2003a: 65).

> Modern natural science is the weapon of choice of these intellectual warriors. Hindu nationalists are obsessed with science. They use the vocabulary of science to claim that the most sacred texts of Hinduism – the Vedas, the Upanishads, which contain the essence of Vedic teachings (also called the Vedanta), and Advaita Vedanta – are, in fact, scientific treatises, expressing in a uniquely holistic and uniquely Hindu idiom the findings of modern physics, biology, mathematics, and nearly all other branches of modern natural science. From the most orthodox priests, to the modern globe-trotting, English-speaking swamis, academics (many of them in American and Canadian universities), pamphleteers and journalists, down to ordinary men and women sympathetic to Hindu nationalist ideology, all proclaim that Hinduism is simply another name for scientific thinking. Some declare the entire Vedic literature as converging with the contents and methods of modern science. Others concentrate on defending such esoteric practices as Vedic astrology, *vastu shastra* (building structures in alignment with the cosmic 'life-force'), Ayurveda (traditional Hindu medicine), transcendental meditation, faith healing, telepathy, and other miracles as scientific. We will call both of these claims 'Vedic science', as their shared aim is to prove that the mythos of the Vedas contains within itself, and even surpasses the logos of modern science.
>
> (Nanda 2003a: 65)

Nanda refers directly to ISKCON when she examines the example of the emerging theory of 'Vedic creationism' which she describes as updating the spiritual evolutionary theories of Sri Aurobindo and Swami Vivekananda. She observes (theologically not entirely correctly) that its chief architects, Michael Cremo and Richard Thompson, claim that Darwinian evolutionary biologists and mainstream biologists, being products of the Western ontological assumptions, have been systematically ignoring and hiding evidence that supports the theory of 'devolution of species' from the Brahman through the mechanism of karma and rebirth. Nanda states: "All knowledge, they claim, parroting social constructivism, is a product of interests and biases. On this account, Vedic creationism, explicitly grounded in Vedic cosmology is as plausible and defensible as Darwinism, grounded on the naturalistic and capitalist assumptions of the western scientists." Nanda (2004) comments of Michael Cremo's *Human Devolution: A Vedic Alternative to Darwin's Theory*:

> As evidence, Cremo cites every possible research in paranormal ever conducted anywhere to 'prove' the truth of holist Vedic cosmology which proposes the presence of a spiritual element in all matter (which takes different forms, thereby explaining the theory of 'devolution').

66   *Anna S. King*

She adds, "Utterly incredible though they are, and utterly devoid of any empirical support, Vedic physics and Vedic creationism are being touted as serious scholarship based upon the assumption that different cultural assumptions sanction alternative methods as rational and scientific."

Nanda therefore argues that, in India, creationism is motivated by ultra-nationalism, Hindu chauvinism and the nationalist urge to declare Hinduism's superiority as the religion of reason and natural law over Christianity and Islam, which are declared to be irrational and faith-based creeds. She maintains that many of the Hindutva arguments for 'Vedic science' find a resonance with the fashionable theories of alternative sciences and postcolonial studies. Postmodernist and multiculturalist critics of modern science are rediscovering and restating many of the arguments that Hindu nationalists have long used to assert the superior 'scientificity' of Hindu sacred traditions. The deep investment of these philosophies in perpetuating superstitions and patriarchy in India was forgotten and forgiven: "Postmodern prophets who promise us a kinder gentler science do indeed face backward to the spirit-soaked metaphysics of orthodox Hinduism, which has, in fact, inhibited the growth of reason, equality and freedom in India" (Nanda 2007, 2005: 49).

Nanda argues that postmodernist attacks on objective and universal knowledge have played straight into the Hindu nationalist slogan of all perspectives being equally true – within their own context and at their own level. The result is the loud – but false – claims of finding a tradition of empirical science in the spiritual teachings of the Vedas and Vedanta. Such scientization of the Vedas does nothing to actually promote an empirical and rational tradition in India, while it does an incalculable harm to the spiritual message of Hinduism's sacred books.

Nanda also accuses scholars of betraying their own profession:

> Long ago, Julien Benda wrote in his *La Trahison de Clercs*, that when intellectuals betray their calling – that is, when intellectuals begin to exalt the particular over the universal, the passions of the multitude over the moral good – then there is nothing left to prevent a society's slide into tribalism and violence. Postmodernism represents a treason of the clerks which has given intellectual respectability to reactionary religiosity. With the best intentions of giving marginalized social groups – especially if they were women and if they belonged to the non-western world – the right to their own ways of knowing, western academics, in alliance with populist Third Worldist intellectuals, have succeeded in painting science and modernity as the enemy of the people. Rather than encourage and nurture a critical spirit toward inherited traditions, many of which are authoritarian and patriarchal, postmodernist intellectuals have waged a battle against science and against the spirit of the Enlightenment itself. As the case of Vedic science in the service of Hindu nationalism in India demonstrates, this misguided attack on the Enlightenment has only aided the growth of pseudoscience, superstitions and tribalism.
>
> (Nanda 2007, 2005: 52, 2003a: 29)

Meera Nanda is one of many critics who believe that there is a strong scientific, rational tradition in India, but not necessarily in the Vedas or religious texts. She reminds readers of the very real dangers posed by the 'Vedic science' demotion of reason and science that leaves people prey to falsehood and mental bondage. She notes that Indian government agencies have subsidised all kinds of traditional pseudoscience, while Vedic Science credits itself with fostering modern discoveries such as quantum mechanics. Reactionary modernism is at work: ideologues champion science while condemning secularism, naturalism, reductionism, the disenchantment of nature, the West, and even the Semitic mentality. "Hinduization of science in India is therefore motivated by a deeply chauvinistic nationalism" (Nanda 2003a: 97). Postmodernism plays into this agenda with its condemnation of Enlightenment rationality, universalism, and objectivity, and hence the universalism of modern science, in their stead proffering social constructivism, standpoint epistemology, and local and situated knowledges. Deep ecologists and prominent feminists rail against the bias of the Western scientific world-view. All this has been a great boon for the 'panderers' of Vedic Science. Not only can the history of ideas be rewritten, but secular Indian modernizers can be accused of succumbing to mental colonization. Nanda notes that ostensibly secular, left-wing intellectuals from India including Ashis Nandy, Vandana Shiva, Claude Alvares, Gayatri Spivak, Partha Chatterjee, Homi Bhabha, Dipesh Chakravarty, Gyan Prakash, Veena Das, Chandra Tolpady Mohanty and many others have been guiding lights of university humanities departments in America. The global prominence of Indian scholars in the assorted postmodernist debates brought them enormous prestige back home. Their critique of 'mental colonialism' and their promotion of local knowledges found a strong echo in literally thousands of 'alternative development' NGOs and social movements (Nanda 2003b).

Reflections: puzzles and perplexities

ISKCON public documents are right to emphasize that physical and biological processes are not a sufficient cause for human thoughts, emotions, and behaviour, and that the worlds of the religious imagination and ethical insights matter. However, Prabhupada's literal understanding of the *Bhagavatam* and other texts means that his disciples today are still taught to accept the texts 'as they are', and to believe that perfect knowledge of the universe is found in the *Bhagavatam* and other texts. Danavir Goswami, for example, attacks any non-literal interpretations of the *Bhagavatam* cosmology as products of the imagination. Indeed, many devotees are deeply disturbed by even the suggestion that the *Bhagavatam* should not be taken literally. As followers of Prabhupada, instead of turning to "science, mental speculation and intellectual juggling", devotees are required to simply "surrender to Srila Prabhupada, surrender to Krishna, and hear from a perfect authority" (Madhudvisa dasa 2011). ISKCON scientists who diverge from received truth are regarded as deviating from the teachings of Prabhupada and "siding with scientists". Even

68　*Anna S. King*

Sadaputa Dasa (Richard L. Thompson), despite his great reputation, was attacked for deviance (ibid.). Thus when ISKCON denounces modern science, it does not seek to understand what modern physics and cosmology tell us about the place of humanity in the natural world nor explore sensitively the dynamic relationships between world-views/cosmologies, socio-cultural practices and technologies. Its scientists seek to convince the public of the authenticity of their own approaches and of the falsity of other approaches.

ISKCON's notion of Vedic science remains vague and is more connected with what might be called religion or *dharma* rather than with what today might be considered science. ISKCON scientists are particularly active when modern scientific hypotheses appear to undermine basic religious tenets, or when theories in contemporary science challenge spiritual views by favouring a naturalistic conception of the world. Notions of evolution, of the age of the Earth and humanity, of life itself are tenaciously opposed, often by a rereading of the scientific data. At the same time devotees read back into the past contemporary scientific achievements – the aeroplane, for example, or nuclear weapons or even relativity or quantum theory. Prabhupada's disciples claim that Western science has been 'disproved' by Thompson and Cremo. I have been assured many times by devotees that *Forbidden Archeology* has completely discredited the claims of Western scientists. In ISKCON's 'official' publications, the complex relationships between 'religion' and 'science' tend to be reduced to one between monolithic entities. There is little recognition that many people – including many practising scientists – believe that modern science and religious belief can co-exist, and that it is possible simultaneously to follow the principles of the scientific method and believe in a particular spiritual tradition.

At the beginning of the chapter I raised the question of whether the public rejection of 'modern' science actually matters. Does it matter that religiously conservative movements like ISKCON aggressively condemn the secular and naturalistic worldview of science? Scientists like Turkish-American physicist Taner Edis speak out against restrictions coming from religious conservatives, and against the recognition of pseudoscientific ideas. Edis laments science and scepticism's standing in society amid "the pseudosciences, new age bunkum and other intellectual hallucinations" (Pietersen 2008). Many scientists make the case that factual knowledge gained through the full range of evidential sources (history, science, and cross-cultural study) can legitimately and easily be interpreted as religiously inspiring, and explain why, at this time in history, it is so urgent and fruitful to do so. They point out that scientists and science educators are committed to presenting the best that today's science has to offer and that today, where the history of life on Earth is concerned, evolutionary biology has no scientific rivals to speak of. Not addressing so-called 'alternatives' is not a limitation of scientific information; it is merely limiting science courses to scientific views that command a consensus within the scientific community. Presenting an artificial 'controversy' over evolution when no significant controversy exists within the scientific community will undermine the efforts of educators to impart basic, accurate information to their students.

On the other hand, those who hold creationist views, like Prabhupada and contemporary ISKCON scientists, argue that scientific institutions, when conflicting with religious views, should not be able to claim a privileged political position. Globally there is a conservative religious rejection of Darwinian evolution. In the USA, the anti-evolutionary movement is strong, and there is much support for the theory of creationism or evolution guided by God despite the fact that creationism and ID are often unacceptable in "intellectual high culture" (Edis 2012). Creationism or guided evolution can enable an affirmation of technology. It could therefore be argued that public hostility to modern science does not greatly affect the wider world of scientific endeavour, and therefore does not matter.

Newly founded religious movements often transform radically, and how they change depends as much on historical contingencies and cultural constraints as doctrine. Scientific information and scientific ways of thinking will continue to influence informed decision-making in practically all areas of life. While this chapter has attempted to clarify the 'official' position of Prabhupada and ISKCON scientists (a position which is itself often ambivalent and complex), it accepts that religion on the ground may not coincide with the official pronouncements of religious leaders.[6] It recognizes that most devotees/Hindus live in a world powerfully affected, even dominated, by science and technology, and that daily life for many involves the use of modern technologies and scientific processes. One only has to access ISKCON's websites to find a range of responses to the cosmology advanced by the Vedic Temple and Planetarium.[7] The charismatic ISKCON guru Radhanath Swami, believes that once global devotion to Krishna is fully established in the world, then more liberal accommodation with science will be possible (personal interview). At present, however, ISKCON is at its most dogmatic in the area of science, constructing its public position upon the assumption that modern science is a prisoner of Western cultural and religious biases. The gaze backwards to a golden age of global Vedic culture and science may bring ontological security in the face of scientific 'advances', but it also diverts the movement away from Krishna consciousness towards a Vedic triumphalism and obscurantism.

Notes

1 I was privileged to have this conversation with a retired nuclear physicist who taught for nine years in Sweden. He is a devotee from Mumbai who was visiting his daughter in Helsinki.

Q: What is science?
A: Science is our daily experience in which we want to know what is happening, and how it is happening, but we don't know why it is happening. The answer to 'why' is Krishna. You know ideas of cause and effect? Who causes the cause? Krishna is the cause of everything.
Q: What is Vedic science?
A: Vedic science is *dharma*. What is your duty, your way of life. One person has created the whole universe, given us limited powers. Just like Newton's law,

70   *Anna S. King*

karma is a scientific law. We should live an ego-free life, free of personal, caste, national ego. *Varnashramadharma* is divinely constituted. It depends upon the qualities. Brahmans are those who are looking for truth. Then there are Kshatriyas and Vaishyas. Sudras are simply the common men. There is nothing like untouchables in Vedas.

The Vedas are very liberal. They contain the knowledge of the material world and the supernatural. Since people had forgotten the Vedas so Krishna came to tell us about them. He came to tell us that 'I am a form.' 'All universes are within me.' The Vedas are ultimate. The Atharvaveda contains everything written about material science. However, Vedic science is almost lost. Most is lost. Some has gone to Germany. We must implore Krishna, please give us knowledge. The God-particle doesn't solve problems. We must surrender everything to God.

Q: What is modern science?

A: Scientists feel that 'I know everything.' I condemn the ego of scientists. Science is a way to know about the material world. Nothing bad. Religion never interferes with science. Religion itself is an experiment, isn't it? Evolution theory is wrong. The body is a temple of God. Scientists feel challenged, threatened. They believe blindly. Even Robert Oppenheimer understood that the nuclear bomb was Krishna in *virat roop*.

The universe is in *maya*, non-existent. Scientists see a time-scale which is just a bubble in the water. It is very limited compared to Brahma's life. The Vedas contain all psychology, mathematics ... today scientists are finding the true science of the Vedas. For example, *tulsi* [holy basil] gives oxygen 24 hours – unlike any other plant. Scientists must work on this. *Aamla* [Indian gooseberry] is given in traditional Vedic medicine, now we know that it is full of vitamin C.

Today the greatest problems are global warming and fossil fuel deficit. But our lives are dependent on the sun. The whole universe will die. We jointly have to think in different religions. Soon every small country will have atom bomb. All countries should join hands and give up 1 or 2% of their total budget to finance research.

2 Prabhupada grounded all knowledge in Krishna, the Supreme Personality of Godhead:

O Arjuna, as the Supreme Personality of Godhead, I know everything that has happened in the past, all that is happening in the present, and all things that are yet to come. I also know all living entities; but Me no one knows.

(*Bhagavad-gita* 7.26)

3 Prabhupada says, for example;

This moon project is childish. Those who aspire to go to the moon are like crying children ... Darwin is a rascal. What is his theory? We kick out Darwin's philosophy. The more we kick out Darwin's philosophy, the more we advance in spiritual consciousness.

([1979] 1981: 48)

4 Like Prabhupada, Singh believed that the primary and singular purpose of the human form of life is to enquire about the nature of the Absolute Truth. Every branch of knowledge should be utilised in searching for answers to these important questions (2005a: 14). Thus, Singh's quest for the synthesis of religion and science turns out to be a very religious project indeed (ibid.: 30).

Vedic science, modern science and reason   71

5 Ward (2005) notes that many believers (the Roman Catholic Church, for example) agree that religion "has to accept the best findings of science on matters of physical fact".

6 In their (1995) Gifford Lectures, John Hedley Brooke and Geoffrey Cantor reject the typological approach to religion and science as simplistic and incapable of explaining the lives and actions of real, historical people. They point out that the relationship between religion and science on the ground is often confusing and contradictory. Someone who accepts and appreciates the integration of religion and science in one context, for example, may find the two in conflict in some other area. Moreover, Stenmark (2010: 292) points out that science and religion are not merely sets of beliefs or theories plus certain methodologies, but two social practices. They are complex activities performed by human beings in co-operation with a particular historical and cultural setting.

7 There are many laudatory comments by devotees. However, there are critical observations also, as can be seen on one of ISKCON's websites: www.indiadivine.org/audarya/spiritual-discussions/446414-latest-3d-animation-model-vedic-planetarium-temple.html:

> I wonder why such a colossal squandering of resources is being indulged in, when far more noble and pragmatic endeavours could be brought to fruition with these millions upon millions of dollars. And all this on what is arguably the least important and most controversial part of the Bhagavata Purana, the empirically unprovable and unverifiable mythic cosmology of the fifth canto. Let the professional astronomers explain the cosmos, that is not the job of religionists. Striving to reach out to God is, on the other hand.
>
> That's amazing indeed, spend billions erecting edifices that have as underlying motivating rationale nothing else than mythology and fantasy, and that in effect amount to no more than ostentatious showing-off; let the hapless indigent living around the compound to their own fates, as deprived of proper nutrition, clean water, adequate education and other basic human necessities as they are. Talk about wanting to uplift society. True spirituality is ineluctably intertwined with humility and simplicity, not fancy Disney theme park-like wonderlands.
>
> And the ultimate irony? Iskcon wants to build a temple devoted to the Vedic vision of the universe while after close to 40 years they still cannot decide whether the Moon is further away from Earth than the Sun. It is a total joke.

References and further reading

Behe, M. (1996) *Darwin's Black Box: The Biochemical Challenge to Evolution*. New York: Free Press.

Bhaktivedanta Institute (2008) *Scientist and Saint: An Introduction to the Life and Work of Dr. T.D. Singh (His Holiness Bhaktisvarupa Damodara Swami)*. Kolkata: Bhaktivedanta Institute.

Clayton, P. and Simpson, Z. (eds) (2006) *The Oxford Handbook of Religion and Science*. Oxford: Oxford University Press.

Cliteur, P. and Gordon, G. (2009) 'The Enlightenment in Contemporary Cultural Debate,' in B. Labuschagne and R. Sonnenschmidt (eds) *Religion, Politics and Law. Philosophical Reflections on the Sources of Normative Order in Society*. Leiden: Brill.

72 Anna S. King

Cremo, M.A. (1998) *Forbidden Archeology's Impact: How a Controversial New Book Shocked the Scientific Community and Became an Underground Classic.* New Delhi: Bhaktivedanta Book Publishing Inc.

Cremo, M.A. (2003) *Human Devolution: A Vedic Alternative to Darwin's Theory.* Los Angeles, CA: Bhaktivedanta Book Trust International.

Cremo, M.A. and Thompson, R.L. (1993) *Forbidden Archeology: The Hidden History of the Human Race.* San Diego, CA: Govardhan Hill Publishing.

Dawkins, R. (2006) *The God Delusion.* London: Bantam Press.

Dennett, D.C. (2006) *Breaking the Spell: Religion as a Natural Phenomenon.* New York: Viking.

Edis, T. (2006) *Science and Nonbelief.* Santa Barbara, CA: Greenwood Publishing Group.

Edis, T. (2012) 'Is There a *Political* Argument for Teaching Evolution?' Paper presented at the Conference on Religions, Science and Technology in Cultural Contexts: Dynamics of Change, the Norwegian University of Science and Technology, Trondheim, 1–2 March.

Geraci, R.M. (2010) 'Science,' in R.D. Hecht and V.F. Biondo (eds) *Religion and Everyday Life and Culture*, vol. 2, *Religion in the Practice of Public Life.* Santa Barbara, CA: Praeger, pp. 703–39.

Goswami, T.K. (1977) *Letter to Jnana das Prabhu*, Vrndavan, 7 August. Available at: http://content.yudu.com/Library/A1qear/SrilaPrabhupadasLett/resources/154.htm

Harrison, P. (ed.) (2010) *The Cambridge Companion to Science and Religion.* Cambridge: Cambridge University Press.

Hitchens, C. (2007) *God Is Not Great: The Case against Religion.* London: Atlantic Books.

Israel, J.I. (2006) *Enlightenment Contested: Philosophy, Modernity, and the Emancipation of Man, 1670– 1752.* Oxford: Oxford University Press.

Kuhn, T.S. (1970) *The Structure of Scientific Revolutions*, 2nd edn. Chicago, IL: University of Chicago Press.

Lalitanatha Dasa (2010) *Rethinking Darwin: A Vedic Study of Darwinism and Intelligent Design.* Petite Somme, Belgium: BBT.

Madhudvisa dasa (2005) 'Vedic Cosmology Debate.' Available at: www.indiadivine. org/audarya/hare-krishna-forum/284108-vedic-cosmology-debate.html

Madhudvisa dasa (2011) 'The Moon – Sadaputa's Is the Bona Fide ISKCON Opinion?', 19 February. Available at: http://krishna.org/the-moon-sadaputas-is-the-bona-fide-iskcon-opinion/.

Nanda, M. (2003a) *Prophets Facing Backward: Postmodern Critiques of Science and Hindu Nationalism in India.* Piscataway, NJ: Rutgers University Press.

Nanda, M. (2003b) 'Postmodernism, Science and Religious Fundamentalism: Religious Fundamentalisms, Modernist and Postmodernist,' *Butterflies & Wheels.* Available at: www.butterfliesandwheels.org/2003/postmodernism-science-and-religious-funda mentalism/

Nanda, M. (2004) 'Postmodernism, Hindu Nationalism and "Vedic Science",' *Frontline*, 21: 01. Available at: www.frontlineonnet.com/fl2101/stories/20040116001408700.htm (accessed 20 November 2011).

Nanda, M. (2005) 'Intellectual Treason,' *Humanist Outlook*, 11(2)(Winter): 45–52.

Nanda, M. ([2005] 2007) 'Intellectual Treason.' *New Humanist.* Available at: https:// newhumanist.org.uk/articles/827/intellectual-treason.

Nussbaum, M. (2007) *The Clash Within: Democracy, Religious Violence, and India's Future.* Cambridge, MA: The Belknap Press.

Vedic science, modern science and reason   73

Pietersen, J. (2008) 'Review of Taner Edis *Science and Nonbelief.*' Available at: www. amazon.com/Science-Nonbelief-Taner-Edis/dp/1591025613.

Prabhupada, A.C. Bhaktivedanta Swami ([1970] 1996) *Krsna: The Supreme Personality of Godhead*. Los Angeles, CA: Bhaktivedanta Book Trust.

Prabhupada, A.C. Bhaktivedanta Swami (1976) Lecture on *Śrīmad-Bhāgavatam* 5.6.8, November 30, Vrndavana.

Prabhupada, A.C. Bhaktivedanta Swami ([1979] 1981) *Life Comes from Life*. Mumbai: Bhaktivedanta Book Trust.

Rosen, S. (2002) *Vedic Archeology and Assorted Essays*. Vrindaban: Ras Bihari Lal & Sons.

Sen, A. (2005) *The Argumentative Indian: Writings on Indian History, Culture and Identity*. London: Penguin Books.

Shapin, S. (2005) 'Science,' in T. Bennett, L. Grossberg and M. Morris (eds) *New Keywords: A Revised Vocabulary of Culture and Society*. Oxford: Blackwell.

Singh, T.D. (ed.) (2004/2005a) '*Savijnanam:* Exploration for a Spiritual Paradigm,' *Journal of the Bhaktivedanta Institute*, 3–4.

Singh, T.D. (2004/2005b) 'Science, Spirituality and the Nature of Reality: A Dialogue between Roger Penrose and T.D. Singh,' in T.D. Singh (ed.) *Sajivnanam: Scientific Exploration for a Spiritual Paradigm*, Vol. 3–4. Kolkata: Bhaktivedanta Institute, pp. 1–45.

Singh, T.D. (2005a) *Essays on Science and Religion*. Kolkata: Bhaktivedanta Institute.

Singh, T.D. (2005b) *God, Intelligent Design and Fine-Tuning: A Dialogue Between T.D. Singh and Michael J. Behe*. Kolkata: Bhaktivedanta Institute.

Singh, T.D. (2006) *Reality of God's Existence*. Vedanta and Science Series. Kolkata: Bhaktivedanta Institute.

Smullen, M. (2009) 'Atheist Nation.' Available at: http://akincanaforum.eponym.com/blog/_archives/2009/7/10/4262022.html (accessed 25 November 2010).

Stengler, V. (2007) *God: The Failed Hypothesis: How Science Shows That God Does Not Exist*. Amherst, MA: Prometheus.

Stenmark, M. (2010) 'Ways of Relating Science and Religion,' in P. Harrison (ed.) *The Cambridge Companion to Science and Religion*. Cambridge: Cambridge University Press, pp. 278–95.

Thompson, R.L. (2004) *God and Science: Divine Causation and the Laws of Nature*. Alachua, FL: Govardhan Hill Publishing.

Van der Velde, P. (2004) 'What Do We Look At? About the "True" Nature of Krishna's Līlā and the Dalai Lama's Secret Paradise,' in I. Bocken, W. Dupre, and P. van der Velde (eds) *The Persistent Challenge: Religion, Truth and Scholarship: Essays in Honor of Klaus Klostermaier*. Maastricht: Uitgeverij Shaker Publishing, pp. 121–45.

Ward, K. (2005) 'Scholarship and Devotion: Can They Co-Exist?', *ICJ*, 11. Available at: http://content.iskcon.org/icj/11/02-ward.html (accessed 22 November 2011).

4 Is the Earth round?

Traditional cosmography and modern science in Jainism[1]

Knut Aukland

Introduction

Developing the claim that Jainism is scientific, that various discoveries of modern science are already found in ancient Jain scriptures or that the Jain religion is compatible with modern science[2] is a salient characteristic of modern-day Jainism[3] (Banks 1991: 253–4; Laidlaw 1995: 72; Flügel 2009).[4] This puts traditional Jain cosmography in an awkward position, given its many and very specific ideas concerning the cosmos and geography ·of the world. Jain cosmography, among other things, postulates the existence of a flat Earth over which two suns and moons rotate around an *axis mundi* in the shape of Mount Meru. The normative position regarding canonical scriptures is that they contain the words of the omniscient Jina. In this regard, the canonical literature has been considered fully authoritative, not unlike the case in many Judaic, Christian and Muslim traditions (Cort 2001: 213, n.12; Dundas 2002: 89).

Jambudweep[5] is the name of a highly popular Digambar[6] pilgrimage site in Hastinapur, the famed, ancient capital of the epic *Mahābhārata*. The name 'Jambudweep' is taken from Jain cosmography and refers to the island *Jambūdvīpa* ('The island of the rose apple tree') which is found in the middle of the universe, and on which the world as we know it from contemporary maps is found. It is also the name of a 101-feet-high model of *Jambūdvīpa* with which visitors can interact by climbing the summit of Mount Meru. From here they can view the whole of *Jambūdvīpa* and the mythical ocean around it, in which one can go boating. The creation of such altogether new types of religious attractions can be seen as the "main markers of the contemporary Jain renaissance" (Flügel 1999: 404), but also points to the increased use of various entertainment technologies as a medium to present religious teachings. An important aspect of this development is the blending of entertainment and religion seen in the various rides offered in Jambudweep including a boat ride, an elephant ride, a train ride with movie screenings, and last but not least, a model of the universe inside which one can travel through the various realms of cosmos with the help of an elevator whose final destination is nirvana.

Cosmography and modern science in Jainism   75

In what follows, I shall present the basic content and application of Jain cosmography, before giving an outline of two recent historical processes I call the *academization* and *scientization* of Jainism. They denote processes by which Jains engage academia and modern science in reformulating and to some extent refashioning their religion. I then turn to the ethnographic case of Jambudweep, which, while displaying signs of academization and scientization, also serves as a modern-day battlefield, not between warring cousins, but between competing ontological claims regarding the world. While classical Jain cosmography is presented through modern entertainment technology, scriptural authority is upheld and defended in the face of competing claims by modern science. This defence consists not only of appeals to traditional religious authorities, but also academia and academic practices.

Jain cosmography

Developing around the same time, the same area and the same milieu, ancient Jainism and Buddhism shared many concerns. Most familiar are probably core soteriological features related to terms such as *karma*, *saṃsāra* and *nirvāṇa*. While the proponents of the two traditions disagreed on many particularities concerning even these concepts, the Jains also distinguished themselves by developing a keen interest in cosmology and cosmography.[7] In fact, this remarkable interest not only surpassed their Buddhist and Brahmanic counterparts (Bossche 2007: xi), it has also enjoyed continued significance for the Jain community until today (Dundas 2002: 92). However, as I shall argue, traditional Jain cosmology and cosmography are now facing resistance on ontological grounds as more and more Jains look to modern science in reformulating their religion and religious identity.

Jain cosmography refers to sections of Jain teachings that deal with the geography of the universe and mapping out its sizes and constituent parts. This universe is a massive one and contains three separate, vertically arranged divisions. The hellish realms are found at the bottom. In the middle (*madhyaloka*) is the realm where plants, animals and humans live. Descriptions of this middle realm also extend to the celestial bodies in the sky, such as the sun and moon. Above this middle realm are the heavenly spheres where gods reside, and finally, at the apex is *siddhaśīla* where the liberated souls dwell. Jain cosmography deals partly with the entire structure of the universe, but pays particular attention to the middle realm, *madhyaloka*. Descriptions of *madhyaloka* include familiar geographical elements such as mountains and rivers that could be linked to the geography of modern-day South Asia, but also more mythical elements such as eternal temples and waters of milk and other substances. In terms of sources, basic Jain cosmography is laid out in early canonical, *āgamic* literature, though the majority of cosmographical works and detailed expansions on the topic are post-canonical (Bossche 2007: xi–xii).[8] The Digambars have divided their canon into four main parts known as 'expositions' (*anuyoga*) that cover the entirety of Jain teachings. It is notable

76   *Knut Aukland*

that the second exposition, *karaṇa* ('calculation'[9]), is devoted only to cosmography. The seminal Tattvārthasūtra (c. fourth or fifth century AD), accepted by both Digambars and Śvetāmbars, also contains a section on cosmography. In short, the Jain doctrine and religion cannot be understood properly without studying Jain cosmography. In the words of Frank von den Bossche, "Jaina cosmography and geography form an essential part of Jainism as a religion" (Bossche 2007: 1).

Madhyaloka, in which humans are found, is believed to consist of innumerable islands that lie in concentric circles around the perfectly circular island Jambūdvīpa, which lies at the centre of the entire universe. Between each island there is an ocean, all of which have their own perfect geometrical shape. Our world as we know it is found in the south of the innermost, central island Jambūdvīpa. Jain cosmographical texts – such as the twelfth-century scripture translated by Bossche (ibid.) – do, in great detail, describe the basic geographical features of the various parts of this and other adjacent islands, focusing particularly on the exact sizes of rivers, mountains and landmasses. The names of various rivers and mountains are given, but also descriptions of the so-called inartificial (*akṛtrima*) Jina[10] temples that have existed as long as the universe, i.e. eternally (Cort 2010: 98–9). They are considered by some to be geographical proofs of Jainism's eternal existence. At the centre of Jambūdvīpa we find Mount Meru, the *axis mundi* of the Jain universe (ibid.: 94ff.). This is where every newborn Jina is taken for a ritual bathing by the gods. As mentioned, this island, Jambūdvīpa, has given the name of the Digambar pilgrimage site we shall visit later: Jambudweep. The site's main attraction is a reconstruction of Jambūdvīpa with its surrounding ocean.

Jain cosmography relates to various aspects of Jainism, including soteriology, ritual culture and the birth and whereabouts of Jinas. It relates to soteriology because it provides a map of the various time periods in which full liberation is attainable and during which Jinas will appear on Earth. While the part of Jambūdvīpa where we live has gone into a stage of decline – with the implication that salvation cannot be reached for thousands of years to come – the central area of Jambūdvīpa remains in a state where salvation is always possible. Moreover, there is always at least one living Jina in this area at any point in time. Only one Jina named Sīmandhara is believed to roam there currently, and there are some temples in India dedicated to him (Dundas 2002: 260–70). The eighth island encircling Jambūdvīpa is Nandīśvara, which plays a particular role in Jain ritual culture. Nandīśvara is the island where the gods, led by the chief Indra riding on his Airāvata, come thrice a year to perform the worship of Jina statues found in the inartificial temples. On fixed dates, following the lunar calendar, they continue this worship for eight days, hence these periods are known as the Eight Day Festivals (*aṣṭānika*) (Cort 2010: 85ff.). The Eight Day Festival is also celebrated by Digambar Jains simultaneously with the gods on Nandīśvara (cf. Babb 1996: 80). The staff at Jambudweep hold special arrangements for these celebrations.

This provides a short introduction to the world of Jain cosmography, the part of Jain doctrine in which Jambudweep specializes. While cosmography has had an enduring significance in Jainism until today (Dundas 2002: 92), I shall now describe processes of fairly recent changes that have put cosmography in a new, and at times, precarious position.

The academization and scientization of Jainism

The study of Jainism has yet to produce a historical narrative of Jainism's development from colonial times until today. Yet, it is clear that Jains adapted well to British rule, taking advantage of the new economic possibilities opening up[11] and thereby laying the basis for their current success as a community. This was also coupled with an increasing interest in professional careers, particularly within the law (Flügel 2005: 1, 5–6). These developments led to the creation of a new Jain elite consisting of Anglophone professionals, who, by their mastery of the new socio-political environment, became community leaders. They did so by creating lay Jain associations from the late nineteenth century onwards.[12] These organizations pushed for reforms on issues such as marriage and caste, along the same lines as other similar religious organizations in India at the time. These organizations were particularly successful in stressing the value of secular, English-medium education, which would soon become related to the Jain identity (ibid.: 5–6).

The British legal framework was important in shaping the Jain community, not just because a number of Jain males opted for legal careers, but also because of the way in which it divided the Indian population into discrete religious groups. Debates on the legal status of Jains and whether Jainism was a separate religion (Flügel 2005: 4, 2014) led the new Jain elite to collaborate with European scholars sympathetic to their views.[13] This, in turn, introduced a novel emic view of Jainism that was not just informed by tradition, but also by academic disciplines such as philology, history and archeology (Brekke 2002: 144; Carrithers 1996: 531–2).

Many of the activities connected to this new Jain elite started what I call the *academization* of Jainism. Academization points to processes by which proponents of a religion, in order to promote their religion, establish institutions and practices modelled on or inspired by Western mainstream academia, actively use markers of academic institutions such as titles of persons (Frøystad 2011) and organizations, create ties with mainstream academic institutions and their scholars, and invite academic appraisals of their religion. The above-mentioned lay Jain associations not only promoted secular education, but initiated these activities by establishing various modern educational institutions such as libraries, colleges and research institutes, and by printing community journals and books (Flügel 2005: 6).[14] The active use of print technology has been of particular importance (Cort 1995: 189), coupled with the impressive growth of Jain literacy rates over the last 100 years (Flügel 2005: 1).

78 *Knut Aukland*

Jains began to approach Indian universities in the 1920s to establish chairs in 'Jainology',[15] and achieved their first success after independence, in the 1950s (ibid.: 6). Research institutions aimed at translation and interpretative work on Jain scriptures were created, such as Parshvanath Vidyapeeth in Varanasi, established in 1937.[16] A separate, and now officially recognized Jain university, with courses in humanities and social science courses related to Jain doctrines, was established 1991. This work was led by the monk Mahaprajna, demonstrating that academization is not purely a lay phenomenon.[17] While these are obvious examples of institutes pushing academization, there are many other Jain organizations, including pilgrimage trusts such as Jambudweep, as we will see, that engage in activities such as publishing (books, periodicals and webpages), organizing conferences and running educational facilities (libraries and courses). Organizations such as the International School of Jain Studies (ISJS)[18] and the Jain Education and Research Foundation[19] work to promote Jainism by actively inviting academic attention and working to spread knowledge of Jainism in secular universities in Asia and the Western world. Through these developments the Jain scriptures became increasingly available in vernacular translations and lay Jains became progressively more interested in and familiar with their contents. Today, lay Jains are heavily involved in composing texts on religious matters, thus taking an active part in shaping doctrines and interpreting them.

Publications by Jains about Jainism represent one tangible result of academization. Many of them are written by lay people and are equipped with references and bibliographies. They often refer to other bodies of knowledge found outside the traditional sources of religious authority, i.e. the Jain scriptures and the ascetics' interpretations of them. Most typically, they draw on modern science. In fact, a prominent anthropologist of Jainism has observed that: 'developing the claim that Jainism is compatible with, or even a part of science, is perhaps the most intense area of intellectual productivity today' (Laidlaw 1995: 72). Other scholars have also noticed this trend (Banks 1991: 247, 253–4; Dundas 2002: 89; Flügel 2009), a development I call the scientization of Jainism.

Scientization points to processes by which proponents of a religion appeal to modern science in thinking and presenting their doctrines and practices. It includes both the production and communication of such appeals. A stimulating volume with case studies from a variety of religions was recently published to similarly explore how religions appeal to the authority of science (Lewis and Hammer 2011). It suggests a typology of various types of appeals that appear to be particularly aimed at NRMs (Lewis 2011: 31f.). Jain appeals to science, I suggest, can be divided into the following three types:

1 *Rhetorical appeals*: appeals where apologetics re-describe their tradition as scientific or a science (cf. Lewis 2011: 31–2, type 1). This can be achieved by reformulating traditional ideas and practices with scientific terminology,

or visually, by employing diagrams and combining images of modern science and Jainism.

2 *Discipline-specific appeals*: appeals supported by referring to the natural sciences, i.e. biology, physics (including mathematics) and chemistry in their widest sense.

3 *Methodological appeals* include the use of or reference to experiments and empirical research – be it mainstream or alternative – and the re-representation of traditional practices as empirical, scientific methods (cf. Lewis 2011: 32–3, types 2, 4, 5, 6).

While there are certainly other ways to categorize Jain appeals to science, this typology is based on reviewing 52 sources written by Jains appealing to the authority of science.

Rhetorical appeals are surely among the most widespread and can be made both in content (claims) and form (use of images). They need not imply much interest or knowledge of Jain doctrines and traditions or modern science. An entry from a popular Jain forum demonstrates how unspecific, rhetorical appeals are circulated: 'I have been reading quite a lot that jainism is scientific ... and i also do believe in the same. But I have never found any systematic stuff on this.'[20] While there are indeed systematic books on the issue, the quote indicates the spread of this general idea. In fact, Jainism itself is often presented as a science, be it the "Science of Salvation" (C.R. Jain 1930: v), the "science of detachment" (S.C. Jain 2012: 200), the "science of living" (D.C. Jain 1981), a "holistic science" (Mardia 1990: 85), the "science of peace" (Bothara 2004), an "ethical science" (Mardia and Rankin 2013) or simply a 'scientific religion' (S.K. Jain 2010). Such rhetorical appeals are also made visually by combining images of modern science with Jain symbols. Examples of this are found on book covers that display Mahāvīra surrounded by Newton, Einstein and other famous scientists (Nandigoshvijay 2000), or use the symbol of an atom (Bothara 2004; Zaveri 1995).

Unlike terminological and rhetorical appeals, discipline-specific appeals point in a much more direct and concrete way to modern science. Appeals of the first type, rhetorical appeals, can be made without any supporting arguments. Discipline-specific appeals are always substantiated in some way. While the notion of science behind the description of Jainism as the "science of detachment" might be somewhat unclear, discipline-specific appeals turn to particular postulates of the natural sciences. The task of harmonizing religious doctrine with discoveries of the natural science derives a peculiar flavour from the nature of Jain scriptures. As with other ancient Indian intellectual traditions, not to mention in the field of grammar and language, many parts of the Jain canon contain highly systematized teachings, numerated in various typologies and categories. In this systematic manner, parts of the Jain scriptures try to break down the basic elements of existence, which includes the idea of matter divided into its smallest property, comparable to what the ancient Greeks called *atomos*. A variety of such Jain ontological concepts are

80 *Knut Aukland*

correlated with concepts in modern physics, chemistry and biology by advocates of scientization or authors of the scientization literature, By re-reading and interpreting ancient scripture in this manner, Jains have found that they contain earlier versions of the Periodic Table, ideas of force and friction, metabolism, microbes, DNA and black holes, to only name a few.[21] Jain epistemology, with its famed doctrine of manypointedness (Dundas 2002: 229–33), is popularly linked with Einstein's theories of relativity and elements of quantum physics.[22]

Jain canonical writings hold that life forms, meaning those things that have a soul (*jīva*), are found not just among humans and animals, but also in plants, water, air, earth and even fire. While the latter element is usually skipped in scientization literature, this is interpreted as proof that Jains have long known about microorganisms (Gandhi [1893] 1993; Mehta 2012: 45) while the practice of boiling water indicates knowledge of epidemiology (V.S. Jain and S.C. Jain 2012a: 8). The Jain taxonomy of living beings is further claimed to be in line with modern equivalents (Shah 2004: 152–8). These various points of claimed confluence have led to publications that deal with these issues systematically, some of which conform to the norms of academic publications in many ways (Sikdar 1974; Mardia 1990; Gelra 2002; Shah 2004). Some works try to give an overview of the various instances of science by going through specific scriptures (N.L. Jain 1996; Pragya 2005; Shah 2011). A recurrent point in all these writings is that modern scientific discoveries were already present in the Jain canon. While many simply use scientific terms to describe theological concepts, others are more creative, inventing new terms such as *karmon* (fusing karma and atom) and *karmasome* (fusing karma and chromosome) (Gelra 2007).

A typical methodological appeal (type 3) among Jains involves the claim that enlightened Jinas or their associated disciples used a scientific method (Sikdar 1974: 289). One might also, somewhat more elaborately, claim that they followed "the four-step methodology of (1) observation, (2) classification and postulates, (3) inference and judgment, and (4) recording and theorization, which suggests that Jain seers had developed a scientific approach to the acquisition of knowledge" (Shah 2004: 132). Mahāvīra, another writer claims, "developed a unique method of analysis which could be applied to any facet of the two cardinal fundamentals: life and matter" (Bothara 2004: xxviii). In a more abstract manner, one might also claim that the karma theory is based on scientific reasoning (Kachhara 2005).

Mahaprajna, the monk behind the Jain university mentioned above, describes the ancient Jain teachers as "ascetic-scientists" who "combined a quest for transcendence with scientific empiricism" (A. Jain 2010: 140). He has also developed a Jain meditation technique (*prekṣa dhyāna*), which is presented as both an ancient and a scientific method (Mahaprajna 2001).[23] I have only come across two examples of the employment of experiments related to Jainism. One relates to the special properties of boiled water and homeopathy (J. Jain 2012).[24] The other is written by a monk and relates aura and Jain concepts with experiments involving aura photography (Nandigoshvijay 2008).[25] The latter is part of an initiative called the Research Institute of Scientific Secrets from Indian Oriental Scriptures (RISSIOS), which besides being part of the academization of Jainism, claims to be "the only institute of its kind in the Jain sect which intends to carry out experimental research."[26] Besides the aura photography experiments mentioned in the book, it is nevertheless somewhat hard to determine exactly what this experimental research consists of.

While RISSIOS serves as a very tangible result of what I have described as the academization and scientization of Jainism, there are many questions related to these processes: it remains to be seen how widespread scientization appeals are, and what the role of lay, monastic and diaspora Jains is in the scientization and academization of Jainism. What is the significance of sectarian differences and English-medium publications versus other languages? In relation to the study of the history of religions and Jainism, it is also natural to ask what the effects of these processes are on Jainism itself. An intended effect vis-à-vis the external surroundings is to elevate the respectability and prestige of Jainism, but what about the 'internal' effects? Academization, clearly, introduces novel perspectives and attitudes towards scriptures and the past, the long-standing debates on lost and inauthentic scriptures in Jainism notwithstanding (Dundas 2002: 67–9, 249–50). Growing interest in both these areas does suggest that there is an "ongoing transformation of Jain lay religiosity from ritual to reflection" (Flügel 2005: 10). In relation to scriptural and monastic authority, scientization and academization could be envisaged as having at least three types of effects:

1 To conserve and reinvigorate traditional interpretations and views; this involves little or no reinterpretation, though it might extend the ramification and meaning of certain doctrines and practices.
2 To reinterpret traditional concepts, thereby downplaying traditional interpretations and views.
3 To modify or remove doctrines or practices; this is often done by claiming that one is not modifying but removing elements that have 'crept in' over time.

Whereas the first effect resonates particularly with rhetorical appeals (type 1), the two remaining effects relate more to the discipline-specific appeals (type 2). While there are clearly overlapping areas in effects as we move from effect (1) to effect (3), there is also a clear tension between these effects, a tension that, as we will see, is found in relation to cosmography, but that is also seen in the scientization literature. In the Foreword to *Scientific Content of the Prākṛta Canon*, the author distinguishes between "sages – traditionalists and moderates", the latter being the only ones who have a suitable scientific outlook (N.L. Jain 1996: x). Another writer contrasts the "die-hard traditionalists" unwilling to open up their views for re-examination with a more open-minded approach (Bothara 2004: xxxii–xxxiv).

82 *Knut Aukland*

There is certainly a decisive lay element to academization and scientization,[27] but there is no clear-cut distinction between lay and monastic participation in these processes. As we have seen, monks are involved in both academization and scientization. While Mahaprajna is behind the creation of a Jain university, Nandigoshvijay founded the RISSIOS and argues that it is "high time to include science in the curriculum of a Jain monk" (2000: 10). This is perhaps indicative of the close relations between lay and ascetics which has been argued to be part of the factors behind the success of Jainism in India compared to Buddhism (Jaini [1979] 1998: 285–6).

Jambudweep: The Digambar Jain Institute of Cosmographic Research

Hastinapur is a small town located a little over a hundred km northeast of New Delhi. This convenient distance from the capital has given me the opportunity to visit the site for a couple of days on three occasions: twice in 2010 and once in November 2012. Arriving in Hastinapur by bus from Meerut, the nearest city, one notices the contrast between the town itself and the Jain pilgrimage sites. Simple houses and shacks line the main road through Hastinapur, before a small side road takes you to the 'Jain Temple Road'. Here one is immediately struck by three very large religious structures (Figure 4.1). They belong to three different temple trusts, two Digambar and one Śvetāmbar,[28] and depict mythical mountains, which visitors can experience by climbing to the top. The most famous of these sites is Jambudweep.

Figure 4.1 The three Jain constructions in Hastinapur

Literary sources reveal that Jain religious activity has taken place in Hastinapur since the fourteenth century (Balbir 1990: 177), while a recovered Jina statue has been dated to the twelfth century (Titze 2001: 138). Hastinapur was abandoned for an unknown reason in the seventeenth century only to be properly revived in the 1950s. This was partly a result of academization, which had sparked an interest in archeology and excavation projects to recover old Jain sites. One such excavation campaign in Hastinapur revealed Jain images and remains. This initiated a new phase for Hastinapur as a Jain pilgrimage site with "a period of great building activity" (Balbir 1990: 177). Typical of this building activity in recent decades is not just the making of Jina statues and conventional temples, but rather new creative constructions with inspiration from various aspects of the Jain tradition, especially cosmography.

Hastinapur is connected to the lives of five different Jinas. A fourteenth-century pilgrimage text explains that three Jinas were conceived, born, became ascetics, and reached omniscience here, while a fourth Jina conducted his first sermon here after reaching omniscience (ibid.: 186–7). The shared focus on cosmography in all three major sites today is partly linked to the story of the first Jina of our era: Ṛṣabha. According to tradition, he once ruled as a king before he eventually became a wandering ascetic and began fasting. One day he reached Hastinapur where he was offered sugar cane juice, which was fit for him to drink. Lay Jains celebrate and re-enact this event annually by fasting and breaking the fast in Hastinapur. All the three Hastinapur sites have managed to attract thousands of pilgrims to Hastinapur for this celebration. Ṛṣabha is later said to have achieved liberation on the mythical mountain Āṣṭapāda, which is sometimes associated with Mount Kailash in the Himalayas. While Jambudweep has a model of *Jambūdvīpa* as its main attraction, the two remaining sites have constructed impressive models of Āṣṭapāda/Mount Kailash.

The official name of Jambudweep is the Digambar Jain Institute of Cosmographic Research (Digambar Jain Trilok Śodh Saṃsthān). The charismatic Digambar nun, Gyanmati Mataji, popularly known as Mataji, founded it in 1972. The story behind the creation of the institute goes back to an episode in 1965 when Mataji had a vision (Candnamati 2010: 6). While meditating, she saw the entire structure of the universe. Discovering later that what she had seen perfectly matched the cosmographical details described in Jain scriptures, she decided to create a pilgrimage site with the aim of creating a model of *Jambūdvīpa* (ibid.: 6). The model was completed and installed in 1985, after the structure had been taken on a tour around India for some years, receiving support from such figures as Indira Gandhi (Balbir 1990: 182). Visiting the site shortly after the construction was completed, Nalini Balbir reported that:

> The main attraction of this vast campus is the Jambudvipa. By its height, this original construction dominates all other buildings. It is meant both for education of the believers, since it shows them the Jaina representation of

the universe, and for their entertainment. One can climb to the top by an inner staircase, or go boating around the Lavanasamudra!

(ibid.: 182)

The climb to the top refers to Mount Meru, hence, one could say that the model enables Jains to rise to the top of their tradition's *axis mundi*. Offering a combination of entertainment, an impressive display of cosmography and an unusual place to perform religious acts, this religious attraction became an "undisputable success" (ibid.: 182). Jambudweep became a famous pilgrimage site.

The popularity of Mataji has been a decisive factor in the success of Jambudweep (ibid.: 183; Shanta 1997: 673–83). Jain ascetics are, under normal circumstances, obliged to be in constant movement, so as not to get attached to the comforts of staying in a particular place. Mataji, however, is said to suffer from some timely illness that has made her permanent presence in Jambudweep since the mid-1970s possible (Shanta 1997: 681). Many of the Digambar visitors therefore have the chance to see her, receive her blessings or teachings and interact with her. While known for her mastery of Jain scriptures and her many publications, she also regularly appears on the new Jain TV channel, Paras TV. She has also appeared on India's biggest religious channel, Aashta.

When first entering the Jambudweep 'campus', as it is called, one quickly recognizes that the site is distinctly modern in that it is not centred around a main temple. Looking to the left, one will see the *jambūdvīpa* model (Figure 4.2), and immediately on the right, there is a kiosk where one can get

Figure 4.2 Jambūdvīpa and Mount Meru

Cosmography and modern science in Jainism   85

snacks, sweets and various Jain memorabilia. As one gazes over the area, one spots a combination of ordinary buildings, children's rides of various kinds and conceptual constructions of things like a mountain, a train and a lotus flower. The more ordinary buildings comprise lodgings for pilgrims, administration and publication buildings, a library, dwellings for ascetics and the people working at the site, and some conventional temples. On Jambudweep's webpage,[29] we find that the terms 'tourist' and 'pilgrim' are used interchangeably. Under the heading *Facilities for Pilgrims* we learn that there are "250 rooms with modern facilities, more than 50 deluxe flats and a number of guest houses (Bungalows)".[30] Under *Recreation*, we read:

> [There are] various means of recreation in the campus such as exhibitions (Jhankis) related to the ancient history of Hastinapur, fountains of laughter, Jambudweep train, Tomato train, various swings, Columbus etc. Tourists come here and sit in beautiful green lawns flooded with flowers to enjoy the natural beauty' (*sic*).[31]

The inclusion of a play area for children is also found at other Jain pilgrimage sites, but in Jambudweep, the entertainment facilities extend into the more clearly defined religious realm, as we shall see.

Considering this emphasis on recreation, it is not surprising that Nalini Balbir, using questionnaires to find out why people come to Jambudweep during a religious festival, concluded that "many of the pilgrims viewed their visit to Hastinapur more as an outing than as a religious ceremony" (1990: 184). In the foreword to one of Mataji's works on cosmography, it is stated that the "Campus has been termed as 'Unparalleled Man Made Heaven' by the tourism department of U.P. [Uttar Pradesh] owing to its natural beauty, peace, maintenance etc." (Mataji 2010: vii). The connections between tourism and religion, which have remained largely unexplored in the study of religion (Stausberg 2011), are clearly visible in Hastinapur where, as in Indian pilgrimage practices in general, the two categories are 'decidedly blurred' (Gladstone 2005: 173). Ian Reader, conducting fieldwork on pilgrimage in Japan, arrived at a similar conclusion, demonstrating that the pilgrim and tourist often work as interwoven roles within individual actors, with "prayer, worship, play and entertainment being part and parcel of the same process" (Reader 2005: 36–7). The same, I would argue, holds true in Hastinapur and elsewhere in India (Figure 4.3).[32]

There are many signs of academization in Jambudweep. It styles itself as a research institute and refers to the site as a 'campus'. It has a library and functions as a publisher of books and a monthly magazine that has been running since 1974. Mataji and her retinue at Jambudweep conduct seminars and conferences on various topics and cooperate with secular universities and the above-mentioned ISJS. They provide an online certificate course that has been running since 2010.[33] Mataji has also been given an honorary degree from Avadh University (Faizabad). The use of academic titles is an aspect of

Figure 4.3 Jambūdvīpa boating

academization aptly pointed out by Kathinka Frøystad (2011: 56–9) in her work on middle-class Indian spiritual self-development circles.

A key focus in Jambudweep's academic and educational activities is Jain cosmography, an interest that is visible everywhere on the campus. The model of *Jambūdvīpa* is the main construction, which combines educational, entertainment and ritual functions. It is educational in that it teaches Jains about their own tradition[34] and entertaining in that it is a ride one can climb up to the top of or, for ten rupees, go boating around (see Figure 4.3). It also has a ritual function in that it is used on special occasions when lay people copy the gods worshipping the Jinas by climbing up a model of the Jain *axis mundi* and conducting rituals at its top. There is also an elephant ride for ten rupees which goes around *Jambūdvīpa* which is based on Airāvata – the mythical elephant Indra rides on when he travels to worship the Jinas. The elephant stands on a platform that is pulled by a tractor and features loud music during its trip around *Jambūdvīpa*. Circumambulation (*parikrama*) is a common feature in Jain religiosity and a picture on Jambudweep's webpage features two men boating around *Jambūdvīpa* with the following text: "Devotees perform the Parikrama of Jambudweep by boating."[35] Candnamati, the nun second in rank to Mataji, has written an article where she invites the reader to "have the view of this Jambudweep to earn great Punya i.e. sacredness" (Candnamati 2010: 7).

The *tīn lok racna* (three-world construction) is another immediately striking model on campus (see Figure 4.4). Its outer shape is that of the entire Jain cosmos, whereas its inside displays the various layers of cosmos with its

Figure 4.4 Tīn lok racnā

hells, the middle world, the heavens and finally the abode of the liberated souls (*siddhaśīla*). In the centre of the construction is a glass elevator "ever-ready to take you to Siddhashila in few seconds".[36] The webpage explains the rationale for the construction, the first being to fascinate, the other, to inspire people to live good lives: "[O]ne will renounce the sinful activities by observing the scenes of cruel atrocities on hellish-beings in different hells along with adopting virtuous deeds and spirits observing the gracious-peaceful life of heavens."[37]

Taken together with the children's rides, these four rides – the *Jambūdvīpa*, the boat and elephant rides and the elevator to nirvana – are reminiscent of other modern temple complexes such as the ISKCON[38] temple and Akshardham in New Dehli in that entertainment technology is used to present religious content (Brosius 2010: 161 ff., 213). Like these places, Jambudweep also offers film screenings. Featuring two music videos, it takes place in a showroom shaped like a train that also holds exhibitions on the life of Mataji and Jinas who have connections to Hastinapur. Entertainment and religion are, in other words, not just offered in the same place or in a combined package, they are also combined and fused into one and the same activity. Visitors can combine recreational and religious activities in one outing, and why, one might wonder, should not religion be fun in the first place? These playful exhibits of religious teachings and other elements attract a mixed audience, some members, some not, but while non-Jains tend to focus on the purely entertaining aspects of the site, Jains engage in a broader range of

88 *Knut Aukland*

activities. Unlike the ISKCON temple and Akshardham, Jambudweep does not appear to attract many foreigners.

The last cosmographical construction I want to mention is that of the first thirteen islands (*terahdvīpa*) of the middle section of the universe, the innermost being *Jambūdvīpa*. The construction is found indoors and is highly instructive as far as Jain cosmography goes. One can see the five Meru Mountains found on the first three islands, islands on which humans and Jinas are born. The reason for showing the thirteen first islands is that these are the only islands on which we find the inartificial Jina temples. Special attention is given to the eighth island *nandīśvara*[39] connected to the mentioned Eight Day Festivals (*āṣṭānika*). The Eight Day Festival is celebrated by Jains and rituals are now conducted in the *terahdvīpa* construction.[40] The construction provides a cosmic stage on which these rituals can be enacted and Mataji has composed new ritual manuals for them (Cort 2010: 98).

This short tour of Jambudweep gives us a glimpse of what has been called the "new communal self-assertiveness" among contemporary Jains, manifesting itself in creative constructions that "boldly embody Jain imagery in their structural design" (Flügel 1999: 2). Mataji's cosmographical project is also bold in that Jain cosmography flies directly in the face of the cosmography of modern science. When standing on top of Mount Meru in the *Jambūdvīpa* model, visitors can see the Earth as we know it as a tiny part of the much larger *Jambūdvīpa* (Figure 4.5). How does this conflict between traditional cosmography and modern science play out in Jambudweep?

Figure 4.5 Southern part of *Jambūdvīpa*

Traditional cosmography meets modern science

Paul Dundas argues that most Jains are "happy to subscribe to two cosmographical systems, one relating to the everyday, transactional world, the other to the more profound symbolic realm of religion" (2002: 93). While we do not have any surveys to support or challenge this assumption, I will contend that there are reasons to suggest that such a combination is becoming increasingly challenged. On the one hand, academization turns attention to the scriptures and their actual content. A literal interpretation of them, such as found in Jambudweep, does not make cosmography symbolic or allegorical. On the contrary, it makes it a factual description of the world given by an omniscient Jina. Scientization, on the other hand, potentially threatens classical Jain cosmography because the descriptions of the world in modern geography and astronomy contradict that of Jain cosmography on several issues. To harmonize the two appears exceptionally difficult.

Academization has made the specific content of Jain scriptures available and better known in lay circles. The general emphasis on education in the community simultaneously means that many Jains are familiar with modern geography and astronomy. India's space ventures, which are, after all, in line with Copernican heliocentrism and modern astronomy, have further been widely covered in the public media in the past few decades. Many of the agents of scientization of Jainism have a background in natural sciences, and one – Narendra Bhandari – has even been involved in both NASA's and India's moon explorations. Given the status of modern science in general, but also these individuals, it is perhaps not that surprising that there are cases in which individual Jains struggle with these issues. The BBC documentary *Frontiers of Peace* (1986) presents us with two such cases: a layman who speaks of the difficulties of accepting the 'flat Earth theory' given his educational background, and a former monk explaining how he left monkhood after having read about the launch of Sputnik 1 and being convinced that the Earth is round. Tradition does not accept such doubt, he concluded, and so he left the order.

Among the scientization literature reviewed above, I found six publications dealing directly with this subject. Two of them favour the traditional Jain view (Nagraj 1959: 190; Nandigoshvijay 2000: 129–30) though not in a straightforward manner as we will see. The four remaining explicitly denounce it (N.L. Jain 1996: 137–8; S.M. Jain 2003; Jain 2012: 84–5; Bhandari 2011: 87). This indicates at least two hierarchical models in vogue among Jains on the issue of cosmography, one favouring modern science, the other religious teachings.[41] The authors in favour of religious teachings, not surprisingly, are both monks. Turning to the lay authors, it is worth noticing that most scientization literature that I have seen does not mention this part of Jain teachings at all. Those more overarching publications that point to the various areas in which Jain ideas and concepts coincide with those of modern science simply skip cosmography all together.[42]

90   *Knut Aukland*

Unlike these writers, the above-mentioned Narendra Bhandari observes that there is no scope to modify Jain cosmography, hence, "Jain concepts need to be corrected in light of modern scientific findings" (2011: 91–2). Recounting how Jain scriptures postulate a flat Earth, another writer concludes that there is an "urgent need to organize broad based conferences of saints and scholars and revise or delete the contents of scriptures which are obviously not correct in the light of glaring scientific facts" (S.M. Jain 2003). While this writer's conclusion is that these elements are due to the distortion of the teachings of Jinas,[43] another writer questions the very notion of the Jina's omniscience considering the odd nature of the 'descriptions of the astral world' (N.L. Jain 1996: 137–8). The scriptures, he argues, "should not be taken as the final word on any matter" advocating the need for a 'historical perspective' (ibid.: 137–8). A retired professor in physics similarly states that the authors of these texts were merely describing the cosmology accepted in their times (D.C. Jain 2012: 84). The impulse to historicize the scriptures, which is connected to academization, is noteworthy here. This can easily lead to effects of the second and third kind described above, and in the case of cosmography, we clearly see the third kind: to "reject scientific facts impoverishes the effort to research into the truth" states one (Zaveri 1994: 1), while another (Bothara 2004: 15) writes of the 'inertia of tradition' that involves "closing the doors in face of up-to-date scientific research". Given the status of the Jain canon as fully authoritative and the words of a Jina, such radical claims are not uncontested.

The two monk authors mentioned above defend Jain cosmography, but not without qualifying and constraining it. Comparing heliocentric and geocentric models, Nagraj (1959: 184) concludes that both the Earth and the sun can be said to be still or moving depending on the perspective. Attempting to delineate a third superior position based on the principle of manypointedness, he claims that both science and Jainism have it partly right on this particular issue. Nandigoshvijay (2000: 124) raises similar issues to the sceptics above, concerning the possible deterioration of the canon over time, and further confesses that Jain ascetics generally do not have the correct information about geography and astronomy (ibid.: 128) and that one cannot expect lay people today to accept the canonical descriptions of the world, as they have telescopes and other equipment (ibid.: 127). Nevertheless, they both rehearse various arguments against the theory of a round earth (Nagraj 1959: 190; Nandigoshvijay 2000: 129–30). While Nagraj employs Einstein to argue against the heliocentric model (1959: 180ff.), Nandigoshvijay (2000: 130) uses insights from modern geography to demonstrate that a theory of a round earth is illogical by listing seven arguments. Hence, they both use elements of modern science to argue against specific postulates of modern geography and astronomy. They are, as Carrie Hersh (2011) observed when looking at Christian televangelists in the USA, "fighting science with science".

Nandigoshvijay and Nagraj are far from alone in taking on modern geography and astronomy. Book titles like *Is the Earth Round?* (*kyā pr̥tvī kā ākār gol hai?), Did Apollo Go to the Moon? (epolo kī candrayātrā)* (Cort 2001: 213, n.12), *The Moon Landing Unveiled (pardā gir cukā hai cāṇd yātrā kā)*, and posters claiming that man did not land on the moon (Flügel 2009), reveal that there are forces in the Jain community resisting modern science on issues that directly clash with Jain doctrines.[44] An educational video entitled *Our True Geography (apnā sacca bhugol)* was posted in 2008 on YouTube.[45] Situated in a classroom setting, this 32-minute-long video sums up many of the arguments used against modern astronomy and geography, concerning the shape of the earth and the moon landing. The film has, from what I can gather, been made by the Shri Jambudweep Vigyan Research Centre. Situated in the Jain pilgrimage area in Palitana, it was founded in the 1980s.[46] Nalini Balbir (n.d.) notes that the site "explains Jain cosmology in a pedagogical manner and justifies it in a polemical manner with posters". While I have not had the opportunity to visit the place, its publications and display of Jain cosmography appear to make it the Śvetāmbar equivalent to Jambudweep.[47]

Turning back to Jambudweep: in what way is modern science is present there? Unlike traditional displays of Jain cosmography, the *Jambūdvīpa* model includes a small, round area with a rough depiction of the continents, as we know them from modern-day maps (see Figure 4.5). Rather than keeping the two maps separate, possibly belonging to different spheres as suggested by Dundas above, this juxtaposition seems to insist that both maps – the religious and the secular – deal with the same physical world 'out there'. In the foreword to the one of many titles by Mataji, we see an example of how the presence of modern science is felt in Jambudweep. The foreword is written by a young female ascetic who completed a degree in biology from a secular university before joining Mataji:

> Whatever has been said by the Lord Jinendra Dev [Jina] is the ultimate truth ... If we see the other side, the development by the modern science & technology is also introducing itself to the whole world most remark-ably. Then, what to do? If we should accept the principles stated by the Lord even when we can-not testify them or we should fully tune ourselves on the line of modern science, which is present before us with full proofs ... Although the latter option is the most approachable for all of us, yet we should accept that modern science is not complete in itself. Completeness lies with the soul who has attained Omniscience ... Thus, we have to be guided by the norms stated by Jinendradev and should be fully convinced about what he has said ... We have not to question whether Sumeru mountain, heavens or hells are there or not, yes! They are there because the Omniscient Lord has seen them (*sic*).
>
> (Mataji 2007: xlvii–xlviii)

This statement comes from an individual standing between two forms of knowledge, one belonging to Jain religion and religious education, the other to modern science and secular education. Having spoken with her on several

92 *Knut Aukland*

occasions she explained that she was familiar with modern geography of the world and the Copernican model of the universe, but that, having become a Jain ascetic, scriptural Jainism had to be given precedence. Jain scriptures are not to be doubted, and, in the end, modern science can never beat the omniscience of a Jina.

While scholars often stress that Indian religions are more geared towards orthopraxy than orthodoxy, the contemporary debate concerning cosmography brings the issue of scriptural authority and faith to the fore. This is seen in the introductory texts to Mataji's *Jain Bhāratī*, a book aiming to cover the whole of Jain teachings. Two of the prefaces remind us that the Jain canon contains the exact words uttered by Mahāvīra (ibid.: xliii, xlvii). In a lecture held by one of the Jambudweep officials, concerning certain aspects of Jain cosmography relating to the existence of the mentioned inartificial temples on far-off cosmic islands, it was stated: "[T]hese facts have been quoted on the basis of ancient Jain Scriptures, written by ancient Acharyas [monks] based on the Sermons of Lord Jinendra [Jina] in His Samavsaran (Divine Preaching Assembly)" (S.B. Jain 2010: 3). Elsewhere, on the same topic, the same writer concludes that: "[W]hatever has been said by Lord Jinendra Dev [the Jina] is the ultimate truth, which has been delivered to us by Gandhar devas [the Jina's disciples] and then by ancient Jainacharyas [monks] through ancient scriptures" (Mataji 2007: xlvii).

Conversing with both of the above-quoted individuals on several occasions, it was stressed that to be a good Jain, one must accept the Jina's teachings. Faith was emphasized. This is not something novel as scriptures such as the influential *Tattvārthasūtra* from the fourth or fifth century AD does the same by listing right faith (*samyak darśana*) as the first of the three jewels of Jainism (Dundas 2002: 86–7). Conversely, 'blind faith' is often criticized by advocates of academization and scientization and in a translation of the *Tattvārthasūtra* carrying the subtitle "through the eyes of a scientist", *samyak darśana* is translated as 'rational perception'. The Jain laity is known as the 'listeners' (*śrāvaka/śrāvika*), meaning those who listen to the teachings of the Jina, but academization and scientization have evidently produced some rather critical and innovative listeners who do indeed reply with questions. We saw above how academization can lead to a historicizing view of the canon. While there are many signs of academization in Jambudweep, such historical perspectives are not accepted. In fact, Mataji is said to have written a letter to the Prime Minister to correct schoolbooks presenting Mahāvīra as the founder of Jainism (Mataji 2007: xxxviii–xxxix): Jainism is eternal, and the inartificial temples are physical proof of that.[48] The traditional view that the canon is fully authoritative is firmly upheld in Jambudweep. To question Jain cosmography is therefore to question the scriptures and the Jina. But in Jambudweep it would also question Mataji's authority, her vision of the entire universe and her cosmography project in general. Her personal vision of the universe was, after all, the very reason for the creation of Jambudweep.

Mataji has produced a popular argument one often hears in Jambudweep concerning the issue of scriptural authority. The argument implicitly acknowledges the difficulty of accepting classical Jain cosmography in our times. It goes as follows: even though you have never seen your forefathers and they cannot be the object of direct observation, you must assume that they existed. You accept this to be true by necessity. Similarly, the argument goes, we should accept the existence of the various islands, oceans and mountains as explained in Jain cosmography. You may not have seen them yourself (this would be impossible unless you become enlightened), but you should accept it with confidence in the unfailing omniscience of the Jina (Mataji 2010: 33).

The official story of the creation of the Jain Digambar Institute of Cosmographic Research is related to Mataji and her special vision, and not the threat of modern science as such. And yet, the various ways in which Jambudweep is pushing academization implies a recognition of 'research' and thus modern science. In this way, the people at Jambudweep are using academic links and associations as a way to fight modern science. This is pushing academization but resisting scientization. Unlike the other defenders of Jain cosmography seen above, there is no attempt to use appeals to science, logics or observation to fight science. Confidence and faith in the bodies of traditional religious authority – the Jina, his ascetic followers and the scriptures – are stressed. So too is entertainment and impressive display. Both the *Jambūdvīpa* model and the elevator to nirvana invite Jains to playfully interact with a part of their own tradition many probably know very little about. In this way Jambudweep combines entertainment and education. In fact, one might say that Mataji and her retinue are using edutainment and academization to defend teachings increasingly threatened by science, secular education and certain advocates of scientization.[49]

Talking to visitors concerning this issue, I found various responses. One senior Digambar Jain lay man, who had studied in the USA in the late 1960s, told me how he had met resistance from ascetics when mentioning the moon landing. Involved in the academization and scientization of Jainism, he concluded that one better not discuss these matters with conservative ascetics. Another senior lay man staunchly defended Jain cosmography, claiming that given the constant changing views of modern science on any given issue, the Jain position is better since it does not change.

In general, I would assume, most lay Jains in the past have encountered the teachings of Jain cosmography and cosmology through visual representations, texts and verbal communication and rituals. In others words, typically via the eyes and ears or through actions governed by ritual prescriptions. The modern-day employment of entertainment technology and practices, and large-scale reconstructions of religious objects allow for a different form of encounter. The interaction facilitated by the *Jambūdvīpa* model and the elevator to nirvana is different in two ways. First, by enabling an embodied and visceral interaction with the ideas and descriptions of Jain cosmography outside the context of a

94   *Knut Aukland*

ritual. Second, by framing it as an entertainment ride akin to those found in an amusement park:[50] unlike the more customary temple buildings in Jambudweep, visitors must pay to access these rides – they require a ticket. The medium through which Jain cosmography and indeed Jainism in general are presented in Jambudweep is defined by modern technology, and modern conceptions and practices of entertainment. The same holds true for Hindu equivalents found in Akshardham and the ISCKON temple.

Conclusion

Cosmography has been a significant part of Jainism for over a thousand years. Scientization and academization, I argue, are crucial characteristics of contemporary Jainism. The effects of these processes do not point in one single direction. While lay religiosity is moving "from ritual to reflection" (Flügel 2005: 10), traditional practices and interpretation are now defended and upheld by appeals to science. In fact, Jainism itself is habitually claimed to be scientific. In these processes some voices are constructing a Jainism that no longer heeds the traditional authorities. As lay Jain scientists and authors directly consult the scriptures to investigate ontological matters, they occupy a position in religious discourse that establishes them as an alternative authority. In this way the implications of academization and scientization do imply a change in the basic sociological structure of Jainism, relegating the authority of the ascetics. The logical monastic response to such a scenario is therefore to suggest changes in the ascetic's curriculum (Nandigoshvijay 2000: 10).

Scientization and academization put Jain cosmography in new contexts. In scientization literature, its teachings are set against completely foreign and different systems of knowledge such as modern geography and astronomy. When writing their publications, agents of scientization can begin with the assumption that Jain scriptures are correct and look for areas where science might confirm the Jain position. This nevertheless brings in the assumption that certain Jain tenets need further legitimization beyond traditional sources of authority. In contrast, some Jain writers begin with the assumption that science has the correct descriptions of the physical world, and then go on to search for passages in the scriptures that can be made to harmonize with such descriptions. This is very difficult in relation to Jain cosmography. As one Jain scientist concludes:

> Surely there are areas of serious disagreement between Jain description related to geography and astronomy, units of time and space and the modern observations, an area in which science has made tremendous progress. They cannot be reconciled and obviously Jain concepts need to be corrected in light of modern scientific findings.
>
> (Bhandari 2011: 91–2)

Cosmography and modern science in Jainism 95

It is noteworthy that some agents of scientization defend Jain cosmography and that they do so by appealing to sources outside the Jain tradition. Monks such as Nagraj (1959) or Nandigoshvijay (2000) use scientific discoveries, observations and coordinates of contemporary maps to argue against the view that the earth is round. 'Fighting science with science' (Hersh 2011), Nandigoshvijay concludes that there is a need for more experimental research (2000: 140). This is why he created the RISSIOS, providing a good example of a tangible result of scientization and academization. In Jambudweep, Jain cosmography is defended by demanding faith and confidence in the traditional authorities – scriptures and ascetics. This is further backed up by academization activities. While the traditional scriptural view of the universe is defended, these projects nevertheless place cosmography in a new context. While the Jambudweep officials can be said to be operating within a hierarchical model where modern science is always subordinate to religious teachings,[51] the engagement with academization does have an impact on traditional teachings. Being a self-proclaimed research institute, the Jambudweep officials turn Jain cosmography into a field of research and a topic of academic investigation. This topic is presented through entertainment technologies that supplant the more traditional lavish temples with religious attractions that boldly materialize Jain cosmography and mythology. They invite its audience to combine a recreational outing with pilgrimage, and entertainment rides with a set of religiously beneficial acts. These edutainment charms speak of another development, which is not unique to the Jains but increasingly found all over India.

Notes

1 Valuable suggestions and comments on earlier drafts were received from Håkon Tandberg, Jane Skjoldli, Knut Melvær and Michael Stausberg.
2 By 'modern science', I refer to those activities we today associate with physics, chemistry and biology in their widest sense, i.e. the natural sciences that started to develop in Europe between 1550–1700, associated with names such as Copernicus, Kepler, Galileo, Descartes and Newton.
3 For the definition of Jainism followed here, see Carrithers (1990).
4 Hermann (Chapter 1 in this volume) makes a similar observation in relation to what he calls Buddhist modernism.
5 I follow the Jains' own spelling in names of places such as 'Jambudweep', and standard Indological procedures (using Sanskrit and not Prakrit) when referring to theological concepts such as *Jambūdvīpa*.
6 Jainism is divided into two major schools – Śvetāmbar ('White-clad') and Digambar ('Sky-clad') – their names referring to their monks' white clothing, or lack thereof. To consider the numerous other sectarian divisions is beyond the scope of this contribution.
7 It is also noticeable that traditional cosmography appears to have been more definitively abandoned in Buddhist modernism in comparison to Jain modernism (see Herman, Chapter 1 in this volume).
8 See the preface and bibliography in Bossche (2007).

96 *Knut Aukland*

9 This name reflects the fact that the lengths and sizes of various parts of the world are given thorough mathematical treatment (see e.g. Bossche 2007: 68–73). See Joseph (2000: 349ff.) for an overview of the various areas of Jain mathematics.

10 The Jina ('Victor') is the Jain equivalent of the Buddha in Buddhism. Another popular term for the Jina is *Tīrthaṅkara* ('Fordmaker').

11 See Luithlie-Hardenberg (2010: 1), footnote 1.

12 See Carrithers (1991, 1996) Humphrey (1991) and Sangave (1991) for more examples of such organizations.

13 See Brekke (2002: 138) and Flügel (2005). For other accounts of interactions between European scholars and Jains, see Babb (2007), Orr (2009) and Numark (2013).

14 See Flügel (1999: 7–8) and Sangave (1980: 265ff.) for lists of specific Jain-run or Jain-supported institutions in the late colonial era.

15 See Flügel (2005) for the history of Jainology and general study of Jainism. Philological and interpretative studies of Jain scriptures appear to be the core activity of Jainology.

16 http://pv-edu.in/ (accessed 15 Nov. 2013). The creation of the Bhaktivedanta Institute by is comparable result of academization in ISKCON (see King, Chapter 3 in this volume).

17 See www.jvbi.ac.in/ (accessed 15 Nov. 2013).

18 See www.isjs.in (accessed 22 October 2013).

19 See www.jaineducation.org/ (accessed 12 January 2014).

20 This entry is dated from 2002 (http://groups.yahoo.com/neo/groups/jainlist/conversations/topics/2973, accessed 1 Sept. 2013).

21 For example, Bhandari (1996), Gelra (2007), D.C. Jain (1954), Modi (2013), Jain and Jain (2012), Sikdar (1974), Pragya (2005), Zaveri (1994).

22 For example, Bhandari (2004), D.C. Jain (1981), Gelra (2002), Zaveri (1995).

23 See Andrea Jain's PhD-thesis (2010) for the history and development of this practice, and especially pp. 119–52 for its connections with scientization.

24 Jain ascetics are only to use boiled water for drinking and washing to avoid killing any minute life forms when using it.

25 The concept of aura appears other places in the literature such as Bhandari (1996: 72–73, 126, 2011: 114) and Gelra (2007).

26 See http://jainscience-rissios.org/ (accessed 19 Nov. 2013).

27 While Carrithers (1991: 273–4, 1996: 523) has briefly used the term 'Protestantization' to talk of modern trends, Flügel (2000, 2009) argues that the term should be reserved to pre-colonial developments.

28 See Balbir (1990), Appendix 3 for a list of various centres and organizations that were present in 1988.

29 See www.jambudweep.org/ (accessed 23 Nov. 2013).

30 See www.jambudweep.org/index.php?option=com_content&view=article&id=61&Itemid=119 (accessed 24 March 2011).

31 See www.jambudweep.org/index.php?option=com_content&view=article&id=59&Itemid=72 (accessed 24 Nov. 2013)

32 The temple trust overseeing the highly popular Śvetāmbar pilgrimage site Nākoḍa (see Aukland 2013) are in the process of constructing a showroom presenting Jain teachings through modern entertainment technology such as three-dimensional figures and film screenings. For other examples of such new constructions, see Titze (2001: 143, 205, 232).

33 See http://jambudweep.org/index.php?option=com_content&view=article&id=280&Itemid=114 (accessed 24 Nov. 2013)

34 Cf. sociologist Erik Cohen (2006) and what he calls "educational pilgrimage".

35 See www.jambudweep.org/index.php?option=com_content& view=article&id=58&Itemid=59 (accessed 16 May 2011).

Cosmography and modern science in Jainism   97

36 See www.jambudweep.org/index.php?option=com_content&view=article&id=57& Itemid=73 (accessed 28 Oct. 2010).
37 See www.jambudweep.org/index.php?option=com_content&view=article&id=57& Itemid=73 (accessed 25 Nov. 2013). This corresponds nicely with scholars' ideas about the function of Jain cosmology for the laity (see Dundas 2002: 92; Cort 2001: 21–2).
38 See King's Chapter 3 in this volume for more on ISKCON.
39 See Cort (2010: Chapter 2) for more on *nandīśvara* in Jain ritual culture.
40 There have been no studies of this festival, as far as I know.
41 The Transcendental Meditation movement's transformation of secular science into something that expresses religious meaning (Rothstein 1996: 199) demonstrates a Hindu alternative to the hierarchical model separating the lower natural sciences and the "higher spiritual science" suggested by Mackenzie Brown in Chapter 2 in this volume as a hallmark of 'Hinduism-science discourse.'
42 See N.L. Jain (1996), Mardia (1990), Gelra (2007) and Shah (2011).
43 See Hermann, Chapter 1 in this volume, for a Buddhist version of this argument in Siam.
44 The religious leader of ISKCON, Prabhupada, similarly speaks of "the moon hoax" indicating that this view is widespread on the religious scene in India (see King, Chapter 3 in this volume).
45 See www.youtube.com/watch?v=hots_z5Xxpk (accessed 18 Oct. 2011).
46 See http://indiatoday.intoday.in/story/jain-research-centre-in-gujarat-still-preaches-that-earth-is-flat/1/301958.html (accessed 26 Nov. 2013).
47 Cf. Cort (2001: 213), n.12.
48 *Jaina Archeology Outside India* (J.D. Jain 2011) provides an example of an attempt to use 'archaeology' to find proof that a range of historical remains of civilizations all over the world have signs that indicate that they were made by people who were once Jains.
49 The ISKCON-planned Vedic Planetarium to be built in 2016 would be an interesting point of comparison with Jambudweep. See King, Chapter 3 in this volume.
50 These two assumptions might be somewhat sketchy considering the history of the board-game 'Snakes and Ladders', whose origins are found in India and which was prevalent among Jains. The Jain version of the game demonstrates one way in which entertainment, play and religious teachings were combined in pre-colonial times. The game focuses on ethics, but also contains information about Jain cosmology. For more information and an online version of the game, see www.vam.ac.uk/content/articles/j/snakes-and-ladders/ (accessed 30 Nov. 2013).
51 See Mackenzie Brown, Chapter 2, in this volume.

References

Aukland, K. (2013) 'Understanding Possession in Jainism: A Study of Oracular Possession in Nakoda,' *Modern Asian Studies*, 47: 109–34.

Babb, L.A. (1996) *Absent Lord: Ascetics and Kings in a Jain Ritual Culture*. Berkeley, CA: University of California Press.

Babb, L.A. (2007) 'Tod and Traders,' in G. Tillotson (ed.) *James Tod's Rajasthan*. Mumbai: Marg Publications.

Balbir, N. (1990) 'Recent Developments in a Jaina Tirtha: Hastinapur (U.P.): A Preliminary Report,' in H. Bakker (ed.) *The History of Sacred Places in India as Reflected in Traditional Literature: Papers on Pilgrimage in South Asia*. Leiden: Brill.

98 *Knut Aukland*

Balbir, N. (n.d.) 'Mount Śatruñjaya', *Jainpedia.org*. Available at: www.jainpedia.org/themes/places/jain-holy-places/mount-satrunjaya/contentpage/2.html?sword_list[]=Palitana&no_cache=1.

Banks, M. (1991) 'Orthodoxy and Dissent: Varieties of Religious Belief Among Immigrant Gujarati Jains in Britain,' in M. Carrithers and C. Humphrey (eds) *The Assembly of Listeners: Jains in Society*. Cambridge: Cambridge University Press, pp. 241–60.

Bhandari, B.S. (1996) *The Science of Reincarnation: The Toll of Karma*. Available at: www.jainlibrary.org/book.php?file=007658 (accessed 5 January 2014). Jain eLibrary.

Bhandari, N. (2004) '"Anekant" as a Physical Reality'. Available at: www.jainsamaj.org/rpg_site/literature2.php?id=247&cat=42 (accessed 5 January 2014). Paper presented at the Jain Doctors' International Conference, Gandhinagar.

Bhandari, N. (2011) *Jainism: The Eternal and Universal Path for Enlightenment*. Ahmedabad: Research Institute of Scientific Secrets from Indian Oriental Scriptures.

Bhattacharya, H. (1925) *A Comparative Study of the Indian Science of Thought from the Jaina Standpoint*. Madras: C.S. Mallinath for Devendra Print. & Pub. Co.

Bossche, F.V.D. (2007) *Elements of Jaina Geography: The Jambudvipasamgrahani of Haribhadra Suri: Critically Edited and Translated with the Commentary of Prabhananda Suri*. Delhi: Motilal Banarsidass.

Bothara, S. (2004) *Ahimsa: The Science of Peaces*. Jaipur: Prakrit Bharti Academy.

Brekke, T. (2002) *Makers of Modern Indian Religion in the Late Nineteenth Century*. Oxford: Oxford University Press.

Brosius, C. (2010) *India's Middle Class: New Forms of Urban Leisure, Consumption and Prosperity*. London: Routledge.

Candnamati, P.A. (2010) 'Jambudweep: The First Geographical Creation,' paper presented at the 6th International Summer School for Jain Studies, Digambar Trilok Shodh Sansthan, Hastinapur.

Carrithers, M. (1990) 'Jainism and Buddhism as Enduring Historical Streams,' *Journal of the Anthropological Society of Oxford*, 21: 141–63.

Carrithers, M. (1991) 'The Foundations of Community among Southern Digambar Jains: An Essay on Rhetoric and Experience,' in M. Carrithers and C. Humphrey (eds) *The Assembly of Listeners: Jains in Society*. Cambridge: Cambridge University Press.

Carrithers, M. (1996) 'Concretely Imagining the Southern Digambar Jain Community, 1899–1920,' *Modern Asian* Studies, 30(3): 523–48.

Carrithers, M. and Humphrey, C. (eds) (1991) *The Assembly of Listeners: Jains in Ssociety*. Cambridge: Cambridge University Press.

Cohen, E. (2006) 'Religious Tourism as an Educational Experience,' in D.J. Olsen and D. Timothy (eds) *Tourism, Religion and Spiritual Journeys*. London: Routledge.

Cort, J.E. (1995) *Defining Jainism: Reform in the Jain Tradition*. Toronto: University of Toronto, Centre for South Asian Studies.

Cort, J.E. (2001) *Jains in the World: Religious Values and Ideology in India*. New York: Oxford University Press.

Cort, J.E. (2010) *Framing the Jina: Narratives of Icons and Idols in Jain History*. Oxford: Oxford University Press.

Dundas, P. (2002) *The Jains*. London: Routledge.

Flügel, P. (1999) 'Review of *Jainism. A Pictorial Guide to the Religion of Non-Violence*. By Kurt Titze. Delhi: Motilal Banarsidas, 1998,' *Internationales Asienforum*, 30(3–4): 403–5.

Flügel, P. (2000) 'Protestantische und Post-Protestantische Jaina-Reformbewegungen: Zur Geschichte und Organisation der Sithānakavāsī I,' *Berliner Indologische Studien*, 13–14: 37–103.

Flügel, P. (2005) 'The Invention of Jainism: A Short Story of Jaina Studies,' *International Journal of Jaina Studies*, 1(1): 1–14.

Flügel, P. (2006) 'Review of "*The Jains.* Second Revised Edition" by Paul Dundas,' *International Asia Forum*, 37(3–4): 396–9.

Flügel, P. (2009) 'Jain Modernism.' PowerPoint presentation received from author.

Flügel, P. (2014) *Jaina Law and Society.* New York: Routledge.

Frøystad, K. (2011) 'From Analogies to Narrative Entanglement: Invoking Scientific Authority in Indian New Age Spirituality,' in J. Lewis and O. Hammer (eds) *Handbook of Religion and the Authority of Science.* Leiden: Brill.

Gandhi, V.A. ([1893] 1993) 'The Philosophy and Ethics of the Jains,' in R. Hughes and R.R. Kidd Seager (eds) *The Dawn of Religious Pluralism: Voices from the World's Parliament of Religions.* La Salle, IL: Open Court.

Gelra, M.R. (2002) *Science in Jainism: Perspectives, Issues and Futuristic Trends.* Ladnun: Jain Vishva Bharati Institute.

Gelra, M.R. (2007) *Jain Studies and Science.* Ladnun: Jain Vishva Bharati Institute.

Gladstone, D.L. (2005) *From Pilgrimage to Package Tour: Travel and Tourism in the Third World.* New York: Routledge.

Hersh, C.L. (2011) 'Fighting Science with Science at Pat Robertson's Christian Broadcasting Network,' in J. Lewis and O. Hammer (eds) *Handbook of Religion and the Authority of Science.* Leiden: Brill.

Humphrey, C. (1991) 'New Jain Institutions in India and Beyond,' in M. Carrithers and C. Humphrey (eds) *The Assembly of Listeners: Jains in Society.* Cambridge: Cambridge University Press.

Jain, A.R. (2010) 'Health, Well-Being, and the Ascetic Ideal: Modern Yoga in the Jain Terapanth,' PhD thesis, Rice University.

Jain, C.R. (1916) *Nyaya: The Science of Thought.* Arrah: Central Jaina Publishing House.

Jain, C.R. (1930) *Jainism, Christianity and Science.* Available at: www.jainlibrary.org/book.php?file=011064 (accessed 5 January 2014). Allahabad: The Indian Press.

Jain, C.R. (2012) *Acarya Umasvati's Tattvarthasutra: Aspects of Reality in Jainism, Through the Eyes of Scientist.* Mumbai: Hindi Granth Karyalay.

Jain, D.C. (1954) 'Matter and Energy According to the Jain Scriptures.' Available at: www.Jainstudy.Org/Jsc7.07dcj.pdf (accessed 27 September 2014).

Jain, D.C. (1981) 'Jainism and Modern Science: A Comparative Study.' Available at: www.google.co.uk/url?sa=t&rct=j&q=&esrc=s&source=web&cd=1&ved=0CC8QFjAA&url=http%3A%2F%2Fwww.jainstudy.org%2FJSC1.08DCJ.pdf&ei=x1TJUs3DAe_H7Ab3jYCADA&usg=AFQjCNFkJlDWCy9qRpD3fJ0eb9M-P51DAA&bvm=bv.58187178,d.ZGU (accessed 5 January 2014), *Jain Study Circular*, October.

Jain, J. (2012) *Science of Dhovana Water.* Jaipur: Samyaggyan Pracharak Mandal.

Jain, J.D. (2011) *Jaina Archeology Outside India.* Lucknow: Shri Bharatvashiya Digamber Jain.

Jain, N.L. (1996) *Scientific Contents in Prakrta Canons.* Varanasi: Parsvanatha Vidyapitha.

Jain, S.C. (2012) 'Ahiṃsā/Non violence: Its Dimensions and Practices,' *ISSJS Study Notes*, 5.0(1): 195–204. Available at:www.isjs.in/ (accessed 10 January 2014).

100   *Knut Aukland*

Jain, S.K. (2010) *Antiquity of Jainism: An Ancient, Scientific and Independent Religion of the Universe*. Delhi: Vishwa Jain Sangathan.

Jain, S.M. (2003) *Pristine Jainism: Beyond Rituals and Superstitions*. Varanasi: Parshwanath Vidyapeeth.

Jain, V.S. and Jain, S.C. (2012) 'Reality (Sat) and Concept of Dravya (Substance) in Jaina Philosophy,' *ISSJS Study Notes*, 5.0(2): 1–14. Available at: www.isjs.in/ (accessed 10 January 2014).

Jaini, P.S. ([1979] 1998) *The Jaina Path of Purification*. Berkeley, CA: University of California Press.

Joseph, G.G. (2000) *The Crest of the Peacock: The Non-European Roots of Mathematics*. Princeton, NJ: Princeton University Press.

Kachhara, N.L. (2005) *Jaina Doctrine of Karma: The Religious and Scientific Dimensions*. Online. Available at: www.jainworld.com/jainbooks/karma/preface.asp (accessed 5 January 2014). Udaipur: Dharam Darshan Sewa Samsthan.

Laidlaw, J. (1995) *Riches and Renunciation: Religion, Economy, and Society among the Jains*. Oxford: Oxford University Press.

Lewis, J.R. (2011) 'How Religions Appeal to the Authority of Science,' in J.R. Lewis and O. Hammer (eds) *Handbook of Religion and the Authority of Science*. Leiden: Brill.

Lewis, J.R. and Hammer, O. (2011) 'Introduction,' in J.R. Lewis and O. Hammer (eds) *Handbook of Religion and the Authority of Science*. Leiden: Brill.

Luithle-Hardenberg, A. (2010) 'The Jaina and the British: Jaina Community in the 19th and the Early 20th Century,' paper presented at the workshop, 'The Jaina and the British,' Tübingen University.

Mahaprajna, A. (2001) *Preksha Dhyana: Perception of Psychic Centres*. Online. Available at: www.herenow4u.net/index.php?id=71314 (accessed 5 January 2014). Ladnun: Jain Vishva Bharati.

Mardia, K.V. (1990) *The Scientific Foundations of Jainism*. Delhi: Motilal Banarsidass Publishers.

Mardia, K.V. and Rankin, A.D. (2013) *Living Jainism: An Ethical Science*. Alresford: Mantra Books.

Mataji, G. (2007) *Jain Bharati*. Hastinapur: Digambar Trilok Shodh Sansthan.

Mataji, G. (2010) *Jaina Geography*. Hastinapur: Digambar Trilok Shodh Sansthan.

Mehta, D.R. (2012) 'Comprehensive Concept of Ahiṃsā and its Application in Real Life,' *ISSJS Study* Notes, 5.0(3): 35–50. Available at: www.isjs.in/ (accessed 10 January 2014).

Modi, M.B. (2013) 'Jainism, Quantum Physics and Evolving Spiritualism.' Available at: www.Herenow4u.Net/Index.Php?Id=90321 (accessed 8 January 2014).

Nagraj (1959) *Jain Philosophy and Modern Science*. Kanpur: Anuvrat Samiti.

Nandigoshvijay, M. (2000) *Scientific Secrets of Jainism*. Ahmedabad: Research Institute of Scientific Secrets from Indian Oriental Scriptures.

Nandigoshvijay, M. (2008) *Aura: A Theoretical and Practical Research*. Ahmedabad: Research Institute of Scientific Secrets from Indian Oriental Scriptures.

Numark, M. (2013) 'The Scottish "Discovery" of Jainism in Nineteenth-Century Bombay,' *Journal of Scottish Historical Studies*, 33(1): 20–51.

Orr, L. (2009) 'Orientalists, Missionaries and Jains: The South Indian Story,' in T.R. Trautmann (ed.) *The Madras School of Orientalism: Producing Knowledge in Colonial South India*. Delhi: Oxford University Press.

Pragya, C. (2005) *Scientific Vision of Lord Mahavira*. Online. Available at: www.here now4u.net/index.php?id=68158 (accessed 5 January 2014). Ladnun: Jain Vishva Bharati.

Reader, I. (2005) *Making Pilgrimages: Meaning and Practice in Shikoku*. Honolulu, HI: University of Hawaii Press.

Rothstein, M. (1996) *Belief Transformations: Some Aspects of the Relation Between Science and Religion in Transcendental Meditation (TM) and the International Society for Krishna Consciousness (ISKCON)*. Aarhus: Aarhus University Press.

Sangave, V. (1980) *Jaina Community: A Social Survey*. Bombay: Popular Prakashan.

Sangave, V. (1991) 'Reform movements among Jains in modern India,' in M. Carrithers and C. Humphrey (eds) *The Assembly of Listeners: Jains in Society*. Cambridge: Cambridge University Press.

Shah, M. (2011) 'Science in Jain Canonical Literature.' Available at: www.herenow4u. net/index.php?id=79265 (accessed 6 June 2013).

Shah, N. (2004) *Jainism: The World of Conquerors*. Delhi: Motilal Banarsidass Publishers.

Shanta, N. (1997) *The Unknown Pilgrims: The Voice of the Sadhvis: The History, Spirituality, and Life of the Jaina Women Ascetics*. Delhi: Sri Satguru Publications.

Sikdar, J.C. (1974) *Jaina Biology*. Ahmedabad: L. D. Institute of Indology.

Stausberg, M. (2011) *Religion and Tourism: Crossroads, Destinations, and Encounters*. London: Routledge.

Titze, K. (2001) *Jainism: A Pictorial Guide to the Religion of Non-Violence*. Delhi: Motilal Banarsidass Publishers.

Zaveri, J.S. (1994) *Neuroscience and Karma: The Jain Doctrine of Psycho-Physical Force*. Ladnun: Jain Vishva Bharati Institute.

Zaveri, J.S. (1995) *Microcosmology: Atoms in the Jain Philosophy and Modern Science*. Ladnun: Jain Vishva Bharati Institute.

5 On 'science' in 'The Science of Happiness'

The Japanese new religious movement *Kōfuku no kagaku*, occult 'science' and 'spiritual technology'

Franz Winter

Introduction

At first sight, a religious movement that presents itself as 'The Science of Happiness' (the literal translation of its official Japanese title, *Kōfuku no kagaku*) or 'Happy Science' (the name used in its international expansion),[1] seems to be an ideal object for a study on concepts of 'science' within a religious movement. However, an in-depth look at the main teachings will soon show that the concept of *kagaku* as purported by the movement is a very special one which draws on a specific view on the function and definition of 'science'. The main aim of this chapter is to give an insight into the religio-historical setting that forms the framework of this understanding and use of the word. As will be shown, the main background can be found in specific religious traditions which can be traced back to the so-called 'New Age' and its historical background, the (Western) 'esoteric' tradition. This idea is also expanded by drawing on a couple of examples to show the importance and the use of 'science' in various contexts within the movement.

On the formation of the main concepts of *Kōfuku no kagaku* and its religio-historical setting

To be able to discuss the references and the way 'science' is perceived within this particular movement, it is important to provide some insight into the development and formation of *Kōfuku no kagaku* which is mainly a history of its founder, Ōkawa Ryūhō, his self-perception, the perception within the group and the developmental changes these concepts underwent in the course of the years. In addition, though *Kōfuku no kagaku* is quite well known in Japan as one of the many 'new religions' (*shin-shūkyō*) or 'new new religions' (*shin-shinshūkyō*),[2] most people outside of Japan are probably unacquainted with it. Even its official English title, 'Happy Science', does not seem to be very familiar to anyone but specialists on the religious history of East Asia or new religious movements.

The official date of the foundation of this movement is 1986, when the then 30-year-old graduate of Tōkyō University, Ōkawa Ryūhō, opened the first branch-office in Tokyo. Ōkawa was born in 1956 as Nakagawa Takashi in the small town of Kawashima on Shikoku island.[3] Already, since 1981, he had claimed to have contact with the 'spirit world' (*reikai*). Its prominent inhabitants allegedly spoke to Ōkawa, who was then working as a businessman in a trading company in Nagoya after a rather successful school and university career. Through 'automatic writing' (*jidōshoki*) Ōkawa began to converse first with Nikkō (1246–1333), one of the disciples of the Buddhist reformer, Nichiren (1222–82), then with Nichiren himself who prepared him for his mission for mankind with the formula *hito o aishi, hito o ikashi, hito o yuruse* ('love others, nurture others, and forgive others').[4] The first publications ever made in the context of *Kōfuku no kagaku* are reports of Ōkawa's contacts with representatives of the spiritual world, which were published a year before the official foundation under the name of a 'friend', whom Ōkawa asked for help after his first encounters with the spirit world.[5] His correspondents cover an impressive sample of various figures of the philosophical and religious history of both the East and the West, including Nichiren, Jesus, Socrates, Laozi, Gandhi, Lincoln and other important teachers, historical figures and various deities like the Japanese sun goddess Amaterasu or the Egyptian god Amon (Winter 2012a: 45–53).[6]

From a religio-historical point of view, the material presented therein may be interpreted as belonging to the vast array of what is called the channelling tradition. This genre was one of the starting points of the Euro-American New Age movement (Hanegraaff 1998: 24–41), and many texts in this vein were translated into Japanese in the 1970s.[7] In Japan, these publications are commonly referred to as belonging to the *seishin sekai* ('spiritual world') literature, which has been interpreted as an adaptation of the Euro-American New Age in Japan (Fukusawa 2001; Prohl 2007). However, there is still some debate whether it is useful to introduce this category and to speak of the *seishin sekai* as the mere 'reception' of the New Age. It is a fact that major issues and topics that are connected to the New Age play a role in Japan (as exactly this example here shows), but the main question is whether they form a separate category. The New Age in the West can be interpreted as a major break with the dominant religious factor, namely the Christian paradigm, and the emergence of an already long-existing current commonly referred to as 'Western Esotericism' (Hanegraaff 1998). Japan, on the other hand, was never under the main influence of specifically one religious tradition but followed several traditions which became important in the course of their adaptation. Therefore the integration of the Western New Age material should not be interpreted as a new chapter in the history of Japanese religions (Pye 2002).[8] Nevertheless, while the idea of contacting a world beyond has been a common feature in the formation of many of the new religions since the nineteenth century (Stalker 2008: 76–8; Staemmler 2009: 112–16), Ōkawa's *reigen* show a clear resemblance to the New Age channelling-genre

104 *Franz Winter*

(Staemmler 2009: 111; Winter 2012a: 324–6). The references are more than obvious with regard to the main content of these publications. There is extensive information on the coming of a 'new age' (*shinjidai*), which will usher in a 'new civilisation' (*shinbunmei*). Certain topics referred to are also well-known features of the Western New Age literature: detailed information on mythical civilisations and 'lost continents', which once flourished but later were destroyed (such as Atlantis or the continent Mu), secret, 'occult' traditions, which have been alive since antiquity and give an insight into the reality behind certain historical events, the importance of the 'spiritual world' (*reikai*), and how to contact it. In addition, Ōkawa himself discusses writings of the Western channelling genre in his *reigen*,[9] and places himself in this tradition. In a separate chapter on the 'secret of channelling' in one of his publications, he refers to the universalistic dimension of the channelling-tradition, when he draws parallels to practices described in the ancient Japanese chronicles *Kojiki* or the *Nihon shoki* (Ōkawa 1994b: 127–58). This stress on the importance of channelling as a tool and master key for the interpretation of any form of religious contact with a world beyond is typical and popular in many presentations of the genre (see Klimo 1988: 2; Bjorling 1992: 3; cf. the critical remarks in Hanegraaff 1998: 25–6). Ōkawa's publications are also part of a specific period in the 1980s when channelling became extremely popular on a worldwide level, a phenomenon that once was labelled the 'popular channelling craze' (ibid.: 41, cf. Gebhardt 2001: 22).

It is important to note that references to a special form of 'science' are already a major issue in this context. The alleged coming of the 'New Age' was combined with a purported 'fresh' look at the way the world and its various features were interpreted. This can be perceived as an important legacy with many connections to its predecessors, mainly Theosophy, as taught by the Russian author and spiritual teacher, Helena P. Blavatsky. From a cultural historical point of view, this approach can be interpreted as a reaction to the explosive growth of modern science, especially in the second half of the nineteenth century, which caused a restructuring of the way the world and its constituents were seen (Zander 2007: 861–6). The traditional religious interpretations of the origin and fate of the world and of mankind were in danger of being neglected or exposed to ridicule and, to a certain extent, many developments were understood as a reintegration of the religious and transcendental factor, which they tried to reconcile with the new 'scientific' discoveries (Barbour 1998). In the academic literature, this claim is referred to as 'scientism' as distinguished from 'science' (Hammer 2004: 201–330). Many authors of the 'New Age' drew on an interpretation of the world, which is commonly referred to as 'holistic' in contrast to the 'analytical' view of traditional 'science'. Its main feature was a special attention to 'the whole' which was interpreted as the opposite of the scientific approaches with their tendency to 'particularise' (and ignore 'the whole'). But this general attitude was not focused on a rejection of modern 'science' *per se* but included a changed attitude towards the way the world and its phenomena

On 'science' in 'The Science of Happiness' 105

should be dealt with. In this regard, Hanegraaff (1998: 62–4) points out a specific dichotomy, namely the 'high regard for modern science' and the 'distrust' of 'academic rationalism', which pervade the New Age current. In particular, (theoretical) physics and biology were the focus of these endeavours since these disciplines were regarded as promising fields which might give insight into the history of the universe, the world and mankind.[10] One of the most important figures of the New Age, the Austrian-born American physicist Fritjof Capra (born in 1939) put forward the main ideas in his influential publication, *The Tao of Physics* and summarised his approach in the famous statement: "Science does not need mysticism and mysticism does not need science, but man needs both" (Capra 1975: 306).[11] The main aim was the search for a 'unified world-view' combining the different and particularised fields of science and the humanities into one coherent concept, including a religious dimension, which was in danger of being neglected by the main propagators of modern science (Hanegraaff 1998: 63).

As will be seen in the detailed description, Ōkawa can be interpreted as a far offspring of this attitude and the heir of major 'New Age' parameters – with a couple of differences and specific adaptations. This becomes particularly clear when dealing with the title the founder gave his own movement, which also draws on a specific history.

The official title of the movement and its background

The name Ōkawa gave his own movement is rather unusual even among the manifold expressions of religion in Japan. Although there is a huge variety of designations used by new religious movements in Japan, the title *Kōfuku no kagaku*, i.e. the 'Science of Happiness', is rather exceptional. Most traditional self-designations used by Japanese new religious movements refer to the common expression in the context of religion and religious teachings, namely the ending in -*kyō* ('teaching', 'doctrine' of/about/on somebody/something). This was the case with nearly all the 'traditional' new religions in the nineteenth century (such as *Tenrikyō*, *Kurozumikyō*, *Konkōkyō*, or *Jikkōkyō*) but also later, for instance, with *Aum Shinrikyō* (founded in 1984). Another widely used type of designation is the reference to the organisational form, the most common form being an ending in -*kai* ('gathering', 'community'), such as in *Sōka Gakkai* or in *Rissho Kōsei-kai*, or an ending in -*kyōdan* ('religious organisation', 'church') as in *PL Liberty Kyōdan*. Other groups coined their own names: the founder of *Mahikari*, Okada Kōtama, referred to the essence of his teachings on the 'true light' (*mahikari*). Rather exceptional is also the use of a non-Japanese expression, as it is the case with the *God Light Association* (commonly referred to in its abbreviated form as *GLA*), which was originally founded as the *Shinkōkai*.

Kōfuku no kagaku clearly belongs to the latter group of non-traditional designations. Interestingly the awkward expression proposed by Ōkawa attracted suspicion that he was orientating himself towards a rather successful but highly controversial non-Japanese new religious movement, namely 'The Church of Scientology'.[12] Contacts and encounters with this movement may well have been possible especially in the course of Ōkawa's one-year stay in New York in 1982, where he studied English at the Berlitz Language School and took courses in International Finance (*kokusai kinyūron*) at New York University (Baffelli 2004: 61). All these assertions, though, were made in the course of the highly critical media discussion on *Kōfuku no kagaku* at the beginning of the 1990s when the movement became ensnared in a major media debate, commonly referred to as the *Kōdansha* or Friday incident (*Kōdansha/ Furaidē jiken*) (Baffelli 2007; Winter 2012a: 82–93). Ōkawa and *Kōfuku no kagaku* always denied any connection and regarded these speculations as futile; the movement even listed 'The Church of Scientology' in their own *Jakyō hihan manyuaru* ('Manual for Criticism on Heretical Movements') as a problematic and dangerous movement.[13]

In addition, there is no need to search for this kind of direct 'foreign' inspiration. The use of the term *kagaku* is not so far-fetched when taking into consideration its history in the context of specific Japanese interests in the 'spirit world'. At the end of the nineteenth and the beginning of the twentieth century there was a highly developed transfer of originally Western ideas and concepts which are commonly referred to as 'spiritualism'. From a cultural-historical point of view, this interest in Japan may be interpreted as a 'romantic' and 'escapist' reaction to the overall trends towards industrialisation, urbanisation and the omnipresent expansion of state power with its stress on nationalism at this time (Hardacre 1998: 133–4). The idea of a common soul to every human being inherent in the spiritualist teachings obviously appealed to a well-educated urban society which was also interested in adopting a Westernised bourgeois salon culture. In addition, there was the possibility of connecting at various times with indigenous religious traditions who proposed various forms of communication with a world 'beyond'.

There is a stream of references to *kagaku*[14] in this context which is particularly relevant to the history of the highly influential new religious movement *Ōmoto*.[15] One example is the *Shinrei kagaku kenkyūkai* ('Research Association for Psychic Science'), founded by the *Ōmoto*-member Asano Wasaburō,[16] which was focused on a 'scientific' approach to all the questions concerning 'psychic phenomena'. A major key in understanding and an important factor concerning all these topics on a worldwide level is the influence of the already mentioned 'Theosophy', which was founded by the Russian author and spiritual teacher Madame Blavatsky (1831–91). It had been known in Japan already since the beginning of the twentieth century (Kasai 2012). One of the colleagues of the above-mentioned Asano Wasaburō translated Madame Blavatsky's last book, *The Key to Theosophy* (published in 1889) into Japanese under the title *Reichigaku kaisetsu* in 1910 (Nishiyama 1988: 184). This influential book is structured as a traditional 'catechism' in a question–answer style and the first sentence shows the clear attitude towards the expression 'science':

ENQUIRER: Theosophy and its doctrines are often referred to as a newfangled religion. Is it a religion?

THEOSOPHIST: It is not. Theosophy is Divine Knowledge or Science.

(Blavatsky 1889: 1)

This short quotation should serve as an example clearly showing the direction and intention that were at the core of *The Key to Theosophy*.

A major bridge and an important further inspiration for Ōkawa is the use of the term in the writings of Takahashi Shinji (1927–76), the founder of the religious movement *God Light Association*. His most important publication is the trilogy, *Kokoro no hakken* ('Discovery of the mind', first published 1971–73), whose second volume is on 'science' (*kagaku*). Therein he mainly gives a description of his own spiritual development and draws heavily on the importance of insight into the 'spirit world' as the basis for everything (Winter 2012a: 191–9).

In *Kōfuku no kagaku* the use of this rather exceptional expression may also be connected with the initial approach of the movement, as explained by Ōkawa in a couple of interviews, namely the fact that it was not meant as a religion, but rather as a kind of 'study institute' or even a 'school' with a definite curriculum. The first official expression used only a short time immediately after the foundation was *Jinsei no daigaku-in: Kōfuku no kagaku* ('Graduate School of Life: The Science of Happiness') and even in later publications Ōkawa draws on the 'school' (*gakkō*) character of his early phase (cf. Ōkawa 2004a: 228, 2004b: 122). One of the reasons was the alleged wish to attract not too many followers in the first phase, since Ōkawa was searching for suitable candidates rather than 'mere' members. In his opinion, this was one of the main failures of many religious organisations, namely a desire to increase the mere numbers rapidly without looking at the quality of the candidates, putting quantity above quality.

New religions today often create problems, because those who are not enlightened try to lead people and draw them by force into their organization ... To avoid similar problems, we must spend time in exploring the Truth and studying it before spreading it. This is why I kept our organization as a study group for the first couple of years. The teachings of IRH will naturally be passed from person to person, as revealed in the fact that there are already many people on the waiting list to become members.

(Okawa 2000: 17)

Limiting the number of members was intended to be a method to promote the quality of the candidates' recruitment.

This focus is also evident when considering the terminology used by the group for the further education of the new members. It is about 'training seminars' (*kenshūkai*), which were started for the inner circle[17] and those who

108 *Franz Winter*

successfully managed these educational procedures would be sent out as 'associated lecturer' (*junkōshi*) or (on the next level) as 'lecturer' (*kōshi*). This terminology is directly derived from academic structures and universities and is another clear indication of the 'academic' claim of Ōkawa (Baffelli 2004: 63). It also makes sense when taking into consideration the official use intended for the publications, namely, to serve as a tool for the 'study of the divine truth' (*shinri tankyū*).[18] Earlier academic publications on *Kōfuku no kagaku* described its character as a 'study group' of spiritual messages purportedly received and transmitted by Ōkawa Ryūhō (Astley 1995: 355–6).

This special approach regarding the structure and aim of the organisation was under constant review more or less until the official registration of the movement in 1991 as a 'religious corporation' (*shūkyō hōjin*) (cf. Ōkawa 1994a: 369, 1996a: 146; Astley 1995: 347). It is evident that there were major concerns regarding the 'religion' character of *Kōfuku no kagaku* when considering its history so far. Even Ōkawa himself argued (in an interview with one of his critics in 1991), that a description of *Kōfuku no kagaku* as something belonging to 'education' (*kyōiku*) or as a 'company' (*kaisha*) made sense – in addition to it being a 'religion' (*shūkyō*). He added that the characterisation as a 'religion' was not done in the beginning since it would have created a bad image in Japanese society. But in the end, he decided to opt for a status as *shūkyō hōjin*, exactly to work against this general view on 'religion'.[19] This change in the general attitude and outlook of the movement also becomes evident in its internal publications, where its perception as 'religious organisation' (*shūkyō dantai*) is marked in the year 1991 (Kōfuku no kagaku sōgō honbu 2001: 29).[20]

This also opened a new chapter in the way the movement behaved. After a rather calm period as a 'study group' of spiritual messages purportedly received by its founder in the 1980s, *Kōfuku no kagaku* began to push itself through big mass events in the surroundings of Tokyo at the beginning of the 1990s and thereby changed its main concepts and beliefs. On the one hand, this self-representation was the starting-point for a rapid growth in membership, which rose dramatically in the following years.[21]

The development is also clear when taking an in-depth look at the publications of Ōkawa which now show major differences and result in a new concept. The first publications, which have much in common with the afore-mentioned channelling material, were soon replaced by new publications, which clearly mark a shift in the self-perception of Ōkawa after the official foundation of *Kōfuku no kagaku* in 1986. After a set of books comprising new spiritual messages, where Ōkawa presented channelled material in a more authoritative way as a spiritual teacher (and not as a 'mere' medium),[22] a new series of books was launched in 1987, which was called the 'law series' (*hō-shirīzu*). The first three books in this collection, namely *Taiyō no hō* ('The Laws of the Sun'), *Ōgon no hō* ('The Golden Laws') and *Eien no hō* ('The Laws of Eternity'),[23] are said to contain

On 'science' in 'The Science of Happiness' 109

all the basic teachings on cosmology, anthropology and ethics and may be regarded as the fundamental doctrinal texts of the group, which underwent a couple of re-editions and changes in the course of the further development of the movement. They were presented as the final revelations of the Buddha, as is evident from the picture used on the cover of the original publications showing a traditional Buddha statue and the subtext with direct references to the *Shakyamuni*.[24] Soon after this presentation of new teachings of the Buddha, Ōkawa began to present *himself* as the reincarnation of the Buddha, not only his spiritual messenger. This was done officially and in public in 1989 in a book whose title was *Budda saitan* ('The Rebirth of Buddha'), though he allegedly had mentioned this insight already to a couple of followers before that time. What follows is a systematic reinterpretation of the main teachings of Ōkawa focusing on his new role. The core message is that Ōkawa represents the reincarnation of Buddha and the doctrine of *Kōfuku no kagaku* is fundamentally Buddhist (Cornille 1998: 288). This is noteworthy as this emphasis on Buddhism changed a little bit later when Ōkawa was presenting the final truth with regard to his nature, which was done officially in 1991 in the so-called *Eru Kantāre sengen* ('El Cantare Declaration') in the Tokyo Dome in a huge mass event (Astley 1995: 360–2; Baffelli 2007: 89–90; Winter 2008: 74–6). The main message of this event, which marked a new phase in the history of this movement, was that Ōkawa is the reincarnation of a spiritual being called *El Cantare*.[25] This 'consciousness' (*ishiki*) already had undergone a couple of reincarnations before Ōkawa and the Buddha, and covered the whole history of humanity, in East and West, North and South, including the 'lost continents' of Atlantis and Mu.[26] This important new version of the doctrine led to a revision of the older publications, particularly changes in the terminology and additions to older versions.[27]

'Science'

The above-mentioned major changes in the general attitude of the movement also brought a changed approach to its character and what it offered. The initial focus on 'studying' and the like, which was so important in the early phase of the movement, became less important. An evident sign is the total absence of any in-depth explanation of the character of 'science' in the newer publications of Ōkawa or introductory books. In a recent bilingual *English Truth Handbook* (Kōfuku no kagaku kokusai-kyoku 2008), which is meant as a guide for members who may meet English-speaking people, there is no information or explanation of the term 'science' (or anything similar). When members are asked what specifically is meant by 'the science of happiness', they commonly draw on the basic 'teachings' of the movement, which are said to be the essence of its 'science'. The actual leader and 'president' of *Kōfuku no kagaku* is regarded as the representation of a spiritual entity which is responsible for the Earth, and as part of an elaborate and not fully

110 Franz Winter

explained hierarchy of beings in a multidimensional universe.[28] This is the main framework that is obviously focused on the function and the authority of its founder and actual leader. It is legitimising his status within the movement's teachings and he claims absolute authority on all matters spiritual and religious. Something like the 'core' of the teachings that are closely interconnected and presented in the publications as the most important essence of the spiritual world (= the essence of the 'science of happiness') are the teachings on the four 'principles of happiness' (*kōfuku no genri*). According to the predominant orientation towards the Buddhist tradition, this feature of the movement's teachings is presented as the new version of the (Buddhist) 'four noble truths', namely the 'fourfold path' (*yonshōdō*) which consists of: love (*ai*), wisdom (*chi*), self-reflection (*hansei*) and progress (*hatten*) (the concept is summarised e.g. in Kōfuku no kagaku kokusai-kyoku 2008: 157–68). The teachings on 'love' are mainly focused on a distinction between different forms of love, which are associated with the various 'dimensions' of the universe. The basic distinction is between the 'love that takes (away)' (*ubau ai*) and the 'love that gives' (*ataeru ai*), the latter being a kind of an altruistic ideal which should be internalised and practised by everyone. 'Wisdom' or 'knowledge' is mainly associated with insight into the teachings of Ōkawa whose authority as the ultimate presentation of the spiritual truth guarantees the truth of this message. 'Self-reflection' is focused on the constant realisation and adaptation of his principles in daily life, particularly through meditation and constant reflection on the main principles. The topic of 'progress' is presented as the more or less logical 'consequence' of the afore-mentioned principles and as a kind of promise for everyone who becomes a member. It is mainly concerned with 'success' (*seikō*), which is the reward for everyone who follows the teachings of Ōkawa. It is 'success' in the context of personal life, which is marriage and family, and also in regard to professional life. The latter topic is of particular importance in many of Ōkawa's publications, which may be perceived as collections of business and management hints and tricks (cf. e.g. Ōkawa 2002: 21–98, with a focus on the 'laws of success', *seikō no hōsoku*, regarding daily life). This is combined with an explicit working ethics in total conformity with the mainstream of Japanese society.[29] Ōkawa stresses the importance of staying within common guidelines and his approach is based on a primarily optimistic view of the world and the way it works. Being reincarnated, for instance, is not interpreted as a burden but as a chance to move towards a better spiritual position. This is summarised in the following quotation:

> This world is a superb training ground for spiritual discipline (*tamashii shugyō no ba*). We are born on earth to learn many lessons in life (*jinsei no kyōkun*) and improve our souls (*tamashii o kōjō saseru*). Life is a workbook of problems to be solved.
>
> (Kōfuku no kagaku kokusai-kyoku 2008: 65)

On 'science' in 'The Science of Happiness' 111

The definition of life as a 'workbook of problems to be solved' (*issatsu no mondaishū*) is used throughout many of Ōkawa's publications even from the beginning (cf. Ōkawa 1990: 29).

Major fields of 'scientific' interests and the 'spiritual technology'

In spite of a certain negligence regarding its own designation (as was shown in the preceding section), there are several fields of interest within the movement, which should be quoted when dealing with its 'science' appeal. An important instance in the writings of Ōkawa is a keen interest in the history of mankind, which is presented in a totally new and exceptional way allegedly based on a fresh look at it. Ōkawa is presented as the current terrestrial representation of a spiritual being, which had already reincarnated a number of times in an imagined history of mankind. This is combined with a specific view on 'history' which is interpreted according to this model as a sequence of different cultures which once flourished and were destroyed in the course of their development – mainly through natural catastrophes but also due to the immoral behaviour of their inhabitants.

Therein the concept of reincarnation is perceived as one of the master keys to understand history. Many pages of the early *hō*-books are filled with detailed information on who was reincarnated as who in the course of the history of mankind.[30] This gives the impression of total insight into the mechanisms of world history that is presented as a permanently interconnected matrix of spiritual entities and powers ruled by the perpetual law of good and evil (see Winter 2012a: 177–237, for further details). Individual members are often very interested in this information that gives the impression of 'secret knowledge' now open to everyone. *Himitsu* ('secret') is – in general – one of the dominant keywords in Ōkawa's publications, often combined with the expression 'occult' (*okaruto*), used extensively without giving a proper definition (see ibid.: 254–7, for further information).

The already mentioned interest in the 'lost continents' is another important area in this context.[31] Ōkawa draws heavily on the various theories of once existing continents with highly advanced cultures that were important predecessors of all the ancient cultures. Therein details of their alleged technological artefacts play a major role in the description. The inhabitants of the continent Mu, for instance, had a special kind of energy which derived from the sun (*taiyō no enerugī*) and which was collected by an elaborated system of 'pyramids' scattered across the country (Ōkawa 1994a: 263–5). On the continent Atlantis, the figure of Thos is introduced as the prototype of the inventor who is responsible for a couple of technological innovations (such as space ships or submarines) and the cities of Atlantis are presented as science fiction utopia in a highly advanced state (ibid.: 273–4); the association with flying objects and submarines is also a recurrent pattern in the visual representations of Atlantis, e.g. Ōkawa 1996b: 180–1). In both continents the references to its most important leaders and reformers (mainly Thos and La

112 *Franz Winter*

Mu) always draw on the symbiosis of their 'scientific' (*kagakuteki*) and their 'religious' (*shūkyōteki*) abilities which have to be combined to produce the quality of a real politician and statesman. This is also very important in the description of the figure of Hermes, who is the subject of a detailed biography of his 'real' life (according to Ōkawa) in a four-volume set entitled *Herumesu – Ai wa kaze no gotaku* ('Hermes: Love is like the wind', Ōkawa 1994c), which was also made into an *anime* film (see Winter 2013, for further details of the character of Hermes in *Kōfuku no kagaku*).[32]

In all these contexts many references are made to the idea of the 'Ancient Astronauts' theoreticians, who concentrate their 'research' on the purported contacts between extraterrestrial cultures, their messengers and mankind. It is mainly about the interpretation of various artefacts and remains of ancient cultures, but also of specific mythological traditions which are studied according to this paradigm. In the publications of Ōkawa, there are several allusions to important instances of this concept which are often presented as common knowledge, which is no longer explained but taken as 'proved'. The introduction to the film *Ōgon no hō*, for instance, which is about the adventure of two teenagers through time and space in a *taimu mashin* ('time machine'), cites major examples of the Ancient Astronauts theories (e.g., iconographic details in Egyptian paintings, the Old Testament story of Ezekiel and his encounter with the heavenly chariot, or the Nacza lines in Southern Peru) without any further comment. This pre-astronautic *tour d'horizon* presupposes a specific acquaintance with these ideas among its consumers.

The idea of combining the 'spirit world' and 'science' reaches its peak in a concept I want to call 'spiritual technology', mainly the claim to have knowledge of technical items that are based on 'scientific' concepts and offer a connection to the 'spiritual world'. An excellent example of this approach is given in one of the recent films that the movement made, namely the *anime* version of the *Eien no hō*. This is the third of the already mentioned fundamental 'law' (*hō*) books which were published in the mid-1980s (and republished and changed in the course of several re-editions, especially in the 1990s) and whose *anime* versions were released in 2000–2007. In the film entitled *The Laws of Eternity* (*Eien no hō*). *Eru Kantāre no sekaikan* the story of the adventure of a group of young students in search of the 'real truth' is told. In the beginning there is a sequence in which the so-called *reikai tsu-shinki* is discussed, a 'device for the communication with the spirit world', which is introduced and presented by (the spirit of) Thomas A. Edison. The context draws on alleged plans of the great inventor for a 'telephone to the dead' which some interpreters found in an interview for the magazine, *Scientific American* in 1921 (Butler and Butler 2003: 6–7).[33] Therein he only mentions the fact that – if there is life after death – there has to be a way to communicate with dead persons. But there is no information available whether Edison ever planned to build anything like that. In the film the technical item works and there is some (pseudo-)'scientific' information on the way it works, but the

On 'science' in 'The Science of Happiness'   113

focus of the story is on the necessity of 'faith' (*shinkō*) and 'religion' (*shūkyō*) in order to make it work. Although a group of young students eagerly tries to start the *reikai tsushinki*, it does not work until a young woman is introduced whose steadfast 'faith' is the additional ingredient missing so far. 'Religion' therein is defined as knowledge about the laws of the 'spirit world' (*reikai*), which is in accordance with its definition by Ōkawa. And 'science' (*kagaku*) only makes sense when it is thoroughly combined with 'religion' in order to give it the right direction. The ideal result is introduced as *reikai kagaku*, which is a 'science' based on insight into the 'spirit world', which is more or less the same as the messages of Ōkawa, as presented in his publications. The film makes it absolutely clear that this kind of science is not just futile study but brings concrete results, for instance, new forms of energy which will enhance the development of humankind. The *reikai kagaku* is perceived as a very practical kind of science, able to fulfil the basic needs of current society and the world.

Some features of this specific interest may also be interpreted as being part of a very important aspect of *Kōfuku no kagaku* and its self-presentation, namely the Manga culture of Japan. It is important to know that this specific medium is a field of expression far beyond the significance of comic literature in the West. Manga was once called a "defining characteristic of Japan's publishing culture" (Cooper-Chen 1997: 98) and its influence on many cultural levels is evident. For this reason, it is no wonder that religion plays a major role in manga and religious movements also took advantage of this important cultural factor to present their contents (Thomas 2012; Winter 2012b; MacWilliams 2012). A specific interest in advanced 'technology' is a constant feature in this context. Many Manga draw heavily on elaborate descriptions of all kind of technical items, special 'energies', or highly sophisticated technologies, which become important in the course of the story. This is closely intertwined with science fiction literature where detailed information on all these aspects is particularly found. This is often presented by referring to a hotchpotch of 'scientifically' sounding terms and expressions, some of them derived from actual research fields in contemporary physics ('black holes', 'antimatter', 'speed of light'), most of them obviously invented and deriving from the imaginative power of the writers and film-makers. It is absolutely justified to introduce a direct connection between these science fiction imaginings and the Manga culture and some features of the publications of *Kōfuku no kagaku*. There is also a close parallel to several aspects of *Aum Shinrikyō*, which also showed the same interest in 'Manga-esque' and science fiction content (cf. Repp 2011). Another example in *Kōfuku no kagaku* would be the 'time machine' in the *anime*-version of the *Ōgon no hō*, which is thoroughly explained in a special book on this film. Therein, Ōkawa makes references to H.G. Wells' famous novel, *The Time Machine* and the alleged 'scientific' foundation regarding the possibility of a journey through time in a future generation (Ōkawa 2003: 10–19).[34]

114　*Franz Winter*

Conclusion

Searching for the meaning of 'science' in 'The Science of Happiness' was not an easy task. As became clear in the material provided, the use of this specific term, even in its self-designation, can be interpreted from a religio-historical point of view as part of a specific tradition which may be linked to various patterns of thought and a specific language, originating in the context of the so-called 'Western esotericism' at the end of the nineteenth century as well as in its adaptation in the 'New Age' literature since the middle of the twentieth century. As has been pointed out, there are various instances and references to the term 'science' in several relevant traditions especially since the beginning of the twentieth century in Japan, where major exponents of religious currents drew on this material in an interesting adaptation process. These instances are mainly referring to alleged contact with the 'spirit world' (*reikai*) and the like, which were said to be based on 'scientific' methods. In addition, the basic concept of 'science' in the above-mentioned New Age context has to be taken into consideration. This is a special attitude towards the function and interpretation of modern natural 'science' which claimed to present a 'fresh' look at it and is mainly focused on a 'unified' world-view with the implementation of the 'religion' factor. It is worth noting that one of the major messages of the so-called New Age referred to the importance of 'science' while it heavily criticised the current state of scientific 'materialistic' research. These concepts should be replaced by a new form which has its basis in a totally changed look at the world and its constituents, since – allegedly – the most essential aspect is missing: a religious or 'spiritual' grounding.

Ōkawa is a direct heir of this tradition, as becomes evident in his writings where he often refers to the necessity to amalgamate 'science' and 'religion'. This is a constant topic in many of his lectures and publications, though a sound definition of both terms is never given. It is also an important factor in his descriptions of ideal leadership and ideal statesmanship, which he exemplifies in a couple of mythical figures in his extensive descriptions of the history of mankind: Hermes (in archaic Greece), King Mu (from the mythical continent Mu) or King Thos (from the mythical continent Atlantis) are said to unify both 'scientific' (*kagakuteki*) and 'religious' (*shūkyōteki*) qualities which are necessary for the ideal 'leader' (*shidōsha*).

However, when going into details, it is evident that Ōkawa does not show any major interest in the progress of modern academic 'science' but is mainly concerned with its adaptation in the particular context cited. The main message is the symbiosis of science and religion with a clear preponderance of the latter since the relevant ideas and patterns of thought should derive from the 'spirit world'. In the case of *Kōfuku no kagaku*, this insight is provided through the authority of its founder and president, Ōkawa Ryūhō, who connects directly to its contents and who is able to give thorough information on its 'doctrine'. The essence of Ōkawa's 'scientific' insight into

On 'science' in 'The Science of Happiness' 115

the 'spirit world' is presented as the teachings on the four 'principles of happiness' (*kōfuku no genri*), which are the guidelines for every devoted member. 'Love', 'wisdom', 'self-reflection' and 'progress' are defined as the main 'doctrine' of the 'spirit world' as presented by Ōkawa and they are closely intertwined as patterns of thought and behaviour which should serve as common guidelines to everyone and which should help to build an ideal society, commonly referred to as 'utopia'.

In addition to this general description, a special case of references to 'science' was described in this chapter as 'spiritual technology'. In several publications and most prominently in the Manga published by *Kōfuku no kagaku*, one encounters a hotchpotch of scientifically sounding terminology, which is closely intertwined with its alleged religious meaning and interpretation. An example cited in this regard is the *reikai tsushinki* mentioned in the *anime* version of the *Eien no hō*. This 'device for the communication with the spirit world' allegedly bridges the gap between modern science and religion through insight into the messages of the spirit world, which is the essence of religion in Ōkawa's interpretation. As was shown, this approach has its closest parallels in the science fiction genre and the Manga and *anime* culture which is a major inspiration for many approaches to 'science' in *Kōfuku no kagaku*.

Notes

1 This is the official title used since 2008; before then, the movement presented itself internationally as the *Institute for Research in Human Happiness*, which was abbreviated either as *IRH* or *IRHH* (depending on copyright issues in the different countries of its missionary endeavours).

2 The concept of *shin-shinshūkyō*, as different from *shinshūkyō*, was originally coined by the sociologist of religion, Nishiyama Shigeru, to distinguish recent developments in the field of new religions. It is mainly used for religious movements which came into being or reached their peak in the last decades of last century and especially since the 1970s. They all share a couple of characteristics, *inter alia* the importance of newer forms of media to promote their ideas, references to a vast array of concepts of a 'spirit world' (*reikai*) as distinguished from the 'real world' or a so-called 'syncretistic'/'eclectic' approach to the various religious traditions. See Clarke (1999: 12–14); Astley (2001: 102–4); and Shimazono (2004: 18–19).

3 Although the official change of name from Nakagawa Takashi to Ōkawa Ryūhō took place in 1986 with the official foundation of *Kōfuku no kagaku*, I shall use this name throughout this chapter, as it is the common and known one.

4 The English translation according to the official version in the publications of Ōkawa; see Ōkawa (1994a: 351, 1996a: 139).

5 As was 'revealed' at the beginning of the 1990s, the 'publisher' and 'interviewer' of Ōkawa in the books, Yoshikawa Saburō, was his father. The use of a pen-name was explained as a device to protect Ōkawa, who was then, i.e. in the first half of the 1980s, still working in a trading company; see Astley (1995: 377). Nowadays the identity of Yoshikawa Saburō is 'officially' acknowledged by the group. Ōkawa's father died in 2003. In the *Seichi Shikoku Shōshinkan*, which was built in 2000 near Naruto on Shikoku island, there is the *Yoshikawa Saburō Kinendō*

116   Franz Winter

('Yoshikawa Saburō commemoration hall'), where the audio instruments used to record the spiritual messages and the notebooks are exhibited.

6   The books published in the mid-1980s are: (first published 1985) *Nichiren shōnin no reigen*; *Kūkai no reigen*; (first published 1986) *Kirisuto no reigen*; *Amaterasu ō mikami no reigen*; *Sokuratesu no reigen*; *Sakamoto Ryōma no reigen*; *Himiko no reigen*; and (first published 1987) *Kōshi no reigen*.

7   It should be noted that the use of the expression *reigen* is typical of this context. This term was used in Japanese translations of the – mainly – American channelling-writings. The books, just to give an example, of the medium Maurice Barbanell, who was channelling a being named Silver Birch, were translated into Japanese in 1981 as *Shirubā Bachi reigenshū*; the so-called 'White Eagle' revelations of the medium Grace Cooke were published in 1986, using the same terminology (Winter 2012a: 315–24).

8   Recent studies challenge the idea of the importance of the *seishin sekai*, which is mainly connected with the assumption of the importance of the so-called 'religious boom' (*shūkyō būmu*) since the 1970s. This has been mainly claimed by the media on various levels, while academic studies in this context show a more differentiated picture. See Ishii (1995) and Roemer (2012).

9   In *Nichiren shōnin no reigen*, he deals extensively with the 'problematic aspects' (*mondaiten*) of the spiritual message of the being *Silver Birch*, which was channelled by the medium Maurice Barbanell from the 1960s to 1981 (Yoshikawa 1985: 191–203). These texts were translated into Japanese in 1984, one year before the publication of Ōkawa's first *reigen* (under the name of Yoshikawa).

10   It is not unfair to speak of (theoretical) physics as the more important aspect in the twentieth century, while biology had a higher standing at the end of the nineteenth century, especially when considering the reception of the work of Ernst Haeckel (1834–1919). See Daum (1998: 303–7) and Zander (2007: 879–81).

11   'Mysticism' here refers to 'Eastern' mysticism, mainly Daoism and Buddhism in its specific interpretation.

12   The expression 'Scientology' is commonly explained by referring to Latin *scire* ('to know')/*scientia* ('knowledge', 'skill') and Greek *lógos* ('word' or 'account [of]'), which gives it the meaning "study of knowing". On the various interpretations, see Cusack (2009: 394).

13   The *Jakyō hihan manyuaru* was published by a *Hikaku shūkyō kenkyūkai* ('Research group for comparative religion'), which was founded and supported by *Kōfuku no kagaku*, and mainly focused on the major Japanese new religious movements as dangerous and problematic developments. It was part of a major publicity campaign of *Kōfuku no kagaku* in the first half of the 1990s where they tried to distance themselves from all other new religious movements, particularly the more important Japanese ones, like *Sōka Gakkai*. The term *jakyō* ('heresy') was the expression most commonly used in regard to the newer religious movements in the nineteenth century and the first half of the twentieth century until it was replaced by the more neutral *shinshūkyō*, on this, see Winter (2012a: 24–6).

14   The expression *kagaku* itself has a specific history in the eager attempts to introduce 'Western' patterns of thought to Japan at the end of the nineteenth century. It was part of the immense modernisation campaign, led by the important Neo-Confucian scholar, Fukuzawa Yukichi. A detailed analysis of the term *kagaku* and its predecessor *kyūri* is given in Tsukahara (2012).

15   *Ōmoto* was founded 1892 by the Deguchi Nao (1837–1918) and mainly organised by her adopted son, Deguchi Onisaburō (1871–1948). The movement was very popular in the first of the twentieth century but it had to suffer major setbacks which led to a constant decrease in membership. Many ideas and concepts propagated by *Ōmoto* were highly influential at several levels and it should be perceived as one of the most important movements especially regarding major topics which became relevant in the course of the further history of Japanese religions. A couple

On 'science' in 'The Science of Happiness' 117

of major new religious movements can be considered as offsprings founded by former *Ōmoto* members, such as *Seichō no ie* (founded in 1930 by Taniguchi Masaharu) or the *Church of World Messianity* (founded in 1935 by Okada Mokichi).

16 Asano Wasaburō (1874–1937), a teacher at Japan's Naval College and a renowned intellectual, was an important figure, since his involvement in the rather small movement made it known to a wider public. See Staemmler (2009: 275–85).

17 See Ōkawa (2000: 17):

> At this stage, an expansion in membership would not be good ... So in the first few years, I would like to produce people who have enough knowledge of Buddha's Truth, lecturers who can teach others and who will become the core of our missionary effort.

In the parallel Japanese text, the equivalent for 'Buddha's Truth' is *shinri* ('divine truth') without reference to the Buddha. This is a common feature of the early texts which were later adapted to the more Buddhist orientation.

18 This is the terminology used in the descriptions of the first *reigen*-publication, namely *Nichiren shōnin no reigen*. On the use of the term *tankyū* which underwent a specific development in the course of the further history of *Kōfuku no kagaka*, see Ōkawa (2004a: 233–42); on this point, see Winter (2012a: 56–7).

19 This interview was published in the monthly magazine *Gekkan Samsāra* 12, 1991, 46f.

20 This new definition is also a kind of explanation for major changes in the structure of *Kōfuku no kagaku* in 1991. Its seven branches, which existed since 1986, were re-arranged into two units and the publishing house was organised independently from the religious organisation. For details and further literature, see Winter (2012a: 72–3).

21 The question, how many members a new religious movement is counting, is notoriously difficult to answer. At the beginning of the 1990s, *Kōfuku no kagaku* claimed to have more members than *Sōka Gakkai* (generally assumed to be the biggest and with several million followers) and they state a membership of 10 million until today. More realistic estimates in the mid-1990s put these figures at between 100,000, 300,000 or 500,000 active members. These numbers were – within certain limits – affirmed by the results of the movement's attempt to establish a political party in the course of the public elections in 2009 and the following years: In the election for the Lower House (the House of Representatives, *Shūgiin*) in 2009, the 'Happiness Realization Party' (*Kōfuku jitsugen-tō*) gained 459,387 votes, which is 0.65 per cent of those eligible to vote; in the election process for the Upper House (the House of Councillors, *Sangiin*) in the following year, this number declined to 229,024. See Winter (2012a: 90, 98); on the estimates in the 1990s, see Reader (2006: 152) and Wieczorek (2002: 167).

22 The new series includes, e.g. *Nichiren shōnin reijishū* (first published in 1987); *Iesu kirisuto reijishū* (first published in 1988). The latter book has been translated into English as *The Spiritual Guidance of Jesus Christ. Speaking on the Resurrection of Love and the Spirit of the New Age* (Tokyo, 1991). With regard to its content, there is not a lot of difference to the material provided in the Yoshikawa book series.

23 All three books were published in 1987, from June to October.

24 The book *Taiyō no hō* is presented as containing "revelations of the Buddha illuminating the new age" (*shinjidai o terasu shaka no keiji*); *Ōgon no hō* recounts "the intelligence of Buddha revealing the new civilisation" (*shinbunmei o hiraku shaka no eichi*); *Eien no hō* is said to give information on "the glory of Buddha illuminating the new world" (*shinsekai o shimesu shaka no kōmyō*). The subtitles have been the object of constant change in the further editions which reflect the

118   *Franz Winter*

doctrinal development. It is also worth noting that the original versions – though referring to the Buddha on the title pages – technically and primarily used the term *shinri* ('God's truth'); this was replaced by *buppō shinri* ('Buddha's Truth') in the following editions. This is a preliminary to the following 'Buddhisation' of the message, which has become important since the end of the 1980s. A picture of the front page of the first editions is given in Winter (2012a: 60).

25 On this rather unusual expression, obviously inspired by terminology used by the founder of the *GLA* movement, Takahashi Shinji, see Ōkawa (1995: 43–6).

26 A canonical list contains the following mythical personalities: El Cantare had been La Mu, a king on the continent of Mu/Thoth, a king on the continent of Atlantis/Rient Arl Croud, a king in ancient South America/Ophealis, acting in Archaic Greece in a time before Hermes/Hermes in Ancient Greece/Buddha in India/Ōkawa Ryūhō in present-day Japan. See Ōkawa (1994a: 358–9).

27 Ōkawa himself spoke of the utmost importance of this new message with consequences for the older publications; see Ōkawa (1996a: 142): "All of my published books will be re-edited to reflect this order in the future." After the official declaration of the new El Cantare-truth, a revised version of the three fundamental *hō* books appeared, which were called the 'new' (*shin*) series. It is worth noting that the mentioning of the *shaka* in the subtitles of the books was now replaced by explicit references to El Cantare. The book *Shin-Taiyō no hō*, for instance, is said to contain *Eru Kantāre e no michi* ('The way to El Cantare'). The most important difference to the first books – beside corrections of some too harsh prophecies and changes in some doctrinal aspects – is the reference to the system of reincarnations of the El Cantare-being, which is now found in the fundamental book *Taiyō no hō* in a special annex.

28 The main argument launched by the group is that Ōkawa has total insight but is not able (or not willing) to reveal 'everything'.

29 This is probably the most distinctive difference between *Kōfuku no kagaku* and *Aum Shinrikyō*, which were both founded in the mid-1980s. Its founder, Asahara Shōkō, called on his followers to become *shukke* ('those who leave their houses') and to break with common society.

30 Examples of these reincarnation connections are also given in the various Manga productions. The Manga version of the book *Ōgon no hō* is full of tables of different important figures of the spiritual, religious, political and cultural history of the world, which are closely intertwined with the help of this interpretative scheme. An example of these tables is given in Winter (2012a: 202).

31 The concept of 'lost continents' and their specific interpretation has its origin mainly in nineteenth-century Europe, but was soon adopted in the Japanese context. It is an important feature of the *seishin sekai*-movement and of particular importance for a specific tradition of 'ancient history', commonly referred to as *chō-kodaishi* ('ultra-ancient history'), which is focused on the prehistory of Japan and its alleged importance in a time beyond the common knowledge of the history of the world. Therefore, the continent Mu, a concept originally coined by the English author James Churchward (1852–1936) and located in the Pacific Ocean, was of particular interest to Japan. See Winter (2012a: 205–38).

32 The film *Herumesu – Ai wa kaze no gotaku* was released in 1997 and is actually the first *anime* produced by *Kōfuku no kagaku* (the first film, *Nosutoradamusu senritsu no keiji*, released in 1994, was a live action film). It is mainly based on the first volume of the afore-mentioned 'biography' of Hermes and deals with the love story between Hermes and Aphrodite.

33 The original quotation of Edison in the *Scientific American* article reads:

> If our personality survives, then it is strictly logical or scientific to assume that it retains memory, intellect, other faculties and knowledge that we acquire on

this Earth. Therefore, if personality exists after what we call death, it is reasonable to conclude that those who leave the Earth would like to communicate with those they have left here. I am inclined to believe that our personality hereafter will be able to affect matter. If this reasoning be correct, then, if we can evolve an instrument so delicate as to be affected by our personality as it survives in the next life, such an instrument, when made available, ought to record something.

34 Here, once again, the Ancient Astronauts theories on encounters with various flying objects are cited as 'proof' of this assumption.

References

Astley, T. (1995) 'The Transformation of a Recent Japanese New Religion: Okawa Ryuho and Kofuku no kagaku,' *Japanese Journal of Religious Studies*, 22: 343–80.

Astley, T. (2001) 'New Religions,' in J. Heisig (ed.) *Philosophers of Nothingness: An Essay on the Kyoto School*. Honolulu, HI: University of Hawai'i Press, pp. 91–114.

Baffelli, E. (2004) 'Vendere la felicità. Media, marketing e nuove religioni giapponesi. Il caso del Kōfuku no kagaku,' PhD thesis, University Ca' Foscari, Venice, Italy.

Baffelli, E. (2007) 'Mass Media and Religion in Japan: Mediating the Leader's Image,' *Westminster Papers in Communication and Culture*, 4: 83–99.

Barbour, I.G. (1998) *Religion and Science: Historical and Contemporary Issues*, 2nd edn. London: SCM.

Bjorling, J. (1992) *Channeling: A Bibliographic Approach*. London: Garland.

Blavatsky, H.P. (1889) *The Key to Theosophy. Being a Clear Exposition, in the Form of Question and Answer, of the Ethics, Science, and Philosophy for the Study of which The Theosophical Society has been Founded*. London: Theosophical Pub. Co.; New York: W.Q. Judge.

Butler, T. and Butler, L. (2003) *There Is No Death and There Are No Dead. Evidence of Survival and Spirit Communication through Voices and Images from Those on the Other Side*. Reno, NV: AA-EVP Pub.

Capra, F. (1975) *The Tao of Physics: An Exploration of the Parallels Between Modern Physics and Eastern Mysticism*. Berkeley, CA: Shambhala.

Clarke, P.B. (1999) *Bibliography of Japanese New Religions. With Annotations and an Introduction to Japanese New Religions at Home and Abroad (plus an Appendix on Aum Shinrikyō)*. Richmond, VA: Japan Library.

Cooper-Chen, A. (1997) *Mass Communication in Japan* (with the collaboration of Miiko Kodama). Ames, IA: Iowa State University.

Cornille, C. (1998) 'Canon Formation in New Religious Movements: The Case of the Japanese New Religions,' in *Canonization and Decanonization. Papers presented to the International Conference of the Leiden Institute for the Study of Religions (LISOR) held at Leiden 9–10 January 1997*. Leiden: Brill, pp. 279–94.

Cusack, C.M. (2009) 'Celebrity, the Popular Media, and Scientology: Making Familiar the Unfamiliar,' in J.R. Lewis (ed.) *Scientology*. New York: Oxford University Press, pp. 389–409.

Daum, A.W. (1998) *Wissenschaftspopularisierung im 19. Jahrhundert. Bürgerliche Kultur, naturwissenschaftliche Bildung und die deutsche Öffentlichkeit*. Munich: Oldenbourg.

120 *Franz Winter*

Fukusawa, H. (2001) 'Die 'spirituelle Welt' (*seishin sekai*) Japans. Einführung und Auseinandersetzungen,' in H. Gössmann and A. Mrugalla (eds) *11. Deutschsprachiger Japanologentag in Trier 1999*, vol. 1: *Geschichte, Geistesgeschichte – Religionen, Gesellschaft, Politik, Recht, Wirtschaft*. Münster: LIT, pp. 647–60.

Gebhardt, L. (2001) *Japans neue Spiritualität*. Wiesbaden: Harrassowitz.

Hammer, O. (2004) *Claiming Knowledge: Strategies of Epistemology from Theosophy to the New Age*. Leiden: Brill.

Hanegraaff, W.J. (1998) *New Age Religion and Western Culture: Esotericism in the Mirror of Secular Thought*. Leiden: Brill.

Hardacre, H. (1998) 'Asano Wasaburō and Japanese Spiritualism in Early Twentieth Century Japan,' in S.A. Minichiello (ed.) *Japan's Competing Modernities: Issues in Culture and Democracy, 1900–1930*. Honolulu, HI: University of Hawai'i Press, pp. 133–54.

Ishii, K. (1995) 'Seronchōsa kara mita kinnen no Nihonjin no shūkyō ishiki to shūkyō kōdō,' *Shumu jihō*, 96: 72–97.

Kasai, K. (2012) 'Theosophy and Related Movements in Japan,' in I. Prohl and J.K. Nelson (eds) *Handbook of Contemporary Japanese Religions*. Leiden: Brill, pp. 433–57.

Klimo, J. (1988) *Channeling. Der Empfang von Informationen aus paranormalen Quellen*. Freiburg: Bauer.

Kōfuku no kagaku sōgō honbu (2001) *Kōfuku no kagaku risshū 15-shūnen kinenshi*. Tōkyō: Kōfuku no kagaku shūkyō hōjin.

Kōfuku no kagaku kokusai-kyoku ([2006] 2008) *Buppō shinri eikaigo handobukku*, 4th edn. Tōkyō: Kōfuku no kagaku shūkyō hōjin.

MacWilliams, M. (2012) 'Religion and Manga,' in I. Prohl and J.K. Nelson (eds) *Handbook of Contemporary Japanese Religions*. Leiden: Brill, pp. 595–627.

Nishiyama, S. (1988) 'Gendai no shūkyō undō. "Rei-jutsu"-kei shinshūkyō no ryūkō to "futatsu no kindaika",' in O. Eishō and N. Shigeru (eds) *Gendaijin no shūkyō*. Tōkyō: Yūhikaku, pp. 169–210.

Ōkawa, R. (1990) *Introduction to the Institute for Research in Human Happiness*. Tōkyō: Institute for Research in Human Happiness.

Ōkawa, R. (1994a) *Shin-Taiyō no hō. Eru Kantāre e no michi*. Tōkyō: Kōfuku no Kagaku shuppan.

Ōkawa, R. (1994b) *The Challenge of Religion: The Wind of Miracles from Japan*. Tokyo: IRH Press.

Ōkawa, R. (1994c) *Ai wa kaze no gotaku*, vols 1–4. Vol. 1: *Herumesu to Afurodīte*; vol. 2: *Ai no eiyū Herumesu*; vol. 3: *Ōji Erosu no tanjō*; vol. 4: *Shūkyōka toshite no shuppatsu*. Tōkyō: Kōfuku no Kagaku shuppan.

Ōkawa, R. (1995) *Buddha Speaks: Discourses with the Buddha Incarnate*. Tokyo: IRH Press.

Ōkawa, R. (1996a) *The Laws of the Sun: The Spiritual Laws and History Governing Past, Present, and Future*. Shaftesbury: Element.

Ōkawa, R. (1996b) *Manga: Taiyō no hō*, vol. 1. *Taiyō no noboru toki*. Tōkyō: Kōfuku no kagaku shuppan.

Ōkawa, R. (2000) *The Principle of Happiness*. Tokyo: Institute for Research in Human Happiness.

Ōkawa, R. (2002) *Jōshō no hō. Jinsei no shōbu ni katsu seikō hōsoku*. Tōkyō: Kōfuku no kagaku shuppan.

Ōkawa, R. (2003) *Ōgon no hō. Kōgi 1*. Tōkyō: Kōfuku no kagaku shūkyō hōjin.

On 'science' in 'The Science of Happiness' 121

Ōkawa, R. (2004a) *Kōfuku no hō. Ningen o kōfuku ni suru yotsu no genri*. Tōkyō: Kōfuku no kagaku shuppan.

Ōkawa, R. (2004b) *The Laws of Happiness: The Four Principles for a Successful Life*. New York: Lantern Books.

Prohl, I. (2007) 'The Spiritual World: Aspects of New Age in Japan,' in D. Kemp and J.R. Lewis (eds) *Handbook of New Age*. Leiden: Brill, pp. 359–78.

Pye, M. (2002) 'Review of: Inken Prohl, Die 'spirituellen Intellektuellen' und das New Age in Japan,' *Marburg Journal of Religion*, 7(1). Online. Available at: www.uni-marburg.de/fb03/ivk/mjr/pdfs/2002/reviews/rev_pye2_2002.pdf (accessed 13 February 2014).

Reader, I. (2006) 'Japanese New Religious Movements,' in M. Juergensmayer (ed.) *The Oxford Handbook of Global Religions*. Oxford: Oxford University Press, pp. 141–54.

Repp, M. (2011) '"When Science Fiction becomes Science Fact": The Role of Science, Science Fiction, and Technology in Aum Shinrikyō,' in J.R. Lewis and O. Hammer (eds) *Handbook of Religion and Authority of Science*. Leiden: Brill, pp. 185–206.

Roemer, M.K. (2012) 'Japanese Survey Data on Religious Attitudes, Beliefs, and Practices in the Twenty-First Century,' in I. Prohl and J. Nelson (eds) *Handbook of Contemporary Japanese Religions*. Leiden: Brill, pp. 23–58.

Shimazono, S. (2004) *From Salvation to Spirituality: Popular Religious Movements in Modern Japan*. Melbourne: Trans Pacific Press.

Staemmler, B. (2009) *Chinkon kishin: Mediated Spirit Possession in Japanese New Religions*. Tübingen: LIT.

Stalker, N.K. (2008) *Prophet Motive: Deguchi Onisaburō, Oomoto, and the Rise of New Religions in Imperial Japan*. Honolulu, HI: University of Hawai'i Press.

Thomas, J.B. (2012) *Drawing on Tradition: Manga, Anime, and Religion in Contemporary Japan*. Honolulu, HI: University of Hawai'i Press.

Tsukahara, T. (2012) 'Kagaku/kyūri,' in *Working Words. New Approaches to Japanese Studies, Center for Japanese Studies*, University of California, Berkeley. Online. Available at: http://escholarship.org/uc/item/4gd8v00m (accessed 24 September 2012).

Wieczorek, I. (2002) *Neue religiöse Bewegungen in Japan. Eine empirische Studie zum gesellschaftspolitischen Engagement in der japanischen Bevölkerung*. Hamburg: Institut für Asienkunde.

Winter, F. (2008) 'Vom spirituellen Medium zum wiedergeborenen Buddha und darüber hinaus. Zum Wandel im Selbstverständnis des Gründers der japanischen Neureligion Kōfuku no kagaku,' *Zeitschrift für Religionswissenschaft*, 8(1): 59–81.

Winter, F. (2012a) *Hermes und Buddha. Die neureligiöse Bewegung Kōfuku no kagaku in Japan*. Münster: LIT.

Winter, F. (2012b) *Von Geistern, Dämonen und vom Ende der Welt*, in *Religiöse Themen in der Manga-Literatur*. Berlin: EZW.

Winter, F. (2013) 'A Greek God in a Japanese New Religion: On Hermes in Kofuku no kagaku,' *Numen*, 60: 420–46.

Yoshikawa, S. (1985) *Nichiren shōnin no reigen. Ima, issai no shūha o koete*. Tōkyō: Chōbunsha.

Zander, H. (2007) *Anthroposophie in Deutschland. Theosophische Weltanschauung und gesellschaftliche Praxis 1884–1945*, Vol. 1. Göttingen: Vandenhoeck & Ruprecht.

6 The synthesis of religious and medical healing rituals in the Song

Philip S. Cho

Introduction

The Northern Song's (960–1127) attempts to standardize medicine and popular religion were part of an integrated whole, especially under the reign of Emperor Huizong 徽宗 (r. 1100–1125) in the twelfth century. The government attempted to establish networks of local medical schools and Divine Empyrean temples that followed state orthodoxy. The state also sponsored the collation of medical texts into compendia such as the *General Record of Sagely Benefaction* (*Sheng ji zonglu* 聖濟總錄) and religious texts into the Longevity Daoist Canon (*Wan shou dao zang* 萬壽道藏). The medical system was to be staffed by state doctors who passed a newly established medical exam that mirrored the civil service test. Huizong also co-opted many leaders of religious movements by grantingd them titles in the imperial court.

These sweeping attempts to bring religion and medicine under imperial order were reflected in the synthesis of ritual healing techniques and medical theories. Imperial Medical Academy physicians in the twelfth century sought to incorporate exorcism and healing rituals associated with contemporary religious movements and explain them using theories of the circulation of *qi* and the various somatic manifestations of possession. One way they did this was by explaining the expulsion and protection against ghosts, otherwise known as interdiction or *jin* 禁, as a matter of praying about the cause of illness *zhuyou* 祝由 to move and transform *qi* in the body.

Religious movements in the Song

During the Song (960–1279), the center of Chinese civilization shifted south of the Yellow River to the coastal region known as Jiangnan 江南. Rebellion, northern raiders, and epidemics had driven nearly two-thirds of the population to this increasingly prosperous area, making it the cultural, intellectual, and commercial hub of China. After Kaifeng 開封, the Northern Song capital, fell to the Jin 金 at the end of Emperor Huizong's reign, the remnants of the imperial government moved to Jiangnan and established Hangzhou 杭州 as the capital of the Southern Song (1127–1279), making the region the political center of power as well.[1]

Religious and healing rituals in the Song 123

Political and commercial changes during the transition from the Northern to Southern Song resulted in a heterogeneous elite who increasingly depended on local connections and influence to maintain wealth and power. In the Song, to a greater degree than in any previous dynasty, political office was less hereditary than a matter of success in civil service examinations, which tested candidates on the classics (Hymes 1986, 1987). Rapid commercial expansion of the porcelain, silk, tea, and other industries brought goods from the interior along the country's waterways to the delta region, creating new opportunities for wealth. Taking advantage of these opportunities, elite families diversified their career strategies by investing in commercial enterprises, taking up new occupations outside of politics, and sponsoring clan schools for the long years necessary to prepare sons for the civil service examinations. The sons of an elite family were likely to become not only bureaucrats, who might be sent to far-off posts, but also merchants, scholars, and even doctors. Elite families cultivated networks and exerted authority within local society as well as in the imperial government.

The main means to exhibit local social influence was to patronize temples. Families in positions of community leadership and prestige were expected to contribute to the temples of popular religion, where the local markets took place (Brook 1993). These communities were linked to networks, especially along pilgrimage routes to temples dedicated to patron gods, such as those for a particular trade or craft.

From the twelfth century on, a number of local cults and Daoist religious movements, notably the Divine Empyrean (*shen xiao* 神霄), Pure and Sublime (*qing wei* 清微), and Celestial Heart (*tian xin* 天心), spread in Chinese society. Their focus was on therapy and healing, particularly through exorcism. Ritual masters, Daoist priests, and other religious healers employed new rites using charms and talismans to call upon gods, such as the Emperor of the North Star (*Bei di* 北帝), the Five Demon Masters (*Wu tong* 五通), the Black Killer (*Hei sha* 黑殺), and Marshal Wen (*Wen qiong* 溫瓊), to drive out disease ghosts and plague demons.[2]

Imperial patronage brought old and new religious traditions into the service of the empire to form a new ritual, cosmological, and religious order. This new order extended through every corner of the empire through the tentacles of the newly established Divine Empyrean Palace Temple network (Chao 2006). Through this network, Huizong ordered a far-reaching search for religious books, that resulted in two compilations of Daoist texts, the *Da Song Tiangong baozang* 大宋天官寶藏 (*The Great Song's Heavenly Palace Precious Canon*) and the *Wan Shou Dao Zang?* (*The Longevity Daoist Canon*).

The Song government sought to assimilate the local gods into this new order. Cult leaders and local elites petitioned country magistrates to have an official title (*fenghao* 封號) conferred upon cult deities. This often involved transforming figures who had originally been worshipped in one place as demons, such as Marshal Wen, into conventional gods who protected people from disease or even from foreign invaders (Katz 1995: 104–6). Petitions

124 *Philip S. Cho*

would then work their way up the imperial hierarchy through a long and often expensive bureaucratic procedure. This process reflected both how local leaders influenced the government to assimilate local gods into the imperial pantheon and how the government imposed imperial order on local religion.

In 1117, Emperor Huizong declared himself the chief deity of the Divine Empyrean movement and ordered the followers of other Daoist and Buddhist organizations to convert to it. Prominent religious leaders such as Lin Lingsu, Zhang Jixian, and Yuan Miaozong 元妙宗 (1086–1116) were granted funds and titles at the court.[3] Local magistrates, particularly in newly settled frontier regions in the South, often took on the dual roles of bureaucratic official and religious potentate.[4] It is not surprising, then, that one of the major changes in Daoist religious practice in the Song was that healing rituals, such as the 'Ritual of Interrogating and Summoning' (*kaozhao fa* 考召法), took the form of judicial inquisitions (Davis 2001: 96–107).

Song exorcism rituals

Exorcism rituals revealed the reason for disorder and whether a person was demonically or divinely possessed. For example, Edward L. Davis notes that from the tenth century onward, the 'Ritual of Interrogating and Summoning' involved the patient's active participation. Unlike the earlier practice, religious texts that explain these rites are addressed directly to the demons, describing the punishments they will receive, rather than serving as a guide for Daoist priests and ritual masters.[5] In a trance, the patient names the spirit and, through a ritual master's interrogation, explains the reason for possession. In this way both the patient and the healer play a role in identifying the disorder.[6] This is in contrast to other forms of exorcism, such as those in medieval Europe, in which the doctor interprets the possessed person's speech and names the disorder, giving the patient little say in his or her illness.[7]

In many elite readings of folktales, such as those in the *Yijian zhi* 夷堅志 (*Records of Yijian*) (Hong Mai 洪邁 1123–1202), this symbolic dialogue between patients and healers often reveals hidden social tensions within a family. Historians and anthropologists usually interpret possession as a symbolic resistance to social norms. Lacking socially acceptable ways to express unhappiness in certain situations, the possessed, often a woman, displays socially abnormal behavior to articulate a desire for attention, respect, or a change in the current situation. "This is how," Mary Douglas suggests, "the fringes of society express their marginality" (Douglas 1973: 83; Lock 1993: 133–55).

Stories abound about how various popular religious healers cured people from all strata of society using only rituals and not drugs. For example, two accounts tell of how a Gentleman with a Way (*dao shi* 道士), Huangfu Tan 皇甫坦 (d.1178), miraculously cured the Empress Dowager, Wei Xianren 韋顯仁, of an eye disease[8] simply by blowing on her eyes.[9] A Gentleman with a Way, like a Gentleman Technician (*fang shi* 方士), was someone who claimed to follow a discipline, that implied that he had deep spiritual knowledge of the cosmos (Sivin 1995: 26–30).[10] Guo Yi 郭翼 (d. 1364), a Yuan official, recounts this tale to question if drugs could cure all ailments. He notes that even the famous physician Pang Anshi 龐安石 (1042–99),[11] who used medicine to cure countless conditions, nevertheless could not cure himself of deafness (*long* 聾). Guo Yi rhetorically asks, "Could it be that [Pang Anshi] lacked a method (*fang* 方) to cure deafness?" Guo Yi's point is that "there are some ailments that human efforts cannot cure ... doctors have a technique called *zhuyou*. Although it is absurd, I cannot reject the principle of ghosts and spirits (*gui shen zhi li* 鬼神之理)."[12]

Medical reforms in the Song and Yuan

Why was healing central to the new religious movements in the Song? Historians of religion have typically pointed to healing as a way for religious groups to attract believers. These explanations overlook another factor already discussed among historians of medicine. Throughout the eleventh century, particularly from 1040 to 1060, a wave of plagues devastated the Northern Song (Liang Jun 1995: 92f).[13]

In response, the imperial government implemented a number of medical reforms that transformed medical careers over the next three centuries. In 1057, the government established a Bureau for Revising Medical Books (*jiaozheng yishuju* 校正醫書局) to survey and revise ancient medical texts to conform with medical orthodoxy. The Imperial Medical Service (*taiyi* yuan 太醫院) was to disseminate these books and promote education through local schools. However, despite edicts in 1061 and 1083 ordering the creation of local medical schools to identify and train young talent, their implementation was erratic and short-lived at best (Liang Jun 1995: 101; Goldschmidt 2006: 286f).[14]

One problem was that, though medicine had a long literary tradition that scholars revered, physicians were traditionally of low status. Few elite families made their sons doctors.[15] Huizong attempted to raise the status of medicine to equal that of classical studies, the basis of the civil service exam, by creating an analogous path into the imperial bureaucracy. Scholar physicians (*ruyi* 儒醫) were to be like classical scholars (*ru* 儒). Huizong created an imperial medical examination to parallel the civil service exam and created an Imperial Medical Academy to mirror the Imperial University (*taixue* 太學) (Chen 1997: 179–224).

It was not until the Yuan (1279–1368), however, that large numbers of elite began to take up medicine as an occupation. When the Mongols overtook the Song, they slaughtered many families of officials and set quotas on the number of Chinese who could serve within the imperial bureaucracy. In fact, when the Mongol armies attacked a city, they were under orders to seek out and spare the lives of Daoist priests, Buddhist monks, craftsmen, fortune-tellers, and physicians. To avoid persecution, many members of the elite slipped into these occupations (Lee and Ho 1968: 83–9).

126 *Philip S. Cho*

The Mongols greatly prized craftsmen and physicians and enacted favorable policies towards them, such as exemption from both labor service and from some taxes. In the 1260s, Khubilai created different hereditary occupational categories, including military households (*junhu* 軍戶), craft households (*jianghu* 匠戶), and medical households (*yihu* 醫戶) (Rossabi 1994: 448–52).[16]

As had the Song, the Mongols sought to promote medicine by mandating the establishment of local medical schools. What distinguished the plans for these schools from the ones sought in the Song was that the Yuan schools were to be in the Temples to the Three Progenitors (*San huang miao* 三皇廟) (Shinno 2007).[17] As one Yuan scholar put it, "With regard to the so-called medical schools and Temples of the Three Progenitors, [they are] the same."[18] Although research by Reiko Shinno has shown that these temples were built and renovated, there is little evidence that they were used as medical schools.[19]

The somatisation of possession in Song medical literature and examinations

In medical literature leading up to the Song, possession was somatically manifested, especially as sores, swelling, and abscesses, and explained as stagnation in the circulation of *qi*. The canonical text that most informed Song medical understanding on this topic was Chao Yuanfang's 巢元方 *Zhu bingyuan houlun* 諸病源候論 (*Discussions on the Origins and Symptoms of all Diseases*). The first medical text on etiology, Chao's seventh-century work greatly influenced how later authors such as Sun Simo categorized diseases. Chao's explanation of possession and disorders caused by ghosts and demons also influenced healing traditions such as *zhuyou* that crossed religious and medical boundaries.

What is striking about Chao's book is the absence of religious or social references. Unlike the Ritual of Interrogating and Summoning, there is no questioning or answering the patient. Illness is not the result of sin, social tension, or emotional conflict. Ghosts, moreover, are not the agents of moral retribution, but one of many causes of possession disorder.

According to Chao, ghosts and demons are forms of pathogenic *qi* (*xieqi* 邪氣) or poison (*du* 毒) that invade one of the visceral systems of function, usually that of the heart or stomach, and disrupt the circulation of *qi*. This occurs when a person's spiritual vitality (*jingshen* 精神), heavenly and terrestrial souls (*hunpo* 魂魄), or spiritual essence (*jinghun* 精魂) are weak or depleted. During possession, a ghost causes pathogens to stagnate in a person's body. These pathogens remain hidden and undetected for a long time, until they suddenly cause acute symptoms.

Chao discusses afflictions caused by ghosts and demons in Chapter 2 on wind disorders (*fengbing* 風病);[20] Chapter 23 on contracting pathology (*zhong' e* 中惡),[21] sudden recalcitrance (*cuwu* 卒忤, *kewu* 客忤),[22] and corpse

Religious and healing rituals in the Song 127

disorders (*shibing* 屍病);[23] and Chapter 24 on possession disorders (*zhubing* 注病).[24] These are the same main categories of possession that appear later in texts such as the *Sheng ji zonglu*. Chao classifies attack by disease demons or ghosts along with other causes of illness including environmental factors such as wind (*feng* 風), water (*shui* 水), cold (*han* 寒), and coolness (*liang* 涼); polluting factors such as birth (*sheng* 生), death (*si* 死), and corpses (*shi* 屍); and invading factors such as pathogenic *qi* and ghosts (*gui* 鬼). Each category leads to possession if the disease pathogen stagnates.

Wind disorders especially are signaled by abnormal behavior and emotional imbalance. Those afflicted curse or talk nonsensically, act wildly and crazily, suffer from extreme mood swings, or become depressed and silent. The cause is pathogenic *qi*, defined as "illness due to ghostly things" (*fan xieqi guiwu suo wei bing ye* 凡邪氣鬼物所爲病也). This is brought on by dreams or contact (especially sexual) with ghosts and spirits. A pulse that slowly (*chi* 遲) falls (*fu* 伏) indicates latent disease. A pulse that is like a bird's peck (*jizhou* 雞啄) or leaves (*qu* 去) signals the onset of sickness.

Discussions of contracting pathology, sudden recalcitrance, and corpse disorders, like those on wind disorders, emphasize how ghosts disrupt the flow of *qi*. In cases of contracting pathology, the *yin qi* and *yang qi* are split apart and the circulation upward and downward is blocked. When the heavenly and terrestrial souls (*hunpo* 魂魄), vital spirit (*jingshen* 精神), or spiritual essence (*jinghun* 精魂) are weak, the ghost *qi* (*guiqi* 鬼氣) attacks the cardiac or sometimes the abdominal system (*wei* 胃), causing acute, sharp pain. The blood and *qi* rush upward, in the wrong direction for these systems, and the patient vomits or eliminates blood. Environmental factors and time are also significant because:

> [I]f [the circulation of *qi*] is not in harmony with the seasonal and climatic changes of the year, month and time, this is called "three-fold depletion." If three fold depletion occurs, the visceral systems are weakened, the vitality and spirit are depleted and emaciated (*weilei* 微羸), and [malignancy] afflicts the patient. Then the true *qi* is used up (*jiejue* 竭絕) and [the patient] dies.[25]

According to Chao, possession is the occult or hidden stagnation of pathogens within the body. Not limited to affliction by ghosts and demons, it encompasses a wide range of illnesses discussed throughout the entire book from cold damage disorder (*shanghan* 傷寒) to swelling. Chao generally describes possession disorders in Chapter 24 of the *Zhu bingyuan houlun* using wording almost identical to the discription of *zhuyou* in the *Huangdi neijing ling shu* 黃帝內徑靈樞 (*Inner Canon of the Yellow Emperor, Divine Pivot*) of *zhuyou*. He then establishes nine basic categories of possession followed by 32 more detailed discussions.

> "To possess" (*zhu* 注) means "to dwell"(*zhu* 住). This is when pathogenic *qi* resides (*ju* 居) within a person's body. Hence, it is called possession.

128   *Philip S. Cho*

This is caused by the loss of protection from *yin* and *yang*, the depletion of the circulation tracts, and the onset of wind, cold, hot, or moist [factors] as well as fatigue and exhaustion. [Besides this, possession results] if: sweating does not occur with Cold Damage Disorder; sweating occurs but is not "true sweating," (*zhenhan* 真汗) capable of sweating out the illness; the disease spreads from the three *yang* tracts to all the *yin* tracts, enters the *yin* visceral systems, and stagnates (*zhi* 滯) [rather than] being expelled; night-time heartburn (*sushi* 宿食) from improperly matched coldness and hotness of food results in pathogenic *qi* entering and possessing [the body]; both the sudden affliction of [polluted] *qi* from birth or death or the unexpected attack of demonic essences. [These cases] can [all] result in this sort of illness.[26] The transformations and symptoms of [possession] are numerous, [some say] there are 36 types, [others say] 99 types. Regardless, technicians (*fang* 方) have not given them all explicit names.[27]

As an occult disruption of the circulation of blood and *qi*, the symptoms of possession are consistent with disorders in the cardiac and abdominal systems. In all cases, patients experience acute pain in the heart or stomach. The cardiac system is intimately related to sweating, controlling the circulation of blood and *qi*, and is the seat of the will (*zhi* 志). Hence the possessed sweat, swell, or become covered in abscesses indicating a stagnation of *qi*, and behave abnormally. The limbs become heavy and the patient feels weak and depressed. Since the abdominal system is in charge of moving the blood and *qi* downward, possession reverses or disrupts this flow, causing the blood and *qi* to rush to the head. Patients either defecate or eliminate blood.

Song medical exams incorporated this somatic understanding of spirit possession. He Daren 何大任, an official in charge of the Imperial Medical Service in 1212, compiled Song medical exams in his *Taiyiju zhu kecheng wen* 太醫局諸科程文 (*Model Examination Papers for Diverse Courses given by the Imperial Medical Service*). Chapter 7 of this collection deals with preventing spirit possession and exorcism.[28] For example, one question asks:

> According to the 'Qian jin yi fang' 千金翼方 (Expanded Formulas Worth a Thousand), in the *Tai bai xian*'s 太白仙 (Great White Immortal) method of exorcising swelling (*zhong* 腫), the healer utters, 'One, two, three, four, five, six, seven all the myriad swellings and ailments (*ji* 疾) be gone! Quickly, quickly as if commanded by law!' (*ji ji ru lü ling* 急急如律令) The specific causes of swelling disorders are not the same, [but] they all form an obstruction (*yong* 壅) and coagulation (*jie* 結) [of *qi*]. Today, how can reciting these seven characters command away the myriad types of swelling and all ailments? How can so few words (*yan zhi shen gua* 言之甚寡) be so quickly efficacious as this? Please discuss the underlying principle of this method.[29]

Religious and healing rituals in the Song 129

Citing Chao Yuanfang, the source explains that, while other diseases arise when pestilent *qi* spreads within the body, swelling, sores, and abscesses are caused when cold, damp, wind, or other pestilent forms of *qi* stagnate (*yong zhi* 壅滯) within the circulation tracts (*jingluo* 經絡). This causes the blood and *qi* to coagulate (*ning se* 凝澀) and cease to flow freely (*bu tong* 不通). In the *Tai bai xian*'s ritual, the number 7 is important in beseeching the god of the Big Dipper (*Bei dou shen* 北斗神) to stabilize the patient's *qi* circulation. Each of the ritual's seven steps evokes a star in the Big Dipper. Each star is a spirit. Seven ceramic cups are arranged in the shape of the dipper representing the four stars that make up the ladle (*kui* 魁) and the three stars that make up the handle (*gang* 罡). The healer ritually paces, gathering *qi* in seven breaths, purifies himself for seven days, and repeats the incantation seven times.[30]

Synthesizing religious and medical rituals in the Song and Yuan

Huizong's vision of synthesizing religious and medical healing into a unified theoretical and bureaucratic order can be seen in the *Sheng ji zonglu*'s Chapters 195–7 on 'Charm Interdiction' (*fujin men* 符禁門). As the emperor's personal mark on medical knowledge, this encyclopedia was to lay the foundations of drug and ritual therapies. In the chapters on charm interdiction, many of the religious leaders of the Divine Empyrean appear as gods to whom healers must pray. On the other hand, the religious practices of ritual interdiction *jin* to protect against ghosts and spirits are explained using classical theory on the circulation of *qi* and phase energetics. These techniques are used to expel not just ghosts and demons but also the somatic manifestations of possession such as abscesses and sores. To ground this new theoretical synthesis, imperial doctors drew on an ancient tradition of medical rituals called *zhuyou* or praying about the cause of illness. Bureaucratically, the assimilation of religious into medical rituals was reflected in the way the Office of *Zhuyou* in the Song and Yuan Medical Academies came to supplant the Office of Interdiction.[31]

The introduction to the *Sheng ji zonglu*'s chapters on charm interdiction explains at length that *zhuyou*, the ritual expulsion of illness through moving and transforming *qi*, was the underlying principle of interdiction, the protection and expulsion of ghosts and demons. The introduction claims that the use of written charms to protect against and expel ghosts (*shu jin* 書禁) was a remnant of this ancient practice. The *Sheng ji zonglu*'s explanation was a radical reinterpretation of *zhuyou* compared to the practice's original meaning in early medical texts such as *Su wen* 問 (*Basic Questions*), *Tai su* 太素 (*Grand Basis*), *Ling shu* 靈樞 (*Divine Pivot*), *Wushi'er bingfang* 五十二病方 (*Prescriptions for 52 Ailments*), and *Huangdi jia yi jing* 黃帝甲乙經 (*Yellow Emperor's AB Canon*). These early medical texts expressly denied that *zhuyou* cured illnesses caused by ghosts and demons. Incantations and prayers about the cause of illness were originally intended to unblock obstructions in the circulation of *qi* caused by unharmonious lifestyles and emotions. These causes were often so minute and subtle that they were undetectable by the

130   *Philip S. Cho*

senses and only appeared *as if* they were caused by ghosts and spirits, but were actually rooted in improper behavior.

According to the chapters on charm interdiction, *zhuyou* was the subtle (*wei* 微) art of using rituals to manipulate the occult (*qian* 潛) circulation of the spirit (*shen* 神), the body's governing vitalities. The circulation of the blood and *qi* carries the spirit. The cardiac system stores it and the blood houses it. If assiduously nurtured, the vital spirit protects the body against illness, rendering the blood channels harmonious and open to flow.

When a person's mind is clouded (*guhun* 汩昏) by lust and desire (*shiyu* 嗜欲) or exhausted (*gonghao* 攻耗) by worry (*lü* 慮), his vital spirit becomes depleted (*xu* 虛) and illness is able to take hold. The vital spirit, blood, and *qi* conflict. This leads to blockages and stagnation, the outward manifestation of which often is abscesses and sores. During the Zhou dynasty, doctors of external therapy (*yang yi* 瘍醫) treated such ailments with incantations (*zhu* 祝), drugs (*yao* 藥), scraping (*gua* 刮), and caustic (*sha* 殺) therapies but considered the use of a ritual expulsion of disorder, *zhuyou*, the most important.[32]

The *Sheng ji zonglu* shows that by Huizong's time, *zhuyou* included the use of incantations, charms and physical movements that were meant to move the gods. Supplicants had to perform the rituals with a pure heart and focused mind. Only those who could channel their utmost sincerity into the talismans and incantations could heal. As *zhuyou* was fundamentally an art of moving and transforming the occult circulation of *qi*, this implied that *qi* was defined through the ritual process.

Many literati and doctors, however, opposed such a synthetic interpretation of religious and medical ritual. Wang Anshi 王安石 (1021–86), for example, stressed that *zhuyou* was not popular exorcism but a form of external therapy. Wang, like many scholars of later generations, sought to uncover the original meaning of *zhuyou* through the examination of the *Zhou li* 周禮 (*Rites of Zhou*), an ancient classic on proper ceremony and ritual. His understanding of ritual drew on the concept of *li* 禮, as did that of many Song intellectuals such as Zhu Xi 朱熹 (1130–1200). One manifests sage virtue through self-cultivation, emotional discipline, and proper behavior and social relations.

In his *Zhou guan xin yi* 周官新義 (*New Interpretations of the Rites of Zhou*, 1075), Wang Anshi sought to model his reform proposals for the Song on the ideal pattern of the archaic kingdom of Zhou. Arguing that the health of the people reflected the proper ordering of the kingdom, Wang Anshi discussed how the kingdom of Zhou categorized physicians into different offices. Doctors who treated external disorders such as swelling sores, ulcerated sores, and incised wounds used ritual and other treatments to nurture health by manipulating *qi*.

> The *Su wen* says that in ancient times there was a method of moving the *qi* that involved incantations. Doctors have used it for a long time. Incantations are especially suitable for external illnesses. Later

Religious and healing rituals in the Song 131

generations used *qi* to cover or seal (*feng* 封) the afflicted area and move (*xi* 徙) it. This is the method, which has been handed down over the ages, of ritually moving and transforming the *qi* to expel the root cause of illness (*bian qi zhuyou* 變氣祝由).

If applying incantations to the afflicted area does not overcome the illness, then use medicine. If medicine does not overcome the illness, then scrape it. If scraping does not work, then kill it using caustics.

Zheng Xuan 鄭玄 is correct when he says that to kill the swollen area means to use medicine to eat away the rotten flesh. Use the five poisons to attack and kill the affected area. Use the five *qi* to nourish the patient and bring him back to health. Use the five medicines to order the disorder and the five flavors to control it and complete the treatment. Moreover, especially for curing sores, use the five *qi* to nourish the patient.[33]

How did ritual allow one to manipulate *qi*? For Wang Anshi, as with other Song thinkers like Zhu Xi, rituals were a way of cultivating the spirit. In Wang's *Liyue lun* 禮樂論 (*Discussion of Ritual and Music*), he states that: "Ritual and music are what kings of the past used to cultivate men's spirits, rectifying men's *qi* to return to proper emotions."[34] This was so because "cultivating *qi* is about calming the heart; calming the heart is the path to perfecting sincerity; cultivating sincerity is in committing the emotions."[35] Thus, "Sage men seek inwardly (*sheng ren nei qiu* 聖人內求) ... ritual and music are what nurtures men's emotions." They did so knowing that the source of all things in the universe was subtle and profound.[36] The real character of the world remained hidden unless one cultivated oneself through ritual. Only then might one have the foresight that went beyond the mere senses. Thus:

When [the sage] does not listen, he can hear things in advance; when he does not look, things become visible in advance; when he does not speak, the meaning of things comes in advance; and when he does not move, there is movement in advance.

In other words, the sage inwardly apprehends the subtle and hidden profundities of the universe.

Conclusion

During the twelfth and thirteenth centuries, physicians in the Office of *Zhuyou* assimilated a variety of popular religious healing techniques into classical medicine. They did this by making *zhuyou*, the ritual expulsion of the cause of illness by moving and transforming *qi*, the underlying principle of exorcism. Exorcism and spirit possession could thus be explained in terms of classical ideas about the somatic circulation of *qi*. This synthesis was

132 *Philip S. Cho*

part of a broad attempt by the imperial government to standardize medicine and the gods.

The values that people asserted through their interpretations of *zhuyou* were diverse. Scholars and elite physicians stressed the cultivation of sage virtue, disciplined conduct, and study as the ways of mastering the art. Religious healers, on the other hand, emphasized faith in the gods, sincerity, and religious authority.

Acknowledgement

This article was supported by the Fetzer Franklin Trust project on Culture and Cognition, the National University of Singapore-Global Asia Institute project on Mapping the Technological and Cultural Landscape of Scientific Development in Asia (grant AC-2010-1-004), and the John Templeton Foundation project on Religion's Impact on Human Life.

Notes

1 Huizong abdicated to his son Qinzong 欽宗 on January 18, 1126. The Jin captured them both when Kaifeng fell on January 9, 1127.
2 For studies of the Five Demon Masters, see Guo (2003), and von Glahn (2004), Chapter 6. For the Black Killer, see Davis (2001), Chapter 4. On Marshal Wen, see Katz (1995), Skar (2000: 412–63).
3 For example Zhang Jixian 張級先 (1092–1126), the thirteenth Celestial Master, is credited with having written the introduction of the *Most High's* manual. In 1116, Yuan Miaozong 元妙宗 (1086–1116) submitted to Huizong the most comprehensive extant treatise on Celestial Heart talismans for healing. In 1117, Lin Lingsu convinced Huizong that the emperor himself was the incarnation of the Divine Empyrean movement's chief deity, The Grand Emperor of Long Life (*changsheng dadi* 長生大帝) also known as the Imperial Lord of the Supreme Empyrean (*taixiao dijun* 太霄帝君). These leaders all appear in the manuals.
4 Boltz (1993: 256f.), and Davis (2001: 58).
5 Davis (2001: 41–3); *Nü qi gui lü, juan* 6, p. 250; *Jinsuo liu zhu yin* (tenth century), *juan* 29, p. 354.
6 Davis (2001: 3, 98).
7 As Michel de Certeau notes, "[T]he possessed woman's speech is nothing more than the words of her 'other,' … she can only have the discourse of her judge, her doctor, the exorcist or witnesses" (1988: 252).
8 In both accounts, the Empress Dowager suffered from a clouding of the eyes (*yi* 翳), possibly cataracts.
9 *Lishi zhenxian tidao tongjian xubian, juan* 3, pp. 6663–67.
10 In some cases, authors applied the term to Buddhist or Daoist monks.
11 Pang Anshi, also known as Pang Anchang 龐安常, was a famous Song clinician and author of four books on cold damage disorder (*shanghan* 傷寒). See He Shixi (1991), *ce* 2, p. 421;
12 *Xueluzhai biji,* p. 653.
13 The demographic shift to the South during the Song was also accompanied by the rise of rice cultivation as a major staple crop. Several historians have noted that medical theories on the influence of climate and seasonal timing on illness, commonly known as phase energetics or the five circulation cycles and six seasonal *qi* (*wu yun*

Religious and healing rituals in the Song 133

liu qi 五運六氣), gained prominence under the Song (Despeux 2001). However, the connection between epidemics, climate, agriculture, and medical theory during this period has not been explored.

14 See also Shinno (2007) for similar attempts under the Yuan to establish medical schools.

15 *Songhuiyao jigao, chong ru* 崇儒 55, pp. 3.11–13.12.

16 In 1262, medical households were exempted from labor service. *Yuan dian zhang, juan* 32, p. 1b.

17 These were the gods Fu xi 伏羲 (The Subduer of Animals), Shen nong 神農 (The Divine Husbandman), and Huangdi 黃帝 (The Yellow Emperor).

18 *Dao yuan lei gao, juan* 23, p. 30b, "若夫所謂醫學三皇廟者, 蓋其一焉."

19 See Shinno's appendix for an extensive list of records on the building and renovation of temples. *Yuan dian zhang, juan* 32, p. 2b; Ibid., *juan* 9, p. 18b.

20 *Zhu bingyuan houlun, juan* 2, pp. 66–68.

21 Ibid., *juan* 23, pp. 667–9.

22 Ibid., pp. 669–79.

23 Ibid., pp. 680–8.

24 Ibid., *juan* 24, pp. 689–713.

25 Ibid., *juan* 23, pp. 668–69. This section describes climatic and environmental influences. Under a full moon, malignant *qi* cannot harm people; however, under a partial moon the blood is empty and susceptible to attack. See also the *Divine pivot* section on 歲露論. In all these cases, even if the patient is treated, some of the pathogenic *qi* remains and stagnates, resulting in possession.

26 The original sentence is "或乍感生死之氣, 卒犯鬼物之精, 皆能成此病." Both *zha* 乍 and *cu* 卒 (also 猝) mean suddenly, abruptly or unexpectedly.

27 *Zhu bingyuan houlun, juan* 24, pp. 689–92.

28 *Taiyiju zhu kecheng wen, juan* 7, pp. 80–91.

29 Ibid., p. 84b.

30 Ibid., *juan* 7, pp. 84b–86b.

31 From roughly the tenth through thirteenth centuries, the Office of Exorcism was also called the Office of Incantations and Interdiction (*zhou jin ke* 咒禁科), the Office of Charm Interdiction (*fu jin ke* 符禁科), the Office of Written Interdiction (*shu jin ke* 書禁科), and the Office of *Zhuyou* and Interdiction (*zhuyou jin ke* 祝由禁科).

32 *Sheng ji zonglu, juan* 195, p. 1a.

33 *Zhou guan xin yi, juan* 4, p. 42f.

34 *Liyue lun*, p. 713, "禮樂者, 先王所以養人之神, 正人氣而歸正情也."

35 Ibid., "養氣在於甯心, 甯心在於致誠, 養誠在於盡情."

36 Ibid., "天下之物 … 其所由來蓋微矣. 不聽之時, 有先? 焉; 不視之時, 有先明焉; 不動之時, 有先動焉."

References

Boltz, J.M. (1993) 'Not by the Seal of Office Alone: New Weapons in Battles with the Supernatural,' in Patricia B. Ebrey and Peter N. Gregory (eds) *Religion and Society in T'ang and Sung China*. Honolulu, HI: University of Hawai'i Press, pp. 241–306.

Brook, T. (1993) *Praying for Power: Buddhism and the Formation of Gentry Society in Late-Ming China*. Cambridge, MA: Council on East Asian Studies Harvard University.

Chao, Shin-yi (2006) 'Huizong and the Divine Empyrean Palace Temple Network,' in P.B. Ebrey and M. Bickford (eds) *Emperor Huizong and Late Northern Song China:*

134 *Philip S. Cho*

The Politics of Culture and the Culture of Politics. Cambridge, MA: Harvard University Press, pp. 324–360.

Chen, Y. 陳元朋 (1997) "Liang song de shang yi shi ren yu ru yi" 兩宋的尚醫士人與儒醫 [Elites Who Esteemed Medicine and Literati Physicians in the Northern And Southern Song]. Taibei: Guoli Taiwan Daxueshi Congkan 國立臺灣大學文史從刊.

Davis, E.L. (2001) *Society and the Supernatural in Song China*. Honolulu, HI: University of Hawai'i Press.

de Certeau, M. (1988) 'Language Altered: The Sorcerer's Speech,' in *The Writing of History*, trans. T. Conley. New York: Columbia University Press, pp. 244–68.

Despeux, C. (2000) 'Talismans and Diagrams,' in L. Kohn (ed.) *Daoism Handbook*. Boston, MA: Brill, pp. 498–540.

Despeux, C. (2001) 'The System of Five Circulatory Phases and the Six Seasonal Influences (*wuyun liuqi*), a Source of Innovation in Medicine under the Song,' in E. Hsu (ed.) *Innovation in Chinese Medicine*. Cambridge: Cambridge University Press, pp. 121–65.

Douglas, M. (1973) *Natural Symbols: Explorations in Cosmology*. London: Barrie and Jenkins.

Goldschmidt, A. (2006) 'Huizong's Impact on Medicine and on Public Health,' in P.B. Ebrey and M. Bickford (eds) *Emperor Huizong and Late Northern Song China: The Politics of Culture and the Culture of Politics*. Cambridge, MA: Harvard University Press, pp. 275–323.

Guo, Q. (2003) *Exorcism and Money: The Symbolic World of the Five-Fury Spirits in Late Imperial China*. Berkeley, CA: Institute of East Asian Studies University of California, Berkeley.

He Shixi 何時希 (1991) *Zhongguo lidai yijia zhuan lu* 中國歷代醫家傳錄 [Record of Biographies of Chinese Physicians Throughout History], 3 vols. Beijing: Renmin weisheng chubanshe.

Hsu, E. (ed.) (2001) *Innovation in Chinese Medicine*. Cambridge: Cambridge University Press.

Hymes, R. (1986) *Statesmen and Gentlemen: The Elite of Fu-chou, Chiang-hsi, in Northern and Southern Sung*. Cambridge: Cambridge University Press.

Hymes, R. (1987) 'Not quite Gentlemen? Doctors in Sung and Yuan,' *Chinese Science*, 8: 9–76.

Hymes, R. (2002) *Way and Byway. Taoism, Local Religion, and Models of Divinity in Sung and Modern China*. Berkeley, CA: University of California Press.

Katz, P.R. (1995) *Demon Hordes and Burning Boats. The Cult of Marshal Wen in Late Imperial Chekiang*. Albany, NY: State University of New York Press.

Kohn, L. (ed.) (2000) *Daoism Handbook*. Boston, MA: Brill.

Lee, S. and Ho, W.-K. (1968) *Chinese Art under the Mongols: The Yuan Dynasty (1279–1368)*. Cleveland, OH: Cleveland Museum of Art.

Liang Jun 梁峻 (1995) *Zhongguo gudai yizheng shilüe* 中國古代醫政史略 [An Outline History of Ancient Chinese Medical Administration]. Hohot: Neimenggu renmin chubanshe.

Lock, M. (1993) 'Cultivating the Body: Anthropology and Epistemologies of Bodily Practice and Knowledge,' *Annual Review of Anthropology*, 22: 133–55.

Rossabi, M. (1994) 'The Reign of Khubilai Khan,' in H. Franke and D. Twitchett (eds) *The Cambridge History of China*, Vol. 6: *Alien Rregimes and Border States, 907–1316*. Cambridge: Cambridge University Press, pp. 414–89.

Skar, L. (2000) 'Ritual Movements, Deity Cults and the Transformation of Daoism in Song and Yuan Times,' in L. Kohn (ed.) *Daoism Handbook*. Boston, MA: Brill, pp. 413–463.

Shinno, R. (2007) 'Medical Schools and Temples of the Three Progenitors in Yuan China: A Case of Cross-Cultural Interactions,' *Harvard Journal of Asiatic Studies*, 67(1): 89–133.

Sivin, N. (1995) 'Taoism and Science,' in *Medicine, Philosophy, and Religion in Ancient China*. Aldershot: Variorum, Part VII.

Tambiah, S.J. (1968) 'The Magical Power of Words,' *Man*, 3(2): 175–208.

von Glahn, R. (2004) *The Sinister Way*. Berkeley, CA: University of California Press.

Further reading

Chinese sources before 1900

Anon. (1303) *Yuan dian zhang* 元典章 [Compendium of Yuan Statutes]. Revised and expanded 1322. Reprint. Beijing: Zhongguo shudian, 1995.

Anon. (n.d.) *Wushi'er bingfang* 五十二病方 [Prescriptions for 52 Ailments]. Probably second century BC.

Chao Yuanfang 巢元方 (610) *Zhu bingyuan houlun* 諸病源候論 [Discussions on the Origins and Symptoms of All Diseases]. Reprinted in Nanjing and edited by Zhongyiyuan 南京中醫院, *Zhu bingyuan houlun jiaoshi* 諸病原候論校釋 [Annotated Translation of the Discussion on the Origins and Symptoms of All Diseases]. Beijing: Renmin weisheng chubanshe, 1980.

Deng Yougong 鄧有功 (n.d.) *Shangqing gusui lingwen guilu* 上清骨髓靈文鬼律 [Demon Code of the "Spinal Numinous Writ" of Highest Purity], ninth century. In *Dao zang* 道藏 (Daoist Canon), 1444, vol. 6.

Guo Yi 郭翼 (d. 1364) *Xueluzhai biji* 雪履齋筆記 [Notes from the Snow Shoe Room]. In *Siku quanshu* 四庫全書 [Complete Library of the Four Treasuries], 1782, vol. 866.

Hanyu da cidian (1986–90) *Hanyu da cidian* 漢語大詞典 [Great Chinese Dictionary]. 13 vols.

He Daren 何大任 (1212) *Taiyiju zhu kecheng wen* 太醫局科程文 [Model Examination Papers for Diverse Courses given by the Imperial Medical Service]. In *Siku quanshu* 四庫全書 [Complete Library of the Four Treasuries], 1782, vol. 743.

Hong Mai 洪邁 (1123–1202) *Yi jian zhi* 夷堅志 [Records of Yijian]. Reprint. Beijing: Zhonghua shuju, 1981.

Huang-fu Mi 皇甫謐 256/282 *Huangdi jia yi jing* 黃帝甲乙經 [The Yellow Emperor's A-B Canon]. Reprinted as *Zhenjiu jia yi jing* 針灸甲乙經 [A-B Canon of Acupuncture] in *Siku quanshu* 四庫全書 [Complete Library of the Four Treasuries], 1782, vol. 733.

Jinsuo liu zhu yin 金鎖流珠引 [Flowing Pearls of the Golden Lock]. Ninth or tenth century. In *Dao zang* 道藏 (Daoist Canon), 1444, vol. 20.

Li Xueqin 李學勤 (ed.) *Zhou li* 周禮 [Rites of Zhou]. Mid-second century BC. In *Zhou li zhu liu* 周禮注流 [Annotations on the Rites of Zhou]. Beijing: Beijing daxue chubanshe, 1999.

Liu Zongzhou 劉宗周 (1578–1645) (1824) *Liu zi quanshu* 劉子全書 [Complete Works of Liu Zongzhou]. *Reprint*. Taibei: Huawen shuju, 1968.

136 *Philip S. Cho*

Nü qing gui lü 女青鬼律 [Demon Codes of Nü qing]. Fourth century, in *Dao zang* 道藏 (Daoist Canon), 1444, vol. 18.

Shen Fu 申甫 *et al.* (1117) *Sheng ji zonglu* 聖濟總錄 [General Record of Sagely Ben-efaction], Chapters 195–97. 1919 edition. Shanghai Wen rui lou 上海文瑞樓 Ancient Books Collection of the Research Institute of Chinese Medicine (Beijing) 中國中醫研究院.

Wang Anshi 王安石 (1021–86) *Liyue lun* 禮樂論 [Discussion of Ritual and Music]. Reprinted in Ningbo in *Wang Anshi quanji* 王安石全集 [Complete Works of Wang Anshi]. Jilin: Jilin renmin chubanshe, 1996.

Wang Anshi 王安石 (1021–86) (1075) *Zhou guan xin yi* 周官新義 [New Interpretation of the Rites of Zhou]. In *Siku quanshu* 四庫全書 [Complete Library of the Four Treasuries], 1782, vol. 91.

Wang Bing 王冰 (ed.) (762) *Huangdi neijing ling shu* 黃帝內徑靈樞 [Inner Canon of the Yellow Emperor: Divine Pivot]. Reprinted in Guo Aichun 郭藹春, *Huangdi neijing ling shu jiaozhu yuyi* 黃帝內徑靈樞校注語譯 [Inner Canon of the Yellow Emperor, Divine Pivot: Commentary and Translation]. Tianjin: Tianjin kexue jishu chubanshe, 1999.

Xu Song 徐松 (1781–1848) (ed.) (978–1243) *Song huiyao jigao* 宋會要輯稿 [Collected Administrative Documents of the Song]. Reprint. Taibei: Shijie, 1964.

Yang Shangshan 楊上善 (666/683?) *Huangdi neijing tai su* 黃帝內徑太素 [Inner Canon of the Yellow Emperor: Grand Basis]. Late recension of the *Huangdi neijing*. Photo-graphic reprint of the Ninnaji Temple edn 任和寺本, edited by *Dong yang yixue yanjiuhui* 東洋醫學研究會. Osaka: Dongyang yinshua zhiben zhushi huishe, 1981.

Yu Ju 虞集, Dao yuan lei gao 道園類槀 [Categorized Papers from the Garden of the Way], thirteenth century. In *Yuan ren wenji zhenben huikan* 元人文集珍本彙刊 [The Precious Collectanea of Yuan People]. Taibei: Guoli zhongyang tushuguan, 1985.

Zhao Daoyi 趙道一 (fl. 1294–1307) *Lishi zhenxian tidao tongjian xubian* 歷世真仙體道通鑒續編 [Supplement to the Comprehensive History of Embodiment of the Dao by Successive Generations of Immortals]. Thirteenth-century? Reprint. Shanghai: Shanghai guji chubanshe, 1989.

Zhu Su 朱橚 (d. 1425) (1390) *Pu ji fang* 普濟方 [Formulas for Universal Benefaction]. In *Siku quanshu* 四庫全書 [Complete Library of the Four Treasuries], 1782, vol. 755.

Zhu Xi 朱熹 (1130–1200) (1190) *Daxue zhangju* 大學章句 [The Great Learning by Chapter and Phrase]. Reprint from Xu Deming 徐德明 (ed.) *Zhu zi quanshu* 朱子全書 [Complete Collection of Master Zhu]. Shanghai: Shanghai guji chubanshe, 2002, vol. 6.

Zhu Zaiyu 朱載堉 (1536–1611) (1606) *Yuelu quanshu* 樂律全書 [Complete Compen-dium of Music and Pitch]. Reprinted and edited by Wang Yunwu 王雲五, *Guo xue jinben congshu* 國學基本叢書 (Basic Sinological Series), vol. 162. Taibei: Taiwan Shangwu yinshuguan, 1968.

7 Medical treatments described in the ritual texts of Kerala

Interaction between religion and science

S.A.S. Sarma

Introduction

India has a unique history of cultural traditions reaching back unbroken for almost four thousand years. Although these traditions have changed and evolved, many ancient practices and beliefs survive even today. The Vedas, the earliest religious documents of a priestly group, are an ancient Sanskrit liturgical literature, which, apart from the praise and worship of the gods, also include prayers for health, long life, healing and matters related to medicine, geometry and astronomy, that give us an idea of scientific knowledge in those early times.[1] Many texts belonging to later traditions, such as the *Dharmaśāstra* (Texts on Hindu Law) and the *Arthaśāstra* (Hindu treatise on statecraft, economic policy and military strategy), also contain information related to scientific subjects.

The Vedas and their insights into scientific thinking

The *Ṛgveda* and the *Atharvaveda*, two of the earliest religious texts, give contemporaneous information about physicians and medicines. The *Ṛgveda* (1.24.9), for instance, speaks of a hundred physicians attending the king[2] and, again, mention a physician who cures diseases (*Ṛgveda* 10.97.6).[3] The ritual works containing directions for domestic rites and ceremonies (*gṛhyasūtras*) and the digests (*prayogas*) of different Vedic schools also prescribe remedies for different types of disease. For example, the *Āgniveśyagṛhyasūtraprayoga* of Abhirāma, a digest āon the *Āgniveśyagṛhyasūtra*, prescribes *Udakaśānti*, a domestic ritual, for conditions of severe illness.[4] Thus we see that, even though the Vedas are essentially religious documents, they not only contain material related to science but even include direct mentions of treatment; this makes it very clear that the Vedic texts gave importance to health and long life and indicates the insights of the Vedas into the scientific thinking of the time.

Does the Indian system of medicine, or *Āyurveda*, give importance to rituals during treatments?

On the other hand, we may see that the texts of *Āyurveda*, or the Indian system of medicine, which deal exclusively with treatments, give great

138   S.A.S. Sarma

importance to *mantra* and rituals while prescribing treatments. In the fifth chapter of the *Suśrutasaṃhitā*, one of the principal reference books for *Āyurveda*, verses 5.8–13 discuss the use of *mantra*s for snakebite:

> An expert in *mantra*s should also tie the tourniquet with *mantra*s. Tied with rope, etc., this is known to stop poison.
>
> *Mantra*s taught by gods and Brahman-seers are full of [the power of] truth and ascetic energy; if they were not (*anyathā*), they would not quickly destroy poison which is very difficult to overcome.
>
> Poison is instantly destroyed by mantras, which are full of vitality, truth, and the ascetic heat of Brahmans; it is not so when medicinal plants are used.
>
> Learning *mantra*s should only be done by one avoiding women, meat, and wine. He must eat in moderation, be clean, and sleep on a bed strewn with *kuśa* grass.
>
> To gain power over the mantras, he must diligently worship the gods with perfume, wreaths, and gifts, chanting and oblations, and also *bali*.
>
> But since *mantra*s that are incorrectly recited, or are deficient a vowel or syllable, do not grant any power, a series of [herbal] antidotes must be used.[5]

We also see that for the treatment of the insane, the *Carakasaṃhitā* (6.9.91–92), another reference book for *Āyurveda*, suggests usage of rituals:

> By worshipping every day, with concentrated attention, the Lord of all creatures, the Supreme Being possessed of great effulgence, the Master of the Universe, one conquers the fear of (catching) insanity. (91)
>
> By offering worship to the retainers, called '*Pramathas*', of Rudra, who wander over the earth, one becomes freed from diverse kinds of insanity (brought about by the action of superhuman beings). (92)[6]

We therefore see that the texts of *Āyurveda* not only give importance to *mantra* but sometimes even proclaimed *mantra*s to be more efficient than medicines in the treatment of poison. It is also worth noting that the texts of *Āyurveda*, apart from dealing with medicine, had a vision for liberation (*Mokṣa*).

As Dominik Wujastyk observes:

> *Carakasaṃhitā* and its commentators stress the fact that the purpose of medicine is to aid the achievement of the canonical goals of life. Both the *Carakasaṃhitā* and *Cakrapāṇi* refer [in this passage] to the four goals of life, i.e., they include *mokṣa* or liberation. This is a prominent passage in the medical literature, but it is also untypical, in fact unique. Elsewhere, the early medical authors always refer to the *trivarga* or three goals as the norm.[7]

Medical treatment dealt with in the early *tantra* manuals

Before we examine how the ritual texts of Kerala deal with medical treatment, it may be useful to see how the early *tantra* manuals discussed treatment related matters in their manuals. It is said that among the five faces of Sadāśiva: Sadyojāta, Vāmadeva, Aghora, Tatpuruṣa and Īśāna, the basic *tantra* texts came out of the Īśāna face of Sadāśiva, and *tantra*s such as *Bhūtatantra*s and *Gāruḍatantra*s, out of the other four faces. While the *Bhūtatantra* texts are exclusively concerned with curing possession and related illnesses the *Gāruḍatantra* texts are concerned with the classification of snakes, treatment of snakebite, and illnesses caused by other venomous creatures.

The unpublished *Kriyākālaguṇottara* is an early Śaiva tantra text that combines these two groups; at the beginning of this text (I.1–9) Kārtikeya (son of Śiva) asks Śiva to explain to him in detail about the *Gāruḍatantra* and *Bhūtatantra*:

> Bowing his head to the Lord Śrīkaṇṭha together with Umā, to that one who is lovely, adorned with the crescent moon, granting welfare via a flood of nectar, (1)
> Kārttikeya said:
> 'I have heard the various *tantra*s which produce miracles in the world of men and grant both magical powers and liberation, all of them spoken by you, O Supreme Lord. (2)
> I have never heard any *Gāruḍam*, which produces immediate proof of efficacy. Tell it to me, O Best of Gods, your devotee, O Śaṅkara! (3)
> [And tell me] the classification of the types of serpents, the birth of their young without omitting any detail, the traits of all the serpents, and the class of indistinct types. (4)
> [And tell me] the classification of Seizers, Yakṣas, Piśācas, and Śākinīs, and those cruel Child-Seizers, which always mercilessly torment [children]. (5)
> And tell me the traits of those spirits which steal women's embryos, and the classification of vipers and scorpions, O Lord of Gods. (6)
> And the various other evil Rāsabha [unknown insect], worms, and spiders. And [tell me] how many types of fevers are known, both incurable and curable. (7)
> And tell me the classification of doctrine, *yoga*, rites, initiation, *mantras*, as well as the classification of teachers, and the post-initiatory obligations of students (*dīkṣita*) and those with regard to advanced students (*sādhaka*) striving for powers. (8)
> Tell the Gāruḍa and Bhūta Tantras, and what [ever other] doctrine is supreme. O Lord of Gods, [tell me] about all of these. Nowhere else is it perfectly known.' (9)[8]

Khaḍgarāvaṇa, Kālakūṭa, Trottala, Trottalottara, Devatrāsa, Sugrīva are some other early tantric texts that belong to the group of *Bhūta/Gāruḍatantra*s.[9]

140   S.A.S. Sarma

Most of these early ritual manuals which provided healing methods, used only mantras and rituals in cures. But, over time, we see that texts begin to add medicinal cures as an additional support for treatment. Some of the manuals even went so far as to provide two separate parts in their manuals, called, *mantrabhāga* (the part which deal with *mantra*) and *auṣadhabhāga* (the part that deals with medicine).[10] Thus, we see that while the early texts rarely dealt with medical science in their manuals, the later ritual texts began to include medical treatments. The ritual manuals of Kerala contain methods of curing through both rituals (*mantra*) and medicine (*auṣadha*).

An introduction to the ritual texts of Kerala

Kerala has a long tradition of enlightened scholarship and the textual corpus of Kerala consists not only of literature on poetry, drama, religion and philosophy but also of a vast collection of writings on technical subjects such as astronomy, medicine, architecture, music and dance, along with an important collection of ritual texts.

Most of the ritual texts produced in Kerala are confined to temple worship and religious rites. Generally the ritual manuals originating from other parts of India tend to be devoted exclusively to a particular system of worship such as *Śaiva, Vaiṣṇava, Śākta* etc. But the ritual manuals originating from Kerala do not differentiate between the *Śaiva* and *Vaiṣṇava* cults. This synthesis of *Śaiva* and *Vaiṣṇava* ritual systems appears to be a unique feature of the theistic ritual literature of Kerala. Even though there exists a vast ritual literature of Kerala, there is little textual evidence to show that any of these ritual texts were written prior to the tenth century.

There are, however, certain other ritual texts of Kerala, which deal not only with rituals but also with topics other than rituals, such as architecture, iconography, toxicology, treatment of the insane, treatment of different kinds of fevers, treatment of children's diseases and infertility. Among these ritual manuals, the *Īśānagurudevapaddhati* of Īśānagurudeva, *Tantrasārasaṅgraha* of Nārāyaṇa, *Prayogasāra* of Govinda and *Yogaratnāvali* of Śrīkaṇṭha particularly deal extensively with medical treatments.

Kerala ritual texts that deal with medical treatments: a brief introduction

Īśānagurudevapaddhati

The *Īśānagurudevapaddhati*, a twelfth-century AD ritual manual consists of nearly18000 stanzas in various metres and is divided into a total of 119 chapters (*paṭalas*) of varying length. Apart from rituals, the text deals with different methods of treatment for averting the evil effects of poison; malicious plants and diseases; the use of medicines; the properties of medicinal herbs; the science of magic and related subjects.

Chapters 39 and 40 of this text deal predominantly with medical treatments, while some of the other chapters contain a few references to medical treatment. Verse 61 of the 31st chapter mentions a Sadāśiva *mantra* that removes poisons, and verses 76–8 describe a method of using the syllables of a (*Vipati*) mantra in a diagram (*yantra*) to cure poison. The thirty-seventh chapter includes a short section about using another *mantra* (*Sudarśana*) for invoking beneficial possession and destroying poisons. Chapter 39 discusses snake bite treatments in detail. Chapter 40 is primarily devoted to herbal remedies; in this chapter, verses 1–23 discuss the treatment for the bite of a cobra and verses 24–33 deals with the remedies for bites from spotted snakes, predominantly vipers. This chapter includes a visualization of the bitten limb as a viper and the eagle (*Garuḍa*) eating it to remove the poison. It also includes a section on striped snakes (particularly banded krait), remedies for any type of snake poison and methods for different kinds of bites by scorpions, spiders, horses, lizards, leeches, cats, monkeys, mosquitoes, etc. Cures for plant poisons are also discussed in this chapter.

Tantrasārasaṅgraha

The Tantrasārasaṅgraha of Nārāyaṇa (fifteenth or sixteenth century AD) is a digest of cures of poisoning and of treatments related to different kind of illnesses. It also contains descriptions of rituals for the worship of certain deities, some of which are meant to attain magical powers. Since the author of this text, whose first ten chapters deal with *viṣa* or poison, is Nārāyaṇa, the text is also called *Viṣanārāyaṇīya*. This text is widely known among experts who specialize in medical treatment for poisoning. The author appears to have extensively used earlier texts written in other regions of India, especially the texts belonging to the *śikhā* and *yoga tantras*.[11] The *Tantrasārasaṅgraha* is a source book for vernacular texts written in Malayalam dealing with the treatment of poisoning.

The *Tantrasārasaṅgraha* contains 32 chapters, the first ten devoted to toxicology. The next four chapters give an account of seizure by evil spirits (*grahapīḍas*) and mental diseases (*unmāda*) and their treatment. Chapters 15 and 16 describe various bodily ailments and prescribe ritual (*tāntrika*) treatments for them. Chapters 17 and 18 give a description of malicious magic (*kṣudraprayoga*) and its remedies. Chapter 19 is devoted to the entertaining magics (*Vinodaprayogas*) and Chapters 20–32 deal with rituals for fulfillment of a desire (*Kāmika-karmas*).

We notice that Nārāyaṇa's *Tantrasārasaṅgraha* and the above discussed *Īśānagurudevapaddhati* share some common features when dealing with topics related to most of the treatments they discuss.[12]

Prayogasāra

Another unpublished ritual manual, the *Prayogasāra* of Govinda written in the same style as *Tantrasārasaṅgraha*, contains two parts dealing with rituals

142   S.A.S. Sarma

(*tantrabhāga*) and treatments (*auṣadhabhāga*) respectively. While the first part deals with rituals related to different deities, the second part deals with topics such as treatment for poisoning, cures for different types of disease, *yoga*, treatment for infertility, methods of protecting the fetus, methods of protecting a child from evil spirits, treatment for the insane, treatment of different types of poison, treatment of different types of fever, etc.

Yogaratnāvali

The unpublished manual *Yogaratnāvali* of Śrīkaṇṭhaśambhu contains nine chapters and deals with cures for different kinds of poisonous stings, snakes and snake bites, treatment of different types of fever, rituals related to *Tripurā* (a goddess), alchemy, methods for preparing fruit syrups, etc. The first chapter of this text is quite remarkable since it contains a detailed description of poison and its treatment and it also draws materials for its description from the 12 *Gāruḍa-tantra* titles.[13]

Some of the important medical treatment topics discussed in Kerala ritual manuals

Toxicology

Kerala is well-known for its prevalent tradition of toxicology which consists of two types of treatment, *Viṣavaidya* and *Viṣavidyā*. While the *Viṣavaidya* is a purely medical practice which uses medicinal plants and mineral drugs for treatment, the *Viṣavidyā* includes the recitation of *mantra*s and other ritual practices in the process of treating poisoning. It is important to note that these treatments are a living tradition, still being followed in Kerala.

Among the *tantra* manuals of Kerala, the *Īśānagurudevapaddhati* may have been the first manual to treat matters related to 'toxicology.' It describes different types of snake (Chapter 39), types of bite and how they affect a person, the inauspicious places to be bitten by a snake, parts of the body where a snake bite could become serious, the omens emitted by certain signs of the messenger who comes to inform the physician about a snake bite, the use of mantras to destroy the poison, treatment for the bites of different types of snake, treatment of the bites of scorpion, rat, etc.

The *Tantrasārasaṅgraha* and the *Īśānagurudevapaddhati* deal with similar topics concerning toxicology. The second chapter of the *Tantrasārasaṅgraha* provides a detailed description of the different types of snake and snake bites, the signs of the messenger, etc. The third chapter of the *Tantrasārasaṅgraha* gives details of treatment and also of the mantras to be used during treatment. The fourth chapter provides the *śaiva* mantras to be used in the treatment. Chapters 5–8 include the treatment of different types of snake bites. The ninth chapter is devoted to the different types of rat and the remedies for their poisons. The tenth chapter describes the poison of a spider and its

Interaction between religion and science 143

treatments. Thus the first ten chapters of the *Tantrasārasaṅgraha* are entirely devoted to describing different types of treatments for poison and hence are extensively used in Kerala even today in snake bite treatments.[14]

The two unpublished manuals, the *Prayogasāra* (Chapters 37–40) and the *Yogaratnāvali* (Chapter 1) also deal with the treatment of different types of poisoning. *Prayogasāra* deals with many aspects of the treatment of poisoning, including the symptoms of poisoning and detailed descriptions of the *garuḍamantra*, one of the formulae (*mantra*) most often recited during the treatment.

Topics related to toxicology described in these manuals

Qualifications for a practitioner

Most of the Kerala texts lay down that it is necessary for a practitioner to know seven facts to be able to provide treatment for snake bite. They are: (1) origin of *Nāga*s (snakes) and their categories, their nature, places where they live, the reason for their bite, etc. (*nāgodyaḥ*); (2) the star, etc. of the day on which the snake bite took place, time of the bite and its merits and demerits (*tārādi*); (3) nature of the bite and its symptoms (*daṃśaḥ*); (4) where the snake bite took place (*sthānam*); (5) part of the body bitten (*marma*); (6) signs observed from the messenger and omens (*sūcakam*); and (7) the signs shown by the one bitten (*daṣṭaceṣṭā*).

According to the current practices followed by some experts in Kerala, a paste-like concoction, smudged on a betel leaf is administered to the victim in order to identify the species of the snake that has bitten. If the extract tastes spicy, the snake is a cobra; if it is sour, it is a viper; if it is sweet, it signifies krait. The extract is extremely bitter if the snake is non-venomous.

Treatment with the mantras

According to the ritual texts of Kerala that deal with treatments, first of all the patient's life should be protected with the recitation of a formula (mantra) called the *nīlakaṇṭha*.[15] Once the life is protected, the treatment may be started. In cases of snake bite, death is most often due to the fear and a victim, once in the hands of the physician (*Viṣavaidya*), usually relaxes and co-operates willingly with the treatment.

The formula (mantra) most used in the treatment of poisoning is namely, the *vipatipañcākṣaramantra* or *garuḍapañcākṣarī*. By installing the syllables of this formula (mantra) in his fingers, the physician becomes powerful enough to be able to destroy the effect of the poison. Among the different type of treatments prescribed in the *Tantrasārasaṅgraha* (4:39),[16] the following treatment is quite remarkable. The text suggests dipping a piece of cloth in water and asks the practitioner to visualize the water in the cloth as poison and to

144   *S.A.S. Sarma*

squeeze it while reciting the formulae (mantra) and imagine that he is taking the poison out of the body of the victim.

Treatments by massaging

The Kerala texts also prescribe treating poisoning by pressing of particular body parts which are located in different parts of the body. It lists two types of body parts, namely *Amṛtakalā* and *Viṣakalā*. If someone has been bitten by a snake, if the *Amṛtakalā* parts are massaged the poison becomes ineffective and if the *Viṣakalā* parts are massaged the poison is prevented from spreading to other regions.

Treatment with the help of medicine

Most of the Kerala texts, after dealing with the formulas (mantras) for the cure of poisoning, discuss in great detail treatments with medicinal plants and mineral drugs to be provided to the patient. These are administered to the body by different methods such as by drinking (*pāna*), smearing on body parts (*limpana*), by giving medication through the nose (*nasya*), or by inhaling smoke generated from herbs sprinkled on embers (*dhūpana*). The Kerala texts prescribe specific types of medicine to cure poisoning according to the part of the body bitten and depending on the type of snake.

Even though there used to exist several families in Kerala who gave treatment using rituals as well as herbs, at present, it is rather difficult to find practitioners who give treatment using rituals. But there still are families who are known to provide treatment for poisoning in Kerala and these families follow a strictly orthodox life. Most of these families provide treatment as a religious service and do not accept any fee. They have been following their tradition of treatment for several generations.

Recalling the snake to take back its own poison

There is another well-known method for snake bite treatment in Kerala, but it no longer seems to be followed and is generally not accepted by strictly orthodox practitioners. In this method the practitioner, with the help of mantras, recalls the snake to come back to reabsorb its own poison. The vernacular as well as Sanskrit texts related to toxicology written in Kerala describe this method of treatment.

It is significant to note that this type of treatment is referred to in the *Jātaka* tales of Buddha (*Visavantajātaka*, 69th story) where the Bodhisattva was born into a family of toxicologists (*viṣavaidya*). A man from the area was bitten by a snake and brought to the Bodhisattva who offered to cure him by one of two methods: through herbs or by magically drawing the snake back and making it reabsorb its own poison. The 41st chapter of the *Mañjuśrīmūlakalpa*, an early Buddhist ritual manual, contains matters related to snake bite treatment, and also describes the technique of recalling the snake to take back its own poison.[17]

The present situation in Kerala with regard to the treatment of poisoning

Even though we have ample textual material written in Kerala for the cure of poisoning with the help of rituals (*Viṣavidyā*), we notice that this practice is slowly dying out. However treatment using medicinal herbs (*Viṣavaidya*) is still followed and there are a number of experts who are keeping this tradition alive.

Moving from religion to science

We note here that by the middle of the nineteenth century, in all three princely states of Kerala, i.e. Travancore, Cochin and Malabar, the system of education had undergone a great change and most royal family members were college-educated and scientifically inclined. The Cochin royal family included at least three kings who were active practitioners of *Viṣavaidya*, and they took steps towards the preservation of this practice, such as setting up *Viṣavaidya* clinics in every village and a *Viṣavaidya* school in Tripunithura, their capital. Most of the living practitioners of *Viṣavaidyam* in Kerala are directly or indirectly linked to the Cochin royal family tradition. All of these *Viṣavaidya* kings were against practicing with mantra, and they saw to it that none of the printed editions of *Viṣavaidya* texts included the parts dealing with mantra.[18]

This might be the reason for the disappearance of treatment through rituals. The Ullanoor Mana family who specialize in the treatment of poisoning, earlier used both rituals and medicines for the cure of poisoning, but presently they limit themselves only to herbal treatment prescribed in the rituals texts of Kerala.

Health and medicine in the Kerala ritual manuals

The Kerala manuals of rituals also contain descriptions relating to the treatment of different types of disease such as treatment for the insane, treatment of different kinds of fever and particularly treatment and protection of children.

Prayogasāra, the ritual text we discussed earlier, gives a detailed description in its 28th chapter of the causes of infertility and its treatment and indicates that it is not only the females but also the males who could be responsible for infertility. Among the different methods of cure, it also prescribes ways to increase the 'sperm count'.

Infertility is often, in the Hindu system, thought of as the outcome of sins committed in a previous life by oneself or by one's forefathers and, due to this belief, astrologers are also often requested to supply remedies. The close

146 S.A.S. Sarma

relationship between infertility and the worship of serpents is worthy of mention; this worship is commonly prescribed for infertility. Rituals, such as 'offering to serpent' (*Sarpabali*), and the visiting of serpent temples are considered efficacious in removing the curse of the serpent gods.

In the 29th chapter of *Prayogasāra*, methods for protecting the embryo are given and in the 30th chapter, health problems of the newborn and their remedies are discussed. Both *Tantrasārasaṅgraha* and *Prayogasāra* also deal with the different types of fever and their treatments.

The reciting of two liturgical hymns, namely, the *Śivakavaca* and *Indrākṣī* is considered to be a method of curing different types of fever which are listed in the text, and this treatment is used even today, as a cure for fever as well as for protection.

The Kerala ritual texts we have been discussing are also concerned with the treatment of possession and related illnesses. Here too mantras and medicines are applied in the cure.

Some of the temples in Kerala closely connected with treatment

The Achankovil Sastha Temple is famous for the cure of poisonous snake bites. The image of Śāstā in this temple holds sandal-wood paste and holy water (*tīrtha*) in his hands and thus the sandal paste and holy water given as *prasāda* (remaining of the offerings) are considered to have medicinal properties for the curing of snake bite; most days, several patients affected with poisons come here for treatment. The 'Garudan Kavu' or 'abode of the eagle god' in North Kerala is another temple where the effects of poison can be cured.

The Tiruvizha Mahadevar Temple in southern Kerala is well known for curing patients who have ingested food that their enemies have poisoned with the help of spells, and also for the treatment of mental illness. After the morning rituals in the temple, 'milk', extracted from medicinal herbs brought from a nearby location, is offered to the god and then given as medicine and it is believed that the patient will vomit out the poison. There are also temples known for curing spider poisoning, paralysis, infertility, possession, etc.

Conclusion

The above brief discussion on the 'medical treatments described in the Kerala ritual texts' makes us aware that the ritual texts were not only meant for rituals but dealt with topics useful in day-to-day life. Even though the practice of curing by mantra is gradually disappearing today, the other traditional method, *viṣavaidya*, curing with herbal medicines, is still widely practiced. We need to remember that the treatments discussed in these texts were written several centuries ago when science, as known today, had not developed and when there were few diagnostic instruments available. Even so, the discussion of more than 20 types of infertility in the *Prayogasāra* itself shows the wide knowledge of medical science the authors of the ritual texts had. The author of *Prayogasāra*, especially, seems to have had a different approach towards treatment since he describes the 'treatment through medicine' (*auṣadhabhāga*) before discussing the 'treatment through rituals' (*mantrabhāga*), which is not the usual order.

In the present day, even when we have an efficient system of diagnosing the reasons for infertility and are able to obtain treatment with modern medicine, many Hindus trust astrological predictions and carry out associated ritual remedies. Rituals for the cure of serious illness are frequently performed everywhere in India.

Kerala is a state with 100 percent-literacy in India, yet we find many experts in *Viṣavaidya* (curing through medicinal plants and mineral drugs) and a large number of Keralites use these methods for treatment.

When it comes to snake bite treatment, it is sad to note that nearly 50,000 lives are lost each year from this cause. Health workers in rural districts are usually poorly trained in the management of snake bite envenoming. It is necessary to note that most snake bite victims presenting at primary health centers receive inadequate doses of anti-venom whereas it is rather rare to hear of traditional methods of cure failing. In fact, treatment through rituals, or what we may call 'Tantric Medicine', is still competitive with respect to *Āyurveda* as well as biomedicine. At this juncture, it would be valuable if scientific investigation into traditionally used plants or herbs to treat snake bite were carried out, as this would provide the source for individual compounds or standardized extracts which would be of benefit in many places where snake bite is a serious public health hazard.

From this discussion it is obvious that a lively exchange between the knowledge contained in texts with a religious viewpoint and the findings of modern science is not only possible but would greatly contribute to the development of medical science.

The ancient knowledge available in these texts needs to be studied not only for its religious aspects, but also for the technical information available in it. These texts may have been written with purely religious aims, but they were used in practice for the benefits they gave in terms of prosperity and healthy living. Whereas much of the world's ancient medical knowledge has been lost to us, these texts have preserved important facts and discoveries and it would be a grave error if all this knowledge were simply abandoned when an intelligent understanding of it would greatly enrich today's medical science.

Notes

1 See also Wujastyk (1998).
2 See *Ṛgveda* 1.24.9.

148 *S.A.S. Sarma*

3 See "He who hath a store of herbs like a king amid a crowd of men-physicians is the name of that sage who is a friend-saver and a chaser of diseases." *Rgveda* 10.97.6.

4 *Āgniveśyagrhyaprayoga* of Abhirāma, Ms. No. T. 1096 of Trivandrum Manuscript Library, p. 21.

5 See Slouber (2012: 33–4).

6 *Carakasaṃhitā* (2006), Vol. III, p. 847.

7 See Wujastyk (2004: 833).

8 Slouber (2012: 254–5).

9 For a detailed study on the subject, see Slouber (2012).

10 For example, *Prayogasāra* of Govinda.

11 *Śikhāyogāditantrebhyaḥ kriyate sārasaṅgrahaḥ / Tantrasārasaṅgraha*, I:2cd.

12 The relationship between the *Īśānagurudevapaddhati* and the *Tantrasārasaṅgraha* is discussed in an article 'Khadga-Rāvaṇa and His worship in Balinese and Indian Tantric Sources', (in *Wiener Zeitschrift fur die Kunde Sudasiens*, 21, 1977, pp. 143–69) by Teun Goudriaan.

13 See '*Pakṣirāja, Śikhāyoga, Bindusāra, Śikhāmrta, Tottala, Kālakūṭa, Krṣṇāṅga, Tottalottara, Kaṭāha, Nāgatuṇḍa, Sugrīva, Karkaṭāmukha* – Śiva spoke these twelve Poison Tantras.' *Yogaratnāvali* 8–9.

14 Sri. Brahmadattan Nambuthiri of Ullannoor Mana, an expert in the treating of cases of poison in Kerala, confirmed this information for me.

15 *Oṃ namo bhagavate nīlakaṇṭhāya ṭha ṭha / oṃ laṃ ṭhaṃ saṃ devadattasya jīvatattvaṃ bandha bandha saṃ ṭhaṃ vaṃ vaṃ //*

16 *Eṣa viṣabhakṣarudro vastrabandhaṃ viṣaṃ kṣipet* (*Tantrasārasaṅgraha* 4:39cd) *vastrabandhaṃ viṣaṃ kṣipedityasyāyam arthaḥ- paṭena jalam ādāyāmuṃ mantraṃ japan daṣṭagataviṣam etadity anusmrtya yatra kvāpi kṣipet tato viṣagamanam iti* (*Mantravimarśinī ad Tantrasārasaṅgraha* 4:39cd).

17 *Mañjuśrīmūlakalpa*, Chapter 41 (Vol. II, p. 462).

18 I am thankful to Michael J. Slouber who confirmed this information to me (personal e-mail communication).

References

Āgniveśyagrhyasūtraprayoga of Abhirāma (n.d.) Manuscript No. T. 1096 of Trivandrum Manuscript Library, University of Kerala.

Āryamañjuśrīmūlakalpa (1920–25) ed. G. Sastri, 3 vols. Trivandrum: Government Press.

Carakasaṃhitā (2006) 2nd rev. edn, trans. C. Kaviratna and P. Sharma. Delhi: Sri Satguru Publications.

Goudriaan, T. (1977) 'Khadga-Rāvaṇa and His worship in Balinese and Indian Tantric Sources,' *Wiener Zeitschrift für die Kunde Sudasiens*, 21: 143–69.

Īśānagurudevapaddhati of Īśānagurudeva (1990) ed. T. Ganapati Sastri, 4 vols. Delhi: Bharatiya Vidya Prakashan. (Reprinted, with a substantial new introduction dated to 1987 by N. P. Unni, from Trivandrum Sanskrit Series Nos. 69, 72, 77 and 83, Trivandrum 1920, 1921, 1922, 1925.)

Kriyākālaguṇottara (forthcoming) see M.J. Slouber (2012) '*Gāruḍa* Medicine: A History of Snakebite and Religious Healing in South Asia,' PhD dissertation. University of California, Berkeley.

Prayogasāra with commentary by Svarṇagrāma Vāsudeva (n.d.) Forthcoming edition by N.V.P. Unithiri and S.A.S. Sarma.

Rgvedasaṃhitā (1990) 2nd enlarged edn. New Delhi: Nag Publishers.

Tantrasārasaṅgraha of Nārāyaṇa with commentary *Mantravimarśinī* by Svarṇagrāma Vāsudeva (2002) ed. N.V.P. Unithiri. 2 vols. Calicut: University of Calicut (Calicut University Sanskrit Series 15 and 16),

Yogaratnāvalī of Śrīkaṇṭha (n.d.) Manuscript No. T. 993 of IFP, Pondicherry.

Singhal, G.D. (ed.) (2007) *Suśrutasaṃhitā*, 2 vols. Delhi: Chaukhamba Sanskrit Pratishthan.

Slouber, M.J. (2012) '*Gāruḍa* Medicine: A History of Snakebite and Religious Healing in South Asia,' PhD dissertation. University of California, Berkeley.

Wujastyk, D. (1998) 'Science and Vedic Studies,' *Journal of Indian Philosophy*, 26: 335–45.

Wujastyk, D. (2004) 'Medicine and Dharma,' *Journal of Indian Philosophy*, 32: 831–42.

Part II
Asian religions and technology

8 New technology and change in the Hindu tradition

The Internet in historical perspective

Heinz Scheifinger

Introduction

In this chapter I begin with the assertion that there is a link between religion and new technology and that therefore it is no surprise that the Internet is being put to religious uses. I point out that such a link is not confined to the West and the discussion then turns to the uses of new technology in the Hindu tradition prior to the introduction of the Internet, and to the effects that the different innovations have given rise to. I then show that, despite the fact that important aspects of (particularly devotional) Hinduism[1] are present online and that this has the potential to exacerbate those processes that have occurred as a result of the earlier technologies and to bring about new effects, the relationship between Hinduism and the Internet has not been given serious consideration within academia until relatively recently. I then discuss the later academic studies that do approach this subject, and exemplify the links between the findings contained therein and the conclusions regarding the implications of the earlier technologies to Hinduism. In addition, I also point out those effects that are unique to the intersection of Hinduism and the Internet before offering some concluding comments.

Religious beliefs and new technology

Throughout history there has often been a link between religion and new technology and this has manifested itself in two distinct ways. First, there has been an actual association between religious beliefs and new technological developments. Second, new technology has been used in order to transmit religious messages and symbols. The former claim has been made by Erik Davis (2004) who argues that there has always been a link between new technology (especially communications technology) and the spiritual yearnings of the population. Deborah Lupton concurs and is of the opinion that through the use of computers we "are searching for a home for the mind and the heart" (Lupton 1995: 98) which leads to her conclusion that "our fascination with computers is ... more deeply spiritual than utilitarian" (ibid.: 98). Lupton's observation regarding computers further suggests that the link between technology and spirituality may especially be the case with the

154 *Heinz Scheifinger*

Internet and such an assertion has, indeed, been made by others. For example, Ziauddin Sardar comments that the Internet's emergent feature of cyberspace "did not appear ... from nowhere" and that instead "it is the conscious reflection of the deepest desires, aspirations, experiential yearning and spiritual angst of Western man" (Sardar 1995, cited in Dodge and Kitchin 2001: 33). Similarly, Tom Beaudoin also suggests that cyberspace itself can be seen in spiritual terms. He believes that it "highlight[s] human finitude and limitations [and thus] provide[s] ... a metaphor for God at an intersection between spirituality and technology" (Beaudoin 1998: 87, cited in Beckerlegge 2001b: 259), while there are also those who believe that cyberspace can be equated with the theologian Pierre Teilhard de Chardin's (1881–1955) idea of the 'noosphere' – "a sphere of consciousness that encircles the globe" (Jenkins 1998: 2). And while the sociologist Douglas Cowan approaches some of the more extreme claims concerning spiritual beliefs and the Internet with caution, he nevertheless comes to the conclusion that "religion and the Internet have become intimately and integrally linked [and that this] is beyond dispute" (Cowan 2005: 257).

The association between new technology and spirituality is highly likely to have also given rise to the fact that the first use of a new form of communications technology has often inspired the user to transmit a religious message, and this, in turn, further strengthens this association. For example, Anthony Giddens points out that in the mid-nineteenth century the first message transmitted by electric telegraph was 'What hath God wrought!' (Giddens 2002: 10), and in 1906 the first extended radio broadcast of the human voice contained a reading from the Bible (Barnouw, cited in Anonymous n.d.: online). There is also similar evidence regarding the Internet. For example, in 1978, when a discussion group went online for the first time, the opening sentence of the prospectus for the inaugural conference was "We are as gods and might as well get good at it" (Stone 2000: 509). Furthermore, citing Howard Rheingold (1985), Christopher Helland notes that religious discussion groups were extremely popular in the early days of the Internet prior to the introduction in 1991 of the user-friendly World Wide Web (Helland 2004: 22) – long before the release of the first commercial Internet browser *Netscape Navigator* in 1995 when, "for most people, for business, and for society at large, the Internet was born" (Castells 2002: 17).

Religious movements and new technology

Regarding the second link between religion and new technology – the actual utilisation of technology to allow for the transmission of religious symbols and messages – James Beckford (2000) points out that, regarding religious movements, it has not just been the case that they have simply made use of technological innovations. Instead, he argues that such movements have actually "been in the vanguard of new technology ever since radical Protestants exploited new printing techniques in order to make the Bible available in vernacular translations to an increasingly literate public in early-modern Europe" (ibid.: 181). He gives the further example of the predecessors of the Jehovah's Witnesses who "perfected an early version of multi-media technology before World War I with their mobile Photo-Drama of Creation show" (ibid.: 181) and mentions that, in addition to employing other forms of new technology, the Jehovah's Witnesses "were also among the first religious organizations to make use of portable phonographs in door-to-door evangelism" (ibid.: 181–2). Beckford also emphasizes the importance of new communications technology to contemporary Seventh-Day Adventists and Mormons, and points to the widespread use of global communications among "American evangelical, fundamentalist and sectarian movements operating in South America and Africa" (ibid.: 182). Similarly, Malcolm Waters (1995: 132) highlights the extensive use of short-wave radio and satellite television by Christian evangelists while Brenda Brasher (2004: 16) also mentions the use of new technology by religious groups in order to communicate their message.

Religion and the Internet

Given the afore-mentioned suggestion of a link between religious beliefs and new technology, and the fact that religious groups have historically utilized new technology, it is therefore no surprise that religious groups are making extensive use of the Internet and that the World Wide Web is awash with religious websites that are rapidly increasing in number (see e.g. Helland 2004: 23–35; Larsen 2004: 17–20). In addition, there is another simple explanation as to why religion is prevalent on the World Wide Web. As Stephen O'Leary notes, "It would indeed be an anomaly if a cultural force of this magnitude were not to find expression in the newly developing world of computer networks" (2004: 37). Lorne Dawson emphasizes the extent of this religious expression when he comments that "there's practically not a religious group or orientation or viewpoint I can think of in the world that haven't gone online ... even if it's something relatively obscure" (Dawson, cited in Pacienza 2005: online). Jeffrey Hadden and Douglas Cowan (2000b: 7) add to this picture when they point out that "religion is one of the most popular items on the web", while Helland notes the extremely large amount of religious websites and reveals that: "No other category – including activism, lifestyle, choices, relationships, sexuality or law – comes close to this level of representation" (2004: 26). Elena Larsen explains that these resources are being extensively used, commenting that: "for comparison's sake ... more people have gotten religious or spiritual information online than have gambled online, used web auction sites, traded stocks online, placed phone calls on the Internet, done online banking, or used Internet-based dating services" (2004: 17). Meanwhile, the influential 2004 Pew Internet and American Life Project study concluded that "64% of the nation's 128 million Internet users [almost 82 million people] have done things online that relate to religious or spiritual

156 *Heinz Scheifinger*

matters" (Hoover *et al.* 2004: i) and this further emphasizes the extent to which the Internet plays a part in the religious lives of individuals.

Hinduism and new technology

In the West, then, a link between religion and technology is unequivocal and it is clear that the Internet is being used for religious purposes. While the claims made regarding the actual association between technology and religion may be particular to Western societies (for example, Sardar's afore-mentioned claim concerning cyberspace and spirituality refers to the West), the transference of religious symbols and messages through new technology is certainly not confined to that part of the world. As Lawrence Babb points out, "In recent times with the introduction of television and video recording, new communications media have profoundly altered the circulation of symbols, including religious symbols, in South Asian societies" (Babb 1995: 1). The Internet is absent in Babb and Susan Wadley's important edited volume in which this statement appears (Babb and Wadley 1995). This is unsurprising as the book has its roots in a 1989 conference on 'religious change and the media' (Babb 1995: 17) held six years before the introduction of the first commercial Internet browser which allowed the World Wide Web to be navigated with ease. The Internet is, however, a crucial addition to the media forms mentioned by Babb. This is because the Internet appears to have the potential to exacerbate the two key trends that he identifies as being associated with new technology: the standardization/homogenization of aspects of religions[2] (Babb 1995: 16–17) and the disembedding of religious symbols/images (ibid.: 17) – developments that will be looked at in more detail in the context of Hinduism as this chapter unfolds.

In South Asia (as well as in the diaspora), technology has been widely used for the transference of Hindu messages and symbols and, as in the case of other religious traditions, this includes the Internet. In fact, as Helland points out; "The assimilation of computer technology into the religious practices of Hinduism is a social and cultural progression that has long been at work in India" (2010: 148). Thus, it is not surprising that Hinduism is prominent online with a plethora of websites concerned with different aspects of this religious tradition. In addition, as in the examples from the Western context briefly mentioned above, the use of new technology in the Hindu tradition is not confined to the Internet or to those relatively recent developments identified by Babb. Instead, technology has been used to transmit Hindu symbols and messages for more than two-hundred years. The historical uses of new communications technologies in the context of Hinduism, and some of the effects that they have given rise to, will now be briefly detailed. This is important because not only does it provide context to my later consideration of the Internet and Hinduism; it also highlights those processes in Hinduism which have been brought about by the use of new technology which may be further exacerbated by the Internet.

The Internet in historical perspective 157

The printing press and chromolithographic technology

Wadley (1995a) informs us that the first printing press arrived in India in 1556 through the Portuguese who published a Christian book there in the same year and that by the late 1800s there were a number of printing presses in India, many of which were owned by Hindus, and that the "the major output of these presses was initially religious works" (ibid.: 21–2). Stephen Jacobs notes the importance of this and even asserts that "it is possible to argue that the printing press was a key factor in the conceptualization of Hinduism as a religion" (2012: 137). The activities of the guru Arumuga Navalar (1822–79), who "developed modern means to communicate through the printed book" (Hudson 1996: 24), provide a specific example of the early use of the printing press in India to allow for the transmission of a religious message. The significance of this development to Arumuga Navalar's lineage in particular, which meant that his religious viewpoint was able to be disseminated far and wide, and to a much larger audience than was previously the case, is hinted at by the fact that his *murti* (three-dimensional Hindu religious image) in Chidambaram, South India holds a book (Hudson 1996: 43–4). Meanwhile, it is apparent that print technology continues to be integral to the evolution of Hinduism, as Jacobs (2012: 138) highlights the fact that the world-wide availability of published material has been an essential factor in the rise of 'transnational guru organizations' – an important development within contemporary Hinduism (see Warrier 2005).

The introduction of chromolithographic technology also occurred in India prior to 1900 (Wadley 1995a: 22) and this enabled, and resulted in, the mass production of coloured images of Hindu deities. The availability of these images in the form of posters and postcard-sized pictures (especially suitable for small shrines) which have become ubiquitous in India is especially noteworthy in a consideration of the intersection of Hinduism and new technology. This is because of the religious practice of *darshan* which is at the core of *puja*, a ritual that involves making offerings to a deity and which, in itself, is the central act within devotional Hinduism (the most widely practised form of the multi-faceted Hindu tradition). *Darshan* involves receiving a deity's grace through the act of gazing at its image and, at the same time, being seen by the deity (see Eck 1985). Thus, religious images are extremely important in any consideration of Hinduism.

H. Daniel Smith investigates the ramifications of the wide availability of coloured pictures of Hindu gods and goddesses and concludes that this development has brought about omnipraxy in worship in which the person beholding the image is simultaneously a *pujari* or priest and a devotee engaging in what he refers to as a new 'democratic devotionalism' (1995: 37). In other words, without the need for a religious specialist to mediate between themselves and a deity, a devotee performs a highly abbreviated and modified form of a *puja* according to their own idiosyncratic beliefs. Because images of deities allow for the practice of *darshan*, the development of chromolithographic

158 *Heinz Scheifinger*

technology has also had the significant effect of disembedding gods and goddesses from their specific locales and has thus contributed to the spread of devotional cults (ibid.). In a similar vein, Stephen Inglis concludes that the wide availability of Hindu god posters means that "the power concentrated in sacred centers is diffused to wherever devotees live, work, and worship" (1995: 67) and he further observes that some images of deities are becoming standardized and more recognizable to Hindus as a result of their mass reproduction (ibid.: 67). Beckerlegge also notes that by the early twentieth century, mass-production meant that devotional prints in India became "increasingly standardized in style and content" (Beckerlegge 2001a: 79) and that this process of standardization has continued (ibid.: 90).

Film and television

Hindu religious films, which, "from the early days of Indian cinema … were part of India's cinematic culture" (Wadley 1995b: 189) have also engendered a process of disembedding of religious symbols and the consequent elevation of previously local traditions to a pan-Indian level (see e.g. D. Smith 2003: 127). While religious films now make up a far lower percentage of the total films made in India than they have done in the past, ostensibly secular films often include Hindu religious themes (Derné 1995) and this strongly explicates the interpenetration of Hinduism and communications technologies in India. As in the case of film, television is another medium which has allowed for the mass dissemination of images of Hindu gods and goddesses and their subsequent disembedding – most famously in the case of the extremely popular serialisation of the Hindu epic the *Ramayana* on the Indian state broadcasting channel Doodarshan in 1987–88. The screening of this serial (*Ramayan*) directed by Ramanand Sagar which has been watched by over one billion people and been shown in 60 languages in over one hundred countries (Anonymous 2005: online), has been considered in detail by Philip Lutgendorf who reveals that "to most viewers, *Ramayan* was a feast of *darshan*" (Lutgendorf 1995: 230). This is the case because, as Carole Cusack who also considers Sagar's *Ramayan* reveals, similarly to the case of printed images of deities, "the mediation of images of the gods through television in no way compromises or diminishes their power" (2012: 288). The serialization of the *Ramayana* on television was also highly significant in another way; according to Carole Cusack, "it is undeniable that *Ramayan* fuelled expressions of Hindu nationalism" (ibid.: 293; see also Jacobs 2012: 141) – an important trend within contemporary Hinduism that will be revisited towards the end of this chapter.

The Internet

As a result of its ability to widely disseminate images across time and space, the Internet appears to have the potential to give rise to, and to exacerbate, the important processes brought about by new communications technologies mentioned above such as standardization and the disembedding of Hindu images with that development's subsequent effects. However, despite this, as Heidi Campbell points out, "Hinduism online [has] until recently been little studied within religion and Internet studies" (2013: 13). For example, in Charles Ess's comments at the panel session concerning religion and the Internet at the 19th World Congress of the International Association for the History of Religions in March 2005, there were references to Buddhism, Judaism, Christianity and Islam but Hinduism was conspicuous by its absence (see Ess 2005). Concerning academic attention to Hinduism and the Internet then, there had been no discernible improvement since Ritamary Bradley gave a paper entitled 'Religion in Cyberspace: Building on the Past' at the Institute for the History of Religions of Abo Akademi University in 1997, where she spoke of Christianity, Buddhism, Judaism and New Religious Movements but neglected Hinduism entirely (see Bradley 1997).

In addition to this, up until 2007 there was no published academic work which focused upon the relationship between Hinduism and the Internet, despite the fact that there was a huge number of websites featuring content regarding the various diverse strands of Hinduism, some of which enabled the actual practising of religion. This, alone, strongly suggests that the Internet was of significance to a sizable number of Hindus and others interested in Hinduism, and to the religious tradition as a whole. This absence of studies dealing with Hinduism online was even brought into sharp focus by the fact that a number of academic articles and books had already been published which analysed the impact of the Internet upon various other religious traditions. Furthermore, a special edition of the journal *Religion* (2002: Volume 32, Issue 4) and three ground-breaking edited volumes (Hadden and Cowan 2000a; Dawson and Cowan 2004a; Højsgaard and Warburg 2005) which dealt exclusively with religion and the Internet had also been published by this time – none of which contained any articles or chapters dedicated to Hinduism.

On those occasions in which Hinduism did feature in academic work, it was largely incidental to the authors' central concerns. So, for example, William Bainbridge points out that in 1995 the Hindu-derived Meher Baba movement and the *International Society for Krishna Consciousness* (ISKCON) had an online presence and he briefly describes their websites (1997: 150–1) while Eileen Barker noted that ISKCON used the Internet in 1995 as a means of communication (2005: 67). Brasher (2004: 3–5) talks of an online *puja* to the Hindu goddess *Kali* in which icons that can be clicked on represent various processes that are likely to be included in a *puja* carried out in a traditional setting, while Dawson and Cowan mention in passing online *pujas* (2004b: 6), online festivals (ibid.: 3), and that *pujas* can be ordered online to be carried out on a devotee's behalf at a Hindu temple in India (ibid.: 3). In their respective chapters which deal with the mediation of religious experience via the Internet, Dawson (2005: 20) and O'Leary (2005: 41) also refer to websites through which *pujas* can be ordered. Gwilym Beckerlegge mentions that the 1998

160   *Heinz Scheifinger*

Durga Puja festival in Calcutta was broadcast via the Internet which enabled people to worship online, and also mentions that, three years later, the *Kumbh Mela* festival was also broadcast using the medium (Beckerlegge 2001b: 229, 231) – something which was also referred to by Manuel Vásquez and Marie Marquardt (2003: 92). In none of these studies though are the implications of the cited online developments given detailed consideration, unlike in the case of the studies mentioned above which analyse the relationship between Hinduism and older forms of new communications technologies.

Hinduism and the Internet: Implications

Since 2007, starting with those published by Jacobs (2007) and Helland (2007) in an issue of the *Journal of Computer-Mediated Communication* (2007: volume 12, Issue 3) which had, as one of its two special themes, 'Cross-Cultural Perspectives on Religion and Computer-Mediated Communication', a relatively small number of academic articles have considered the intersection of Hinduism and the Internet. In particular, the implications of online *pujas* and the facility to order *pujas* online that were referred to by the authors mentioned above but which were not explored further, have been investigated. In addition, the two key trends that had been identified by Babb in relation to the earlier forms of new technology recur in these studies. Thus, attention has been paid to the Internet's possible role in contributing to standardization in Hinduism and to its capacity to exacerbate the process of the disembedding of Hindu images. In both cases, the subsequent effects that did not arise as a result of the earlier forms of new technology and which, instead, are unique to the Internet, are also revealed and considered. As well as considering these trends below, I will also take into account the role of the Internet in contributing to other developments within contemporary Hinduism – developments which are inextricably linked to the Hindu diaspora.

Standardization/homogenization

Both the afore-mentioned online *pujas* which involve a devotee viewing an image of the deity on a screen and clicking on icons in order to simulate processes involved in a *puja* in the offline context (see Jacobs 2007, 2010: 97–8; Scheifinger 2008: 243–7, 2013) and the ordering online of *pujas* to be carried out on a devotee's behalf at a temple in India – an activity carried out by thousands of Hindus on a regular basis (Helland 2007) – have resulted in the Internet contributing to a process of standardization in actual forms of worship. It is not just the case, then, that the *puja* ritual undergoes a process of standardization in its migration to an online form. Instead, worship carried out in the offline context is also subject to standardizing tendencies.

Standardization is clearly apparent in the case of actually performing worship online because the various online *pujas* that can be undertaken via the World Wide Web display an extremely high degree of homogenization. They are

The Internet in historical perspective   161

almost identical both in terms of their appearance on the screen and in the way that they must be performed. The only significant difference between them is that the image of the actual deity that is the focus of the *puja* is different (Scheifinger 2008: 244–5). The fact that devotees are only able to perform the *puja* in a certain way and there is thus no scope for innovation contrasts with *pujas* in a conventional setting where there is a high degree of heterogeneity. In the latter case, worship is carried out according to the particular wishes of the devotee – a situation which, as noted above, has, according to H.D. Smith (1995), developed as a result of the introduction of chromolithographic technology to India. However, despite this, through allowing for the possibility to partake in the *puja* ritual online, the Internet also contributes to the new omnipraxy in Hindu worship identified by H.D. Smith. This is because this form of the ritual does not require the services of a *pujari* to mediate between the deity and the devotee and, furthermore, it also constitutes a highly abbreviated version of the ritual compared to a traditional orthodox *puja* in which the services of a *pujari* are engaged.

In the case of online *pujas*, that the Internet contributes to standardization in forms of Hindu worship is straightforward. However, the situation is more complex when its role in enabling the ordering of *pujas* to be carried out at a temple in India is considered. Here, although homogenization of worship forms does occur, there is evidence of the Internet also engendering a process of heterogenization. On the one hand, services which allow for *pujas* to be ordered through a website give rise to a degree of homogenization because the devotee is not performing a *puja* according to his or her own method. Instead, the *pujari* at a temple will perform *pujas* requested by different people in the same way. On the other hand, there are a number of websites offering the opportunity to order a *puja*, and those responsible for them have different ideas about the conditions attached to worship and to how it should proceed. This determines aspects of the overall process which means that diversity is also an important component when *pujas* are ordered via the Internet to be carried out at temples in India (Scheifinger 2010a). This combination of homogeneity and heterogeneity fits well with the globalization theorist Arjun Appadurai's claim that both of these processes can occur simultaneously. Appadurai argues that "globalization involves the use of a variety of instruments of homogenization ... that are absorbed into ... cultural economies, only to be repatriated as heterogeneous dialogues" (1990: 99). In the case of *pujas* ordered online, the Internet can have a homogenizing effect yet individual agency ensures that a process of heterogenization also occurs.

Disembedding

On the one hand, because the Internet facilitates the world-wide availability of Hindu images, it has continued the process of the disembedding of local deities and religious figures with the consequent elevation of local cults to a pan-Indian level that was associated with the mass production of colourful religious posters, following the introduction of chromolithographic technology. Moreover, the fact that images can easily be accessed by those living outside of India means that certain expressions of Hinduism, such as those typically put forward by the afore-mentioned transnational guru organizations, can flourish online. Although these organizations sometimes emphasize particularistic aspects of Hinduism, they also commonly seek to transcend a direct association with India in favour of a universalized version of Hinduism that is not tied to India. They can thus derive benefit from the Internet as images of their respective gurus (as well as their messages which derive from traditional Hinduism but which may be claimed to be universal) undergo the, for them, welcome process of disembedding online. In unintended relation to this, Jacobs (2010: 97) intriguingly notes that "the ability to access the guru from anywhere at any time, via a computer terminal, reinforces the notion of the omnipresence of the true guru".[3] Thus, there is a further consequence of being able to see (and hear) Hindu religious figures online (whether they seek to overcome particularity or not) that have become disembedded from India – or, in this context, from temporal space itself.

That the availability of Hindu images on the World Wide Web can further the process of disembedding previously associated with Hindu god posters is only one side of the story. Because webcams have been installed in the inner sanctum of some temples, the Internet allows live images of deities to be broadcast around the world (see e.g. www.siddhivinayak.org; www.shrika shivishwanath.org). At first, it might appear that this development exacerbates the disembedding process. Live images engender a more tangible link than mass-produced posters, and the world-wide availability of deities in this form to those with access to an Internet connection makes it seem like they have become almost completely disembedded from their traditional sacred sites. Significantly, via the Internet, *darshan* can now be received through gazing at actual *murtis* in temples without attendance at the actual site. However, empirical research shows that, despite this, the images, and, by extension, the deities themselves, retain a strong link to their physical locations. This is for a number of reasons. First, although online *darshan* is considered to be valid, it is also a commonly held belief that it is not as beneficial as *darshan* taken from the *murti* at the physical site. Second, there is the belief in Hinduism that actions at the physical site have a direct effect upon the efficacy of *darshan*. If *pujaris* do not serve the deity adequately, then the quality of *darshan* – whether experienced at the temple or online via a webcam – will diminish. Third, devotees who access websites offering live *darshan* do so in order to worship particular favoured deities that are particular due to the very fact that they are inextricably related to their sacred physical site with its attendant mythology. Therefore, the physical site retains importance which means that live images of deities on the World Wide Web have far from become fully disembedded from their original locations (see Scheifinger 2009, 2010b).

This conclusion, though, does not mean that the presence of deities online is devoid of important implications for Hinduism. Because online, deities are

The Internet in historical perspective   163

available to all regardless of ethnicity, socio-cultural status and temporary
state of perceived pollution – all factors which can prohibit individuals from
entering certain temples – live images of deities online can further contribute
to the afore-mentioned universalization of Hinduism (see Scheifinger 2009,
2010b). However, this should not simply be interpreted as leading to a
'potential democratization' (Mallapragada 2010: 119) of Hinduism. Instead,
there is the danger that those who are discouraged from entering some
temples (as in the case of Varanasi's celebrated *Vishwanath* temple which
offers a webcam facility) will be encouraged by high-caste Hindus to avail
themselves of online *darshan* instead, and this would perpetuate the existing
inequality. It is clear that while online deities may well engender a process of
universalization, levels of exclusivity within Hinduism remain (Scheifinger
2010b: 340).

Other effects: the Internet and diasporic Hindus

Other forms of new technology such as satellite television (see Saha 2007:
493–4; Jacobs 2012: 142) and video cassettes (see Little 1995) have been useful
in enabling diasporic Hindus to keep in touch with religious figures and
sacred centres in India. Used as a tool, the Internet has further enabled this
and has also given Hindus living overseas (who may be widely scattered) the
opportunity to keep in touch with each other and with Hindus in India. As
Helland points out, this is achieved in a number of ways: through participation
in online discussion forums; by accessing informative websites; through the
afore-mentioned ordering of *pujas* online; and by using the medium to
engage in philanthropic activities such as awareness raising and fundraising
on a wide scale with very little time-lag (Helland 2007: online). Shandip Saha
(2007: 493–5), Phyllis Herman (2010), Jacobs (2012: 142) and Heinz Scheifinger
(2014) also highlight the importance of the Internet in allowing Hindus in the
diaspora to connect with religious figures and sacred places in India in a way
that was not previously possible. Furthermore, Jacobs (2012: 145) also points
out that, in addition to the afore-mentioned continued importance of printed
matter to transnational guru organizations which are popular among Hindus
living outside of India (as well as among middle-class Hindus in India
and non-ethnic Indians around the world), the Internet – along with other
media forms – is also used in a sophisticated manner by these organizations.
This co-opting of the Internet is noteworthy because of the fact that the
growth of transnational guru organizations is an important development
within contemporary Hinduism.

An increase in Hindu nationalism since the early 1990s – most markedly
among Hindus living in the USA (see Kurien 2007: 144–62) – is another
important development and is one in which the Internet also plays a crucial
role. In her book that considers the growth of an 'American Hinduism',
Prema Kurien (2007: 149–83) details the way in which diasporic Hindus in
the USA are using the Internet extensively to propagate Hindu nationalist

164 *Heinz Scheifinger*

views. Significantly, in her study, Kurien (ibid.: x) comes to the conclusion that supporters of Hindu nationalism:

> [W]ere becoming the central authority and hegemonic voice that Hinduism had so far lacked, defining Hinduism, Indian identity, Indian history and culture, and the obligations of good Hindus. Thus many elements of the Hindutva discourse were manifesting themselves in the self-definitions and explanations of lay Hindu Indian Americans, even those who were uninterested in or opposed to Hindu nationalism.

Moreover, although Kurien recognizes that American Hindu nationalists draw upon "ideologies and networks first articulated in India", she discovers that "ideas and practices of Hinduism that are made or remade in the United States are also exported back to India" (ibid.: 2). The fact that nationalist views are permeating 'mainstream' Hinduism (both in terms of beliefs and in outside perceptions of the tradition) means that the extensive use of the Internet to promote Hindu nationalism heavily implicates the medium in one of the most significant developments within contemporary Hinduism.

Conclusion

In this chapter I have pointed out that there has historically been a link between religion and new technology, and that a relationship between Hinduism and communications technology has existed for more than two hundred years. Studies which have considered this relationship have been discussed, and trends within Hinduism that have occurred as a result of this – namely standardization/homogenization and the disembedding of images – have been considered in the light of the Internet. The Internet was shown to contribute to standardization within Hinduism through the medium offering the possibility to conduct *pujas* online, but, despite this, I asserted that online *pujas* also engender omnipraxy in worship. When the Internet is used as a tool in order to facilitate the ordering of *pujas* to be carried out in India, both homogeneity and heterogeneity occur simultaneously.

Images of deities online can exacerbate the process of disembedding that began with the mass production and the consequent wide availability of Hindu god posters, and the disembeddedness that the Internet gives rise to is a boon for transnational guru organizations. However, I have also shown that, though the Internet, through hosting live images of deities residing in Hindu temples, might at first appear to have the ability to fully wrench these images – and ultimately deities themselves – from their original locations, this is not happening. Importantly, though, I suggested that this development can contribute to the universalization of Hinduism. Finally, I highlighted the Internet's role in two significant developments within contemporary Hinduism – both of which involve Hindus in the diaspora. It is a factor in the rise of transnational guru organizations and it plays a crucial role in the growth of

The Internet in historical perspective   165

Hindu nationalism – an ideology which is an especially important ingredient in the evolution of the Hindu tradition because of the fact that it is permeating mainstream Hinduism. Thus, it is undeniable that, as in the case of the earlier forms of new technology, in a number of ways the Internet is having a considerable impact upon Hinduism.

Notes

1 There is no homogenous religion that can be termed Hinduism. Therefore, 'Hinduism' is a problematic term but it retains utility as it is able to refer to a diverse range of practices, beliefs, and groups which share a 'family resemblance' because they are 'held together by a complicated network of similarities overlapping and criss-crossing' (Eichinger Ferro-Luzzi 1997: 295). At certain points in this chapter I refer to specific aspects of Hinduism when the all-encompassing term would be too general to adequately refer to certain processes that are taking place.
2 Although standardization/homogenization is one of the two key trends identified by Babb, he does also mention that in some instances diversity may occur (Babb 1995: 17).
3 In relation to this, the belief that Hindu gods and goddesses are omnipresent is sometimes mentioned by Hindus in order to justify the validity of online worship (see Jacobs 2007: 11; Karapanagiotis 2010: 180–2).

References

Anonymous (2005) 'Mythological "Disneyland" in India,' *Indo-Asian News Service*, March 14. Available at: www.rn.org/articles/15920/?&section=hinduism (accessed 10 April 2013).

Anonymous (n.d.) 'The First Radio Broadcast,' *Worldwide Faith News*. Available at: http://archive.wfn.org/story.html (accessed 1 April 2013).

Appadurai, A. (1990) 'Disjuncture and Difference in the Global Cultural Economy,' in J. Beynon and D. Dunkerley (eds) (2000) *Globalization: The Reader*. London: The Athlone Press, pp. 92–100.

Babb, L.A. (1995) 'Introduction,' in L.A. Babb and S.S. Wadley (eds) *Media and the Transformation of Religion in South Asia*. Philadelphia, PA: University of Pennsylvania Press, pp. 1–18.

Babb, L.A. and Wadley, S.S. (eds) (1995) *Media and the Transformation of Religion in South Asia*. Philadelphia, PA: University of Pennsylvania Press.

Bainbridge, W.S. (1997) *The Sociology of Religious Movements*. London: Routledge.

Barker, E. (2005) 'Crossing the Boundary: New Challenges to Religious Authority and Control as a Consequence of Access to the Internet,' in M.T. Højsgaard and M. Warburg (eds) *Religion and Cyberspace*. London: Routledge, pp. 67–85.

Beckerlegge, G. (2001a) 'Hindu Sacred Images for the Mass Market,' in G. Beckerlegge (ed.) *From Sacred Text to Internet*. Milton Keynes: The Open University Press, pp. 57–116.

Beckerlegge, G. (2001b) 'Computer-Mediated Religion: Religion on the Internet at the Turn of the Twenty-First Century,' in G. Beckerlegge (ed.) *From Sacred Text to Internet*. Milton Keynes: The Open University Press, pp. 219–64.

Beckford, J.A. (2000) 'Religious Movements and Globalization,' in R. Cohen and S.M. Rai (eds) *Global Social Movements*. London: The Athlone Press, pp. 165–83.

Bradley, R. (1997) 'Religion in Cyberspace: Building on the Past,' paper presented at the Institute for the History of Religions of Abo Akademi University, Turku,

166 *Heinz Scheifinger*

Finland, April 23. Available at: www.geocities.com/Wellesley/1114/cyberspa.html (accessed 9 February 2005).

Brasher, B. (2004) *Give Me That Online Religion*. New Brunswick, NJ: Rutgers University Press.

Campbell, H.A. (2013) 'Introduction: The Rise of the Study of Digital Religion,' in H.A. Campbell (ed.) *Digital Religion: Understanding Religious Practice in New Media Worlds*. London: Routledge, pp. 1–21.

Castells, M. (2002) *The Internet Galaxy: Reflections on the Internet, Business, and Society*. New York: Oxford University Press.

Cowan, D.E. (2005) 'Online U-Topia: Cyberspace and the Mythology of Placelessness,' *Journal for the Scientific Study of Religion*, 44(3): 257–63.

Cusack, C. (2012) 'The Gods on Television: Ramanand Sagar's *Ramayan*, Politics and Popular Piety in Late Twentieth-Century India,' in A. Possamai (ed.) *Handbook of Hyper-Real Religions*. Leiden: Brill, pp. 279–97.

Davis, E. (2004) *TechGnosis: Myth, Magic and Mysticism in the Age of Information*. London: Serpent's Tail.

Dawson, L.L. (2005) 'The Mediation of Religious Experience in Cyberspace,' in M.T. Højsgaard and M. Warburg (eds) *Religion and Cyberspace*. London: Routledge, 15–37.

Dawson, L.L. and Cowan, D.E. (eds) (2004a) *Religion Online: Finding Faith on the Internet*. London: Routledge.

Dawson, L.L. and Cowan, D.E. (eds) (2004b) 'Introduction,' in L.L. Dawson and D.E. Cowan (eds) *Religion Online: Finding Faith on the Internet*. London: Routledge, pp. 1–15.

Derné, S. (1995) 'Market Forces at Work: Religious Themes in Commercial Hindi Films,' in L.A. Babb and S.S. Wadley (eds) *Media and the Transformation of Religion in South Asia*. Philadelphia, PA: University of Pennsylvania Press, pp. 191–216.

Dodge, M. and Kitchin, R. (2001) *Mapping Cyberspace*. London: Routledge.

Eck, D.L. (1985) *Darśan: Seeing the Divine Image in India*. Chambersburg: Anima Books.

Eichinger Ferro-Luzzi, G. (1997) 'The Polythetic-Prototype Approach to Hinduism,' in G.-D. Sontheimer and H. Kulke (eds) *Hinduism Reconsidered*. New Delhi: Manohar, pp. 294–304.

Ess, C. (2005) 'Respondent's comments,' paper presented at the 19th World Congress of the International Association for the History of Religions, Tokyo, 30 March.

Giddens, A. (2002) *Runaway World: How Globalisation Is Reshaping Our Lives*. London: Profile Press.

Hadden, J.K. and Cowan, D.E. (eds) (2000a) *Religion on the Internet: Research Prospects and Promises*. New York: JAI.

Hadden, J.K. and Cowan, D.E. (eds) (2000b) 'The Promised Land or Electronic Chaos? Toward Understanding Religion on the Internet,' in J.K. Hadden and D.E. Cowan (eds) *Religion on the Internet: Research Prospects and Promises*. New York: JAI Press, pp. 3–21.

Helland, C. (2004) 'Popular Religion and the World Wide Web: A Match Made in (Cyber) Heaven,' in L.L. Dawson and D.E. Cowan (eds) *Religion Online: Finding Faith on the Internet*. London: Routledge, pp. 23–35.

Helland, C. (2007) 'Diaspora on the Electronic Frontier: Developing Virtual Connections with Sacred Homelands,' *Journal of Computer-Mediated Communication*, 12(3): article 10. Online. Available at: http://jcmc.indiana.edu/vol12/issue3/helland.html (accessed 10 April 2013).

The Internet in historical perspective   167

Helland, C. (2010) '(Virtually) Been There, (Virtually) Done That: Examining the Online Religious Practices of the Hindu Tradition: Introduction,' *Online: Heidelberg Journal of Religions on the Internet*, 4(1): 148–50.

Herman, P.K. (2010) 'Seeing the Divine Through Windows: Online Darshan and Virtual Religious Experience,' *Online: Heidelberg Journal of Religions on the Internet*, 4(1): 151–78.

Højsgaard, M.T. and Warburg, M. (eds) (2005) *Religion and Cyberspace*. London: Routledge.

Hoover, S.M., Clark, L.S. and Rainie, L. (2004) 'Faith Online – 64% of Wired Americans Have Used the Internet for Spiritual or Religious Purposes.' Available at: www.pewintern et.org/~/media/Files/Reports/2004/PIP_Faith_Online_2004.pdf (accessed 1 April 2013).

Hudson, D. (1996) 'Winning Souls for Shiva: Arumuga Navalar's Transmission of the Saiva Religion,' in R.B. Williams (ed.) *A Sacred Thread: Modern Transmission of Hindu Traditions in India and Abroad*. New York: Columbia University Press, pp. 23–51.

Inglis, S.R. (1995) 'Suitable for Framing: The Work of a Modern Master,' in L.A. Babb and S.S. Wadley (eds) *Media and the Transformation of Religion in South Asia*. Philadelphia, PA: University of Pennsylvania Press, pp. 51–75.

Jacobs, S. (2007) 'Virtually Sacred: the Performance of Asynchronous Cyber-Rituals in Online Spaces,' *Journal of Computer-Mediated Communication*, 12(3): article 17. Online. Available at: http://jcmc.indiana.edu/vol12/issue3/jacobs.html (accessed 10 April 2013).

Jacobs, S. (2010) *Hinduism Today*. London: Continuum.

Jacobs, S. (2012) 'Communicating Hinduism in a Changing Media Context,' *Religion Compass*, 6(2): 136–51.

Jenkins, M. (1998) 'Surfing the Net for Souls,' *Network+*, *The Independent*, April 28, 2–3.

Journal of Computer-Mediated Communication (2007) 12(3). Available at: http://jcmc. indiana.edu/vol12/issue3/ (accessed 10 April 2013).

Karapanagiotis, N. (2010) 'Vaishnava Cyber-*Puja*: Problems of Purity and Novel Ritual Solutions,' *Online: Heidelberg Journal of Religions on the Internet*, 4(1): 179–95.

Kurien, P.A. (2007) *A Place at the Multicultural Table: The Development of an American Hinduism*. New Brunswick, NJ: Rutgers University Press.

Larsen, E. (2004) 'Cyberfaith: How Americans Pursue Religion Online,' in L.L. Dawson and D.E. Cowan (eds) *Religion Online: Finding Faith on the Internet*. London: Routledge, pp. 17–20.

Little, J.T. (1995) 'Video Vacana: Swadhyaya and Sacred Tapes,' in L.A. Babb and S.S. Wadley (eds) *Media and the Transformation of Religion in South Asia*. Philadelphia, PA: University of Pennsylvania Press, pp. 254–83.

Lupton, D. (1995) 'The Embodied Computer User,' in M. Featherstone and R. Burrows (eds) *Cyberspace/Cyberbodies/Cyberpunk: Cultures of Technological Embodiment*. London: Sage, pp. 97–112.

Lutgendorf, P. (1995) 'All in the (Raghu) Family: A Video Epic in Cultural Context,' in L.A. Babb and S.S. Wadley (eds) *Media and the Transformation of Religion in South Asia*. Philadelphia, PA: University of Pennsylvania Press, pp. 217–53.

Mallapragada, M. (2010) 'Desktop Deities: Hindu Temples, Online Cultures and the Politics of Remediation,' *South Asian Popular Culture*, 8(2): 109–21.

O'Leary, S.D. (2004) 'Cyberspace as Sacred Space: Communicating Religion On Computer Networks,' in L.L. Dawson and D.E. Cowan (eds) *Religion Online: Finding Faith on the Internet*. London: Routledge, pp. 37–58.

O'Leary, S.D. (2005) 'Utopian and Dystopian Possibilities of Networked Religion in the New Millennium,' in M.T. Højsgaard and M. Warburg (eds) *Religion and Cyberspace*. London: Routledge, pp. 38–49.

168　*Heinz Scheifinger*

Pacienza, A. (2005) 'New Passover Website Latest Example of Religious Groups Using Web to Teach,' *Canadian Press*, April 14. Available at: http://wwrn.org/articles/16439/ (accessed 1 April 2013).

Rheingold, H. (1985) *Tools for Thought: The People and Ideas Behind the Next Computer Revolution*. Online. Available at: www.rheingold.com/texts/tft/ (accessed 1 April 2013).

Saha, S. (2007) 'Hinduism, Gurus, and Globalization,' in P. Beyer and L. Beaman (eds) *Religion, Globalization, and Culture*. Boston, MA: Brill, pp. 485–502.

Scheifinger, H. (2008) 'Hinduism and Cyberspace,' *Religion*, 38(3): 233–49.

Scheifinger, H. (2009) 'The *Jagannath* Temple and Online *Darshan*,' *Journal of Contemporary Religion*, 24(3): 277–90.

Scheifinger, H. (2010a) 'Internet Threats to Hindu Authority: *Puja* Ordering Websites and the *Kalighat* Temple,' *Asian Journal of Social Science*, 38(4): 636–56.

Scheifinger, H. (2010b) 'On-line Hinduism: World Wide Gods on the Web,' *Australian Religion Studies Review*, 23(3): 325–45.

Scheifinger, H. (2013) 'Hindu Worship Online and Offline,' in H.A. Campbell (ed.) *Digital Religion: Understanding Religious Practice in New Media Worlds*. London: Routledge, pp. 121–7.

Scheifinger, H. (2014) 'Online Connections, Online *Yatras*: the Role of the Internet in the Creation and Maintenance of Links Between *Advaita Vedanta* Gurus in India and Their Devotees in the Diaspora,' in J.G. de Kruijf and A. Kumar Sahoo (eds) *Indian Transnationalism Online: New Perspectives on Diaspora*. Farnham: Ashgate.

Smith, D. (2003) *Hinduism and Modernity*. Oxford: Blackwell.

Smith, H.D. (1995) 'Impact of "God Posters" on Hindus and Their Devotional Traditions,' in L.A. Babb and S.S. Wadley (eds) *Media and the Transformation of Religion in South Asia*. Philadelphia, PA: University of Pennsylvania Press, pp. 24–50.

Stone, A.R. (2000) 'Will the Real Body Please Stand Up? Boundary Stories About Virtual Cultures,' in D. Bell and B.M. Kennedy (eds) *The Cybercultures Reader*. London: Routledge, pp. 504–28.

Vásquez, M.A. and Marquardt, M.F. (2003) *Globalizing the Sacred – Religion Across the Americas*. New Brunswick, NJ: Rutgers University Press.

Wadley, S.S. (1995a) 'Introduction,' in L.A. Babb and S.S. Wadley (eds) *Media and the Transformation of Religion in South Asia*. Philadelphia, PA: University of Pennsylvania Press, pp. 21–3.

Wadley, S.S. (1995b) 'Introduction to Section 3,' in L.A. Babb and S.S. Wadley (eds) *Media and the Transformation of Religion in South Asia*. Philadelphia, PA: University of Pennsylvania Press, pp. 189–90.

Warrier, M. (2005) *Hindu Selves in a Modern World: Guru Faith In the Mata Amritanandamayi Mission*. London: Routledge.

Waters, M. (1995) *Globalization*. London: Routledge.

Websites

shrikashivishwanath.org. Available at: www.shrikashivishwanath.org/en/online/live.aspx (accessed 13 April 2013).

siddhivinayak.org. Available at: www.siddhivinayak.org/virtual_darshan.asp (accessed 13 April 2013).

9 Japanese new religions and social networks

Toward a 2.0 interactive religious discourse?

Danilo Giambra

Introduction

In this chapter I explore how new religions in Japan make use of social networks. In particular, I focus on the cases of two religious organizations, namely Tenrikyō and Seichō no Ie, as relevant examples of this phenomenon.

Japanese new religions are increasingly making use of the Internet for a variety of purposes. They are building new websites, providing a range of religious services via email and instant messaging (IM), uploading audio and video materials that can be streamed or downloaded, as well as digital copies of sacred texts to read online, through the computer or other portable devices that can connect to the Internet. Some religious movements share videos of a selection of public lectures given by their leader or other officially recognized religious authorities, as well as digital recordings of religious festivals and rituals. Less frequently, religious rituals can be practised directly online, in 'cyberspace' or 'virtual reality'. In other words, Japanese new religions are progressively extending the religious space beyond the limits of the physical world, to include the always *in fieri* digital dimension of life. Thus, the Internet can be used to create new digital spaces where the religious organizations present and re-present themselves publicly online,[1] and where users can talk about religion, can receive religious advice, and can in some cases experience and practise religion in a variety of ways.

To some degree, and with different outcomes according to the cultural contexts and the religion involved, religious communication on the Internet is contributing to the re-shaping of religion itself. The Internet as a medium of communication with its own characteristics is in fact not merely reverberating opinions and thoughts found offline, but is actively affecting the way users perceive, interact with, and practise religion. This, in turn, is brought back into the offline dimension of life, in a circular communicative scheme (Figure 9.1).

In this way, it is possible to go beyond the offline vs. online dichotomy, using the two terms to demonstrate that these two dimensions of life are in fact just one interdependent reality in the case of metropolitan Japan. Thus, religion is mediated through the Internet. However, it is brought back into

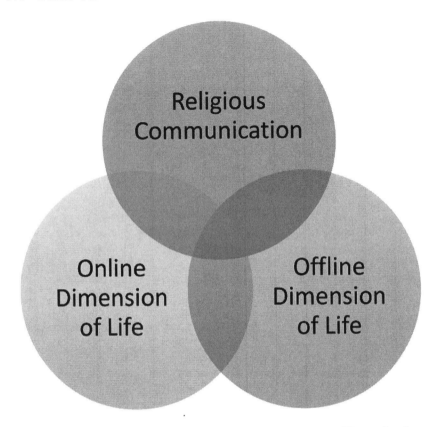

Figure 9.1 Religious communication and the interaction between offline and online

our offline life, sometimes showing new traits acquired during its mediation. Indeed, the Internet is providing new ways of interacting and gathering official and unofficial, authoritative and less authoritative information about religion. Depending on the different types of online platforms, users can exchange thoughts and materials synchronously and/or asynchronously, and can send private messages or post publicly in forums, bulletin boards (BBS), social networks, blogs, and other platforms that allow users to interact with each other.

New Religions can use the Internet both for internal and external communication. As technology has influenced much of the daily communicative practices, the organization of religious and non-religious services and events via email and multiple online social platforms has become common practice, at least at the individual level. This innovative standard of communication has changed not solely the rapidity with which messages are conveyed from the sender to the receiver, but has also added characteristic features. For instance, religious correspondence now includes hypertext and links, attachment of digital files, and sharing of documents, just to cite a few examples. However, there are many groups, including those among the Japanese new religions, who resist the change, rejecting the use of new media to communicate religion. At the organizational level at least, they prefer to use more 'traditional' media such as printed materials (i.e. books, pamphlets, magazines).[2] There are, in fact, numerous problems associated with the adoption of new communication technologies. Highly interactive online environments, such as the social networks, are often perceived as spaces that are difficult to control. Communication can be volatile, and important religious content can be discussed potentially by anyone, regardless of their understanding of the matter and knowledge of the doctrine (Reader 2011: 7–38). Furthermore, the Internet is sometimes perceived as alienating people from the 'real' world, and in doing so, is breaking important social bonds that can only be built through traditional face-to-face interaction within the religious community of people. Issues such as this lead a number of religious organizations in Japan to use mainly printed materials, or else to make use of the Internet and social space in ways that closely resemble traditional approaches to printed advertising.

Religion and the social space

First, let us consider on the meaning of social space, as it is used in this chapter. The term itself has been used historically in many disciplines, mainly to define the category of space from a sociological perspective (Zieleniec 2007). The concept of space is usually considered along with the category of time, and it has been central in many of the academic publications in the field of geography, including human and cultural geographies. These latter approaches create a connection between the physical and the cultural, to cover more complex typologies of space. In this chapter, we concentrate our attention on the social space, a complexly connoted portion of the space. As the term itself reveals, the social space is a combination of two emblematic elements: a socially interactive environment set within a portion of the digital space.[3] In other words, the space we explore is *social*, as human interaction is paramount, and it occurs under the following conditions:

- always through the Internet, as the principal medium of communication;
- in variable modalities (i.e. synchronously and/or asynchronously, through written text and/or voice and/or video streaming, from home or on the move);
- within platforms that enable users to create, modify and join networks of users (i.e. family, friends, colleagues, simple acquaintances), similar to the networks of people we find in the 'offline reality';
- through a multiplicity of technologically advanced devices (i.e. home computers and laptops, mobile phones, smartphones, tablets, advanced mp3 players, Internet TVs, game consoles);

- allowing users to use multimedia features (i.e. sharing links to web pages, adding pictures or videos or music, sharing documents, chatting, calling and video-calling) and to share thoughts and comments (i.e. status updates, diaries, notes, general comments).

Space here indicates the location where interaction occurs, as well as the environment of social interaction. My research is on online religious communication. Hence, the space in question is not necessarily materially defined. However, it is possible to name it, to describe it, and to provide a 'link' to the web page, in the same triangular relationship as the one occurring between a 'real' referred place (the actual platform where the interaction occurs), its geographical coordinates (the IP address of the web page, numeric), and its geographical name (the www address of the web page, alphanumeric) (Figure 9.2).

Users, who are people and friends and relatives in the so-called 'offline reality', get in touch and exchange opinions or share information in social space, which becomes a lived and intertwined extension of the places we go, and of who we are.[4] Expanding the number of acquaintances through social interaction is certainly one of the principal goals of accessing all sorts of social networks, however, it is not always the ultimate intention for many. Sociologists have long described the dynamics of creating and maintaining

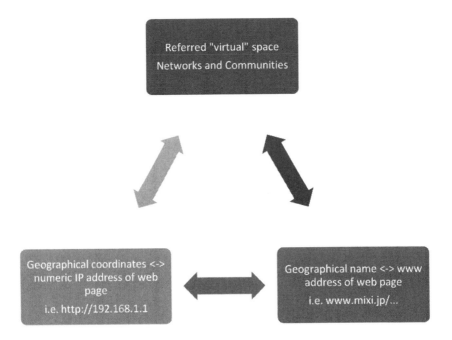

Figure 9.2 Digital space semiotic triangulation

Japanese new religions and social networks 173

friendships, which are replicated and expanded in social space, but with characteristics directly linked to the medium. In order to understand religious communication in social space,[5] it is helpful to think about the networks we create around us, and the way these are recreated online in the social networks.

Thus, in this chapter, I will provide some examples of how Japanese new religions are building their presence on the Japanese Internet, and more specifically, within the Japanese social space. For this, we will focus on two properly defined social networks, namely, Mixi and Facebook. I will also introduce the case of Twitter, a multilingual micro-blogging platform, as this cannot be disregarded when taking into account religion and the Internet in Japan.

Self-centred networks around religion: creating and maintaining (religious) networks of friends and acquaintances online

Within social space, social networks play an important role in connecting users to one another, facilitating the process of knowing other users, but more importantly creating a space where it is possible to manage the existent networks of friends and acquaintances, while making those connections visible to others (Boyd and Ellison 2008). This is not to say that the idea of social networks is anything new, as it existed long before the Internet developed. People just keep connecting with others. Starting with the family relationships, people make friends, work with other people, and join various communities. People learn how to manage their social networks in everyday life, meeting people in person, sending them a letter, calling them on the phone, or praying with them at church. Through the people we know, we get to know new people. This behaviour has been studied under a variety of perspectives. Scholars of sociolinguistics, such as Lesley Milroy, for example, have written extensively about language variation and social networks (Milroy 1987). More recently, advances in social network analysis has facilitated the study of the connections between a node (a person, or a group) and its ties (the relationships) within the Social Network Theory frame (Prell 2012). This approach has been adopted by some scholars in the social sciences and partly by scholars whose research focuses on communication and the Internet. For instance, Susan Herring, who has published extensively on computer-mediated communication (CMC), proposed integrating social network analysis into a more complex methodological set for researching communication on the Internet (Herring 2009).

In addition to CMC studies, many scholars of religion have decided to devote some time and quite a number of papers and publications to the study of religion and the Internet. In 2000, Christopher Helland introduced the distinction between 'religion online' and 'online religion' to describe two main attitudes toward the new media, where 'online religion' is used to describe those groups which really make use of the Internet and provide services and

174 *Danilo Giambra*

experiences online (Helland 2000). As communities of users were perceived as one of the most important social institution found on the Internet, several studies on 'virtual', and then online communities appeared. In particular, Heidi Campbell has devoted a whole book to this matter, and introduced an important discussion on the Internet as a social network for communicating religion (Campbell 2005: 25–51).

In Japan, 79.5 per cent of the population has access to the Internet via a variety of devices (Anon n.d.b) Many users register on one or more social networks, according to the popularity of these social platforms through time. Mixi, for instance, was for a long time one of the most popular social networks in Japan. However, lately it has begun losing popularity and many users have migrated elsewhere. Facebook, on the other hand, was unsuccessful for a while in Japan (Tabuchi 2011), but it gained about 10 million users alone in 2012, reaching 13.5 per cent penetration rate (Anon n.d.b). Along with Mixi and Facebook, Twitter continues to attract a great number of users, especially because of its ease of use and minimal hardware requirements. Within the complex and various digital space of Japan, religion remains one important reason for aggregation. Individuals use social networks to post comments on their religious life, their beliefs, and their fears. Communities are created to facilitate discussion and the sharing of experiences and materials. Religious organizations create group profiles, and sometimes the leader finds in the social networks a powerful tool to communicate directly with the followers. However, the use of social networks for religious communication requires us to think about the main levels of communication we find in these digital social environments.

Levels of communication within social networks

The individual level

This is the most common level of communication for many users. As social networks are self-centred networks (Facebook is a clear example) (Papacharissi 2011), users create personal profiles. Using the terminology of Network Analysis, users become the nodes of their network. They will develop a series of ties, which are connected to them, the node. Those are their relationships with other users. At the individual level, the user coincides with the person. Therefore, the contents published on the social networks by individuals will generally be perceived as personal thoughts. Nonetheless, holding a position of authority could change everything.

In the case of religious communication, the leader of a religious organization who starts a personal page on social networks will post as an individual, but because of his or her role within the community, his or her thoughts might be perceived differently – more authoritatively – by other users of the network. In most cases, the leader's thoughts might be interpreted as representative or core ideas of that religion. The head of a single church that is part of a larger religious organization will be in a similar position. He or she will be both a person and a representative. So, how do we distinguish official religious communication from what we could call a bunch of personal thoughts about religion? The line between official and personal blurs when it comes to religion and the Internet.

The group level

Groups assemble a plurality of users. Usually, groups are built around a theme, such as a shared interest, a common geographical location, or a religious preference. Groups can be open or closed, according to the characteristics present on each social platform. Within the group, users can speak for themselves, as their publications will remain linked to the single, as in the individual level. The creators and moderators of the group might be granted a greater level of authority on the matters relevant to the group's theme, creating verticality in the communication. In the case of religious groups, the creators and moderators might be just members of the religious organizations. Their understanding of the doctrine might not be complete, but they might be trusted because of their status within the group. This latter typology of religious groups is very common, and representatives of the religious organizations do not always agree with the contents presented. Sometimes, these groups can even be representative of a fringe movement within the movement. Finally, groups can be created to criticize a specific religious organization, or religion in general.

The organizational level

The organizational level is probably the most official way for a religious organization to enter the world of social networks. The religious organization will create a page or similar space, which is immediately recognizable by users in the network as official. This page is expected to be at least partly public, as it usually aims primarily at advertising the presence of the religious organization on social networks. The creators of the page will choose the modalities of interaction among users. A rather vertical communication frame is to be expected, though this is not always the case. The official contents do not necessarily reflect the ideas of one single person, but are often created by a team of users, who work for the religious organization. At the organizational level, a third party, usually a company in the advertising industry, can be in charge of managing the space on the social networks. Once again, at this level, creators might interact using their personal account to keep their personal ideas separate from the official contents stream. In this model, the religious organization becomes the node of the (religious) network, and the ties can be individuals (i.e. followers and sympathizers), groups (i.e. local religious groups), and even other organizations (i.e. other religious organizations, NGOs).

176 *Danilo Giambra*

Introducing two Japanese 'other religions'

Tenrikyō

Tenrikyō, translated into English as 'the Religion of Heavenly Wisdom' or 'the Teaching of the Divine Reason' (Lewis 2004: 506; Clarke 2006: 562–4), is one of the oldest new religions in Japan. Founded in 1838 by Nakayama Miki (formerly Maegawa Miki), the movement went through the Meiji Restoration (1868), and was nested under the Sect Shinto umbrella during the war period in Japan. In 1970, Tenrikyō was officially recognized as a divergent, or distinct religion.[6] Nowadays the group claims to count more than two million believers in Japan and abroad,[7] and its headquarters are located in Tenri city, close to Nara.[8] The city of Tenri has been named after the religious movement, and is also known as Oyasato, literally 'Village of the Parent'.

Nakayama Miki, commonly called *Oyasama* (Venerable Mother) by the members of the group, is the central figure of the movement. She is believed to have served as the shrine for the divinity named Tenri-o-no-Mikoto, who is also known as 'God the Parent'. According to the doctrine of Tenrikyō, God created humankind, and the Jiba represents the centre of creation, where Nakayama Miki is believed to be residing for eternity after she 'withdrew from physical life'. Pilgrimage to the Jiba is a very important aspect of the religious life of Tenrikyō believers, who also devote a lot of time helping others as a form of purification called *hinokishin*. The main goal of Tenrikyō members is to live a 'joyous life', *yōkigurashi*, while understanding their body as a thing borrowed from God that must be returned (*karimono kashimono*) (Translation Section 1998).

Seichō no Ie: the House of Growth

Seichō no Ie, 'the House of Growth,' (Clarke 2006: 514–15; Staemmler n.d.) was founded in 1930 by Taniguchi Masaharu. The founder was a graduate of Waseda University (English literature) and he was previously a member of a religious movement called Ōmoto.[9] Taniguchi was also strongly influenced by the American New Thought current, as the leader himself translated into Japanese *The Law of Mind in Action* by Fenwicke Holmes (Clarke and Somers 1994: 40). The founder of Seichō no Ie also wrote *Seimei no Jissō* (Truth of Life), which is commonly considered the most important multi-volume religious text of the movement. Taniguchi Masaharu was followed by Taniguchi Seicho (1985), and then by his son, the current president of Seichō no Ie, Taniguchi Masanobu (2009).

Seichō no Ie members believe in one universal God. According to the doctrine of this group, God created a perfect world. It is possible to experience the real perfect world of God, or the True Image (*jisso*), by meditating. Human beings are the children of God, and for this reason share with God his divinity. However, the divinity of humans needs to be rediscovered

Japanese new religions and social networks 177

following the teachings of Seichō no Ie. The environment perceived by human beings is believed to be merely a reflection of the people's mind, and thus is not the ultimate reality, which is in fact God's perfect world. As part of the Seichō-no-Ie God's main teachings, world religions all derive from 'one universal god' (Anon n.d.e), in so doing explaining in part the syncretic attributes of this religion. As with Tenrikyō, Seichō no Ie is a Japanese new religion that falls into the 'other religion' category we find in the *Shukyō Nenkan*, edited by the Japanese Ministry of Education. The group claims currently on its English website to have 1,683,227 members, of which 651,119 are in Japan (ibid.). Seichō no Ie has expanded overseas, in particular to Brazil, where it has gained a great number of followers.

Mixi, Facebook, and PostingJoy: local and global social networks around religion

Mixi: the Japanese way of social networking

Among the many social platforms available on the Internet, Mixi represents an interesting case of a geographically and culturally defined Japanese social network (Anon n.d.h). Founded by Kenji Kasahara in 2004 for the Japanese public (ibid.), Mixi takes its name from the combination of the English words 'mix' and 'I', delivering in a simple way the idea of creating a network between a central self and its acquaintances. Unlike Facebook, Mixi is only available in Japanese. Registering for Mixi requires users to be in possession of an email address, which is linked to a Japanese mobile phone. This represents a further step to limit the registration of users who do not actually reside in Japan, with the consequence of homogenizing the cultural frame of reference within the network. Mixi recently changed its policy on this matter. In the past, it was in fact possible to register on the social network after receiving a friend's invitation. The developers intended this limitation to help keep Mixi a safer environment, purged by users whose intention is to annoy others under a false identity. However, Mixi allows its user to use nicknames or pseudonyms, instead of real names, once the email address has been provided. This characteristic is very important to understanding the success of this social platform in Japan. Users are not always keen to reveal their true identity to others, even if they have good intentions. Further evidence of the disinclination of Japanese people to disclose their identities online may be drawn from the early failure of Facebook to attract users in Japan.

Mixi claims to have about 27.1 million users as of 2012 (ibid.) and can certainly be described as one of the most popular social networks in Japan. However, many argue the network is progressively losing popularity in favor of other social networks, as is also shown by a relatively slower increase in the number of users in the last year. Mixi presents a series of characteristics that makes it unique. For example, users visiting a page leave a footprint (*ashiato*). This makes it possible to monitor who is accessing the contents. Writing a

178   *Danilo Giambra*

diary, sending private messages and deciding the level of privacy (among friends, friends of friends, public or private) when adding contents are also features available.[10]

In Mixi, users can create *communities*, to discuss various topics. Users can officially join multiple communities, though it is often possible to access some of the contents without being a member (this is commonly referred to as lurking behavior, and it is not generally perceived as polite by the members of the online community). Among the various communities in Mixi, a number are religious ones that are created by or directly linked to a Japanese new religion. In particular, some can be linked to Tenrikyō. Among them, we can distinguish official and unofficial ones. Generally, official religious communities are created by representatives of the religious organization after the decision is taken at the highest levels within the group, or by committees in charge of establishing an official presence for the organization on the social space. However, users browsing the communities on Mixi have a hard time recognizing when a community really is official or not. Sometimes, descriptions are made up, or do not tell the whole story. This can generate uncertainty, especially when religion is the central topic. A borderline case is that of communities that actually are created and run by members of Tenrikyō, including some representatives, but which have not obtained official recognition from the highest levels of the group. These are in fact at least partly official, though it might be problematic to decide whether the contents always reflect the official understanding of the doctrine. In most cases such communities are spontaneous, as they are often started by individuals acting as pioneers for the offline community.

The number of users joining Tenrikyō-related communities is relatively high. The largest group, named after the religious organization, counts 1971 registered members (Anon n.d.c). However, the number of 'active' users certainly is much lower. This Tenrikyō community was created in December 2005 and is still active. It offers several topics for discussion, and it is open, allowing everyone registered on the social network to contribute thoughts, questions, and experiences. The community is also open to sympathizers and non-members of Tenrikyō, as can be seen from some of the threads that focus on discovering this religion.[11]

It is common practice to begin by introducing oneself when joining a community. Tenrikyō community is no exception. Other links on the home page of the community open pages where discussion focuses on counseling, exchange of personal experiences, social status and life, request for more information about Tenrikyō religion, how to improve one's life and conditions, sentiments of thankfulness, and open discussion. The Tenrikyō community on Mixi also provides a space where users can discuss religion. However, it is noticeable that this community has not been particularly active recently. This might be because of both a very slow interest in Tenrikyō in social media, but could also be a result of the decrease in popularity of Mixi in the last few years. Regardless, recent trends do not suggest that the Tenrikyō community

Japanese new religions and social networks   179

will be generating more interactive and innovative discussion of religion on Mixi in the near future.

Facebook: where religion put its face

Despite the incredible notoriety of this social network in many countries all over the world, Facebook struggled to convince the Japanese audience, including Japanese new religions, to accept it. However, the last figures reveal this platform is quickly gaining popularity in the country, now numbering over 17 million users (Anon. n.d.b). While Facebook has many features in common with other social networks such as Mixi, it handles registration matters and privacy settings in a slightly different way, requiring its users to reveal their real names.[12] The core idea behind this network is in fact to connect 'people' online, amplifying pre-existent offline social relationships, and supporting the establishment of new relationships among the so-called weak ties, or the friends of our friends.

Facebook *wall* functions as a micro-blogging environment where users add contents and receive comments from other users.[13] Private messaging, video-calling, instant messaging, email services (… @facebook.com), online games and applications, questions and discussion areas, as well as open and private groups and a rich multilingual platform make Facebook a very complete social platform. Recently, after the launch of the new social network from Google, namely Google+, Facebook has introduced new privacy options, making it easier for users to choose with whom they want to share contents. Japanese new religions are starting to build Facebook pages. However, frequently the level of interaction has been limited and the contents are merely mirrored from other platforms, mostly Twitter.

A different case is that of Seichō no Ie, with quite a few Facebook pages created by this religious organization. Masanobu Taniguchi, the president of Seichō no Ie, has his own Facebook profile, which is available both in Japanese and in English (Anon. n.d.d, n.d.g). The president does not seem intimidated by the possibility of receiving criticism on the social space, and decided to keep the comment feature on his wall. Users are welcome to interact and express their ideas, and it is evident that interaction is taking place among them and their leader through this digital network.[14] Taniguchi's profile pages on Facebook are public pages. In other words, everyone can see what he puts there. The pages can be searched online using a web search engine like Google.com or Yahoo.co.jp, and the product of the contents is not restricted to registered users of Facebook. Nevertheless, only registered users can post comments.

Seichō-no-Ie president Taniguchi updates his page frequently. He shares pictures of the food he had with his wife, he writes about himself, but he also uses the page to communicate his thoughts about religion. His personal thoughts are highly regarded by the people who comment on his posts, based on the many positive comments he receives. His offline authority is in fact

180   *Danilo Giambra*

brought online, as he is both the man and the leader. He represents the individual, Taniguchi Masanobu, and the religious organization Seichō no Ie. Taniguchi also uses Facebook to advertise his lectures and to share religious materials, some of which he wrote. In his notes Taniguchi shares his greetings for a happy new year, but he also transcribes the 'Song in Praise of Nature', mixing the religious with the non-religious. Another relevant page built by the religious movement Seichō no Ie on Facebook is the community page for the relief of Japan after the 2011 Tohoku earthquake and tsunami.[15] In spite of the time-limited function of the page, it remains a good example of how religious organizations can use the social space not only to inform people, but also to organize events, to raise funds, and ultimately, to help society.

PostingJoy: an example of a Japanese religious social network

Mixi and Facebook certainly represent two of the most accessed social networks in Japan, and thus must be considered when researching religious communication online. Nevertheless, smaller social networks are also available in the social space. Some of them are designed specifically to host religious communities, to expand the space of gathering and communication about religious topics beyond the constraints of the physical world. That is the case of *PostingJoy* (Seicho no Ie n.d.) a religious social network created to spread joyful messages among the members of Seichō no Ie, from all over the country, but also from overseas. Seichō no Ie created localized versions of the social network PostingJoy in Japanese, English and Portuguese. The availability of these three languages reflects the diffusion of the religious organization in the world, and it aims to reach out to everyone everywhere.

Given that Seichō no Ie members' ultimate goal is that of living a 'joyful life', a series of communities have been created to encourage the sharing of joyful messages, pictures and poetry. The social network is accessible through multiple devices, including a web version, but also an iPhone and iPod mobile application. Accessing the Internet on the move is in fact a very common practice in Japan, and it reduces even further the gap between the offline and online dimensions of life, as everything can be shared immediately. More recently, Seichō no Ie has implemented a geo-tag function, to facilitate the meeting of users also in person. It is easy to know who has posted from where, and then arrange a time to meet. PostingJoy requires users to be registered in order to post, but as is usually the case, most of the contents are publicly available for scrutiny. Anyone can register, even non-members of Seichō no Ie. However, because of the very nature of this social network, it is unlikely that people other than members and sympathizers will ever join this community of users.

Presence on multiple online social platforms

Having introduced the cases of Tenrikyō's and Seichō no Ie's presence on specific social networks, I now consider how these religious movements make the most out of the countless opportunities available on the social space. It is relevant to emphasize that both these religious organizations extend their presence beyond a single social platform. It would be rather restrictive in fact to limit the presence of the group to one social network, especially if proselytization is one of the aims of being social online.

Beyond the so-called 'proper' social networks, other social platforms can make good bases for further religious communication. Blogging and micro-blogging platforms, such as Twitter, but also video-centered Social Networks, such as YouTube, along with a myriad of mobile phone apps, constitute a portion of the social space too important to be ignored. Indeed, there is no need to ignore any of these opportunities, since it is now possible for the content that users place on one platform to be available on many others. Users can follow updates about religious events and lectures on Twitter, join communities that discuss doctrine on Mixi, as well as post comments on the president's Facebook page, discussing topics such as what the president did during his visit to Brazil, when he met the local religious community. Therefore, it is likely that Japanese new religions deciding to establish an active presence on the social space will extend their presence over multiple social platforms. The reasons behind this are different for each religious organization. However, it is possible to focus on some general reasons:

- Extending the presence over multiple platforms guarantees a greater visibility to the religious group, its leader, its representative, and its community.
- Extending the group's presence on multilingual platforms better suits the needs of internationalized religious organizations, which can find a maximized audience and can merge communities of followers located in different geographical locations.
- Extending the group's presence to multiple platforms allows religions to create ad hoc messages, according to their present needs.

New religions will employ personalized communicative strategies, and will choose the most suitable platforms accordingly.

In particular, internationalized Japanese new religions, such as Seichō no Ie, are expanding rapidly over the social networks, providing online religious environments where members can gather and form communities that transcend geographical distances and that promote the formation of new social bonds, while strengthening the old ones within a common religious faith. Furthermore, it is also possible to observe that some emerging Japanese new religions are making use of the social networks, as they find in such environments a more accessible public square and a potentially more receptive audience in order to spread their messages and grow.[16]

To sum up, the presence of Japanese new religions and related groups and communities on multiple social platforms, along with the creation of

182 *Danilo Giambra*

customized religious digital spaces, indicates that religious discourses on these environments are growing to include an interactive model of religious discussion that goes beyond the sharing of simple information.

Conclusion

This chapter discussed how new religions in Japan are increasingly making use of the Internet and are establishing a stronger presence over the social platforms available online. Social space represents both an opportunity and a threat to these religious organizations. Nonetheless, it seems that even 'established' Japanese new religions, such as Tenrikyō, eventually will have to deal with the social media, as their influence cannot be ignored. The multilevel communication model we find online is a further element that makes religious communication on the social networks even more complex and difficult to avoid

What is official religious communication in the social networks? When does official end? Where does unofficial start? It is obvious that these questions will require a different analytic frame. Facebook seems to suit the needs of spiritual leaders, as it provides a space where the self can be presented and re-presented, and where charismatic authority can be re-confirmed. Furthermore, as a globalized social platform Facebook also suits the needs of internationalized religious organizations. Localized social networks, such as Mixi, facilitate the reconfirmation and re-interpretation of the social relationships found in the offline world. A more homogeneous cultural frame helps religious organizations keep in touch with the local communities.

On the other hand, social platforms such as Twitter guarantee a faster transmission of information, and are easier to access. Religious social networks, such as PostingJoy, focus on religion and religious communities. Nonetheless, PostingJoy does not really offer much in terms of communicating about religion. People can share beautiful pictures and talk about their experiences, but a meta-discourse about religion seems to be absent, as yet.

To conclude, Japanese new religions are changing their way of communicating. However, they seem to be embracing the change at a very slow pace, or with modest results. Despite this, there is evidence of a greater presence of these religious organizations on the Internet, and in the social space, but most of the interactive religious discourse remains at the level of individuals. At the organizational level, the social networks have not yet been exploited, leaving the role of representing the organization as a whole to the official website. However, the Internet is changing continuously, and it is likely that these religious organizations will increasingly progress toward a more interactive use of social media, to keep up to date with the lfestyles of younger generations.

Acknowledgements

I would like to thank Helen Bradstock and Nicole Aaron for reading this chapter and providing valuable comments.

Notes

1 Not only the religious organization is presented and re-presented online, but also its spiritual leader and the whole religious community often are too. Presentation and re-presentation of religious persons and groups, along with the mediation and mediatization of religion, are major topics of research when it comes to understanding religion on the Internet. Studies on (traditional and new) media and religion (Baffelli 2007, 2008; Helland 2000; Campbell 2010; Stout 2012; Inoue 2012) are very important to understand how new media are used by these groups today. In many cases, the new media do not replace the traditional media, but are integrated, instead.

2 Japanese new religions continue to make use of a large array of printed materials. Many, including Tenrikyō and Seichō no Ie, own their own publishing house. For this reason, scholars and journalists in the field sometimes refer to them in Japanese as *shuppan shūkyō*, translated in English as 'Publisher Religions'.

3 The two terms, separately, have already been the object of academic discussion for a long time within different disciplines, including philosophy, sociology and geography, to mention but a few. Like most of the definitions we find, however, these two terms now have to be reinterpreted according to the needs and the reality of contemporary society.

4 Recently, some social networking services have added features allowing users to share their position (often through the use of a GPS antenna). This emphasizes the fact that these platforms are not meant to alienate people from their usual social contexts, instead they aim to provide an extended social space, linked to the real world, where users can continue to behave socially.

5 In this chapter I employ the locution 'religious communication' aware that this might lead to positive criticism. I could have used instead 'communication about religion', or similar expressions, to avoid misunderstandings. However, 'religious communication' works better to define the general object of scientific enquiry I am focusing on in this research.

6 According to the Ministry of Culture's classification of Japanese religions, the following categories are available in the *Shukyō Nenkan*: Shinto-related religions, Buddhism-related religions, Christian-related religions, Islam-related religions, and Other Religions (*shokyō* 諸教). This last category covers a number of Japanese new religions, which do not fully fit into the other existing categories.

7 It is not always easy to determine the actual number of adherents. In fact, we must distinguish at least between the figures published by the religious organization (i.e. online), and the official figures published yearly in the *Shūkyō Nenkan*, or Religious Yearbook, by the Japanese Ministry of Education. According to the *Shūkyō Nenkan* of 2009 (Bunkacho 2011: 86–7), Tenrikyō had 1,211,565 members. Also, it must be considered that the number of members is greater when also counting the members from outside Japan.

8 Nara, with the Kansai region in general, is a very important place when it comes to religion in Japan. Buddhism first arrived in this area from continental Asia, and *Kojiki* and *Nihonshoki* – associated with Japanese cosmogony – were written during the Nara period (710–94 CE). Thus, the region is traditionally associated with a more 'classical' idea of Japan.

9 It is important to stress Taniguchi Masaharu's relationship with Ōmoto, and in particular with its syncretic Shintoism and healing practices, which combined with the later New Thought ideas allowed him to create Seichō no Ie as we know it.

10 These features were not all available when the SNS was first launched, but they have been added in a similar place to other American SNSs.

11 When creating a community, a description is generally present. Many users also provide a policy for entering and behaving in the community, sometimes limiting the access to specific typologies of users.

184 *Danilo Giambra*

12 As a matter of fact, this requirement is not always met by Facebook users.
13 Comments on the wall can be switched off by the user.
14 Comments can be deleted by the owner of the page.
15 In Japanese, *Seichō no Ie Higashi Nihon Daishinsai Kyūen Komyuniti* 生長の家東日本大震災救援コミュニティ.
16 For example, this is the case of Hikari no Wa, a Japanese new religion born from the ashes of Aum Shinrikyō, after this latter movement collapsed as a consequence of the Aum affair in 1995. For a more detailed account of the Aum Affair, see Reader (2011).

References

Anon. (n.d.a) 'About Social Network – mixi, Inc,' *About Social Network*. Available at: http://mixi.co.jp/en/about/ (accessed 16 January 2013).

Anon. (n.d.b) 'Asia Internet Stats: Facebook Subscribers and Population Statistics.' Available at: www.internetworldstats.com/asia.htm#jp (accessed 15 January 2013).

Anon. (n.d.c) '[mixi] Tenrikyo,' *Tenrikyo Community*. Available at: http://mixi.jp/view_community.pl?id=457161 (accessed 16 January 2013).

Anon. (n.d.d) 'Seicho no Ie Sosai,' *Facebook*. Available at: www.facebook.com/pages/%E7%94%9F%E9%95%B7%E3%81%AE%E5%AE%B6%E7%B7%8F%E8%A3%81/280856148591794 (accessed 16 January 2013).

Anon. (n.d.e) 'Seicho-No-Ie – What's SNI – Summary.' Available at: www.seicho-no-ie.org/eng/whats_sni/index.html (accessed 14 January 2013).

Anon. (n.d.f) 'Seicho-No-Ie – What's SNI – Teachings.' Available at: www.seicho-no-ie.org/eng/whats_sni/teaching.html (accessed 14 January 2013).

Anon. (n.d.g) 'Seicho-No-Ie President,' *Facebook*. Available at: www.facebook.com/Seichonoie.President (accessed 16 January 2013).

Anon. (n.d.h) 'Social Network Mixi.' Home Page. Available at: http://mixi.jp/ (accessed 16 January 2013).

Baffelli, E. (2007) 'Mass Media and Religion in Japan: Mediating the Leader's Image,' *Westminster Papers in Communication and Culture*, 4(1): 83–99.

Baffelli, E. (2008) 'Media and Religion in Japan: The Aum Affair as a Turning Point,' working paper presented to the EASA Media Anthropology Network. Online. Available at: www.philbu.net/media-anthropology/baffelli_mediareligion.pdf (accessed 25 January 2013).

Boyd, D.M. and Ellison, N.B. (2008) 'Social Network Sites: Definition, History, and Scholarship,' *Journal of Computer-Mediated Communication*, 13(1): 210–30.

Bunkacho (2011) *Shukyo nenkan: 2009*. Tokyo: Gyosei.

Campbell, H. (2005) *Exploring Religious Community Online: We Are One in the Network*. New York: Peter Lang.

Campbell, H.A. (2010) *When Religion Meets New Media*. London: Routledge.

Clarke, P.B. (2006) *Encyclopedia of New Religious Movements*. London: Routledge.

Clarke, P.B. and Somers, J. (1994) *Japanese New Religions in the West*. London: Routledge.

Helland, C. (2000) 'Online-Religion/Religion-Online and Virtual Communitas,' *Religion and the Social Order*, 8: 205–24.

Herring, S.C. (2009) 'Web Content Analysis: Expanding the Paradigm,' in J. Hunsinger, M. Allen, and L. Klastrup (eds) *The International Handbook of Internet Research*. New York: Springer, pp. 233–49.

Inoue, N.(2012) 'Media and New Religious Movements in Japan,' *Journal of Religion in Japan*, 1(2): 121–41.

Lewis, J.R. (2004) *The Oxford Handbook of New Religious Movements*. Oxford: Oxford University Press.

Milroy, L. (1987) *Language and Social Networks*, 2nd edn. Oxford: Basil Blackwell.

Papacharissi, Z. (ed.) (2011) *A Networked Self: Identity, Community and Culture on Social Network Sites*. New York: Routledge.

Prell, C. (2012) *Social Network Analysis: History, Theory and Methodology*. London: SAGE.

Reader, I. (2011) 'The Shikoku Pilgrimage Online. Official Sites, Promotion, Commerce and the Replication of Authority,' in E. Baffelli, I. Reader, and B. Staemmler (eds) *Japanese Religions on the Internet: Innovation, Representation and Authority*. New York: Routledge, pp. 80–100.

Seicho no Ie (n.d.) 'Postingjoy.' *PostingJoy.com*. Available at: http://postingjoy.com/ (accessed 20 April 2012).

Staemmler, B. (n.d.) 'World Religions and Spirituality | Seicho noe.' Available at: www.has.vcu.edu/wrs/profiles/SeichNoIe.htm (accessed 19 November 2013).

Stout, D.A. (2012) *Media and Religion: Foundations of an Emerging Field*. New York: Routledge.

Tabuchi, H. (2011) 'Facebook Wins Relatively Few Friends in Japan,' *The New York Times*. Available at: www.nytimes.com/2011/01/10/technology/10facebook.html?_r=1&scp=1&sq=mixi&st=cse (accessed 25 November 2011).

Translation Section (1998) *Tenrikyo, the Path to Joyousness First*. Tenrikyo Overseas Mission Department.

Zieleniec, A.J.L. (2007) *Space and Social Theory*. London: Sage.

10 #Hashtag meditation, cyborg Buddhas, and enlightenment as an epic win

Buddhism, technology, and the new social media

Ann Gleig

Introduction

Sitting in front of a massive neon projector screen, which constantly flashed with Twitter updates, and surrounded by an intergenerational audience united by iPads and iPhones, I perused the schedule booklet for the 2012 Buddhist Geeks Conference. Alongside popular Western Buddhist teachers such as Stephen Batchelor, featured speakers included Amber Case, a 'cyborg anthropologist' and 'contemplative scientist,' Willoughby Britton. The conference began not with the standard 'dharma talk' but with an 'opening keynote' by American Tibetan Buddhist popularizer, Lama Surya Das. After leading the audience in a short-guided meditation, Surya Das's provocatively entitled presentation, 'The Future of Buddhism, Which is Now: Does Buddhism Have to Die to Be Reborn in the West?' introduced several of the key themes that were to be vigorously debated over the next two days. These included questions such as how the Buddhist principles of awareness and compassion can be applied to the use of social media, and warnings such as Buddhist communities risked becoming stagnant or even obsolete unless they embraced modern technology. The message was clear: Buddhism needs technology and technology needs Buddhism.

Through a focus on Buddhist Geeks, an online media community based in Boulder, Colorado, which produced the conference, this chapter will explore intersections between Buddhism, modern technology, and the new social media. Buddhist Geeks is an online Buddhist media company that launched in 2007. It consists of a weekly audio podcast and a digital magazine component, and in 2011 launched the first of what is expected to be a series of annual conferences. The motivation behind Buddhist Geeks is to explore and celebrate the ways in which technology and the new social media have begun to shape contemporary Buddhist practice and make it more accessible and relevant for the twenty-first century. The appeal of this project is indicated by the size of their audience: the Buddhist Geeks website records between 75,000 and 100,000 downloads each month, and they have 11,000 followers on the

Buddhism, technology, and new social media   187

social networking site Facebook and around 16,000 followers on Twitter. The majority of traffic on the website comes from the United States (between 60–70 percent) but there is also a sizable percentage from the United Kingdom, Canada, Australia, India, and France.

Drawing on ethnographic research and discourse analysis, this chapter will tease out and examine three distinct intersections between Buddhism, technology and the new social media in the Buddhist Geeks network. First, it will consider the ways in which participants reframe traditional Buddhism through a scientific-technological lens. Second, it will explore the ways in which Buddhist teachings and practices are utilized to combat the types of afflictive mind states that social media can generate, and refashion the use of social media as a potentially contemplative activity. Third, it will examine the ways in which contemporary technology and social media are being used to both extend traditional Buddhist practices and enable the emergence of radically innovative forms of Buddhism. In conclusion, it will reflect on the ways in which these technological and social media interactions are shaping Buddhism in the twenty-first century.

Buddhism, technology, and the new social media: prior studies and trends

Studies of the interactions between Buddhism, technology and the new media are in their infancy. As Scott Mitchell (2010) notes, in his annotated bibliography of Buddhism and the new media, Buddhist studies has come late to the conversation between religion and media studies. There is no authoritative monograph on Buddhism and the new media, though Mitchell provides a comprehensive and useful overview of primary resources—such as popular Buddhist magazines, Internet sites, blogs—and existing secondary sources—mostly journal articles and a few edited book chapters, as well as relevant related (but not Buddhist-focused) academic books—to begin an investigation. While no means exhaustive, this section aims to give a taste of existing academic studies of and emerging trends between Buddhism and new media.

The first and only full-length book treatment on Buddhism, technology and the mass media is Peter D. Herschock's *Reinventing the Wheel: A Buddhist Response to the Information Age* (1999), a critical constructive study of mass media and the new information technologies from a Buddhist perspective. Herschock draws on Buddhist thought, particularly the doctrines of dependent origination, emptiness and karma, to critique what he calls the 'colonization of consciousness,' i.e. the homogenization of personhood, an undermining of cultural diversity, and a degradation of relationality, produced by the global spread of mass media. Conceding, however, that the use of new technology is unavoidable, he advocates utilizing it within a Buddhist framework of intentionality and skillful means.

While Herschock uses Buddhist thought to analytically critique mass media and the new information technologies, Charles Prebish (1999: 203–33) provides

188 *Ann Gleig*

the first detailed history of how both Buddhist scholars and practitioners have used the Internet and the World Wide Web to reach and promote their respective interests and goals. Prebish traces the beginning of formal Buddhist interest in computer technology to the establishment of a 'Committee on Buddhist Studies and Computers' at the 1983 Tokyo meeting of the International Association of Buddhist Studies and discusses the proliferation of Buddhist Internet activity, such as online and email discussion forums, newsgroups, databases, archives, electronic journals, in the 1990s. His main focus is on the increasing growth of Buddhist 'cybersanghas,' a term coined in 1991 by Gary Ray to signify an emerging online Buddhist community. Prebish delineates three major types of Buddhist cybersanghas: (1) WWW pages created by many American Buddhist groups as a useful communication tool for their members; (2) virtual communities created by traditional sanghas as an addition to their existing programs; and (3) a number of communities that only exist in cyberspace (ibid.: 225). He cautiously concludes that while cybersanghas should be celebrated for enabling Buddhist practitioners to participate in either exclusively virtual communities or non-local actual communities, their potential value could be undermined by the "loss of face-to-face encounter, personal support, and shared practice in real space" (ibid.: 231).

Given the accelerated development of information technologies and the new social media, much of Prebish's data is somewhat outdated, however, his study does highlight the two main overlapping areas of research conducted into Buddhism and media: cybersanghas, and the impact of the Internet on Buddhist teaching and research. In terms of the former, though focused on email discussion lists rather than cybersanghas, Richard Hayes (1999) shows how Buddhist forums create an alternative Buddhist community in which practitioners can ask controversial questions regarding authority, doctrine, practice, and cultural identity in a safe space. Mun-Cho Kim (2005) offers an empirical sociologically investigation into one online Korean Buddhist community. Kim concludes positively that the Korean cybersangha provides multiple relational needs and is better understood through a community 'sanctuary model' rather than a utilitarian 'tool model' (ibid.: 148). Using a similar ethnographic methodology, Ally Ostrowski (2006) asks what types of people are accessing online Buddhist resources and for what purposes. From a short and self-acknowledged limited sample, Ostrowski discovered that users were mainly white, between the ages of 23–40, and were unaffiliated with any specific Buddhist tradition. She identified the main purpose as the convenient collection of information on Buddhism rather than a search for spiritual community (ibid.: 97–98). In contrast, Laura Busch (2007) analyses three Buddhist forums to explore the intentional creation of a nonsectarian, transnational 'global cybersangha' whose specific aim is to promote the goals of socially engaged Buddhism.

In terms of the impact of the Internet on Buddhist research and teaching, Jamie Hubbard (1995) was the first to ask how the computer revolution—particularly word processing, electronic communication and archives—was affecting Buddhologists. Noting both opportunities and obstacles, Hubbard encouraged scholars to harness new technology while at the same time resisting the wider commodification of education it participates in. Mavis Fenn (2002) offers a similarly cautious evaluation of the emergence of distance education courses on Buddhism. A much more optimistic approach to 'digital dharma' is advocated by Brett Greider (2002), who encourages Buddhist scholars to fully welcome the Web not only as unprecedented and invaluable pedagogical tool but also as a type of Buddhist phenomenon—an embodiment of Indra's Net and analogous to interdependent arising—in its own right.

From this brief review of some of the main studies on Buddhism and the new technologies, it should have become apparent that attitudes range from a suspicious reservation to an enthusiastic embrace. As I will show, the Buddhist Geeks network is firmly situated in the celebratory camp. While it does consider the possible dangers of the new media—particularly, the dilution of classical Buddhism and the afflictive mind states that unmindful use of technology can generate—its basic project is to promote the ways that new technology can enhance and enrich Buddhist practice in the twenty-first century.

"The leading edge of Buddhism, technology and global culture": the history and mission of Buddhist Geeks

Buddhist Geeks is an online Buddhist media company that launched in 2007. It consists of a weekly audio podcast and a digital magazine component and in 2011 hosted the first of what is expected to be a series of annual conferences. Vincent Horn and Ryan Oelke, who at that time were both students at the Buddhist-inspired liberal arts college, Naropa University, in Boulder, Colorado, began the podcast to explore issues that were particularly relevant to them as young Buddhist practitioners in the twenty-first century, but were rarely addressed in prevailing Buddhist circles. Joined later by a third member, Gwen Bell, the three wanted, they explained, to provide a public forum for the kind of discussions they were having among themselves such as what was actually happening in their meditation practice and how to think more positively about the way "practice is changing to meet the culture."[1]

Their original idea was to interview a different figure every week as an audio podcast and then post it on the Buddhist Geeks website where it would be available for free download. The innovative and interdisciplinary nature of the podcast is emphasized in its advertisement as "an ongoing conversation with the individuals and communities who are experimenting with new ways of practicing Buddhism, as well as new ways of bringing Buddhist and contemplative insights into other disciplines."[2] Horn reports that there is no specific criterion for who is interviewed and that he has tended to choose people, both Buddhist and non-Buddhists, he is personally interested in learning more about.[3] The result is nearly 300 interviews with a range of

190   *Ann Gleig*

figures cutting not only across Buddhist traditions and lineages but also from fields as diverse as neuroscience, technology, business, social justice, and the creative arts.

Horn and Oelke report that after a few years, and over a million downloads of their weekly podcasts, "it became clear that Buddhist Geeks was something closer to a movement or community, rather than just a podcast." The thought of bringing this community together inspired the first 2011 Buddhist Geek conference at the University of the West in Los Angeles. Given the size of the conference—around 150 participants—the international media coverage it received was quite extraordinary. In large part due to Horn's media savviness, it received enthusiastic reviews in a number of newspapers including the *Los Angeles Times* and the British broadsheet, *The Guardian.* In August 2012, a second conference that was twice the size took place at the University of Colorado at Boulder, and a 2013 conference followed at the same location.

Reflecting on the development of Buddhist Geeks, Horn notes:

> Like every good question, each time I ask, the answer changes. In the beginning the answer was, "It's a podcast where we interview geeky Buddhists about things we don't see being talked about anywhere else." …
> At a more recent point the answer was that Buddhist Geeks exists to serve a question. The question being: "How can we serve the convergence of the time-tested practices and models of Buddhism with rapidly evolving technology and a global culture?" Put another way: "How can we help bring Buddhism into the 21st century?"[4]

The Buddhist Geeks website has been recently redesigned and highlights three main features: the podcast, the conference, and the Life Retreat.[5] The latter is an exclusively virtual practice or 'new delivery model' that includes weekly one-to-one instruction with a teacher and group meetings.[6] Another new feature on the revamped site is 'The Lab,' which contains a series of reflections on emerging trends in Buddhism by the major figures in Buddhist Geeks.[7] Included in the 'koan' that functions as a mission statement for Buddhist Geeks is the statement that all of the Buddhist Geeks projects are motivated by the observation that Buddhism is a dynamic and heterogeneous tradition that has always shaped and been shaped by the different cultures it has come into contact with. Moreover, not only has Buddhism crossed geographical boundaries, it has also moved through cultural epochs from the Agrarian Age, to the Industrial Age, and now into the Information Age, a period in which rapid technological development is "altogether changing our understanding of what it means to be human."[8]

Before examining some of the trends emerging from this particular historical and cultural juncture, an explanatory word on my designator the 'Buddhist Geeks community' is necessary. The Buddhist Geeks core team has undergone various transformations with Bell and Oelke leaving and new influential members, including Horn's wife, Emily Horn, and Daniel Thorson joining the organization.[9] This chapter draws heavily on the views of the two most vocal and featured members on the Buddhist Geeks website, Horn and *vipassana* meditator and design consultant, Rohan Gunatillake. However, also included are the perspectives of other significant members of the Buddhist Geeks organization as well as the multitude of interviewees, particularly ones who have been repeatedly featured. 'Buddhist Geeks community' functions therefore as a loose signifier for a diverse network of people who share some common interests but are not united by any specific ideological consensus.

Updating the scientific Buddha: Buddhism through a technological lens

Since the nineteenth century, Asian and Western Buddhists have commonly presented the Buddha as a rational empiricist and Buddhism as a religion that is compatible with science (Lopez 2008, 2012). Buddhist Geeks can be seen as continuing and also updating this scientific lineage through the translation of classical Buddhist teachings and practices into contemporary technologically associated language and concepts. For example, many of the popular speakers on the Buddhist Geeks podcast or conferences are committed to integrating science and Buddhism and use scientific language to interpret or reframe classical Buddhism. These include former Buddhist monk and *vipassana* teacher Shinzen Young, who has collaborated with neuroscientists from UCLA and Harvard Medical School in order to chart how meditation affects the brain. In his 2011 Buddhist Geeks Conference keynote speech, "Towards a Science of Enlightenment," Young calls the Buddha "the first and greatest scientist of human happiness" and claims Buddhism can be improved upon by incorporating the insights of science.[10] In a related vein, Pragmatic Dharma teacher, Kenneth Folk, draws from Buddhism, developmental psychology and neuroscience to conclude, "enlightenment is an old word, maybe an outdated word for human development." He cites a 2007 University of Toronto study that used fMRI scans to examine the brains of meditators and posited two modes of attention: an experiential focus and a narrative focus. It discovered that meditation changed the actual wiring of the brain through a shift from the default narrative setting to the experiential, which allowed for a more immediate experience of reality. Folk describes Buddhism as essentially "a set of technologies for awakening" that enables one to effectively "perform neurosurgery" on oneself.[11]

Similarly, one of the most popular areas of inquiry on Buddhist Geeks is the dialogue between Buddhism and science, particularly in relationship to the 'Emerging Science of Mindfulness Meditation.'[12] In fact, it presents itself as signifying not just the continuation but also the updating of the scientific lineage through the participation of "a new generation of contemplative hybrids" who are equally trained in the "inner and outer technologies," or classical Buddhism and neuroscience and unlike their closeted predecessors are willing to talk openly about the "enlightenment game."[13]

192   *Ann Gleig*

The updating of the scientific lineage is also seen in the adoption of technological language and concepts that are likely to speak to a younger, technologically savvy demographic. One example of this is Horn's refashioning of the Buddhist doctrine of *anatta* or no-self and *vipassana* meditation through the lens of hacking, the illegal entry into and exploitation of a computer system. Horn compares the target of *anatta*—an illusory sense of a permanent, unchanging self—to 'Windows ME,' a human operating system that is pre-programmed to have a mistaken but persistent sense of a solid, essential self and world. He envisions meditation as a form of 'mind-hacking,' which is used to hack into and rewrite this illusory 'Windows ME,' so that self and reality are experienced as they actually are: fluid, changing, and impermanent.[14]

Another different but related area of makeover comes from Gunatillake who calls on Buddhist communities to adopt a contemporary technological design aesthetic. In his 2012 Buddhist Geeks conference presentation, 'Disrupting the Awakening Industry,' Gunatillake argues that Buddhism must learn from other systems such as the entertainment, publishing, and mass media industries. He notes that with the revolutionary 1998 appearance of the Apple MAC, the computer became a design item, and aesthetic as well as functional considerations became integral to modern technology. In an analogous manner, he wants Buddhist communities to incorporate a more modern design aesthetic into their teachings or 'delivery product.' He frames the Buddha's first teaching of the Four Noble Truths as the 'start of the awakening industry' in that it shifted from the realization of an individual to the birth of a religious system or industry. Rather than a 'proto-scientist,' he presents the Buddha as the 'first management consultant' because of his extraordinary ability to codify complex information in simple and accessible ways. For Gunatillake, Buddhism, like any other industry, must be updated to remain relevant and accessible to a constantly shifting 'market' or audience.[15]

The adoption of technological language to interpret and frame classical Buddhism can be seen as serving two main functions. On one level, it explicitly functions as a pragmatic pedagogy or 'skillful means' way to teach traditional Buddhism in a language that will resonate more with a twenty-first-century audience. On another level, it implicitly serves a legitimating function in implying that technological innovations are structurally compatible or even inherent to Buddhism. For example, many speakers on Buddhist Geeks frame Buddhist mediation as a 'spiritual technology' or an 'internal technology.' As Horn puts it:

> The spiritual technologies are also technologies. Prayer and meditation and yoga—so many of these things are inner sciences, inner technologies, tried and true technologies, and spiritual traditions all use them. So maybe we could just think that some of these things we're talking about are more like the new outer technologies. Technology has always been part of the spiritual traditions.[16]

Contemplative design and the wise use of technology: how Buddhism can aid technology and social media

One of the main questions of the Buddhist Geeks community is how to apply Buddhist principles and practices to the use of social media and refashion it as a contemplative activity. Soren Gordhammer, Buddhist and best-selling technology author, suggests that consciously cultivating interior life and uniting internal and external worlds is the way to ensure "we can use technology, rather than technology using us." Drawing from a Zen Buddhist story of the importance of emptying the mind, he recommends both periodically unplugging and bringing mindfulness practice to the use of technology:

> So I think that for those of who are trying to balance this life of mindfulness and technology, it's extremely important to have some time where we're not taking in information and we're bringing attention to our breath and our internal world. And we're not as focused on our external world. But then the challenge, of course, is to not become a good meditator. The challenge is to become awake, right? And to bring that sense of awareness and full engagement no matter what we're doing. And if we're checking email, can we do that fully? If we're tweeting, can we do that fully? Whatever it is, can we bring our full attention to that?[17]

Similarly, Lama Surya Das advises drawing from Buddhism to bring discipline and self-control to the skillful use of technology and social media.[18] Other recommendations from participants at the Buddhist Geeks conference included doing periodic body-scan practices whilst using a computer as an antidote to technological disembodiment and having regular breaks from technology and bringing attention back to the breath.[19] One specific example of applying Buddhist qualities of compassion and mindfulness to the use of social media is Horn's technique of '#hashtag meditation,' which melds *vipassana* practice with the use of Facebook and Twitter. Horn acknowledges that bringing awareness to the use of social media is a challenge and shares that his motivation for developing '#hashtag meditation' was his realization that it often generates many of the afflictive mind states and self-aggrandizing that Buddhism guards against. He draws a parallel between the social media use of the '#hashtag' as a way to notice and emphasize activity and the identification of thoughts, emotions, or sensations that occur in *vipassana* 'noting' practice. Working from this basic analogy, he advocates the practice of meditation hashtags to make transparent to self and others the underlying intentions—including both wholesome and unwholesome mind states—fueling the practice of social media posting.[20]

Going even further, Gunatillake suggests that Buddhism can change the ways people not only use but also actually design technology. He acknowledges that technology can fragment attention, but argues that this is not an inherent feature of technology but rather reflects its normative driving force, namely

194 *Ann Gleig*

the intention to sell products. By changing the 'core mission' of technology from consumerism to spiritual development, however, he believes that it can be transformed into a contemplative activity. Further, Gunatillake notes that technological design has developed from a purely functional to a creative aesthetic stage and suggests that the next step or 'evolution' for the digital medias is the incorporation of contemplative design. He sees this occurring through people who are interested in contemplation—Buddhists, meditators, psychologists, and neuroscientists—becoming involved in technology design. According to Gunatillake, one result of the current "democratization of manufacturing" is that people who have contemplative expertise now also have access to "the tools to make the difference."[21] The emerging collaboration between contemplative and technological experts is also signified by the popularity and success of the 'Wisdom 2.0' conferences. Hosted by Gordhammer since 2010, these events have brought together technological pioneers including the founders of Facebook and Twitter with American Buddhist teachers, such as Jack Kornfield and Joan Halifax, to explore questions such as "How can we live with greater presence, meaning, and mindfulness in the technology age?"[22]

Meditation on the go, practice as play, and Buddha helmets: how technology and social media can aid Buddhism

Another major area of inquiry on Buddhist Geeks is how new technologies and social media can be used to both aid classical Buddhist practices and innovate radically new ones. This discussion ranges from the present use of common technologies to promote classical Buddhist practices to radical future technological possibilities, such as creating an 'enlightenment machine' or 'Buddha helmet,' which would accelerate the process of liberation.[23] At one end of the spectrum there is much celebration of how the Internet and social media have positively enhanced practice by providing easy access to Buddhist resources and fostering new forms of Buddhist communities. Horn, for example, shares how the popular technologies of Skype and Twitter have enhanced his dharma practice. Skype has enabled him to have more "real interaction" and "oral conversation" with his geographically distant teachers while Twitter has enabled him to connect with other practitioners and socially reinforced his practice commitment.[24]

In addition to utilizing prevailing technologies, members of the Buddhist Geeks community are also advocating the development of new ones to help Buddhist practice. One example is Gunatillake's iPhone and Android cell application, the 'mindfulness-based' buddhify, which he designed to introduce meditation practice in an urban environment. Users or 'players' select one of four locations—traveling, walking, at the gym, or at home—and the app plays an audio-guided meditation, which is designed specifically for that environment. buddhify has had significant media and market success, being featured in a number of international newspapers such as *The Guardian* and exceeding initial sales predictions.

Gunatillake designed buddhify after repeatedly having conversations with people who expressed an interest in Buddhist meditation but stated they either had no time for traditional teaching formats or felt alienated from its association with "hippy or new age culture." He sees these obstacles or "design challenges" as indicating that the "aesthetic of meditation is broken" and claims that Buddhist meditation must be re-packaged if it is to attract a young urban demographic.[25] He designed buddhify with a team of people who had experience both in classical Buddhist meditation and also in contemporary design and technology and presents it as a "meditation service" or "delivery model" that is accessible, convenient and relevant for contemporary lifestyles. Gunatillake acknowledges that buddhify is primarily targeted at and most beneficial for people who are new to meditation and he recommends that users who want to develop their practice further should work with a qualified teacher. Buddhify's aim is not to enhance depth of practice, however, but rather to "widen the funnel of people who will practice" and to inspire a wave of "authentic modern translations of contemplative traditions."

Integral to Gunatillake's way of thinking about Buddhist practice in the twenty-first century is the idea of "practice as play" and he includes "the emerging culture of urban and pro-social gaming represented by people like Hide & Seek and Jane McGonigal" as inspirations for buddhify. Social gaming culture also has a strong presence on Buddhist Geeks. Horn has interviewed three leading game designers—Jane McGonigal, Jonathon Blow and Michael Harbourn—about the interface between game culture and Buddhism. McGonigal (2011) is a leading game consultant and pioneer of "alternate reality gaming" which applies game design and game theory to business and public issues such as poverty, climate change, education, and healthcare. Describing herself as "23% Buddhist, 77% geek," McGonigal reveals that in addition to the influence of positive psychology, her work is inspired by and draws deeply from Buddhist philosophy, particularly "the Buddhist goal of ending suffering on Earth." McGonigal claims that her research has shown that video games can "alleviate all kinds of suffering" and suggests that there are multiple similarities between gaming and Buddhist practice. To begin with, she argues that both gamers and Buddhists share an attitude of "wholehearted participation," a sense of "being fully present, open, curious and joyful about whatever challenges the moment bring."[26] Further, she sees significant parallels between the goals, methods and practices of Buddhists and gamers.[27] In terms of goals, both are "trying to end suffering, are trying to help people wake up and be the best versions of themselves and then to bring those virtues and abilities to the world around them to help others."[28] In terms of method and practices, she suggests that there are interesting overlaps between Buddhist techniques such as mind training and the qualities and skills that gamers are developing. For example, she claims that gaming has the potential—both as a natural by-product and as an intentional aim—to cultivate the seven factors of awakening delineated in Theravada Buddhism or "the seven positive traits that Buddhists believe can help end

196 *Ann Gleig*

suffering: mindfulness, investigation, energy, joy, relaxation, concentration, and equanimity."[29]

While McGonigal suggests the emergence of a "future form of Buddhism that can be played together," fellow designer Jonathon Blow is in the actual process of developing a game called 'The Witness,' which though not explicitly Buddhist was inspired by his exposure to the Indian guru Ramana Maharshi and Western Neo-Advaita.[30] Similarly, Michael Harboun advocates a "contemplative design" approach to gaming that balances inner contemplation with external technology. He laments the way is which social media currently functions to reify and aggrandize a sense of self, and intuits a shift towards Buddhist-inspired games and a "transpersonal social network" in which the self is de-centered and the aim is "to go with the flow of experience."[31]

A related vision of using technology to promote contemplative experience is sketched in the dialogue between neuroscience and Buddhism. Buddhist meditator and neuroscientist Daniel Rizutto, for example, offers some radical 'conjectures' in his exploration of the intersections of neuroscience, technology and Buddhism with Horn. Rizutto conducts clinical research into the 'brain machine interface,' specifically the use of technology to manipulate neural brain correlates in order to treat chronic depression. Applying this to Buddhism, Rizutto and Horn discuss the possibility of developing a neural map of the Buddhist meditation process and creating a device or 'enlightenment machine' that would accelerate its development.[32] In the 'Neural Correlates of Enlightenment: The Buddha Helmet,' Jean-Paul Wiegand further investigates the idea that Buddhist meditation could be improved by technology and that one could recreate the Buddhist enlightenment experience using modern scientific techniques. He suggests that neuroscientists could pinpoint characteristic qualities of the Buddha and identify their neurological or chemical localization. Further, in reviewing existing scientific studies on neurons that appear to be related to compassion and those which structure our sense of self, he concludes, "Buddhism has found intriguing middle ground, if not complete compatibility with the concept of Technological Singularity," the attempt to redefine and recreate God.[33]

In a similar vein, bioethicist, transhumanist and long-term Buddhist practitioner, James Hughes enthuses on how developments in biotechnology could produce a 'Cyborg Buddha.'[34] He claims that a disproportionately large percentage of transhumanists are Buddhist and attributes this to the fact that Buddhist philosophy is more compatible with the transhumanist project than many Western frameworks. For example, he notes that the Buddhist concept of *anatta* or no self circumvents the Jewish-Christian notion of an essential, authentic self that is threatened by and objects to transhumanist manipulations of subjectivity.[35] Moreover, Hughes argues that biotechnology could be used to facilitate or complement Buddhism in a number of ways, such as stimulating brain waves to enhance meditation practice and manipulating biology to cultivate the *paramitas*, the highest virtues or ethical qualities of

Mahayana Buddhism. In response to the concern that transhumanism would eradicate the inherent suffering of life that motivates Buddhist practice, Hughes draws from Buddhist cosmology to distinguish between 'god realms' in which humans are lost in the pursuit of pleasure and have no incentive to spiritually awaken and 'Techno-Utopian Pure Lands' in which conditions are optimal for Buddhist practice such as found in the classical Buddhist concept of the Pure Lands.[36]

"The new normal" and the NextGen: emerging trends in technology and Buddhism

Across the diversity of speakers and the wide range of discussions on intersections between Buddhism, technology and the new social media, one can identify a number of dominant themes on Buddhist Geeks. First, there is a fundamental optimism towards the impact of technology on Buddhism in the twenty-first century. While there is acknowledgment of the dangers of technology, such as the fragmentation of attention or the sense of disembodiment it can produce, the main emphasis is on its spiritual and pragmatic benefits. This basic affirmation and embrace of technology signify a discernible shift in the dialogue between Buddhism and technology. As Horn notes, Buddhist communities are starting to think about and utilize technology as a spiritually transformative tool rather than dismiss it as a hindrance to practice or reluctantly accept it as a necessary evil.[37]

A second theme is that as the 'new normal,' technology can facilitate the integration of Buddhist practice into everyday life. One of the reasons Buddhist practitioners are utilizing different forms of technology for practice is because it has become such a common and normative aspect of daily life across the globe. Hence, as Gunatillake puts it, through technology, "spirituality can reclaim its seat as an accessible and central part of people's lives."[38] This signifies a wider integrative and world-affirming approach to Buddhism in which all aspects of contemporary daily life—technology, business, relationships, social justice, and creative work—are affirmed as potential sites for Buddhist awakening.

Related to the integrative approach is a third theme of the technological reconfiguration of both traditional Buddhist and Buddhist modernist forms of space and place. The most obvious shift here is from the actual to the virtual, the real to the digital, seen most visibly in the fact that Buddhist Geeks is primarily a cyber community and also signaled by the Life Retreat—an intensive, exclusively online meditation program, which is one of the main features of the Buddhist Geeks website.[39] There is also a turn from the rural to the urban as the privileged site of Buddhist practice. One of Gunatillake's main aims, for example, is to facilitate Buddhist practice in an urban environment. He sees the location options of buddhify—traveling, walking or at the gym—as questioning normative associations of sacred space and place in Buddhism. Buddhify challenges the assumption that meditation should occur

198   *Ann Gleig*

in a distinct "quiet, controlled and supportive place" and establishes urban spaces as equally valid sites of practice. The sacralization of unorthodox spaces is seen even more radically in the use of social media sites and video games as potential sites of awakening.

In addition to destabilizing normative sites of Buddhist practice, a fourth theme is the ways in which technology challenges traditional forms of Buddhist authority and hierarchy and furthers the democratization of Buddhism. Technology is playing a fundamental role, for example, in the emergence of 'DIY Buddhism,' which was one of the roundtable topics of the Buddhist Geeks conference in 2012. One of the participants, 'Buddhist agnostic' and well-known author and teacher, Stephen Batchelor, suggested that the first form of DIY Buddhism is located in and legitimated by the Buddha's Parable on the Raft, in which he likens his teachings to a raft to be used as a provisional means to cross the river and then discarded. Gunatillake offered a more contemporary spin by comparing the assembling of the raft to 'hacking' and declaring that:

> Everyone here is a hacker of the dharma. We take methodologies, systems, techniques, teachings and we make them personal to ourselves. We sort of cobble together teachings with bits of string and tape and we sort of make it all work and we get results and progress and what we're looking for. And that's the experience of hacking.[40]

Social technology is essential in this hacking process, as it has enabled unprecedented direct access to Buddhist teachings without the mediation of a teacher or community.[41] Similarly, with the rise of the cybersangha, the teacher–student model is being either replaced or at least joined by a peer-to-peer approach. This democratizing thrust is further seen in Gunatillake's promotion of 'co-design,' in which the user is encouraged to become involved in Buddhist teaching models.

Closely related to the democratizing role of technology is a fifth theme that celebrates the relational and collective aspects of technology. Technology is promoted as a means to foster community from cybersanghas to new inter-personal practice modes. Horn, for example, compares Facebook to a "small town" and sees it as providing a virtual equivalent to the development of spirituality in traditional communities where relationships were a central means of learning. He describes the Internet as allowing people to "gather in this sort of virtual collective or virtual pods that are geared around particular styles of practice of shared aims."[42] The relational angle is also visible in the advertisement of the Buddhist Geeks conference as an "interactive event," which includes "community-led sessions," and the Buddhist Geeks Life Retreat, which declares, "awakening is a team sport." In addition to celebrating the relational components of prevailing technologies, the Buddhist Geeks community is also developing new specifically relational practices. Horn has designed a practice called, 'Two Player-Meditation,' which adds a

Buddhism, technology, and new social media **199**

dimension of interpersonal exploration to individual sitting practice and buddhify also has a mode called the 'Two Player Meditation,' which is designed for two people to practice meditation together.[43]

A sixth theme is a stress on a dialogical both/and approach between Buddhism and technology as captured in the podcast opening slogan "seriously Buddhist, seriously Geeky." The commitment to both discourses and fields—Buddhism and technology—is seen on multiple levels. One is through the repeatedly stated concern of preserving the depths of Buddhist wisdom and practices and forging a middle way between preservation and innovation. Another is through an emphasis on the Buddhist credentials of innovators or the importance that new practice technologies are co-designed by people with both contemplative and technological expertise.

This collaborative ideal leads us to our final theme that a new generation of Buddhist practitioners is emerging—a generation that, unlike previous ones, is comfortable and fluent in both Buddhist and technological worlds. The biographies of the Buddhist Geeks team, for example, include information on both their Buddhist and technology histories. Similarly, as noted earlier, the leading figures in the conversation between neuroscience and Buddhism are touted as "a new generation of contemplative hybrids" who are equally trained in both disciples.[44] In a related vein, participants on Buddhist Geeks recognize a "generation divide" and explain the emergence of new technological innovations, in part, as being produced by and reflecting this generational difference.[45]

Conclusion: it's Buddhism, (Jim) but not as we know it

In conclusion, I want to reflect on what type(s) of Buddhism this "NextGen" is producing. In an associated press article on the 2011 Buddhist Teacher's Council, differences between what were identified as the "pioneers" and the "NextGen" of Western Buddhist teachers were represented as signifying the difference between "traditional and innovative" forms of Buddhism.[46] Claiming earlier Euro-American adaptations as traditional is, however, a gross misrepresentation. Such forms are captured rather by David McMahan's recently refined category of Buddhist modernism, a historically unique form of Buddhism that has emerged as a result of a process of modernization and reform that has been taking place in Asia and the West for over a century. As McMahan states, Buddhist modernism is neither unambiguously "there" in classical Buddhist texts and lived traditions, nor is it merely a fantasy of an educated, white, Western, elite population. This new form of Buddhism has been fashioned by modernizing Asian Buddhists and Westerners deeply engaged in creating a Buddhist response to the dominant problems and questions of modernity (McMahan 2008: 4–5).

At first glance, Buddhist Geeks with its cutting-edge technologies appears to be a clear iteration of Buddhist modernism. I suggest, however, that Buddhist Geeks can be more usefully understood as a response to certain limitations of

Buddhist modernism and displays characteristics more associated with the postmodern than modern. As noted, Buddhist Geeks participants distinguish themselves not from traditional forms of Buddhism but rather from the preceding generation of Buddhist modernist 'baby boomer' or 'hippy' practitioners.[47] Further, the Buddhist Geeks community demonstrates a postmodern sensibility in destabilizing Buddhism as a totalizing metanarrative or absolute system. This occurs on multiple levels from its pluralistic embrace of other discourses and technologies, to its reluctance to exclusively identify with the signifiers 'Buddhism' or 'Buddhist.' In several places, for example, Horn relativizes Buddhism as just one way to perceive or point to a much larger reality. Similarly, both Horn and Gunatillake caution against holding a Buddhist identity too tightly and note that it can be both skillful and unskillful to explicitly identify as a Buddhist.

Yet, at the same time as undercutting Buddhism as an absolute system, a main concern of Buddhist Geeks is to preserve the depths of Buddhist wisdom and to avoid the dilution of Buddhism to mere "stress reduction tools." In calling for a serious engagement with classical elements of Buddhism, Buddhist Geeks hase resisted the linear process of secularization seen in various Western assimilations of Buddhism such as the secular mindfulness movement. It fits more rather with McMahan's observation that within contemporary Western Buddhism there has been a reclaiming of tradition and the appearance of various combinations of tradition and innovation alongside the existence of an increasingly detraditionalized Buddhism (2008: 246). Moreover, as he points out, these various combinations of the traditional and modern, innovative and reconstructive are more characteristic of postmodern rather than modern conditions. As such, I conclude that Buddhist Geeks—with its dialogical approach to contemplative and technological discourses, commitment to preservation and innovation, and its undercutting of Buddhism as a metanarrative—is indicative of the emergence of a new distinctive postmodern state in the North American assimilation of Buddhism.[48]

Notes

1 'BG 001: Meet the Geeks.' Available at: www.buddhistgeeks.com/2007/01/bg-001-meet-the-geeks/ (accessed 7 November 2012).
2 'Our Koan.' Available at: www.buddhistgeeks.com/koan/ (accessed 2 April 2013).'
3 V. Horn, personal interview. 20 September 2012.
4 Ibid.
5 'A New Buddhist Geeks is Here.' Available at: www.buddhistgeeks.com/2013/03/a-new-buddhist-geeks-is-here/ (accessed 2 April 2013).
6 'The Life Retreat.' Available at: www.buddhistgeeks.com/liferetreat/ (accessed 2 April 2013).
7 'The Lab Archives.' Available at : www.buddhistgeeks.com/category/lab/ (accessed 2 April 2013).
8 'Our Koan;' see note 2.
9 'Our Team.' Available at: www.buddhistgeeks.com/team/ (accessed 2 April 2013).

Buddhism, technology, and new social media 201

10 S. Young, 'Towards a Science of Enlightenment.' Available at: www.buddhistgeeks. com/2011/10/bg-conference-2011-towards-a-science-of-enlightenment/ (accessed 22 March 2013).

11 K. Folk, 'Enlightenment for the Rest of Us.' Available at: www.buddhistgeeks.com/ 2012/01/enlightenment-for-the-rest-of-us/ (accessed 22 March 2013).

12 D. Vago, 'BG 262: The Emerging Science of Mindfulness Meditation.' Available at: www.buddhistgeeks.com/2012/07/bg-262-the-emerging-science-of-mindfulness-meditation/ accessed 3 April 2013).

13 K. Sosan Bearer, 'The Scientist and the Contemplative.' Available at: www.bud dhistgeeks.com/2013/02/the-scientist-and-the-contemplative/ (accessed 3 April 2013).

14 V. Horn, 'Mind Hacking: Upgrading from Windows ME.' Available at: www. buddhistgeeks.com/2013/01/mind-hacking-upgrading-from-windows-me/ (accessed 3 April 2013).

15 R. Gunatillake, 'Disrupting the Awakening Industry.' Available at: www.buddhistgeeks. com/2012/10/disrupting-the-awakening-industry/ (accessed 12 March 2013).

16 V. Horn, 'Uniting Technology and Wisdom.' Available at: www.buddhistgeeks. com/2011/12/uniting-technology-and-wisdom-video/ (accessed 12 March 2013).

17 S. Gordhammer, 'BG 161: Happiness—There's an App for That.' Available at: www.buddhistgeeks.com/2010/03/bg-161-happiness-theres-app-for-that/ (accessed 13 March 2013).

18 Lama Surya Dass, 'BG 189: The Tao of Twitter.' Available at: www.buddhistgeeks. com/2010/09/bg-189-the-tao-of-twitter/ (accessed 13 March 2012).

19 Fieldnotes from Buddhist Geeks Conference 2012, Boulder, Colorado.

20 V. Horn, 'Hashtag Mediation.' Available at: www.buddhistgeeks.com/2013/01/ hashtag-meditation/ (accessed 22 March 2013).

21 V. Horn and R. Gunatillake, 'BG 275: Buddhism, Technology and Quarter Pounders.' Available at: www.buddhistgeeks.com/2013/01/bg-275-buddhism-technology-and-quarter-pounders/ (accessed 22 March 2013).

22 For details of the Wisdom 2.0 conferences, see www.wisdom2summit.com/ (accessed 22 March 2013).

23 D. Rizzutto, 'BG 043: Neuroscience and The Enlightenment Machine.' Available at: www.buddhistgeeks.com/2007/10/bg-043-neuroscience-and-the-enlightenment-machine/ and J.P. Wiegand, 'Patient Suffering from Chronic Samsara.' Available at: www.buddhistgeeks.com/2010/08/doctors-notes-patient-suffering-from-chronic-sam sara/ (accessed 22 March 2013).

24 V. Horn and K. McLeod, 'BG 250: Crossing the Generational Divide.' Available at: www.buddhistgeeks.com/2012/04/bg-250-crossing-the-generational-divide/ (accessed 28 March 2013).

25 R. Gunatillake, 'BG 217: The Aesthetic of Meditation is Broken.' Available at: www.buddhistgeeks.com/2011/05/bg-217-the-aesthetic-of-meditation-is-broken/ (accessed 13 March 2012).

26 J. McGonigal, 'BG 205: Gaming as Spiritual Practice.' Available at: www.bud dhistgeeks.com/2011/01/bg-205-gaming-as-a-spiritual-practice/ (accessed 22 March 2013).

27 J. McGonigal, 'BG 254: A Buddhist Game Designer.' Available at: www.bud dhistgeeks.com/2012/05/bg-254-a-buddhist-game-designer/ and J. McGonigal, 'BG 255: Is Super Mario a Buddhist?' Available at: www.buddhistgeeks.com/2012/05/bg-255-is-super-mario-a-buddhist/ (accessed 3 March 2013).

28 Ibid.

29 McGonigal, 'Gaming as Spiritual Practice.'

30 J. Blow, 'BG 272: Quantum Gaming.' Available at www.buddhistgeeks.com/2013/ 01/bg-272-quantum-gaming/ and J. Blow, 'BG 273: The Witness.' Available at: www.buddhistgeeks.com/2013/01/bg-273-the-witness/ (accessed 22 March 2013).

202 *Ann Gleig*

31 M. Harboun, 'BG 271: Contemplative Design: Less is More.' Available at: www.buddhistgeeks.com/2012/12/bg-271-contemplative-design-less-is-more/ (accessed 23 March 2013).
32 D. Rizutto, 'BG 043: Neuroscience and the Enlightenment Machine.' Available at: www.buddhistgeeks.com/2007/10/bg-043-neuroscience-and-the-enlightenment-machine/ (accessed 23 March 2013).
33 J.P. Wiegand, 'The Buddhist Singularity.' Available at: www.buddhistgeeks.com/2010/08/the-buddhist-singularity/ (accessed 23 March 2013).
34 Institute of Ethics and Emergent Technologies: Cyborg Buddha Project.' Available at: http://ieet.org/index.php/IEET/cyborgbuddha (accessed 23 March 2013).
35 J. Hughes, 'BG 077: Transhumanism and the Authentic Self.' Available at: www.buddhistgeeks.com/2008/06/bg-077-transhumanism-and-the-authentic-self/ (accessed 23 March 2013).
36 J. Hughes, 'BG 078: Cyborg Buddhas and Techno-Utopian Pure Lands!' Available at: www.buddhistgeeks.com/2008/07/bg-078-cyborg-buddhas-techno-utopian-pure-lands/ (accessed 22 March 2013).
37 Horn and McLeod, 'Crossing the Generational Divide.'
38 Gunatillake, 'BG 275: Buddhism, Technology and Quarter Pounders.'
39 See www.buddhistgeeks.com/liferetreat/ (accessed 25 March 2013).
40 R. Gunatillake, 'Practice, Play and Products.' Available at: www.buddhistgeeks.com/2012/11/video-practice-play-and-products/ (accessed 25 March 2013).
41 R. Gunatillake, 'The Rise of the Social Meditator.' Available at: www.buddhistgeeks.com/2010/12/the-rise-of-the-social-meditator/ (accessed 26 March 2013).
42 Gunatillake, 'Buddhism, Technology and Quarter Pounders.'
43 V. Horn, 'The Two-Player Meditator.' Available at: www.buddhistgeeks.com/2011/03/two-player-meditation/ (accessed 26 March 2013).
44 Bearer. The Scientist and the Contemplative.
45 For example, Horn and McLeod, 'Crossing the Generational Divide.'
46 'At the Crossroads: Buddhism in America is facing a generation shift.' 01 September 2012. *TuscaloosaNews.com.* Available at: www.tuscaloosanews.com/article/20110716/NEWS/110719820 (accessed 3 March 2012).
47 For a provocative critique of "boomer Buddhism," see D. Chapman, 'BG: 239 Consensus Buddhism and Mindful Mayo.' Available at: www.buddhistgeeks.com/2011/12/bg-239-consensus-buddhism-and-mindful-mayonnaise/ (accessed 28 March 2013).
48 The expansion of my reading of Buddhist Geeks as a form of postmodern Buddhism is detailed in A. Gleig (2014) 'From Buddhist Hippies to Buddhist Geeks: The Emergence of Buddhist Postmodernism?' *Journal of Global Buddhism,* 15: 15–33.

References

Busch, L. (2007) 'Global Cybersanghas: Strategies for Constructing Global Buddhist Community,' in *Conference Papers of National Communication Association.*
Fenn, M.L. (2002) 'Teaching Buddhism by Distance Education: Traditional and Web-Based Approaches,' in R. Hayes, V. Sogen Hori and J.M. Shields (eds) *Teaching Buddhism in the West: From the Wheel to the Web.* London: Routledge, pp. 197–211.
Greider, B. (2002) 'Academic Buddhology and the Cybersangha: Researching and Teaching Buddhism on the Web,' in R. Hayes, V. Sogen Hori and J.M. Shields (eds) *Teaching Buddhism in the West: From the Wheel to the Web.* London: Routledge, pp. 212–24.

Hayes, R. (1999) 'The Internet as a Window onto American Buddhism,' in C. Queen and D. Ryuken Williams (eds) *American Buddhism: Methods and Findings in Recent Scholarship*. New York: Routledge, pp. 168–79.

Herschock, P.D. (1999) *Reinventing the Wheel: A Buddhist Response to the Information Age*. Albany, NY: State University of New York Press.

Herschock, P.D. (2006) *Buddhism in the Public Sphere*. London: Routledge.

Hubbard, J. (1995) 'Upping the Ante: budstud@millenium.end.edu,' *Journal of the International Association of Buddhist Studies*, 18(2): 309–22.

Kim, M.-C. (2005) 'Online Buddhist Community: An Alternative Religious Organization in the Information Age,' in M. Hojsgaard and M. Warburg (eds) *Religion and Cyberspace*. London: Routledge, pp. 138–48.

Lopez, D.S. (2008) *Buddhism and Science: A Guide for the Perplexed*. Chicago, IL: The University of Chicago Press.

Lopez, D.S. (2012) *The Scientific Buddha: His Short and Happy Life*. New Haven, CT: Yale University Press.

McGonigal, J. (2011) *Reality Is Broken: Why Games Make Us Better and How They Can Change the World*. London: Penguin Books.

McMahan, D. (2008) *The Making of Buddhist Modernism*. Oxford: Oxford University Press.

Mitchell, S. (2010) *"Buddhism in New Medias," Oxford Online Bibliographies: Buddhism*. Oxford: Oxford University Press.

Ostrowski, A. (2006) 'Buddha Browsing: American Buddhism and the Internet,' *Contemporary Buddhism: An Interdisciplinary Journal*, 7(1): 91–103.

Prebish, C. (1999) *Luminous Passage: The Practice and Study of Buddhism in America*. Berkeley, CA: The University of California Press.

Prebish, C. (2004) 'The Cybersangha: Buddhism on the Internet,' in L. Dawson and D. Cowan (eds) *Religion Online: Finding Faith on the Internet*. New York: Routledge, pp. 135–47.

Prebish, C., Husted, W. and Keown, D. (1995) 'Indra's Net and the Internet,' *Religious Studies News*, 10(1): 14.

11 The technology of tradition

Javed Ahmad Ghamidi and the contemporary Pakistani media's participatory construction of women's *shari'a*

David A. Doss

Introduction

On Thursday, 24 August 2006, two unknown men shot Syed Manzoorul Hassan, editor of the Islamic education and research journal *Ishraq*, as he was exiting his office building in Lahore, Pakistan ('Al-Mawrid Will Forgive Hassan's Attackers' 2006: 7). Hassan, though critically injured, with a bullet lodged in his neck, remained alive, and was eventually released from hospital care (Khan 2006: 1; 'Al-Mawrid Will Forgive Hassan's Attackers' 2006: 7). Some news media sources suggest that the attack was a politically and religiously motivated assassination attempt (Khan 2006: 1).

Such violence is by no means uncommon in the realm of Pakistan's religious and intellectual sphere. A relatively new country, only independent from the United Kingdom since 1947, Pakistan is a changing society with both changing ideologies and changing technologies. In the past decade or so, during the coming of age (both in terms of content and in terms of technical skill/resources) of Pakistan's academic and social media, the role of religion, and of the public religious scholar, has been an extremely volatile one (Ahmad 2010: 2). The Pakistani government no longer considers the Taliban or *jihad* as supportive of its interests (ibid.). The traditional *'ulama'*,[1] the Taliban, and, generally speaking, the conservative forces, are beginning to fade in influence, whereas the power of the public religious scholars is beginning to grow. These scholars are usually not traditionally trained. However, they are usually not only more adept at reading the ideological needs of their target audience but also increasingly savvy in finding the appropriate technological means of reaching them (Ahmad 2010: 2). Understandably, the opposition of conservative forces to more non-traditional ones is also beginning to grow. In 2007, Abdul Rashid Ghazi, a formally trained Pakistani cleric, demanding implementation of *shari'a*[2] and overthrow of the Pakistani government, led a group of Islamic militants to an armed occupation of the Red Mosque, confronting the Pakistani army (Roggio 2007).

In these rising conflicts, members of ultra-conservative groups have targeted many public scholars and activists. Salman Taseer, governor of the Punjab province, was shot dead because of his opposition to Pakistan's blasphemy laws (International Crisis Group 2005: i) – laws resulting from Islamism.[3] Islamist religious parties in favor of these laws "warned that anyone who expressed grief over the assassination could suffer the same fate," and the Taliban stated, "anyone offering prayers for Mr. Taseer would be guilty of blasphemy." As the *Daily Guardian* mentions, "Sherry Rehman, a PPP (Pakistan People's Party) parliamentarian who proposed changes to the (blasphemy) legislation, was ... charged with blasphemy this week ... (and) confined to her Karachi home after numerous death threats, some issued publicly by (*'ulama'*)" ('Islamic Scholar Attacks Pakistan's Blasphemy Laws' 2011). Further, due to public opposition and argumentation against these same blasphemy laws since 2006, public Islamic scholar Javed Ahmad Ghamidi has begun to be criticized for producing work that is *fitna* (Fitna of Javed Ahmad Chamidi 2006).[4] He received death threats, which in 2010 escalated to a (foiled) plot to bomb his family's home, causing him to flee with his family into exile in Malaysia (Mufti 2007). The major objections that such leading figures have raised in traditionalist circles revolve around tradition and change, and involve varying technologies and concepts of informing and performing with respect to ethics and religion.

As a start toward understanding such issues, it is useful to examine a key concept. The word 'contemporary' can describe many things. First of all, for example, it can be seen as an ideology (or group of ideologies). For each area or society, such a type of ideology is influenced by specific historical and cultural factors unique to specific national and cultural memories. However, some of the defining characteristics include a focus on interconnections between people, and interconnections between ideas – the power of knowledge that is spread and shared among peers for the growth of a community. Further, it is tied to the scientific knowledge and methodology of the post-Enlightenment world. In other words, such an ideology places a high value on connection and on development. Second, however, 'contemporary' also evokes something not only symbolic but also more physical than the previous concept: it evokes technology, and the productions resulting from this scientific knowledge and methodology – the newest development, the latest gadget. Like the ideological aspect, the technological aspect places emphasis on the need both for connection and for development. This ultimately involves sharing and building of connections – in mutually beneficial relationships between technological development and a community. Such a building of connections is achieved through technological networks. The two concepts – of contemporary medium and of contemporary message – are highly interrelated.

In principle (distanced from the blurred boundaries of everyday life), contemporary ideals might be seen to oppose those of a traditional ideology – such as most religious ideologies – which can tend to look back at the past as the main yardstick for value and meaning. Traditionalists often see this 'contemporary' (in either the ideological or the technological sense – or even both) as a threat to tradition, and often see it in relation to the West and to secularism. On the

206   *David A. Doss*

other hand, it is nearly impossible for most people not to be participating in the contemporary world in some way or another, ideologically and/or technologically – even as a relative outsider or a potential dissident. Many people, for instance, have experienced such incongruous events as seeing a medieval-looking, robed Franciscan friar standing in line to order at a McDonald's, and it should also be noted that radically conservative groups such as the Taliban have often used relatively advanced contemporary technologies to achieve their radically traditionalist ideological goals.

Some Pakistani traditionalists can indeed be said to be employing violent measures of prevention (attempts to preserve the status quo that extend to the permanent and brutal silencing – or attempted silencing – of dissident voices such as in the above paragraphs). However, it does not necessarily follow that tradition in and of itself is an enemy of the contemporary. Rather, the twin forces of preservation and change are key in many aspects of life – not the least of which are religious aspects. In other words, the religious atmosphere is one that necessitates two forces. The first is the *informative* function, which is preservation of the religious network by instilling/socializing religious information – a consciousness, and a memory – in religious individuals and thus in the religious group. The second is the *performative* function, which entails expressing the sacred memory of a society/community, and with that, developing and changing the religious memory and the religious community (Hervieu-Léger 2000: 103–4; Assmann 2006: 66).

The selection and the use of not only contemporary ideologies but also contemporary technologies can (and do) support religious agendas in Pakistan, as can be seen by the country's recently developing socio-religious media-technology revolution. This chapter will examine one voice as a key example of that revolution: Javed Ahmad Ghamidi. His strategy of combining contemporary ideology and technology, for all of its potential issues (some of which are examined in the third section and the conclusion) has at base a unified vision fusing the informative with the performative in a way that is mirrored and maximized by his movement's use of contemporary media and social networking technologies.

Ghamidi: a brief biography

As mentioned before, the attack on Hassan (again, a public religious scholar) may very well have been an assassination attempt by traditionalist opposition, and though the attackers remain unidentified, these suspicions of political foul play are by no means unreasonable, given Hassan's affiliations. As editor of the monthly Urdu journal, *Ishraq*, organized by the Al-Mawrid Foundation,[5] Hassan represents the interests of that institution and its founder, Javed Ahmad Ghamidi.

An Islamic theologian, poet, and public intellectual, Ghamidi was born on 18 April 1951 in the Sahiwal village of Pakistan's Punjab province. He was raised studying Arabic, Persian, traditional Islamic studies, and Qur'an exegesis privately under various teachers (Zaidl 2009: 80; Ahmad 2010: 4). In 1972, he achieved an honors BA in Philosophy and English Literature from the Government College of Lahore, Pakistan (Zaidl 2009: 82). Remaining in Lahore after these studies, he then made a decision to turn his intellectual efforts from the secular to the religious (ibid.). As "an extremely disciplined and avid reader with a well-conceived plan to educate himself in Islamic religious literature" (Ahmad 2010: 5), he dedicated himself to studies under the respected theologian and exegete Amin Ahsan Islahi (Zamman 2011: 192) as well as with the renowned Islamist revivalist Syed Abul A'ala Maududi and his group, the Jamaat-e-Islami, but broke off contact with the latter in 1977, ostensibly due to Ghamidi's own less Islamist views (Hassan 2009: 172; Zamman 2011: 193). He taught Islamic studies in the Pakistan Administrative Services' Civil Services Academy in Lahore, and founded the *Al-Mawrid* Foundation for Islamic Research and Education, the backbone of his other endeavors (such as *Ishraq*) (Research Team at Al-Mawrid: Javed Ahmad Ghamidi 2011).

Ghamidi never officially studied theology at a professional academic level, pursuing a study of Western humanities at a colonial school (Zamman 2011: 192) rather than obtaining the *ijazah*[6] that is considered traditional for an *'alim*[7] at a *madrasah*.[8] Nonetheless, he appears to be a dedicated and learned scholar of Arabic and of the Qur'an (ibid.: 192), and in the sense that he maintains a prominent place as a widely received public religious figure, he has an influence similar to that of a traditional *'alim*, though with a different voice from many of them and from some of the Muslim community at large. He certainly does differ, as can be seen by many confrontations.

The incidents of hardship mentioned in the preceding section illustrate how high the personal stakes really are in this changing society. In Pakistan, as in many Islamic countries, religious issues and social issues are one and the same. In this context of great tension over how Islam ought to be interpreted and socially implemented, we see the role of the Islamic scholar (not only the traditional *'alim* but perhaps more so the non-traditional ones such as Ghamidi) as key. But what exactly is so key? When we compare Ghamidi and his ideological opponents, we can draw several comparisons. Ghamidi favors the implementation of *shar'ia*, like some Islamists that have threatened his life. Yet his voice is one that many such Islamists seek to silence. As was already touched upon, the susceptibility of those like Ghamidi to violent reactions within Pakistan (primarily stemming from traditionalist groups) is one of many related effects of the conflicting nature of an infrastructurally and ideologically contemporary mission to encourage and maximize religious information and performance in the country. In other words, this is a mission involving a technological medium, as combined with a technologically-oriented message. The following two sections of this chapter will explicate conceptions of science and technology in Ghamidi's media and message: The next section will focus on analysis of his ideological and infrastructural strategy, and the penultimate section will bring this to bear on desired or effected changes of socio-religious *shari'a* ethics surrounding Pakistani women's rights issues.

208   *David A. Doss*

The concept of a Muslim science and technology

As we have seen above, Islam in Pakistan is struggling to adapt its message to a modern world. Several figureheads of this adaptation have faced at best difficulty, and at worst death. Some Islamic influentials favor westernization and modernization, while others, viewing this as *bid'a*,[9] have in response to these perceived evils proposed radical fundamentalist strategies, a few effects of which were already mentioned in the Introduction. The Islamic state of Pakistan, whose laws and society are influenced by the principles of *shari'a*, is always facing these issues of tradition vs. adaptation. In the post-colonial era, it has been common for Muslim socio-religious and political movements to polarize into two main factions: Islamic traditionalism[10] and Islamic modernism.[11] Where does one place Ghamidi's analytical strategy in these polarized issues? Many see Ghamidi as neither an Islamic modernist nor an Islamic traditionalist, neither liberal nor fundamentalist – or rather, as both: a "fundamentalist moderate" (Mufti 2007).

Many socio-religious leaders in Pakistan are increasingly involving themselves in contemporary spheres of influence – moving outside of mosques and into the secular sphere (Ahmad 2010; Aziz 2011). At least in the case of leaders such as Ghamidi, this sought-after blend of sacred and secular involvement has led to his self-professed prioritization of a scientific-technological strategy and ideology with regard to religion. In other words, regardless of whether or not this holds true on a practical level, his works clearly state that his method and priorities are supposed to be characteristic of the definitions of science – derived from the idea of knowledge/discernment as based on cutting or dividing of one concept from another – just as much as his methods and priorities are supposed to be characteristic of religion.[12] Ultimately, Ghamidi perceives religious information – and thus, religious meaning, or religious truth – as something reached through progressive construction of evidence.

Scientific method

One of the reasons why Ghamidi is called the "fundamentalist moderate" lies in his very method. His scientific and technically oriented strategy – with which he on the one hand appeases the more traditional groups (holding himself rigidly accountable to method), and on the other hand renders himself adaptable to the increasingly savvy and technologically-oriented generation – is so called because, rather than attacking fundamentalism on the grounds of needing to modernize, or even on the grounds of its violation of human rights, he attacks Islamism fundamentalist extremism on religious grounds and on grounds of Qur'anic analysis (Mufti 2007; 'Islamic Scholar Attacks Pakistan's Blasphemy Laws' 2011). As Ghamidi maintains, "I have come across people who agree with me and many who do not. All I can say is that I base my research and knowledge on the Holy Qur'an and Sunnah of the Holy Prophet, pbuh"[13] ('A Misreported Interview' 2005). Influenced by the

The technology of tradition 209

Qur'anic thought of his mentor Amin Ahsan Islahi, he sees the writings of the Prophet as gifted with a consistency and necessary clarity (Aziz 2011: 615–16). This clarity is something that Ghamidi claims many, including both the modernists and the pro-*jihad* Islamist fundamentalists, tend to misunderstand (Mufti 2007).

Ghamidi's Islam, that is, claims to be based on rationality and procedure. According to the Qur'an, it is the duty of a messenger of Allah to "to proclaim (the message) in the clearest manner" (5.797). Ghamidi puts forth his understanding of Islamic scientific-religious logic in several books, including *Mizan* (a comprehensive introduction to his understanding of Islam) and *Burhan* (a critical analysis of contemporary religious thoughts) (Research Team at AlMawrid: Javed Ahmad Ghamidi 2011). To him, Islam has a clear and coherent message – admonition to the people – and that is the basis of the *shari'a*, the revealed religious law (Aziz 2011: 54).

The rationality that Ghamidi ascribes to Islam, and to the Qur'an, is an internal one. In other words, training within and knowledge of Islam – scientific expertise – are required to understand the Quran's meaning and style (Masud 2007: 615). He argues for an inductive coherence of all parts taken together, rather than a deductive coherence (Ghamidi 2011). He emphasizes the *nazm*[14] of each *sura*[15] of the Qur'an: each is a complete linguistic, literary, and thematic structure (Hassan 2009: 178). In asserting that the meaning of the Qur'an is tied to the meaning of its literary structures, and that its meaning is thus to be taken within their context, one can see a further inherent assertion that the religious information (or rather the perceived religious truth) contained in it is obtainable only by methodological and inductive observation (Research Team at Al-Mawrid: Javed Ahmad Ghamidi 2011).

In other words, basic information within Islam is in Ghamidi's system collected inductively as if in a process of scientific experimentation, to reach evidence-based conclusions. Even though the form of evidence may not be the same as that which a scientist such as a chemist or a neurologist would consider legitimate, it is evidence that nearly all Muslims would consider legitimate, and the method is undeniably similar to that which the said chemist or neurologist would employ in a laboratory.

To Ghamidi, every verse has its own context-specific meaning, and all verses must be studied together in order to reveal the difference between general and context-specific issues (Masud 2007: 359, 362). To him, the Qur'an is an absolute authority, the revealed word of Allah, but the interpretation of any single verse into a general *shari'a* should not be overextended past its context. "[E]ach verse of the Qur'an (and any directive emanating from it) is specific to its first addressees and their times unless its universality and generality can be proved from the context" (Iftikhar 2004: 62). The truth comes out of unity of all the contexts. In this interpretation, there is no abrogation[16] among these verses, but rather a mere difference in their contexts. He seeks to maintain the fundamental, traditional value of the Qur'an, while coming to a contemporary-friendly conclusion. His idea of the text is a sort of a post-modern

210   David A. Doss

one, in that it treats the religious text as something that has just as much to do with its reader and the *reader's context* as with its writer and the *writer's context*. Further, his interpretation treats the religious relationship between Allah and the *jamaa*[17] as mediated through text with context and agreement. Thus, what was once considered true (much like scientific acceptance of a flat earth or of a geocentric universe) can – and in fact should – be revised and reconstructed when further methodological observation proves it false.

All evidence is not created equally, according to Ghamidi, and everything within Islam is not even considered by him to be valid evidence. These ideas are underscored by his refusal to accept an Islam that is dictated by every single Islamic text and tradition with an equal weight of authority. The *sunna*[18] and *hadith*[19] are to him merely the primary and secondary supports, respectively, for the hermeneutic, context-driven textual criticism of the Qur'an that he regards as the base of *shari'a*. He maintains that the authority of the *sunna* is secondary to that of the Qur'an, and that they together make the base for *shari'a*. He holds that the beliefs (information) of Islam are contained within the Qur'an alone, while the practices (performance) of Islam are guided by both the Qur'an and the *sunna* (Ghamidi 2009). The *sunna* are those practices of Muhammad passed down via a combination of the Islamic community's agreement (*ijma'*) and continual adherence (*tawatur*) (Iftikhar 2004: 66). He argues that *sunna* can explain what is not completely clear from the context of the Qur'an alone, but that it may not add to or abrogate anything in the Qur'an (Masud 2007: 371). He sees the Qur'an as God's law, even if it is often misinterpreted – the rest in Islam is in comparison merely undeveloped hypothesis, an ever-changing performance.

Several further taxonomical prioritizations of Islamic thought reflect this general idea. Separate from and below the *sunna* are the *hadith*, which are "vague and full of internal contradictions that require a critical and careful reading" (ibid.). Coming up with a complete list of what practices are *sunna* means that he is drastically reducing, or even rejecting, the authority of those *hadith* passages outside of his *sunna* conception (Iftikhar 2004: 66). Although the *'ulama'* and the *mujtahidun*[20] tend to cite these sources in order to pass laws based on *shari'a*, Ghamidi wants to "restrict the hadith as a source of religious norms, thereby facilitating the revaluation of legal norms" (Zamman 2011: 192). To him, *hadith* is not a revelation from Allah, so it must be returned to a status secondary to the Qur'an, and when it conflicts with the Qur'an, it should be rejected. To restrict the *hadith*'s authority would by nature bring about a re-evaluation of the *hadith*, and vice versa (Islahi 2011), thus also leading to a re-evaluation of the religiously oriented laws based upon that *hadith*. In sum, while he finds the Qur'an is immutable, a matter of belief whose practice is contextual, the *sunna*, of which the *hadith* may be a part, is purely a matter of practice, encompassing the *hadith*, that ought always to be regarded skeptically.

Ghamidi further differentiates between the concepts of *shari'a* and of *fiqh*.[21] His distinction between Divine guidance and its understanding and interpretation

The technology of tradition   211

is also a distinction between *shari'a* and *fiqh* (Iftikhar 2004: 51). When the state adopts the *mujtahidun*'s educated understanding of the Divine directives, it is this understanding that becomes practiced Islamic law (*fiqh*) (ibid.). But the contents of religion, the divine directives (*shari'a*), are what are pure and unchanging, and not the understanding of them, the practiced laws (*fiqh*). In Ghamidi's system of thought, due to this human nature of *fiqh*, Muslims should not be obliged to adhere to it (Masud 2007: 361), in contrast to the divine *shari'a* according to which they must direct their lives.

As Iftikhar argues, in order for the change of Pakistan's religious environment to be productive, a "convincing alternative epistemology and methodology" are needed (2004: 8). Ghamidi consciously seeks such a methodology, painstakingly scientific in its skepticism. Regardless of whether one approves of his method, or agrees with the conclusions that he uses this method to reach, his analytical agenda is at base a systematic one, well calculated insofar as it relies on an in-depth reading of the Qur'an. His analytical methodology is one that views Allah and the Prophet as the only sources truly to be trusted, and yet he treats the Qur'anic text as a living and literary document whose meaning is dependent not only upon the actual words, but also upon the intent of the writer and the understanding of its readers. He uses solely the traditional framework, but with an analytical strategy different from the traditionalists, employing a postmodern understanding of text and a double hermeneutic – understanding the relationship between text and reader as two-way. In doing so, he often comes to conclusions similar to those of Islamic modernists, whose methods would differ from his. This could effect change by defining Islam and the Qur'an itself as fundamental – fundamentally Qur'anic – yet also as a communal network of readers and thinkers – fundamentally interpreted by group contexts. He rallies himself, and rallies the post-modern reader, relying on her "perspicacity" in moving toward a fundamental, respectful skepticism, not toward the Qur'an itself, but toward the assumptions about the Qur'an that he attributes to Westernizers and Islamists alike (Research Team at Al-Mawrid: Javed Ahmad Ghamidi 2011).

In most Islamic cultures, the power of the leader is primarily based on his intellectual method's credibility (Iftikhar 2004: 93), so method is a characteristic crucial to the public Islamic scholar, and especially so for one like Ghamidi, who does not have the customary credibility of the traditional *'alim*'s religious education. Since "[t]he 'laws of Islam,' as interpreted by the *'ulama'*, are considered by many Muslims to be the *shari'a* and, therefore, are followed religiously, even when they do not have the force of state authority," Ghamidi, in re-casting these laws as non-mandatory *fiqh*, and not as *shar'ia*, has all the more need of a credible method, since "[t]he authority behind such 'laws' derives … from the strength of the arguments given by scholars or reformers" (Iftikhar 2004: 93). The movement of the Islamic religious leadership's cautious and skeptical method (seemingly so vital for their credibility) into a more expanded 'secular'/public sphere influence (as in the case of neo-religious Muslim media-preachers such as Ghamidi) could thus arguably further the

212   *David A. Doss*

potential for Pakistan's reduced socio-religious conflict with contemporary scientific/technological ideologies within that same expanded realm. This same cautious and skeptical inductive method seems to be one of the reasons why the Western hemisphere is, on the one hand, relatively sympathetic to Ghamidi's kind (for example, as evidenced by comparatively high levels of news and social media coverage of him and his followers) and, on the other, harshly critical of the same people who harshly criticize Ghamidi (Islamic traditionalists who do not view truth as needing adaptation based on scientific observation).

Scientific ideology

As the American biologist and science historian Steven Jay Gould says, science is more than just a method:

> Science, since people must do it, is a socially embedded activity. It progresses by hunch, vision, and intuition. Much of its change through time does not record a closer approach to absolute truth, but the alteration of cultural contexts that influence it so strongly. Facts are not pure and unsullied bits of information; culture also influences what we see and how we see it. Theories, moreover, are not inexorable inductions from facts. The most creative theories are often imaginative visions imposed upon facts; the source of imagination is also strongly cultural.
>
> (1996: 53–4)

In other words, science is a group/community ideology that demands ties to many spheres of influence and prioritizes not only a thirst for information (even though that information is human and imperfect) but also a desire for performance/adaptation of that information according to changing contexts. It should be emphasized that Ghamidi claims an epistemology that is 'scientific' not only in its method of scholarly accountability and credibility, but also in his vision of truth(s) – for example, religious truth(s) – as constantly in need of development: the informative process is a path to the divine.

He offers hope of getting the public attention with a convincing, effective ideology, based on a systematic, and thus ostensibly credible, method. In his turning away from the traditional role of the *'ulama'*, Ghamidi faces all the more pressure to fulfill this analytically sound role beyond reproach. It is therefore not surprising that this focus on informative and performative scientific knowledge is integrated into his ideology, "acknowledging himself as a student ... an obsessive personality who believes in continuous learning" (Zaidl 2009: 81). Further, Ghamidi cultivates an environment of information. His Al-Mawrid Institute, which awards fellowships "to established intellectuals ... accredited with academic work of original and seminal value" and develops collaborative projects, seeking to offer the "necessary environment to

The technology of tradition 213

facilitate the work of Fellows and scholars, which includes maintenance of library and provision of other requisite logistics" (Al-Mawrid, Institute of Islamic Sciences 2011). His dedicated, literary, and analytical method, the double hermeneutic interpretation of divine law – participatory/performative (in the sense that it relies on a context-dependent community network interpretation) – is the basis for an ideology intended to be for and of the Islamic network. Thus, to Ghamidi, the *umma*[22] must come together in a performative *ijma'* regarding religious knowledge.[23]

Rather than choosing to accept the *hadith*-based *fiqh* decisions relying on the *ijma* of the scholars and lawyers, Ghamidi seeks (through *ijma*) a performative, collaborative consensus of the scholarly community together with the popular community – an ongoing "scientific conferencing" of an Islamic *umma* that is (at least in theory) all-inclusive. He prefers *sunna* to *hadith* not just on the analytical level, but also on the ideological level. His analysis of *sunna* and how Islamic practice was carried out in the past speaks to his ideology and to the way that he handles the contemporary Pakistani Islamic community. In other words, just as *sunna* are those practices of Muhammad that were passed down via the Islamic community's agreement (*ijma'*) and their continual adherence (*tawatur*) to Muhammad's teachings (Iftikhar 2004: 66), so (to Ghamidi) must the *shari'a* discourse in the contemporary era involve a coherent, interactive community *ijma*, firmly planted in *tawatur*, firmly linked to the discourse of past networks of Islam. In turning away from the *'ulama'* and downplaying the role of their *fiqh* interpretation as what his website calls a "maze of sectarian prejudices and political wrangling" (Al-Mawrid, Institute of Islamic Sciences 2011), Ghamidi makes it clear that his is an ideology in which *fiqh* does not control *shari'a*, in which scholars and *fiqh* and political wrangling should not control the *umma*. Ultimately, in such a method as his, it appears that it is a priority for knowledge obtained in the past (Pakistani Muslim religious tradition) to live on and be an aid to the further performative development of knowledge about Pakistani socio-religious development – much like previous hypotheses leading to a more definitive but never completely provable theory. Tradition is taken scientifically, and as Gould would say, does not consist of "unsullied bits of information."

The need for the social integration of knowledge (as Gould so emphasizes) is similarly prioritized in Ghamidi's agenda. He portrays himself as a public-oriented community scholar, "producing results by taking people along" (Zaidl 2009: 81). He sees the role of the Islamic scholar as essential to the proper functioning of the Islamic *umma*, since he sees a false (or absent) understanding of Islam as leading to Islam's abuse. He looks to the Qur'an to maintain that Muslims must receive a well-rounded education in order to understand Allah and the religion of Islam to the fullest – the "unlearned" do not "submit (them)selves" (Qur'an 3.20). To him, *jihad*-lobbying groups pursue their behaviors because they are unlearned (Zaidl 2009: 80) – and as such, are not true Muslims:

214   *David A. Doss*

> [He] envisions the revival ... of the Muslim Ummah. The Holy Qur'an ...
> is (n)o longer ... resorted to for guidance toward moral reformation and
> intellectual development of the Ummah ... [T]he objectives of the Institute
> are to conduct and facilitate academic and research work on Islamic
> Sciences, to educate people on its basis and to publish and disseminate it
> through all available means.
>
> (Al-Mawrid, Institute of Islamic Sciences 2011)

Thus, while a scholar, his primary goal seems to be the maximization of access to information, and the ability to perform (that is, create, develop, or act) based on that information – as tied to the revival of Islam as a force of scientifically oriented force knowledge encompassing all aspects of life.

This knowledge-is-power approach is, in a sense, a non-political approach to politics – an approach that, though admittedly deeply involved with politics, takes political action out of the legal sphere and into the social sphere. In other words, he views religion as an all-encompassing community. Particularly relevant for the purposes of this discussion, this conception of the community's scope includes the realms of both science and of politics. In this community approach, power is equivalent to encouraging the internalization of values of self-education. The goal of this scholarly education-activism is apparently to help the people to formulate the *shari'a* law and government. This is the community's "public mandate and continues to exist as long as it commands the support of the majority" (Ghamidi 2005: 2). In this sense, Ghamidi's is an ideology of ethics: "moral reformation and intellectual development of the Ummah" are necessary in order for this community to make its own ethical, *shari'a*-based decisions (Al-Mawrid, Institute of Islamic Sciences 2011). As would follow from his above-mentioned differentiation of *fiqh* and *shari'a*, the Ghamidian community ideal is one that democratically controls *shari'a*, reducing the legal *fiqh* aspects of it, and increasing its social ethics aspect of personal and communal responsibility and decision. Iftikhar describes Ghamidi's ideology: "ethical foundations ... and guidelines for ... personal and social life in relation to ... submission to God ... aim at purification ... to become true servants of God ... This excellence, not any Islamic global order, is the pinnacle of a Muslim's faith and religion" (2004: 78).

So it is exactly because of ethics that he finds the systematic pursuit and development of knowledge to be so important: it is the basis of the individual, and thus of the *umma*.[24] He sees his 'religious science' as capable of planting the seeds of this "excellence" in individuals, encouraging ethics – in Islam, ethics involves behaviors showing to Allah that the human being is his true servant. As Ghamidi himself says:

> [An] important requirement of religion is purification of morals ... [A]
> person should cleanse his attitude both towards his creator and towards
> his fellow human beings ... a righteous deed. All the *shari'ah* is its

The technology of tradition   215

corollary ... the *shari'ah* has indeed changed; however, faith and righteous deeds ... the foundations of religion, have not undergone any change.

(Ghamidi 2011b)

Thus, in this view, *information* shapes individual excellence and ethics, and individuals in turn form the *umma*'s development of *shari'a*-based social ethics by their *performance* of ethical knowledge (Mufti 2007). This inductive-scientific ideology makes *shari'a* the *umma*'s social responsibility toward dialogue on ethical action (a bottom-up approach) rather than a set of laws that the state independently enacts and controls (a top-down approach).

This Ghamidian ideological strategy of development exclusively from the starting point of well-understood tradition is ultimately one that regards Pakistani Islam as a living community – an unbroken network from past to present, from decision to decision. In his view, Islamist fundamentalism that lobbies *jihad* errs due to its misinterpretation and glorification of a misunderstood past, disrupting this past–present network rather than returning to it. Thus from an interactive, network-approached scientific ideology and method, Ghamidi professes a striving towards a fundamental, intertextual, and thus network-oriented ideology of a democratic *umma*.

Such an ideology, in short, is one that fuses religious tradition not just with a scientific methodology (as examined in the previous subsection) but also with science-based technology – joining and highlighting what the two have in common. A message that is constructed on the expectation of accountability with respect to an ever-developing informative and performative network is one that appears in most ways true not only to the spirit of Islamic religious tradition, but also to the spirit of post-Renaissance and post-Enlightenment scientific thinking and methods (as well as to the spirit of the Information Age).

Network and social media technologies

The recently developing technical- and media-driven socio-religious renaissance in Pakistan is much like the philosophical and technological "Islamic Renaissance" that preceded the European one, in that technology is intimately tied to a scientific method and ideology (Ullmann 1979; Gutas 1998). In other words, it was a scientific method and ideology (the intellectual culture) just as much if not more than the *resulting* technological products (the physical culture) that spurred the Islamic Renaissance, which in fact led to the European one. Similarly, a politically and socially religious movement of any significant sophistication is also quite likely to have its own (religiously and socially oriented) scientific method (and ultimately ideology) that will back up (and in fact drive) its use of science and technology.

Inductive-scientific method and ideology mirror not only technology but also that technology's use and development. This means that contemporary

216 *David A. Doss*

epistemological and physical culture are in a feedback loop with each other. Scientific methods are ultimately supposed to effect practical results. Technology – connected with the concept of the representation and physical embodiment of techniques in a use or product, particularly in the form of network connections and social media application (Harper 2001b) – is thus understandably just as much a part of Ghamidi's self-professed priorities as the scientific ideology and method that he turns toward social/religious/political issues of ethics.

Ghamidi heavily relies on technologies – particularly media and social network technologies – to reach out to this Islamic *umma*. He relies primarily on electronic media for his educational mission. The objectives of his Institute, as stated above: "are to conduct and facilitate academic and research work on Islamic Sciences, to educate people on its basis, and to publish and disseminate it through all available means" (Al-Mawrid, Institute of Islamic Sciences 2011). Ghamidi and the Al-Mawrid Institute do indeed use nearly every available means imaginable. As mentioned, Pakistan is undergoing a media-based social revolution, in which "new popular Islamic religious leaders have been able to spread their influence to groups previously alienated by more traditional religious authorities, particularly the middle classes and educated women" (Ahmad 2010: 2). Ghamidi is just such a new religious leader and is taking full part in this media revolution. Those who follow his work are primarily "educated, urban-based, middle-class men between the ages of 20–35" as well as educated women, yet his television audience also "includes not only modern educated youth but also lay Islamic intellectuals and professionals" (ibid.: 5) in Pakistan and worldwide, who are aware of issues in contemporary Islam (especially Islamic controversies relating to the nature and implementation of *shari'a*), and view him as a moderate, since they are dissatisfied with the stance not only of the traditional *'ulama'* but also of the secular and the Western-educated classes that form the Pakistani elite.

This relationship of the popular intellectual religious leader to an electronic media audience is one in which the religious authority is slipping out of the hands of the *'ulama'*. In discussing Islam's relationship with contemporary issues, he uses contemporary media. As one news article says:

> The popular media gravitates to him for his impeccable oratory and the ease with which he makes common sense out of millennium-old religious texts. Of late he has become a bit of a rock star – adored, hated, popular, and notorious all at once.
>
> (Mufti 2007)

This demonstrates that he is making headlines in the press, for example, in the *Boston Globe*, the *Chronicle*, and *BBC News*. He frequently makes appearances on various television channels. Television and radio interviews, lectures, and debates are a key strategy in bringing his views into line with

Pakistani middle-class socio-cultural practices. He makes regular appearances on government-operated and independent television channels, such as GEO (including the interactive talk show *Ghamidi*[25] and several airings of the talk and contest show *Alif*), ARY, AAJ News (the question-and-answer show *Live with Ghamidi*, and other programs) Duniya News, and PTV (Pakistan Television Corporation) (Zaidl 2009: 80; Ahmad 2010: 3). Granted, several of these were cancelled due to the opposition of various traditional *'ulama'* (Mufti 2007). One of his websites[26] includes audio and video lectures from television and radio appearances as well, all from Al-Mawrid's own video recording system,[27] and the Institute publishes his work and that of his associates on audio and video cassettes, CDs, and DVDs (Al-Mawrid, Institute of Islamic Sciences 2011).

In addition to the education that he and his associates offer through courses, seminars and workshops on Islam, and to the training of "fresh apprentices, assistants, and scholars for the planned projects," he takes advantage of the Internet to create live online lectures and online distance-learning courses (ibid.). His social mission, one of developing social ethics, relies on the Internet and its social media. In addition to his numerous books and articles (most of which are available online for free), and sources on him (mostly available through the Internet), he is the Chief Editor of the Urdu monthly magazine, *Ishraq*, and the English monthly magazine, *Renaissance*,[28] both organized through his Al-Mawrid Institute, and both available online for free.[29] His has numerous affiliated websites.[30] In several of these, one can find links to his Facebook and Twitter pages.[31] Also, there is an immense number of clips from his television appearances available on YouTube, for example, on his personal channel.[32] In terms of the technology, the movement is as contemporary as can be.[33]

Ghamidi and his associates seek not only the "clearest manner" of analysis (Al-Mawrid, Institute of Islamic Sciences 2011), but also the "clearest manner" of presentation. As mentioned at the beginning of this subsection, this form of religious revival based on technological (media and social network) mobilization is intricately connected to the scientific nature of the method and ideology. Mobilization of technology not only fuels his intellectual work and his ideology, but also mirrors them. As Foucault says, "[K]nowledge is not made for understanding; it is made for cutting" (1984: 88). It is exactly this power to use scientific method and technological application (to maximize the potential to cut to the heart of ethical issues) that Ghamidi attempts to take from the Qur'an via a networked, hermeneutic interpretation based on group considerations and context, shared through the network of the *'ulama'* in electronic media networks.

One of the main goals of religion is to create a network of ideological, symbolic, social and physical devices promoting an individual and group awareness of belonging to a meaning synchronically and diachronically surpassing this individual or group (Hervieu-Léger 2000: 103–4). Technological ideologies and structures (especially, social media platforms), inasmuch as

218 *David A. Doss*

they share this same priority of interconnection spurred by preservation of information (tradition) and creative performance of new information that is spurred by the past information (development), are useful tools (literally/physically and metaphorically/ideologically) for such an endeavor.

It is not only religious ideology and apparatus but also scientific/technological ideology and apparatus that drive this Ghamidian vision of contemporary Islam in Pakistan. Such a vision is one that seeks to place religious power within an expanded realm of developing issues and inventions based on a prioritization of technologically oriented methodology and strategies. Such a maximization of a developed and transformed religious influence can be seen in the case of Ghamidi's involvement with Pakistani women's rights issues.

Implications of sociotechnological information and performance in relation to a *shari'a* of human rights

Through his extensive use of this electronic media, Ghamidi has been addressing the public on his ideas of *shari'a* ethics and their relationship to women's rights issues currently debated in Pakistan. Ghamidi and his followers have been employing scientific methodology and ideology, coupled with network and social media technologies, to shape and alter religiously oriented societal information on and performance of ethical issues that include women's rights, and human rights in general. This activity is related not only to their advocating in relation to the Pakistan's Women's Protection Bill, but also in relation to others extending beyond this range.

As mentioned, educated women form a significant part of Ghamidi's audience (Ahmad 2010: 4) – with good reason. In his analysis of the Qur'an, Ghamidi asserts through public media the right for women to have equal status as witnesses in court – and further, to lead public prayer, to own property, hold public office, etc. ('A Misreported Interview' 2005). These assertions testify to his view of the *umma* as majority (not just of men, but of women, which is, to say the least, not the most common position for a respected socio-religious leader in Pakistan). Ghamidi's vision of Pakistan is a society that should be "based on the vote of the majority" – the totality of Muslims functioning together as a network (ibid.). He sees the *'ulama'* as the source of *shari'a*, and therefore as needing to be educated on the true meaning of Qur'anic injunctions (which, according to his analytical method, exclude the need for several relatively common practices in Pakistan, such as stoning women as punishment for adultery, requiring women to cover every single part of their bodies, or preventing women from owning property and participating in public life, for example, testifying in court).[34]

In other words, it is ultimately on a Qur'anic basis that Ghamidi challenges the terminology and interpretations of Pakistani religious-civil laws such as the Hudud Ordinances on stoning. He attacks them as un-Islamic, arguing that they actually go against the Qur'an. In 2006, he began to participate in the

The technology of tradition 219

Council of Islamic Ideology (CII) (Mufti 2007), "a constitutional body that advises the legislature whether or not a certain law is repugnant to Islam, namely to the Qur'an and Sunna" (Council of Islamic Ideology: Government of Pakistan 2011). This is one of many ways in which Ghamidi reaches out into the socio-political sphere.

Not only this strong desire to bring about social change (through methodological pursuit of religious information that is questioning of the status quo), but also this use of social media technologies (to maximize the participatory performance of contemporary Pakistani Islam) seems to display bright prospects for the further development of a human rights discourse within Pakistani society. Yet it nonetheless appears that his scientific-like ideology and method of Qur'anic investigation, coupled with the maximizing power of technology, are ultimately used to optimize the reach of a primeval religious conception of an all-encompassing sphere of Islamic influence, rejecting the conception of religion as being confined to a specific sphere. In other words, the inductive approaches of science (gathering information from all usable sources in all usable environments) and technology (maximizing the performative potential of that knowledge across as many demographics as possible) are here used to make Islam be what many people argue Muhammad originally conceived it as – not a religion, but an all-encompassing social force that does not take into account the idea of secularization (thought in such Muslim circles to be merely Western/Christian remedy to Western/Christian social problems) (see Lewis and Churchill 2009). The implications of this will be explored in the following section.

While Ghamidi's movement at base claims a search for truth and ethics, it looks for them exclusively within the context of an Islamic community, aiming for a *shari'a* based solely on the authority of the Qur'an and of the *umma*. As he says, "Muslims cannot enact any law in their country which is contrary to the Qur'an and Sunnah or without taking into consideration the guidance these sources provide" (Ghamidi 2005: 7). He further maintains:

> Secularism for the West emerged as a reaction from the theocratic environment imposed by the Christian church. Since Muslims do not have the theocratic environment, there was never a need to rebel against ... religion in that manner. Secondly, Islam is pure democracy. The majority's say in society has more significance. Thus if a people want religious laws, they are welcome to do so through a legislative process.
>
> ('A Misreported Interview' 2005)

Thus, even though Ghamidi affirms gender equality and political equality, he does at base rejects the separation of Church and State, seeing the movement of religion out of the public sphere as a necessity only in the West.

A possible bone of contention is this very emphasis he places on the democratic majority of the *umma*. He seems to understand democracy as "majority rule." In this understanding of democracy, the Ghamidian system

220   *David A. Doss*

will work, as long as the majority is Islamic. Yet if democracy is to be a system in which all people have an equal say in decisions that affect their lives (rather than the majority having the say on decisions that affect all of the people's lives), it cannot survive on the basis of a purely Ghamidian system. Civil disobedience, or freedom of conscience, would be limited since he maintains, "Muslims must fully cling to state authority in all circumstances" (Ghamidi 2005: 7). So the truth, the ethics, and the laws must remain what the majority holds to be true. In contrast, the United Nation's understanding of democracy, and thus of social ethics and of human rights, is one that includes the minority, and that protects the rights of the minority ('Multi-ethnic States and the Protection of Minority Rights' 2011). While women – not a minority – are protected within a Ghamidian framework that improves social and sexual ethics and thus the status of women, minorities such as homosexuals are not protected in it, but rather are to be punished ('A Misreported Interview' 2005). This practice of majority rule is equivalent to using a large body of evidence – for example, observing 100 brown birds in a forest – to draw a conclusion that is too general, for example, that all birds in the forest must be brown. The difference is that the potentially generalizing ethical system in question involves potentially serious harm to human lives.

Such potential for harm due to inductive fallacy, which can also be a danger of a scientifically oriented method, also includes the possibility of leading to several unfortunate effects. Ghamidi rejects all Qur'anic readings except the most generally accepted one, and wishes this majority reading to dictate behavior, ethics, and laws. Yet in Pakistan, even though the majority of the society is Muslim, as many as 20 percent of these Muslims are Shiite ('How Many Shia Are There in The World?' 2011). It is questionable whether non-Muslims or Shiites are properly represented if the Sunni majority has control. Such a Ghamidian conception would almost certainly fail outside of Pakistan in a pluralistic society with no clear majority religious interests and with a wider variety of competing cultures, competing priorities, values, and ethics. Yet in the former examples, we can see elements in which it could also even be problematic in a Muslim majority society such as Pakistan, even for a substantial minority of Muslims.

Conclusion

In his ideology, Ghamidi is searching for a greater coherence and inclusiveness than he perceives either in the traditionalist Islamist context or in Western society. His is a philosophy that seeks to avoid not only compartmentalizing religion into obscurity but also the pitfall of holding on to traditionalism or past religion. His stance on the ethical treatment of women in Pakistani culture is part of a *shari'a*-based social ethics system, and an agenda that is both thorough and logically structured. Through a non-political, media- and education-based strategy, Ghamidi has been seeking to change the Pakistani public opinion, and to influence the community. In so doing, he has found a

The technology of tradition   221

way to engage them on important issues of religion and social ethics. His system deals a solid blow to the Islamist traditionalism of many of the *'ulama'*.

Nonetheless, the implications of a Ghamidian ideology are not likely to include the secularization of religious power through the curtailing influence of scientific method/ideology and through the extensive use of technology. Rather, they are more likely to include an increasing control of Islam over society and politics via this same scientific method/ideology and through the extensive use of technology. His community-based informative and performative priorities seem to avoid politicizing Islam or using religion as a tool for political purposes, instead seeking to promote a social and legal flexibility by rejecting a top-down approach to laws and social ethics. Yet the system embodying these priorities is in danger of remaining in favor of Islamizing politics, and thus of keeping society, government, and ethics in the control of the religious majority. Further, such a system fails to provide a confident answer to the question of whether Ghamidi's conception of a majority-decided, community-decided *shari'a* is compatible with international conceptions of human rights.

On a more positive note, it should be reiterated that Ghamidi seeks to face the inevitability of interplay between ideology and technology, between medium and message. In doing so, he begins to address issues such as those of ancient vs. modern, of East vs. West – even if he does not give definitive resolution to such issues. Further, as mentioned before, Ghamidi is one of many new religious leaders employing similar media and messages. While the details of each social media preacher may vary, the ideal of a plurality of participation put forth by new religious leaders such as Ghamidi (using web-based media with open access for all) stands strongly in contrast to the restriction and guarding of religious knowledge by such groups as the (often) traditionalist Pakistani *'ulama'*. These new ideological and technological strategies, in comparison to those of preceding (more traditionalist) generations, are more conducive to a tolerant form of Islam that could encourage social equality, inasmuch as the strategies are of a participatory nature and involve non-exclusive control over religious truth and religious authority. In such a blend of scientific method/ideology and maximizing technological application, religious authority nevertheless remains an encompassing power that attempts a complete (or near-complete) *relevance* to all aspects of Pakistani life, and thus represents a continued potential for Islam to *dominate* all aspects of Pakistani life.

Thus, beginning to blossom in Pakistan is a discourse, of which Ghamidi is only a part, though granted, a significant one. This discourse gives hope for a more effective blend of the performative and informative aspects of Pakistani Islam, involving a striving to develop yet also preserve in a changing and conflict-ridden religious environment, and offering the potential of moving toward a more equalizing, network-based community. For better or worse, a more maximized yet more functional Islamic religious power in Pakistani politics and society, driven by an adaptive scientific investigatory method and ideology, and by changing network and media technologies.

Notes

1 "Community of trained of Muslim scholars" (Glassé and Smith 2003: 461). Note: an attempt is made to explain all Arabic terms in the notes, for the sake of continuity and brevity.
2 Islamic law. Note: due to the wide variety of systems used to transliterate words from Arabic into English, a variety of spellings for one Arabic word may be found in this chapter, though every effort towards consistency has been made. For example, though this chapter uses the transliteration "*shari'a*," this word may be spelled as "sharia," "Shari'ah," etc. in quotes from other authors.
3 That is, fundamentalist movement for the political unification of Muslims and the integration of Islam and politics.
4 Sedition or rebellion, a sign of the impending Day of Judgment (Glassé and Smith 2003: 142).
5 For a list of examples, see www.al-mawrid.org/pages/download_books.php.
6 "Academic Degree in Islamic law and jurisprudence" (Glassé and Smith 2003: 208).
7 Member of the *'ulama'* (ibid.: 461).
8 A "Center of Islamic higher education" (ibid.: 278).
9 Sinful or spiritually harmful innovation (ibid.: 87).
10 The tendency to make tradition the supreme criterion and rule of assurance.
11 A person who, in seeking to "facilitate interpretations consistent with the demands of modern society" fuses Western secularism with Islamic spirituality; see Rahman (2005: 4).
12 Consider standard definitions of science (for example, Harper 2001a). This idea is also related to the informative and performative treatments of religious information. See Introduction to this chapter, as well as Hervieu-Léger (2000).
13 Pbuh: 'peace be upon him' (a traditional pious practice when mentioning the name of the Prophet Muhammad).
14 Indicating structural and thematic coherence in Urdu poetry.
15 A chapter of the Qur'an.
16 Contradiction.
17 Muslim community (Glassé and Smith 2003: 236).
18 The practices of Muhammad and of Islam (ibid.: 441).
19 Traditions related to Muhammad's sayings and deeds, as handed down by his followers (ibid.: 159).
20 Islamic canon law jurists (ibid.: 327).
21 Laws practiced by Muslims (ibid.: 141).
22 Community network of believers, transcending national/ethnic definition, for which Islam encompasses all aspects of life (ibid.: 464).
23 Community consensus on *shari'a* (ibid.: 208).
24 Cf. the Islamic concepts of *akhlaq*, the practice of virtue, morality and manners, and *adab*, referring to refinement, morals, decency, and humaneness, and how these concepts are formative of the normative order.
25 *Ghamidi, Geo Television Network.*
26 Useful examples are available at: www.tv-almawrid.org.
27 See www.al-mawrid.org/pages/audio_video.php.
28 Other resources are also available in Arabic. See Al-Mawrid, Institute of Islamic Sciences (2011).
29 Note: Ghamidi himself does not usually write or speak publicly in English, but his associates have translated the overwhelming majority of his work into English. See Ahmad (2010: 3).
30 See www.javedahmadghamidi.com, www.monthly-renaissance.com, and www.al-mawrid.org. See www.al-mawrid.org/pages/channelsandaffiliates.php for a complete list of affiliated websites.

31 See www.facebook.com/JavedGhamidi and a few dozen other, smaller groups, plus www.twitter.com/JavedGhamidi.
32 See www.youtube.com/user/javedghamidi.
33 Compare Ghamidi's tactics to that of Yusuf al-Qaradawi's global youth movement and its large-scale implementation of social media. See Gräf and Skovgaard-Petersen (2009) *The Global Mufti: The Phenomenon of Yusuf al-Qaradawi*.
34 There is much to be read on these issues. For example, Faruki (1983); Amjad (2000); Mydans (2002); Ghamidi (2004, 2005, 2011a); 'A Misreported Interview' (2005); Hasan (2006); Protection of Women (Criminal Laws Amendment) Act 2006; Usmani (2006): 287–96; 'A Victory for Pakistani Women' 2006; Masud (2007); Mufti (2007); Hassan (2009); Aziz (2011); Council of Islamic Ideology: Government of Pakistan (2011); Hashmi (2011). Some of Ghamidi's positions on these topics are expressed in more detail in Iftikhar (2004). See also the work of the Human Rights Commission of Pakistan and their website: www.hrcp-web.org/default.asp.

References

Ahmad, M. (2010) 'Media-Based Preachers and the Creation of New Muslim Publics in Pakistan.' Available at: www.nbr.org/publications/element.aspx?id=421 (accessed 11 August, 2011).

Al-Mawrid, Institute of Islamic Sciences (2011) *Renaissance*. Online. Available at: www.renaissance.com.pk/intro.html (accessed 14 August 2011).

'Al-Mawrid will forgive Hassan's attackers.' (2006) *Daily Times*, August 28, p. 7. Available at: www.dailytimes.com.pk/default.asp?page=2006/08/28/story_28–8–2006_pg7_33 (accessed 14 August 2011).

'A Misreported Interview.' (2005) *Understanding Islam*, June 21. Available at: www.understanding-islam.com/articles/miscellaneous-issues/a-misreported-interview-239 (accessed 9 August 2011).

Amjad, M. (2000) *Punishment of Rajam* (i.e. Stoning to Death in Case of Adultery). Online. Available at: www.understanding-islam.com/ (accessed 14 August 2011).

Assmann, J. (2006) *Religion and Cultural Memory*, trans. R. Livingstone. Stanford, CA: Stanford University Press.

Association of Muslim Social Scientists. *Annual Conference: Muslims and Islam in the Chaotic Modern World: Relations of Muslims among Themselves and with Others.* Online. Available at: www.amss.net/pdfs/34/finalpapers/HabeebRahmanIbramsa.pdf (accessed 21 August 2011).

'A Victory for Pakistani Women.' (2006) *The Washington Times*, 2 August. Available at: www.washingtontimes.com/news/2006/aug/2/20060802-095409-1513r/ (accessed 18 August 2011).

Aziz, S. (2011) 'Making a Sovereign State: Javed Ghamidi and 'Enlightened Moderation,' *Modern Asian Studies*, 45(3): 597–629. Cambridge: Cambridge University Press.

Council of Islamic Ideology: Government of Pakistan. (2011) 'Homepage.' Available at: www.cii.gov.pk/ (accessed 23 August 2011).

'Dr. Farooq: an academic silenced by the Taliban.' (2010) *Channel 4*, October 7. Available at: http://blogs.channel4.com (accessed 14 August 2011).

Faruki, K.A. (1983) "The Islamic Resurgence: Prospects and Implications," in J.L. Esposito (ed.) *Voices of Resurgent Islam*. Oxford: Oxford University Press, pp. 277–91.

224 David A. Doss

'Fitna of Javed Ahmad Ghamidi.' (2006) *Sunni Forum*, June 25. Available at: www. sunniforum.com. (accessed 17 August 2011).

Foucault, M. (1984) "Nietzsche, Genealogy, History," in P. Rabinow (ed.) *The Foucault Reader*. New York: Pantheon.

Ghamidi, J.A. (2004) *The Penal Shari'ah of Islam*, trans. S. Salim. Lahore: Al-Mawrid. Online. Available at: www.renaissance.com.pk/The%20Penal%20Shari'ah%20of% 20Islam.pdf (accessed 19 August 2011).

Ghamidi, J.A. (2005) *The Political Shari'ah of Islam*, trans. S. Salim. Lahore: Al-Mawrid. Online. Available at: www.renaissance.com.pk/The%20Political%20Shari'ah%20of% 20Islam.pdf (accessed 18 August 2011).

Ghamidi, J.A. (2009) *The Fundamentals of Understanding Islam*. Online. Available at: www.javedahmadghamidi.com/index.php/renaissance/view/fundamentals-of-under standing-islam (accessed 12 August 2011).

Ghamidi (Television program) (2011) *Geo Television Network*. Available at: www.geo. tv/geonews/program.asp?pid=530 (accessed 12 August 2011).

Ghamidi, J.A. (2011a) *Etiquette of Sexual Intimacy*, trans. S. Saleem. Online. Available at: www.renaissance.com.pk/JulIslaw2y3.html (accessed 21 August 2011).

Ghamidi, J.A. (2011b) *Morals and Morality: The Religion of Islam*, trans. S. Saleem. Online. Available at: www.monthly-renaissance.com/issue/content.aspx?id=949 (accessed 7 August 2011).

Ghamidi, J.A. (2011c) *Principles of Understanding the Hadith*, trans. S. Saleem. Online. Available at: www.renaissance.com.pk/JulHadi2y6.htm (accessed 15 August 2011).

Glassé, C. and Smith, H. (2003) *The New Encyclopedia of Islam: A Revised Edition of the Concise Encyclopedia of Islam*. Walnut Creek, CA: Rowman/Altamira.

Gould, S.J. (1996) *The Mismeasure of Man*. New York: Norton.

Gräf and Skovgaard-Petersen (2009) *The Global Mufti: The Phenomenon of Yusuf al-Qaradawi*.

Gutas, D. (1998) *Greek Thought, Arabic Culture: The Graeco-Arabic Translation Movement in Baghdad and Early 'Abbasaid Society (2nd-4th/5th-10th c.)*. London: Routledge.

Harper, D. (2001a) 'Science,' in *Online Etymological Dictionary*. Online. Available at: www.etymonline.com/?term=science (accessed 25 August 2011).

Harper, D. (2001b) 'Technology,' in *Online Etymological Dictionary*. Online. Available at: www.etymonline.com/index.php?term=technology (accessed 21 August 2011).

Hashmi, T.M. (2011) 'Punishment of Rajam and the Qur'an.' Available at: www.al mawrid.org/ (accessed 21 August 2011).

Hasan, S.S. (2006) 'Strong feelings over Pakistan rape laws,' *BBS News*, November 15. Available at: news.bbc.co.uk/2/hi/south_asia/6152520.stm (accessed 23 August 2011).

Hassan, R. (2009) 'Islamic Modernist and Reformist Discourse in South Asia,' in S. Hunter (ed.) *Reformist Voices of Islam: Mediating Islam and Modernity*. New York: Sharpe, pp. 159–86.

Hervieu-Léger, D. (2000) *Religion as a Chain of Memory*, trans. S. Lee. Cambridge: Polity Press.

'How Many Shia Are There in The World?' (2011) *Islamic Web*. Available at: http:// islamicweb.com/beliefs/cults/shia_population.htm (accessed 25 August 2011).

Ibn Ishaq (2011) *Sirat Rasulullah*, trans. A. Guillaume. Online. Available at: http:// answering-islam.org/Index/A/adultery.html (accessed 24 August 2011).

The technology of tradition 225

Iftikhar, A. (2004) '*Jihad* and the Establishment of Islamic Global Order: A Comparative Study of the Worldviews and Interpretative Approaches of Abu al-A'la Mawdudi and Javed Ahmad Ghamidi,' Master's thesis. Institute of Islamic Studies at McGill University, Canada.

International Crisis Group (2005) 'Understanding Islamism,' *Middle East/North Africa Report*, March 2, 37. Online. Available at: http://merln.ndu.edu/archive/icg/Islamism 2Mar05.pdf (accessed 20 August 2011).

Islahi, A.A. (2011) 'Difference Between Hadith and Sunnah,' trans. S.A. Rauf. Online. Available at: www.renaissance.com.pk/jafelif986.html (accessed 13 August 2011).

'Islamic Scholar Attacks Pakistan's Blasphemy Laws' (2011) *The Guardian*, January 1. Available at: www.guardian.co.uk/world/2011/jan/20/islam-ghamidi-pakistan-blas phemy-laws (accessed 18 August 2011).

Khan, S. (2006) 'Attempted Murder of Ghamidi's Magazine Editor: Cops Say Street Crime, Others Disagree,' *Daily Times*, August 25, p. 1. Available at: www.dailytimes. com.pk/default.asp?page=2006%5C08%5C25%5Cstory_25-8-2006_pg1_3 (accessed 9 August 2011).

Lewis, B. and Churchill, B.E. (2009) *Islam, the Religion and the People*. Upper Saddle River, NJ: Wharton School Publishing.

Masud, M.K. (2007) "Rethinking Shari'a: Javed Ahmad Ghamidi on Hudud," *Die Welt des Islams*, 47(3–4): 356–75.

Mufti, S. (2007) 'The Fundamentalist Moderate,' *The Boston Globe*, July 22. Available at: www.boston.com/news/globe/ideas/articles/2007/07/22/the_fundamentalist_mode rate/ (accessed 8 August 2011).

'Multi-ethnic States and the Protection of Minority Rights' (2011) Paper presented at World Conference against Racism. Online. Available at: www.un.org/WCAR/e-kit/ minority.htm (accessed 24 August 2011).

Mydans, S. (2002) 'In Pakistan, Rape Victims Are the "Criminals",' *The New York Times*, May 17. Available at: www.nytimes.com/2002/05/17/world/in-paki stan-rape-victims-are-the-criminals.html?pagewanted=all (accessed 24 August 2011).

Protection of Women (Criminal Laws Amendment) Act (2006) *Pakistani.org*, December 1. Available at: www.pakistani.org/pakistan/legislation/2006/wpb.html (accessed 27 August 2011).

Rahman, H. (2005) 'Muslim Modernists and New Hermeneutic Approach to the Prophetic Tradition: Special Reference to the Injunction of Sariqah and Hirabah,' *AMSS 34th*.

Research Team at Al-Mawrid: Javed Ahmad Ghamidi (2008) *Al-Mawrid: A Foundation for Islamic Research*. Online. Available at: www.al-mawrid.org/pages/research_ detail.php?research_id=5 (accessed 18 August 2011).

Roggio, B. (2007) 'The Battle at the Red Mosque,' *The Long War Journal: A Project of the Foundation for the Defense of Democracies*. July 5. Available at: www.long warjournal.org/archives/2007/07/the_battle_at_the_re.php#comments (accessed 10 August 2011).

Ullmann, M. (1979) *Islamic Medicine*. Edinburgh: Edinburgh University Press.

Usmani, M.T. (2006) 'The Islamization of Laws in Pakistan: The Case of Hudud Ordinance,' *The Muslim World*, 96: 287–304. Online. Available at: www. globalwebpost.com/farooqm/study_res/islam/fiqh/usmani_hudud.pdf (accessed 21 August 2011).

Zaidl, E. (2009) 'Spiritual Leaders: Javed Ghamidi,' in J. Laghari (ed.) *Leaders of Pakistan*, vol. 1, 78–85. Online. Available at: www.szabist.edu.pk/Publications/Books/LeadershipBK-CP-09.pdf (accessed 2 September 2011).

Zamman, M.Q. (2011) 'Pakistan: Sharia and the State,' in R. Hefner (ed.) *Sharia Politics: Islamic Law and Society in the Modern World.* Bloomington, IN: Indiana University, pp. 207–43.

12 New technologies and new funeral practices in contemporary Japan[1]

Fabienne Duteil-Ogata

Introduction

Since the 1990s, new technologies have spurred true revolutions in the field of funerals in Japan. The first technological revolution I will examine deals with the new cremation process, which reduces the human corpse to ashes. New cremation processes afford new forms of burial places for funerary objects. In fact, businessmen and NPOs (non-profit organizations) have created new objects called *temoto kuyôhin* 手元供養品 ("close-at-hand funerary items"). They are composed of ashes reduced to powder and constitute new forms of funerary objects, such as memorial diamonds. Other processes consist in mixing human ashes with other substances like metal to create hybrid objects in ceramics or crystal.

The second revolution that occurred in Japanese funerals is directly related to the new process of cremation and deals with the use of digital technology. In fact, with the high temperature involved in the cremation process, which reaches up to 1000°C, all traces of DNA disappear. This is the reason why Matsushima Nyokai, a Buddhist monk, tried to find a solution to recreate the identity of the deceased person by using digital technology through the database system. He invented the grave-computer and the online-grave.

After a quick overview of Japanese traditional funeral practices from a historical perspective, I will illustrate the context in which such new practices arose. I will closely examine the following questions: How do technologies influence Buddhist practices and ancestor worship? How do they change the predominant representation of death in the examined societies? Can technology change religion? Do new technologies announce the end of Buddhism's monopoly on funerals in Japan? Is technology a new religion in itself?

Traditional Japanese funeral practices: Buddhism and cremation

In contemporary Japan, funerals are obviously associated with Buddhism and cremation. In fact, nowadays, 99.8 percent of the Japanese are cremated (Yoshiyuki 2006: 73) and the majority of them follow traditional Buddhist funeral practices.[2] How were funerals initially associated with Buddhism in

228 *Fabienne Duteil-Ogata*

Japan and how did the technology of cremation arise and become the main technology process for the treatment of corpses?

First of all, I will provide a brief introduction to the Japanese religious system in order to elucidate the key role played by institutionalized Buddhism in Japanese funerals. Currently, Japanese popular religion is a secular syncretism that merges the religions of Shinto and Buddhism with Confucianist and Taoist thought. While Buddhism and Shinto are established as historical religions, Confucianism and Taoism remain merely schools of thought. However, nowadays, the diversity of religious practices and beliefs through the ages provides a consistent and more or less unified religious world-view. Although Japanese people are involved in both Shinto and Buddhist institutions in different ways, they tend to share a basic religious framework. In fact, many are members of local Shinto shrines in their particular regions (every region in Japan is protected by a Shinto deity *kami* enshrined in a Shinto shrine), and many also belong through their families to the Buddhist (household) temple where they worship their ancestors through a patrilineal affiliation.

The main concept of the syncretic Japanese religion deals with purity and impurity, associated with vital forces. Popular Japanese religion considers that all beings, deities, living things such as natural elements, animals or human beings, and inanimate objects, embody a vital force named *tama* and fall into the category of purity. But little by little, through the process of time or due to natural or social disasters or even physiological states (menstruation, illness, pregnancy, death), human beings, like other beings, including the deities and objects mentioned above, lose their *tama* and become impure, polluted *kegare*.[3] To manage the decline of the vital forces and restore purity, the Japanese rely on rituals to revitalize the *tama*. I would say that, in essence, the Shinto religion is mainly involved in these rituals during the individual's lifetime, while Buddhism provides a framework to perform funerals and postmortem rituals. However, both participate equally in the same project, which aims to restore order to the purity of beings that have degenerated into an impure state.

The death and post-death processes follow different steps: the first process implies cleaning the being of the extreme impurity of death (through the funeral), while the second process involves purifying the family member, whereby, through postmortem rituals of ancestor worship, the family member becomes an ancestor. It takes roughly 33 to 50 years (depending on the doctrines of the various Buddhist sects), and requires at least more than one generation to purify the death of a family member. It is through this last process (the last postmortem ritual) that the final step is achieved: an ancestor surmounts their status as a dead person and becomes a protective local deity, a Shinto *kami*. This process exemplifies the syncretism that characterizes this Japanese religion, and the important role played by rituals in the transformation of entities, whether human or otherwise, from an impure into a pure state, and thus in the elevation of deceased human beings belonging to the Buddhist sphere to the status of a Shinto *kami* (Yanagita 1970: 193).

As mentioned earlier, in Japan, funerals and postmortem rituals are the duty of the Buddhist institution, which means that the majority of the Japanese are parishioners of their local Buddhist temple. The reason why Buddhism was directly related to the treatment of deceased dates back to Edo period (1603–1868) when the Tokugawa Shoguns legally decided to delegate the task of constituting registers of the whole population to Buddhist temples all over Japan, and requested that every household be affiliated with a local Buddhist temple. The first of these orders was promulgated in 1638 and it compelled every Japanese household to register with a local Buddhist temple, and thereby to obtain a certificate of affiliation, called a *terauke shômon* (Tamamuro 1997). This certificate was used during the Edo Period as a verification of people's disassociation from Christianity, a prohibited religion at the time. Essentially, it ensured that every household was bound to a local Buddhist temple. A second order issued in 1671 required that Japanese households declare their dead to their local Buddhist temple and then proceed to hold a Buddhist funeral. In those days, just a few families could afford Buddhist funerals, but the orders of the Tokugawa Shogun allowed for the development of Buddhist funerals among all members of the population, irrespective of financial disparities. Cremation was not the rule but started to spread among wealthy people, who tended to follow the tradition of erecting a funeral gravestone inside the Buddhist temple. The last order, promulgated in 1700, reinforced Buddhist funerals in Japan, obliging the whole population to practice rituals in commemoration of the dead that aligned with specifically Buddhist beliefs (postmortem rituals) and respected the Buddhist annual calendar. If people did not follow these practices, the household would not be eligible to receive the Buddhist Certificate and could be suspected of association with Christianity, and therefore prosecuted and sentenced to death.

The impact of the these three orders remains visible to this day in three fundamental ways: (1) the relationship between the family (the household) and the local Buddhist temple; (2) the generalization of the Buddhist temple as the site of funeral practices (cremation) and postmortem rituals; and (3) the widespread erection of household gravestones inside Buddhist temples.

The relationship between Japanese families and their local Buddhist temple still persists, being based on parishioner membership and is known as *danka seido* 檀家制度 (the parishioner system).[4] The family or household contributes financially to the economy of the temple through offerings for rituals (funerals and postmortem rituals) and gravestone maintenance. In return, the Buddhist monk performs critical rituals for the family's ancestors, reaching back generations, and even maintains the family grave. The second impact of the above-mentioned orders is the generalization of Buddhist practices for funerals and the development of numerous postmortem rituals throughout the whole of society. Since the second part of the Edo period (1603–1868), the association of Buddhism with funerals and the use of cremation among wealthy people has become a reality.[5] The third aspect attesting to the persistent reverbera-tion of these ordinances today is the long-standing family practice of building

230 *Fabienne Duteil-Ogata*

a 'family gravestone' (*iebaka* 家墓) inside the enclosure of the local Buddhist temple, which strengthens the relationship between the Buddhist priests or monks and the families.

In the beginning of the Meiji era in 1868, Japan was forced to open its boundaries to Occidental countries for trade. In 1889, Japan adopted a new Constitution that permitted the practice of Christianity and other religions: Article 28 stipulated the freedom of religion. But at the same time, in reaction to the powerful Occidental cultural invasion, the Japanese government proclaimed Shinto as the unique and national religion of Japan, while Buddhism was considered a foreign religion and cremation became a controversial practice. In fact, throughout the entire period of the Shinto State (1868–1945), the government promoted Shinto not only for rituals during lifetime but also for funeral rituals (Hardacre 1989). Burial was promoted and cremation was considered impure, a *kegare* or a pollution practice, because the smoke that escaped from the crematoria constituted a menace to public health. The government forbade cremation from 1873 to 1875 (Berstein 2006), but the Shinto shrines and their priests were too weak to impose this change upon the whole society. Thus, the Japanese continued to practice funerals and postmortem rituals in Buddhist temples.

Also during this period, new technologies and new concepts arose through Japan's relations with Occidental countries. Electricity was introduced in Japanese industries, and the crematoria started using it in 1922 (Picone 2007: 136). The concept of urban planning introduced the idea of hygiene, and Western medicine was put forward as an argument in favor of such pursuits. Cremation was regarded as a new opportunity: it allowed space-saving in urban areas, unlike gravestones and cemeteries, and was considered to be a hygienic process. The corpse would not spread diseases and epidemics as it would not rot in the earth and or be disturbed by animals. Cremation also prevented dissection and other medical examinations.

After World War II, cremation became the rule for Japanese[6] funerary practices, especially in urban areas. The crematorium was rendered more effective with the change of the source of energy from coal, oil, and gas to electricity, and the time required for burning a corpse decreased to one hour. Nowadays most crematoria use gas burners monitored by computers. The corpse is burned in temperatures ranging from 300° to 800°C and takes from 45 minutes to one hour and a half to be transformed into ashes, depending upon its size and weight.[7] The bones are not pulverized, because in traditional funeral ceremonies the Japanese 'bones-picking ceremony' (*kotsu age* 骨あげ) is an essential step in ancestor worship: this ritual signifies the attainment of buddhahood. When the cremation is completed, the family goes to the 'ash/bones-collecting room' (*shûkotsu-shitsu* 収骨室) to collect the remains of the deceased and place them into the urn. In order to place the deceased in a standing position, the bones are collected from the toes to the skull. Performed by family members and relatives who pass

Technologies and funeral practices in Japan   231

the bones to one another, using two pairs of chopsticks, one made of bamboo, the other of wood (inversion ritual), this ritual ensures the transformation of the corpse of the deceased from flesh into white bones. All the bones cannot be collected for several reasons. In fact, all of them cannot be put into the cinerary urn because it is small, even if the cremator breaks the big bones such as the femur or the skull. Secondly, for religious reasons, some bones are more important than others, especially the Adam's apple bone, literally called the 'Buddha throat' in Japanese (*nodo-botoke* 喉仏), as it resembles the shape of a Buddha sitting in meditation. This bone is usually packed with great care at the top of the urn, just under the bone of the skull. After 49 days, the urn is buried in the grave. The monk of the family temple assigns a Buddhist posthumous name (*kaimyo*, see Shintani and Sekisawa 2005: 86–7) written in a mortuary spirit tablet (*ihai*, see ibid.: 235–6) to the dead, which is worshipped in the Buddhist household altar (*butsudan*) in the home of the heir for 33 or 50 years. At the end of the 33 or 50 years of worship (depending upon the sect of Buddhism), the deceased ancestor loses his individual identity and enters the realm of the ancestor spirits (becoming a Shinto deity): the mortuary tablet is burned or thrown into the river, or given to a Buddhist temple, or even buried in the grave. This marks the end of all the rituals performed by the living for the dead.

By the end of the 1980s, with the introduction of the high temperature cremation process that reached temperatures as high as 1,000°C, the corpse was directly reduced to powder ashes and the bones-picking ceremony disappeared. If the most important ritual of the funeral is changed, the disjunction between the spirit and the corpse becomes more abstract. The mourning process thus must undergo reconsideration. In fact, according to psychologists, in order to mourn properly, the loss must be faced momentarily to mark the permanent separation between the living and the dead.

At the end of the 1980s and at the beginning of the 1990s, the background of the funeral industry changed for the technological reasons mentioned above, but also for economic reasons (the economic crisis, the bursting of the land asset bubble) as well as social changes. The extravagant and expensive funerals and their meaning were beginning to be questioned. New forms of funeral practices appeared, such as the scattering of ashes in a natural environment – rivers, seas, mountains or forests – or funeral practices through objects (*temotokuyō*[8]), which both used high-temperature cremation procedures. At the same time, in the 1990s, due to media campaigns by the well-known Japanese journalist Mutsuhiko Yasuda that promoted the scattering of ashes, the legislation concerning mourning changed (Rowe 2003) and the Japanese people began to change their mourning practices. The book written by journalist Tokutome Yoshiyuki (published in 2006) and entitled 'For Those Who Neither Can Nor Wish to Have a Grave' stresses the fact that Japanese people refuse to be buried in a stone grave and would rather be disposed of in other ways.

232 *Fabienne Duteil-Ogata*

The new high-temperature cremation process: creation of 'close-at-hand cinerary objects'

'Close-at-hand cinerary objects' (*temoto kuyôhin*) use new technologies also based on high-temperature cremation and appeared in Japan at the end of the twentieth century. They consist of small objects (plaques, diamonds, pendants, accessories) made from the ashes of the deceased.[9] These objects were promoted by a non-profit organization[10] and sold by a handful of private companies. Frequently called 'funeral goods', in other countries, in Japan they are referred to as *temoto kuyôhin* which literally means "the object for the funeral practices that you have close-at-hand." I would like to emphasize that the Japanese term *temoto-kuyô-hin* focuses on two very important features. First, the term 'object' (*hin* 品) is appended to an expression meaning 'close-at-hand' (*temoto* 手元), and *kuyô* 供養 refers to "ritual offerings in a Buddhist tradition."

I will analyze two types of cinerary objects. The first are made exclusively of the ashes of the remains of the dead, such as a memorial diamond. The second type of funeral objects is made from a combination of the ashes of the remains of the dead with other substances.

A memorial diamond: a new technology for a new ontology of death

The new technology which can transform the ashes of cremated deceased persons into diamonds (Figure 12.1) was invented in Chicago in 2001 by Greg Herro, the manager of the American Company LifeGem,[11] and a similar technology was used by the Swiss company Algordanza in 2004.[12] This technology is available in Japan through the Japanese branch companies of those two foreign companies.

I will present the case study of the second company, the process of its transformation and the motivation of the Japanese director that initiated this new branch. Through the new technology invented by Professor Blank in the Technological Institute of Superhard and Novel Carbon Materials (TISNCM) in Switzerland, the ashes of the cremated deceased can be transformed into diamonds. To make a diamond from the cremated remains of a dead person requires usually about 500 grams of ashes, but Algondanza Japan asks for all the ashes (i.e. 2 or 3 kilograms per person). Then, all of them are sent to Switzerland, and the laboratory proceeds with the process. At the beginning of the process, all inorganic substances (such as salts, oxides) are chemically separated from the carbon. For a couple of weeks, the carbon is placed under up to 60,000 bars of pressure and up to 2,500°C in temperature. The greater the intensity and the duration, the larger the diamond created. At the end of this process a diamond emerges. The rough diamond is cut and polished according to the client's request: 8 sizes are available from 0.2 carat to 1 carat (0.2 gram), the cost ranging from 400,000 yen (about $4,000) to 2,500,000 yen (about $25,000). The bluish tint depends on the

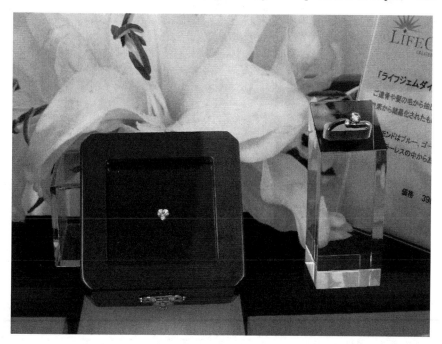

Figure 12.1 A memorial diamond displayed in the LifeGem Japan branch company, Tokyo

quantity of an element called Boron in the carbon. The memorial diamond can be engraved in microscripture by means of laser inscription. A text of a maximum 75 characters may be carved to provide such information as the name or the life data of the deceased. When the diamond is cut and polished, it is sent back to Japan and the client may wear it as jewelry. It can become a pendant made in different shapes such as a dolphin, a leaf or a cross. These diamonds can also be worn as rings, earrings or as bracelets. The director of the Japanese branch of the Swiss company explained that he created the branch in Japan in 2005 primarily because he wanted to leave a beautiful trace of himself to his wife after his death, a trace that would be eternal, natural, and visible. He mentioned other reasons as well, which dealt with aesthetics, eternity, or environmental issues, but focused on proximity in terms of both space and time. Indeed, having a diamond made from the ashes of the remains of the dead eliminates the visit to the grave (*o-haka mairi*) and reduces the distance between the remains of the dead and the living. The dead is no longer settled in a special space such as a grave or Buddhist household altar (*butsudan*), represented by the mortuary spirit tablet (*ihai*). The dead person is close to the living, touching their skin all the time. He or she can be carried and touched. As mentioned above, the transformation of all the ashes of the dead into diamonds eliminates the process of the ancestor worship (no grave, no mortuary tablet, no Buddhist rituals) and removes the 'traditional

234 *Fabienne Duteil-Ogata*

household' that is based on these elements. The dead is not the ancestor of the family but a diamond, an individualized object, which emphasizes the sense of touch. The deceased person seems to have changed its ontology, passing from a human being into an object, but not an ordinary one: an object with many other functions such as a financial asset, an aesthetic artifact (a piece of jewelry). It is not simply a representative artifact such as a mortuary spirit tablet. The deceased is now an eternal and mobile object that has a new relationship with time and is holding a new position with the living person. The diamond is regarded as a symbol of love, commemoration and imperishability. A diamond is unique, just like a human being.

Hybrid cinerary objects: ashes mixed with metal alloy

Less expensive than the memorial diamond, the second kind of funeral object includes those made with ashes mixed with other substances to create ceramic artifacts. Several companies are involved in these new goods. I will present these different activities and the motivations that drive them respectively through the eyes of their creators.

Mr. N. is the first person in Japan to have created this hybrid object. Mr. N. stated, "When my mother-in-law died in 1987, I thought that all these rituals for funerals were ridiculous, that they cost a lot. We didn't understand the meaning of the sutra read by the Buddhist monk and the people who participated in the funeral were mostly unknown to the family." As a result of this first experience with a Buddhist funeral, Mr. N. thought that his own funeral should be conducted differently. He first felt that he wanted his ashes scattered into nature, but he refrained from this option, because he realized that, in this case, he would not be able to leave any trace to his children. They would have no material references. "I am not religious, but we need to look at something to create the relationship," he said. So, in 1993, he studied ceramics with a specialist and started in 1999 his company *Eternal Japan*.[13] In the beginning it was difficult, but the company began to grow in 2002. He stated that, for him, the Eternal Plate is a new concept, which is not a grave, nor the scattering of ashes: it is a third path. "My idea was that we could touch the deceased, take it in our hands; the object could have a simple shape, more sober than the Buddhist ritual object."

The process of the Eternal Plate resembles the one for the memorial diamond. First, the ashes have to be reduced to powder of about 1 millimeter in size, and are then mixed with metal-based substances. Following a process involving high pressure and high temperature, a ceramic plate is created. The size of this object looks about the same as that of a standard business card. Inscribed upon it are elements allowing the identification of the dead – the name of the deceased in Japanese characters or in the Roman alphabet, and the dates of his or her birth and death. These are words that also typically appear on gravestones (except for the Buddhist posthumous name). In addition, an illustration such as a photograph can be added. The Eternal Plate

Figure 12.2 An Eternal Plate displayed in the Eternal Japan Company, Tokyo

(Figure 12.2) costs 150,000 yen (about $1,500). Since 2000, it can also be displayed as a pendant of various designs and colors and called the Eternal Pendant. "Women gave me the idea to create a pendant; they wanted the 'Eternal Plate' in the shape of a jewel. 80 percent of women buy an 'Eternal Pendant,'" said Mr. N. He has also created the same range of products for pets at the customers' request.[14] Some 70 percent of his customers have no grave, or the grave is too far from their residence. With the cinerary object, the person maintains a sensitive relationship with the departed or loved one.

These two managers of cinerary objects make no mention of religious statements, particularly those pertaining to ancestor worship as practiced in the household descendant traditions. Their objects seem to reflect a new response to religious practices, even if they emphasize the similarity of the data that appear on them. The concept of eternity is also a leitmotif involved in the naming and the materiality of these objects.

Another company uses more or less the same technological process, but creates different artifacts in ceramics. Mr. R. was aware of environmental issues. He thought that building a cemetery was not good for nature, especially in Japan, where space is rare. He explained that he wanted also to create a substitute for the Buddhist household altar, because the space in his apartment was needed for furniture. When he retired, he performed

236 *Fabienne Duteil-Ogata*

experiments with crystals and discovered the process of making a gem with ashes and metals as strong as quartz. In the beginning, he created pendants and later he started creating rings, bracelets in the shape of a *Juzu*, a Buddhist prayer bead, or the Buddhist rosary itself. Furthermore, funeral objects are not strictly dedicated to humans in Japan. Since the end of the 1990s, the ashes of pets are also mixed to create objects, such as ceramic representations of them, with photographs used as models. Miniature cats, dogs, hamsters, and horses are typically made.

The motivation of Mr. R. to create funeral objects is down to space constraints and is not explicitly formulated against religion. Some of the objects' shapes are directly related to religious practices such as the Buddhist rosary. This means that the dead (a part of his corpse reduced to ashes) becomes a religious tool and not only an aesthetic artifact. Both these funeral objects, made with powered ashes combined with other substances, point to another of their features: the remains of the cremated dead are divided between several objects.

Indeed, all of these objects emphasize aesthetics and represent a perceptible (visual and tactile) and individualized relationship with the deceased, which often does not involve a religious ritual. This raises several questions. First, having been transformed into an object (ceramic or diamond), the corpse in the form of ashes can be touched: it seems to be no longer considered impure and does not affect the person who handles it, as if by becoming an object, it has changed its ontological status and becomes a guardian being or deity without the need for a ritual, a sort of relic with talismanic powers. Note that according to animist belief, objects contain the same vital force as animated beings.[15] We may be facing a sort of democratization of relics: the ordinary person's remains can become a relic, not just the Buddha's or of famous Buddhist monks! Second, the cinerary object questions the work of mourning, the grieving process: how can the proximity to the deceased (through the close-at-hand cinerary objects) allow spatial distancing, a separation between the living and the dead necessary to the grieving process?

The other question raised by this practice involves the increase in the number of graves for one single person. Systems that allow multiple representations of the dead to be erected in several places exist in the Japanese religious tradition. This is the case of the double grave system (*ryôbosei*, see Shintani and Sekizawa 2005: 210–13), which consists in constructing a second, empty grave close to one's workplace and the 'system of separating memorial tablets' (*ihai wake*[16]), involving the creation of several memorial tablets for the deceased to be displayed on different household altars. However, in the case of small cinerary objects, it is not the representation of the dead that is multiplied, but the corpse itself, which occupies several locations. It seems possible then to see a parallel with the process of 'dividing a deity among several shrines' (*bunrei*). After death, the corpse (the ashes) can be divided and located simultaneously in several places.

Technologies and funeral practices in Japan   237

From high-temperature cremation to digital technology: the grave-computer and the online grave

The grave-computer (dennôhaka 電脳墓)

The concept of *dennôhaka* 電脳墓, which I translate as 'grave-computer,' was initiated by Matsushima Nyokai, a Buddhist monk and the headmaster of the Shingon Buddhist school (Mahâyâna Esoteric School) of Kôtokuin, in Tokyo on April 1st, 1997: "Although it is April Fool's Day, it's not a joke," he said. He explained his idea of a new type of grave in his book entitled, *Revolution of the Internet Grave: Virtual Graves* (Matsushima 1997).

Matsushima explained that factors such as the emergence of technology, social changes and environmental issues led to the creation of the grave-computer and the cyber-stone. In the beginning of his book, Matsushima Nyokai mentions the cremation revolution that took place in the 1980s. The corpses of the deceased were reduced to powdered ashes with a temperature reaching 1,000°C. Thus, in Japan, human bones that constituted the last mortal remains to be buried prior to the development of high-powered incineration technology became useless. "It's a boneless new age," he said, and cremation implies the disappearance of DNA and therefore the impossibility of individual identification. Then he concluded that gravestones or cemeteries were no longer useful. Using computers and the Internet, the digital technological revolution generated recordings of the memories of an individual, recordings involving visuals, sounds and words. These means avoided any lack of individual information about the identity of the deceased. His conclusion was that grave-computers would provide a good solution: it created a grave in a virtual space that gave personal records through digital tracks instead of DNA.

The grave-computer is located in the Sugamo Peace Graveyard of the Kôtoku Buddhist Temple in Tokyo (Figure 12.3). In July 2011, about 130 people had signed a grave computer contract while still living, but the currently planned overall capacity amounts to 8,000. The subscriber of the grave-computer pays 350,000 yen (about $3,500). This fee includes the insertion of ashes into the grave, the eternal rituals realized by the monk of the temple and the visit to the grave (*ohaka mairi*) on the screen of the grave-computer by the people chosen by the subscriber.

Open to all confessions, Buddhist, Christian, Shinto and others, as the grave-computer website mentions (in English and in Japanese),[17] in reality, it is mainly dedicated to people who are seeking an 'eternal ritual grave' (*eitaikuyôbo*):[18] a collective grave for the cremated remains of unrelated people where a ritual is performed every month for the pacification of the deceased. Unlike the regular grave, the subscriber of the grave-computer is an individual and does not belong to a household (*ie*, based on patrilineal affiliation). Furthermore, the purpose of the ritual is not to render the dead person an ancestor of the household but rather to pacify him or her.

238 *Fabienne Duteil-Ogata*

Figure 12.3 Grave-computer in the Kôtoku Buddhist temple, Tokyo

Despite the collective approach – collective ashes and collective rituals – the individuality of the person is taken into consideration. Indeed, the subscriber decides upon the series of visits to the grave and the rights of access with an ID-card login to the grave-computer located in the Kôtoku Buddhist temple in Tokyo. The future deceased can create his own virtual

Technologies and funeral practices in Japan 239

sequence within 90 seconds – it should fit with his personality, on a partially fixed frame. He can integrate his autobiographical portrait and use two types of data: words and photographs. A sample frame provided by the Kôtokuin to their clients is available on the website mentioned above.[19] The given name of the deceased appears to the right of the photograph, while the Buddhist posthumous name appears on the left. The birthday is mentioned alongside the death date and the age of the deceased. These four data are usually carved in the graves. But the main words first shown on the front of the grave are the name of the patrilineal affiliation followed by the ideogram of *ie* (household) and the ideogram of the grave itself. On the side of the traditional grave, the Buddhist posthumous name, the given name and the dates of birth and death are usually written, but these individual data are not the main data, as the household's name remains the most important. In order to correct this lack of personal data, a new part of the gravestone named *boshi* was recently created to emphasize the personal data, as well as to add a personal epitaph.

The grave-computer also provides various designs for the background on which these personal data are written. Patterns, such as natural patterns, colors, clouds, cherry blossoms, sea and waves can be selected. The patterns and data organization can be rearranged, and the orientation of the writing can be changed as well (verticality corresponding to the traditional Japanese, horizontality to Western types of writings). Obviously, in the case of traditional graves the color is restricted to a natural stone color. Although recently wealthier people have asked for designs upon their gravestones or specifically carved designs, the possibility of performing such modifications is drastically limited due to the mineral artifact and the price.

The sample photography is a traditional one named *iei*. It is a photograph of the deceased selected when still alive or by a relative in case of accidental death. According to the Buddhist tradition, the heir who stands at the head of the procession holds the framed portrait of the deceased. At the end of the mourning period, it is placed at the top of the Buddhist household altar. The black and white photograph is usually formatted according to traditional standards; a black kimono is simply added. Photography in the grave-computer practice is used as a traditional material *iei* (black and white picture of the deceased), but is also used as a new one with album sheets composed of four pictures featuring everyday life. The future deceased can choose four pictures – the narrative portrait refers to various life stages – in the sample provided by the website and test visits. The sample includes periods such as motherhood and grand-motherhood, which focus on family life but also on neighborhood life (meeting friends in the street). In the case of traditional graves there is no photography. There is no visual record of the death, only words that mention affiliation to the household, no information pertaining to individual life. The grave-computer device includes few references to Buddhism as compared to secular items and questions the funeral practices.

First, the grave-computer emphasizes individual records, photographs for a personal touch, a sensory mediation, emphasizing creativity based on pictures,

240 *Fabienne Duteil-Ogata*

sounds, and words, which create a hypertext and new aesthetics based on special computer features such as visuals and sounds. Second, the mediation is directed towards several chosen people, creating a new type of affiliation, which is not a traditional one, but a *chosen affiliation* that often includes friends as well. And, finally, the grave-computer seems to change the usual relationships between the living and the dead because it gives the most important role to the deceased whose position is reversed: the grave is established in such a way that it is as though the deceased is acting through their own decisions on the visitors. These visitors can do nothing but comply.

From the grave-computer to the online grave: the cyber-stone[20]

In May 2008, the Kôtoku Buddhist temple opened a new website called *Cyber-stone*[21] and a new type of grave was created, based on the pattern of the grave-computer: the cyber-stone. As it states on the website, "It is a virtual grave." This means that the ashes are located in a grave in another cemetery, so it is not a fully virtual grave (the person must keep the ashes somewhere). The subscriber has to pay 150,000 yen (about $1,500) to have their own cyber-stone homepage, the contract of managing the homepage lasts 33 years according to a first version of the website and 30 years according to a further version of the website. This length refers directly to the duration of Japanese ancestor worship. The cyber-stone homepage can be modified by the owner while alive, but it is not changeable after death. It costs also 6,000 yen (about $60) for a one-year service contract.

For this price, the subscriber has their own ID and password, and they can create their own top page, a memorial page that includes photography and text on a slide show display. Optionally, it is possible to create a profile page (by registering the chronological data), a page including a text, a photo-album page, a movie/audio page and a space information page on which one can register important places on maps such as those provided by Google map. The whole option costs 100,000 yen (about $1,000) and allows about 100 MB (10 pages of A4 size sentences, 20 photographs, 5 minutes of audio and 10 minutes of movies) or 20,000 yen (about $200), for each optional page. But unlike other online graves, no offerings are available on *Cyber-stone*. According to the website, the subscriber is free to choose the color and the design of each page. The subscriber is free to give the ID and password for login to visitors (family or friends) to access their cyber-stone homepage via the Internet, and is free to manage the contents of the homepage and its length. It means that it is possible for the owner to select some content accessible to certain visitors during a limited length of time. For example, owners may click on an option specifying that "this page is only accessible to my children five years after my death." Access to all the owners of the cyber-stone website is also available to create a cyber-stone site community, but nowadays there is no other cyber-stone homepage available than Matsushima Nyokai's own page.[22] The subscriber can also create a cyber-stone for a pet and a

Technologies and funeral practices in Japan 241

human, both together, as was the case for some real cemeteries in Japan since 2003 (Duteil-Ogata 2012b: 207).

The common assumption that these new funeral practices are the end of the Buddhist monopoly on funerals in Japan is not accurate: Matsushima Nyokai and his grave-computer and cyber-stone are counterexamples. However, *Cyber-stone* utterly eliminates the reference to Buddhism, as it seems to be more a memorial website than a religious device for funeral practices: there are no offerings, no rituals. 'The visit to the grave' (*ohaka mairi*) becomes a connection to the Internet. Furthermore, Internet connections between the living and the dead create a new relationship with space and time. Mediation is immediate and does not follow calendar rituals. As in the case of the relationship with time, the geographical distance to the deceased is abolished. Could we not argue for the hypothesis that the monk Matsushima Nyokai and the clients of *Cyber-stone* have been converted to Internet worship, as analyzed by Philippe Breton (2000)? Do they not share the same vision of the world in which the truth would be composed of digital data, a new kind of technological immortality? In other words, do we not face a new religious belief or utopia that human beings could be immortalized in digital data?

Conclusion

Technologies alter religious representations and practices. First of all, these new forms of funeral no longer stress the traditional family unit, but focus rather on the individual: emotional bonds replace the rules of affiliation. The relationship between the dead and the living is more individualized and sensitive, through visual or object devices. These new forms of graves will be notably aesthetic, they are more creative: the uniqueness of the individual is highlighted.

The use of technology generates a new relationship to time: a relation based on eternity and the immediate link. A new relation to space is also visible in both discourse and practice. The people who created new forms of funeral practices are aware of the environmental issue at stake: the necessity to limit the construction of cemeteries and avoid damaging mountains and forests. Furthermore, the physical separation, the distance between deceased persons and living human beings is not wanted and seems no longer regarded as necessary to perform the mourning process.

Regarding the practices themselves, ancestor worship seems to have been abandoned and replaced by a memorial practice that is no longer focused on the dead but on the living. Thus, the representation of the dead is undergoing a radical transformation; the corpse is no longer seen as a polluting and impure *kegare*. The high temperature cremation eliminates the 'Bones-picking ceremony' and the bone funeral culture in Japan. Powered ashes become the last remains. The practice of dividing the dead among several places or objects bestows upon it the status of a guardian of the living without the need to perform ancestral rites. It is difficult not to see in these practices an

242 *Fabienne Duteil-Ogata*

expression of individual freedom, a manifestation of religious freedom and a revival of animist thought.

The use of technology in new funeral practices does not mean the end of the Buddhist monopoly on the funerary market, as the examples of the grave-computer and the online graves created by the Buddhist monk Matsushima show. However, these new forms of practices represent an alternative to Buddhist practices and also a criticism of or a challenge to traditional religious frameworks. They thus perhaps provide a new form of religious belief: the belief in technology itself.

Notes

1 This article has been annotated and updated, based on Duteil-Ogata (2011), an article published in French.
2 In Tokyo, 85 percent of people perform Buddhist rituals for funerals (Shimane 2012: 37).
3 The concept of pollution (*kegare*) was mainly defined by Namihira Emiko (1987, 1992) and Miyata Noboru (1997) to explain the meaning of ritual in Japanese popular religion.
4 The word *danka* 檀家 (parishioner of Buddhist temple) is written with two ideograms, *dan* 檀 and *ie* 家. *Dan* comes from the Sanskrit word *dâna* which denotes offering, alms, donation. In that case, the offering is addressed to the Buddhist monk. *Ie/ka* 家 refers to the household. *Danka* is the household involved in the Buddhist temple from generation to generation and financially participating in the daily expenses of the Buddhist temple. This word is still used nowadays even if legally the status of household (*ie*) has disappeared since the new Constitution in 1946. In fact, Japanese people consider themselves as *danka* (parishioner-household of a Buddhist temple) and they also use the word *iebaka* (household grave) to designate their family grave.
5 The practice of cremation was used in Japan for more than a thousand years. Even though the earliest archeological traces go back to the third century BC (Jomon period), the first cremation mentioned in historical documents is from 700 AD, dealing with the Buddhist monk Dôchô. The most frequent reason mentioned to explain the link between cremation and Buddhism is the cremation of Shakyamuni (the historical Buddha) himself. Cremation has been probably practiced in Japan since the introduction of Buddhism in the sixth century. From that time, cremation among Buddhists was looked upon as a prestigious custom. Cremation spread among high-ranked aristocrats, including Buddhist monks and the imperial family (Empress Jito). However, in the thirteenth century, only very few (wealthy) families practiced cremation. Corpses were usually abandoned in natural spaces (mountains, rivers) far from residential areas.
6 The cremation rate in Japan was 30 percent at the beginning of the twentieth century. Cremation spread through the country during the High Growth period (1955–73). See Shimane (2012: 45).
7 See Suzuki (2000: 116).
8 See Yamasaki (2007: 203). This book written by the President of the Society for the Promotion of 'Funeral object' is the first book explaining these new practices.
9 The micro-containers of ashes (accessories, pendants) belong to a category of close-at-hand funerary objects but new technologies were not involved in making them, so I do not mention this type of objects here.

Technologies and funeral practices in Japan   243

10 The marketing policy of the NPO named *temotokuyô kyôkai* is based on the publication of articles in the mass media, a quarterly report for members, the organization of events (exhibitions-conferences) throughout Japan and televised interviews.

11 See www.lifegem.com/ (accessed June 2013).

12 See www.algordanza.co.jp/ (accessed June 2013).

13 See the *Eternal Japan*-website: www.eternal-j.co.jp/ (accessed June 2013).

14 In Japan, the funeral for animals is not a new trend. Since the Edo Period (1603–1868), several funerals have been performed. But since the 1980s a pet boom has emerged, especially in urban areas. The adoption of pets by Japanese people has become popular and also the funerals for animals (Duteil-Ogata 2007b).

15 See Matsuzaki (2004: 16). The author mentions that since the 1980s and 1990s there has been a revival in animist thinking regarding objects, notably those directly linked to the corpse in daily life.

16 Several memorial tablets are made for an individual so that all members of the family can represent the deceased on their Buddhist household altar (Shintani and Sekisawa 2005: 151–3).

17 The website is available in English or in Japanese, this latter including more details. In Japanese, www.haka.co.jp (accessed June 2013) and in English, www.haka.co.jp/CyberStoneInfo/english/index.html (accessed June 2013).

18 This kind of ritual started to spread in Japan in the 1990s. This particular choice implies that there is no possible individual ancestors worship based on patrilineal affiliation which corresponds to the traditional worship in Buddhist temples.

19 See www.haka.co.jp/CyberStoneInfo/profile/display.html (accessed June 2013).

20 See Baffelli *et al.* (2011: 22–3).

21 See www.cyber-stone.jp/HP/index.html (accessed June 2013).

22 See www.cyber-stone.jp/CyberStone/PublicView.aspx (accessed June 2013).

References

Baffelli, E., Reader, I. and Staemmler, B. (2011) *Japanese Religions on the Internet.* London: Routledge.

Berstein, A. (2006) *Modern Passings: Death Rites, Politics, and Social Change in Imperial Japan.* Honolulu, HI: Hawai'i Press.

Breton, P. (2000) *Le culte de l'Internet* [The Worship of the Internet]. Paris: La Découverte.

Duteil-Ogata, F. (2002) 'La vie religieuse dans un quartier de Tôkyô' [Religious Life in a Tokyo District], doctoral thesis. University of Paris X-Nanterre.

Duteil-Ogata, F. (2007a) 'L'espace funéraire au Japon, un espace diversifié en pleine mutation: vers un nouveau lexique?' [The Funerary Space in Japan: A Varied Space in Transformation. Toward a New Vocabulary?]. English summary and paper available at: www.reseau-asie.com/cgibin/prog/pform.cgi?langue=fr&Mcenter=collo que&TypeListe=showdoc&email=&password=&ID_document=434 (accessed June 2013).

Duteil-Ogata, F. (2007b) 'Les pratiques funéraires des animaux de compagnie ; nouveaux traitements, nouvelles corporéités' [New Funeral Practices for Pets: New Forms, New Bodies], in A. Brotons and C. Galan (eds) *Japon Pluriel 7.* Arles: Philippe Picquier, pp. 39–48.

Duteil-Ogata, F. (2011) 'Nouvelles technologies et pratiques funéraires contemporaines' [New Contemporary Funerary Technologies and Practices], in N. Berliguez-Kôno and B. Thomann (eds) *Japon Pluriel 8.* Arles: Philippe Picquier, pp. 295–308.

244 *Fabienne Duteil-Ogata*

Duteil-Ogata, F. (2012a) 'Emerging Burial Spaces and Rituals in Urban Japan,' in N. Aveline (ed.) *Invisible Population*. London: Lexington Books, pp. 50–71.

Duteil-Ogata, F. (2012b) 'La place de l'animal de compagnie dans les mégalopoles japonaises: un animal urbanisé?' [The Place of Pets in Japanese Megacities: Toward an Urbanized Animal?], in G. Teissonnières and D. Terolle (eds) *A la croisée des Chemins*. Paris: Éditions du Croquant, pp. 195–228.

Gamba, F. (2007) 'Rituels postmodernes d'immortalité: les cimetières virtuels, comme technologie de la mémoire vivante' [Postmodern Rituals: Virtual Cemeteries as a Living Memory of Technology], *Sociétés*, 97: 109–23.

Hardacre, H. (1989) *Shinto and the State*. Princeton, NJ: Princeton University Press.

Matsushima, N. (1997) *Saibâsuton intânetto jô no haka, kakumei* [Revolution of the Internet Grave: Virtual Graves]. Tokyo: Mainichi Komyunikêshonzu.

Matsuzaki, K. (2004) *Gendai kuyô ronkô* [Essay on Contemporary Memorial Rites]. Tokyo: Keiyûsha.

Miyata, N. (1997) 'Le concept de souillure et la structure des rites populaires' [The Concept of Contamination and the Structure of Popular Rituals] in École Pratique des Hautes Études, Ve section (ed.) *Cahiers d'études et de documents sur les religions du Japon* [Book of Research and Documents on Japanese Religions]. Paris: Alpha Bleue, pp. 63–82.

Namihira, E. (1987) 'Pollution in the Folk Belief System,' *Current Anthropology*, 28(4): 65–74.

Namihara, E. (1992) *Kegare no sôzô* [Structure of Pollution]. Tokyo: Seidosha.

Picone, M. (2007) 'Cremation in Japan: Bones Buddhas and Surrogates Bodies,' *Études sur la mort*, 132: 131–40.

Rowe, M. (2003) 'Grave Change: Scattering Ashes in Contemporary Japan,' *Japanese Journal of Religious Studies*, 30(1–2): 85–118.

Shimane, K. (2012) 'The Experience of Death in Japan's Urban Societies,' in N. Aveline (ed.) *Invisible Population*. London: Lexington Books, pp. 29–49.

Shintani, T. and Sekisawa, M. (2005) *Shi to sôsô kojiten* [Small Dictionary of Death and Funeral Practices]. Tokyo: Yoshikawa Kôbunkan.

Suzuki, H. (2000) *The Price of Death: The Funeral Industry in Contemporary Japan*. Stanford, CA: Stanford University Press.

Tamamuro, F. (1997) '*Jidan*: idéologie des rapports qui liaient monastères bouddhiques et familles paroissiales à l'époque d'Edo' [Jidan: Ideology of the Relationships between Buddhist Temples and Parishioners' Families during the Edo Period], in École Pratique des Hautes Études, Ve section (ed.) *Cahiers d'études et de documents sur les religions du Japon* [Book of Research and Documents on Japanese Religions]. Paris: Alpha bleue, pp. 87–110.

Tokutome, Y. (2006) *Ohaka ni hairitakunai hito hairenai hito no tame ni* [For Those Who Neither Can Nor Wish to Have a Grave]. Tokyo: Hamano Shuppan.

Yamasaki, J. (2007) *O-haka no shinpai muyô temoto kuyô no susume* [No Need to Worry about the Grave: Recommendations for Close-at-hand Funerary Practices]. Tokyo: Shôdensha Shinshô.

Yanagita, K. (1970) *About our Ancestor Worship in Japan*. Tokyo: Japanese Society for the Promotion of Science.

13 Producing deities?

Ritual as technology

István Keul

'Ritual': between discomfort and disutility

In a number of seminal contributions to ritual studies, scholars have repeatedly expressed their discomfort with the concept of 'ritual' and reflected on possible alternative conceptualizations. Goody (1977: 25) included 'ritual' among the terms he deemed "virtually useless for analytic purposes", given its wide occurrence in fields and disciplines ranging from ethology and sociology to archaeology and anthropology. Goody's and others' unease with 'ritual' as an analytical category are probably rooted in what Catherine Bell described as the development of the idea of ritual, "a category or tool of analysis built up from a sampling of ethnographic descriptions and the elevation of many untested assumptions" ([1997] 2009: 21), the latter part being the problematic element in the concept's formation. The questioning of the category's universal validity has led to the search for conceptual alternatives, an endeavor seen in the specialized theoretical literature as "not only challenging but also necessary for theorizing rituals" (Kreinath *et al.* 2006: xx). While not intending to offer any real alternative to a category he opposed and considered universalistic and vague, Goody reasoned nevertheless that "perhaps it is better to build up from nothing than break down from everything" (1977: 27). As a possible solution, he proposed to 'translate' (that is, to find alternative concepts for) the term every time the need of using it seems to occur. Another approach suggested by Goody follows the lines of Goffman's (1967) 'sociology of occasions' and the study of so-called 'small behaviors,' seen as basic components of even large-scale rituals (ibid.: 33–4).

A more recent critique of universal definitions and monothetic classification of ethnographic instances of 'ritual' was put forward by Handelman (2006), who pointed out that the positing of an abstract meta-level or roof rubric of 'ritual' hinders reflection about conceptual alternatives. As a way out, Handelman suggested suspending the operation of the global concept and roof category 'ritual', focusing on the various ethnographic instances and their interior logics, and using the term 'public event' instead of 'ritual', looking at meta-designs that "generate events as dynamic micro-worlds that are powerful transformers of person and cosmos" (ibid.: 46).[1]

246 *István Keul*

Building on some of the suggestions outlined above, this chapter intends to look at an ethnographic instance of ritual, temporarily suspending the use of the all-encompassing term and broad category, and proposing to 'translate' or re-conceptualize this particular ritual as a 'sociotechnical event'. The composite and complex nature of the event in question, the consecration of a temple image in North India, makes it a useful starting point for manifold theoretical reflections and perspectives. I will attempt elsewhere to look at the morphology (units of meaning), syntax (organizational structure), and 'ritual grammar' (rule-based description) applied in its performance.[2] The focus of this chapter lies in the technological and social aspects of the consecration. I will begin by inquiring into the usefulness of 'technology' as a model for possible forms of such events and their interior dynamics, looking at examples from classical anthropological works for associations of 'ritual' and 'technology' and continuing with a brief excursus into the problem of 'ritual efficacy' before turning to the consecration itself.

Ritual as technology

The association (or disassociation) of ritual and technology occurs quite conspicuously in major anthropological works published in the 1960s. Anthony Wallace, in his *Religion: An Anthropological View* (1966: 107), defines religion as basically a 'set of rituals' with the "purpose of achieving or preventing transformations of state in man and nature". As the first of five categories of transformations of state,[3] Wallace introduces the category of 'ritual as technology', and mentions at first two 'obvious and ubiquitous' subcategories, namely divination and rites of intensification, the latter rooted in the domains of hunting and agriculture. Later he adds the subcategory of protective rituals. All these technological rituals, he writes, "are aimed at one goal: the transformation of man's external environment into states favorable to man" (ibid.: 113). While this might not be the place to assess the applicability of Wallace's typology and taxonomy, his predominantly teleological and utilitarian approach to the rituals he classifies as technological tends to play down their systemic, epistemic, and processual aspects. Whether discussing dowsing or scapulimancy,[4] calendrical ritual cycles related to agriculture or ceremonial hunting practices related to bears, Wallace emphasizes the pragmatic aims and results of these rituals that are "rarely, if ever, pursued without corresponding activities that are practical and 'rational' (by which we mean efficacious in terms of the cause-and-effect relationships recognized by scientific knowledge)" (ibid.: 113). We do not have to stretch Wallace's definition of technological ritual too far in order to accommodate the consecration outlined below: it is an activity with a clearly defined goal, namely – and I am formulating it somewhat pointedly – of producing a deity, and contributes hereby considerably to the favorable transformation not only of the temple owner's and his family's environment, but that of the entire neighborhood as well. However, in addition to duly considering goals, this

Producing deities? Ritual as technology 247

chapter looks primarily at processual and systemic aspects related to the long and elaborate ritual transformation of a profane statue into a temple image fit for worship.

In an oft-quoted passage from *The Forest of Symbols*, Victor Turner defined ritual as "prescribed formal behavior for occasions not given over to technological routine, having reference to beliefs in mystical beings or powers" (1967: 19). While Turner's definition has been widely influential in the history of ritual studies, his limiting of ritual to non-technological formal behavior leads us to the question of whether and how the categories and perspectives of the ritual actors might differ from those of the academic observers.[5] As the present chapter will show, instances of ritual *can* be interpreted as a certain type of 'technological routine'. And contrary to Wallace's statement (see above), such actions *are* considered practical, rational, and efficacious by the participants and do not need to be accompanied by additional 'corresponding activities'.

Ritual efficacy

Frazer's differentiation between magic, religion and science was among the early scholarly attempts to assess the efficacy of rituals ([1890] 1922). He saw the belief in the efficacy of magic as the 'universal faith' of mankind.[6] While magical rituals have the aim to produce an effect on the course of nature, they are based – according to Frazer – on false premises and therefore instrumentally ineffective. At the beginning of the twentieth century, Hubert and Mauss defined rituals as "actes traditionels d'une efficacité *sui generis*" (1902–3: 12).[7] Another decade later, Durkheim attributed a social function or 'moral efficacy' to rituals, which he characterized as 'real', in contradistinction to an imagined (and believed) 'physical efficacy'.[8] This dichotomy of efficacious versus symbolic/expressive/non-efficacious actions can be found also in Turner's above-quoted definition of ritual as non-technological formal behavior, followed by his statement that "[t]he symbol is the smallest unit of ritual which still retains the specific properties of ritual behavior" (1967: 19), and his emphasis on the symbol's importance for the preservation of social structure.[9] It can also be found in the use of the word 'ritual' in Western languages, both in ethnographic writing and in contemporary popular contexts, often implying an activity that is non-rational, ineffective, deficient, and therefore in need of change.[10]

In a recent contribution, William Sax mentions the rain dance, initiatory tattooing, and the curing of diseases by prayer as examples of activities that are called 'ritual', as they do not comply with modern meteorological or medical theories (2010: 3f.).[11] However, Sax also shows that participants in such rituals refer to their actions in terms that present these activities not at all as non-rational or ineffective, which leads us back to the question raised earlier regarding Turner's definition and the problem of the differing perspectives.[12] In South Asian contexts, many of the words that come close to

248   *István Keul*

'ritual' are derived from the Sanskrit verbal root *kṛ*, 'to do', 'to make'. One example of such a term is *devakārya*, which could be translated as '[the] work to be done for the deities' (ibid.: 4). Other important Sanskrit analogues to 'ritual' are *karma(n)* ('work', 'action'), which in Vedic texts (ca. 1750–500 BCE) stands for a religious ritual, most often the sacrifice;[13] *saṃskāra* ('the [act of] making perfect', 'the [act of] putting together'), which has come to mean the 12, 16 or more life-cycle rituals (the most important of these being the initiation, marriage, and death ritual); *pujā* ('worship', 'respect'), the worship of deities following a prescribed ritual choreography that includes five or 16 sequences/services (*upacāra*).[14] The consecration of a temple image is called *prāṇapratiṣṭhā*, a technical term that can be translated as the 'establishment or instilment of vital breath/life', this being another example of how, from an emic perspective, these activities are seen as methodic and systematic ritual work, and not as placebo or as-if actions.[15]

Reconceptualizing ritual

Working methodically, systematically, and effectively with the aim to control or modify the natural environment is a defining characteristic of technological activity. The present chapter argues that it is possible to approach the image consecration from a technological perspective also etically, enabling a reconceptualization of this particular ritual as a 'sociotechnical event'. While the terminological proximity to the sociotechnical system concept is not incidental, the degree to which sociotechnical system research is relevant to describe and analyze this type of event remains to be established. The focus on the social aspects of human technological activity, or on methods for the study of the relations of technologies and organizational forms in various settings (Trist 1981: 9f.) are only two of the general areas of common interest.

The sociotechnical system concept was developed collectively in a number of related fields, such as the sociology of scientific knowledge, the history and sociology of technology, and science and technology studies.[16] By including the social dimension, the common-sense, 'hard' view of technology and material culture is decisively broadened. Instead of operating with a definition of technology as the means by which humans seek to modify or control their natural environment, the social anthropologist of technology Brian Pfaffenberger, suggests two alternative approaches, namely, to view *technique* as "the system of material resources, tools, operational sequences and skills, verbal and nonverbal knowledge, and specific modes of work coordination", and the *sociotechnical system* as "the distinctive technological activity that stems from the linkage of techniques and material culture to the social coordination of labor" (1992: 497).

In our case, it is especially the first approach that seems useful for an attempt to reconceptualize the consecration as a 'sociotechnical event'. The *pratiṣṭhā* described below is a multi-layered, highly complex technical event in which material resources, skills, verbal and nonverbal knowledge, and the

Producing deities? Ritual as technology 249

division and coordination of work are combined to transform a sandstone artifact, a statue of the god Hanumān into a 'living' divine image. At the same time, the consecration was an event of high social relevance. Dubbed an *utsav*, festival, by those in charge of its organization, it brought together numerous members of the sponsor's extended family and was a visible event in the life of one of the southern neighborhoods of the North Indian city of Vārāṇasī. In what follows, I give a brief (and necessarily selective) overview of the main activities performed on the first day of this three-day event, and mention the most important sequences from days two and three.[17]

The consecration (in fast-forward mode)

Early in the morning five priests and the temple owner, who sponsored the event and acted as *yajamāna* ('sacrificer'), took their places in the special space marked off for the consecration and, reciting Vedic hymns, started the preliminary sequences. These included purifying the vessels and instruments, the sacrificial ground, and the people in the sacrificial space by means of Ganges water; expiation rites performed by the temple owner; an announcement of the place, time, method, and purpose of the ritual; the worship of Gaṇeśa; and the ritual entreaties for an auspicious day. At the rice diagram (*maṇḍala*) of the 16 mothers, the priests and the sacrificer invoked these goddesses, who were represented by areca nuts placed on the diagram. In the next step, the sponsor's (deified) ancestors were honored. The elaborate invocation of the deities of another diagram was preceded by sequences dedicated to the serpent deities, such as the symbolic insertion of iron pegs. Then, two priests and the sacrificer walked around the enclosure invoking the protectors of the directions distributed around the area in the form of clay pots. After a detailed worship of the deities of the main *maṇḍala*, Hanumān stood in the center of attention for the first time: The deity was invited to take his seat in the coconut on the brass pitcher placed in the middle of this diagram. The priests carried out a rapid process of instilling life-breath into a small, golden Hanumān image that was then wrapped into a betel leaf and placed under the coconut. For the following sequences the sacrificer and the priests moved to the so-called bathing place, to the large Hanumān statue made of sandstone. After invoking the protectors of the world, the sponsor and two of the priests rubbed the image with oil, melted butter, and a mixture of the five cow products. The statue was then cleaned and covered with a damp white cloth, which represented the (abbreviated) rite of the purification rite with water during which the images to be consecrated are usually immersed overnight in a water tank. Under the cloth, the sacrificer drew the eyes of the image (the first phase of the eye-opening ritual), and held a mango in front of the statue's face. Back at the ritual area, the group of 64 Yoginīs were invoked and worshipped at their *maṇḍala*, and so were Sarasvatī, Kālī, and Lakṣmī. Then the celebrants turned to the diagram of the protectors of the field and invited them, too, to the consecration. Returning to the bathing place, the sacrificer

250 *István Keul*

poured water over the image eight times. Hidden by a brocade cloth he then performed the second and decisive part of the eye-opening ritual: With the help of a golden needle he drew the contours of the image's eyes, while a priest held up a mirror to catch and neutralize the deity's first energy-laden gaze. The purification rite with food followed; a box with a glass front was set up around the image, and the priests poured chickpeas and wheat over the statue until it was completely covered. Hidden by a cloth, it remained thus until the morning of the next day. The rites of the first day of the consecration ended, about 12 hours after they started, with the light-waving sequence (*ārtī*) and a circumambulation of the ritual space. While a thorough description of days two and three is beyond the space limitations here, some of the most important sequences should be mentioned nevertheless. On the second day, the image was purified with Ganges water and a mixture of the five cow products, and then covered with flowers. The priests kindled the sacrificial fire with traditional utensils (kindling sticks), prepared a fire altar, and performed a fire sacrifice. The image was then purified and bathed with various substances. The circumambulation of the area followed, during which the image (or here: a copy of it) was taken in a procession around the territory over which the deity is supposed to watch. Near the end of the second day, the sponsor touched various parts of the image, imposing on them different verses/seed syllables. The main sequences of the third day included the installation of the image in the temple and the final stages of the instilment of life force, followed by another fire sacrifice. Finally, the priests were offered food and given their honorariums.

The consecration as a sociotechnical event: a brief assessment

During three days of ritual, a 'profane' statue was transformed into an 'animated' cultic image. The event was carefully choreographed, following a script laid down in handbooks. Taking into account the various characterizations and definitions of 'technological rituals' that we touched upon, as well as Pfaffenberger's approach, the consecration qualifies as technology/technique: It was goal-oriented and conducted by a team of highly trained specialists. The senior member of the team was a widely recognized and respected authority in ritual matters, often invited to act as head priest in various contexts at similar events not only in Vārāṇasī. The remaining priests were well versed, and the team functioned harmoniously during the three days of the event. At (almost) all times, the priests made sure that both non-verbal and verbal knowledge were applied as correctly as possible. Non-verbal knowledge refers here, for example, to the setting-up of the *maṇḍalas*, the sprinkling of Ganges water during the initial purification of the ritual enclosure, the various movements in the invocation of the myriad of deities (such as the touching of the areca nuts on the diagrams with the sandalwood paste-covered tip of the right hand's ring finger), the eye-opening sequence, the various hand gestures, the kindling of the fire, the building and purification of the fire altar,

Producing deities? Ritual as technology 251

as well as the pouring of libations into the fire, all of which were performed with the utmost care. The priests assisted each other in these tasks, complementing possible lacunae and correcting flaws. Verbal knowledge includes primarily the recitation of verses and the utterance of so-called seed syllables. Whenever there was doubt about the accuracy and the clarity of the pronunciation of a word, about the coherence of a phrase, or the correct recitation of a verse, the respective passage was repeated. To the specialists, most of the sequences were clearly routine procedures, ubiquitous components of South Asian ritual constellations. They knew many of the verses well and recited them at great speed, with occasional lapses into unintelligibility. In such cases, one of the priests would disapprovingly raise his voice, returning to and reiterating the passage in question. Especially susceptible to such lapses were the rather monotonous, long lists of deity names; nearing the end of a long enumeration, and realizing he was mumbling, the head priest repeated the names he had not pronounced clearly.

As for the event's efficacy, it became manifest on various levels. The consecration was declared serially effective, and was considered integrally effective. At several stages, the head priest declared that the aim for that particular stage had been accomplished, and he announced the next sequence and its respective goal. Perhaps the most memorable of these units was the preparatory sequence intended for the expiation and purification of the sponsor. After the rhythmic regulation of his breath, he was asked to repeat the Sanskrit verse word-for-word after the head priest, which he did. The priest then recited the whole verse once again, the sponsor drank the mixture of the five cow products, and the purification was declared complete. As for the integral efficaciousness: at the end of the consecration, the statue was installed in the temple, and the main priest performed a worship ceremony with the 16 services, acknowledging the statue's new status as a fully-fledged divine image. From that day (in 1995) until the present, the 'reactivated' small Hanumān temple on Assīghāṭ in Vārāṇasī has attracted numerous devotees from the area who visit regularly and worship there.

The social dynamics that unfolded around the event deserve a much more extended treatment than can be given here. The description and analysis would have to begin with the religious history of the sponsor's family, which includes Vaiṣṇava and Śākta traditions. It would have to take into account his social status in the city (he is a member of the traditional landed aristocracy), as well as his regional and supra-regional family constellations. The consecration was a major event, and the sponsor invited numerous people from his local social network to attend. In addition to friends and relatives living in the city, invitations were sent to important members of the local community, such as the area's police chief, or the head of the largest temple in the area. In the days preceding the event, a large number of relatives arrived from the neighboring federal state of Bihar, and were put up in the sponsor's guesthouse and in adjacent buildings. Uncles, aunts, cousins, nieces and nephews populated the large house during the event, met in smaller or larger groups on the

252 *István Keul*

rooftop terrace, or in one of the many rooms, or sat on the mattresses covered with white sheets laid out around the ritual space watching and commenting on the ritual sequences performed by the religious specialists and the sponsor. In key moments, such as the evening light-waving ceremony, the circumambulation of the city, or the first extended worship of the freshly 'enlivened' deity, the numbers of people attending were larger, while during the lengthy consecration proceedings there were fewer people watching. The event had thus the characteristics of a family reunion, with an opportunity to socialize and to enjoy each other's company in a calm and relaxed, but nevertheless engaged and committed atmosphere. On the evening of the third day, additional guests joined the family and friends at a reception in the garden in front of the house, with a group of musicians playing Indian classical music. Earlier, food had been distributed to a large number of needy families in the area, as well as to beggars gathered in front of the building. These aspects, closely connected to status, hierarchy, family and kinship, agency, and participation, – along with the aforementioned classification of the consecration as a technological or technical ritual – are the basis of the attempt to reconceptualize the consecration as a 'sociotechnical event'.

Notes

1 The two meta-designs discussed in Handelman (2006) are 'modeling', exemplified by a central African initiation (*Chisungu*) and 'virtuality', a term proposed by Bruce Kapferer in the context of his analysis of Sinhalese exorcism (*Suniyama*). See also Handelman (1998).
2 A collected volume on consecration rituals in Asia is currently in preparation.
3 The others are: ritual as therapy, social control, salvation, and revitalization (Wallace 1966: 107).
4 Dowsing is a form of divination employed to find ground water ('water witching'), but used also in the search for metals, oil or other materials and substances hidden in the ground. Scapulimancy is divination performed with the help of shoulder blades.
5 Already Goody's rather cautious critique of Turner points in the same direction (Goody 1977: 27).
6 According to Frazer:

> We shall find underlying them all a solid stratum of intellectual agreement among the dull, the weak, the ignorant, and the superstitious … This universal faith, this truly Catholic creed, is a belief in the efficacy of magic … We seem to move on a thin crust which may at any moment be rent by the subterranean forces slumbering below.
>
> ([1890] 1922: 55–6)

7 See also Sørensen's (2006: 522–3) discussion of this definition.
8 "C'est ainsi que les hommes en sont venus à attribuer à des gestes, vains par eux-mêmes, des vertus créatrices. L'efficacité morale du rite, qui est réelle, a fait croire à son efficacité physique, qui est imaginaire" (Durkheim [1912] 1990: 513).
9 On the history of the question of efficacy in ritual theory, see Töbelmann (2013: 222f.).

Producing deities? Ritual as technology 253

10 According to Dücker (2004: 250), some of the connotations of 'ritual' in everyday language are: idle repetition ('leerlaufende Wiederholung'), stagnation management ('Verwaltung des Stillstands'), and lack of efficacy.
11 For the following, see also Sax (2009: 231f.).
12 "What we see as ritual, they see as technique" (Sax 2010: 4).
13 Beginning with the early Upanishads, the term *karma* is also used to denote the individuals' actions and their consequences in the cycle of rebirths and redeaths (*saṃsāra*).
14 For the discussion of Sanskrit terms equivalent to 'ritual', see Axel Michaels' contribution in Stausberg (2006: 86–90). Also in ancient Greek, terms from the semantic field of 'to act', 'to do', and 'to perform' are used in connection with rituals, such as *teleîn*, *drómena*, *órgion* (Chaniotis, cited in Stausberg 2006: 69f.).
15 On ritual and the 'placebo response', see Brody (2010).
16 See for this paragraph, Pfaffenberger (1992).
17 For a detailed description of the event, see Keul (2002).

References

Bell, C. ([1997] 2009) *Ritual Perspectives and Dimensions*. Oxford: Oxford University Press.

Brody, H. (2010) 'Ritual, Medicine, and the Placebo Response,' in W.S. Sax, J. Quack and J. Weinhold (eds) *The Problem of Ritual Efficacy*. Oxford: Oxford University Press, pp. 151–67.

Dücker, B. (2004) 'Ritus und Ritual im öffentlichen Sprachgebrauch der Gegenwart,' in D. Harth and G.J. Schenk (eds) *Ritualdynamik: Kulturübergreifende Studien zur Theorie und Geschichte rituellen Handelns*. Heidelberg: Synchron, pp. 219–57.

Durkheim, E. ([1912] 1990) *Les formes élémentaires de la vie religieuse: Le système totémique en Australie*. Paris: Quadrige/Presses Universitaires de France.

Frazer, J.G. ([1890]1922) *The Golden Bough: A Study in Magic and Religion* (abridged edn). New York: Macmillan.

Goffman, E. (1967) *Interaction Ritual: Essays on Face-to-Face Behavior*. New York: Anchor Books.

Goody, J. (1977) 'Against "Ritual": Loosely Structured Thoughts on a Loosely Defined Topic,' in S.F. Moore and B.G. Myerhoff (eds) *Secular Ritual*. Assen and Amsterdam: van Gorkum, pp. 25–35.

Handelman, D. (1998) *Models and Mirrors: Towards an Anthropology of Public Events*. Oxford: Berghahn Books.

Handelman, D. (2006) 'Conceptual Alternatives to "Ritual",' in J. Kreinath, J. Snoek, and M. Stausberg (eds) *Theorizing Rituals: Issues, Topics, Approaches, Concepts*. Leiden: Brill, pp. 37–49.

Hubert, H. and Mauss, M. (1902–3) 'Esquisse d'une théorie générale de la magie,' *L'Année Sociologique*, 7: 1–146.

Keul, I. (2002) *Hanumān, der Gott in Affengestalt: Entwicklung und Erscheinungsformen seiner Verehrung*. Berlin: de Gruyter.

Kreinath, J., Snoek, J. and Stausberg, M. (2006) 'Ritual Studies, Ritual Theory, Theorizing Rituals: An Introductory Essay,' in J. Kreinath, J. Snoek, and M. Stausberg (eds) *Theorizing Rituals: Issues, Topics, Approaches, Concepts*. Leiden: Brill, xv–xxvii.

Pfaffenberger, B. (1992) 'Social Anthropology of Technology,' *Annual Review of Anthropology*, 21: 491–516.

254 *István Keul*

Sax, W.S. (2009) *God of Justice: Ritual Healing and Social Justice in the Central Himalayas*. Oxford: Oxford University Press.

Sax, W.S. (2010) 'Ritual and the Problem of Efficacy,' in W.S. Sax, J. Quack and J. Weinhold (eds) *The Problem of Ritual Efficacy*. Oxford: Oxford University Press, pp. 3–16.

Sørensen, J.P. (2006) 'Efficacy,' in J. Kreinath, J. Snoek and M. Stausberg (eds) *Theorizing Rituals: Issues, Topics, Approaches, Concepts*. Leiden: Brill, pp. 523–31.

Stausberg, M. (2006) '"Ritual": A Lexicographic Survey of Some Related Terms from an Emic Perspective,' in J. Kreinath, J. Snoek and M. Stausberg (eds) *Theorizing Rituals: Issues, Topics, Approaches, Concepts*. Leiden: Brill, pp. 51–98.

Töbelmann, P. (2013) 'Wirksamkeit,' in C. Brosius, A. Michaels and P. Schrode (eds) *Ritual und Ritualdynamik*. Göttingen: Vandenhoek & Ruprecht, pp. 222–8.

Trist, E. (1981) *The Evolution of Socio-Technical Systems: A Conceptual Framework and an Action Research Program*. Ontario: Ontario Quality of Working Life Centre.

Turner, V. (1967) *The Forest of Symbols*. Ithaca, NY: Cornell University Press.

Wallace, A.F.C. (1966) *Religion: An Anthropological View*. New York: Random House.

Index

academia 75, 77, 153
aesthetics 233, 236, 240
agriculture 133n13, 246
ancestors 227–28, 230, 233, 235, 240–41
ambivalence 55–56, 69
anthropology 7, 28, 109, 134, 245, 253
archaeology 3, 60, 97n48, 245
artefacts 61, 111–12
astronomy 14, 26, 89–91, 138, 140; and
  life science 31; modern geography and
  11, 19–21, 94; Western 2, 16
axis mundi 3, 74, 76, 84, 86

biology 46, 60, 65, 68, 79–80, 95n2, 196;
  and theoretical physics 105; degree in
  91;
  evolutionary 51; higher standing of
  116n10
blasphemy 205, 207, 225

calendar 76, 229, 241
canonical literature 56, 74–75, 80, 126
cardiac system 128, 130
cells 40, 45–46
chemistry 60, 62, 79, 80, 95n2
chromolithographic technology 5, 157,
  161–62
circumambulation 86, 250
commemoration 116n5, 229, 234
controversy 25–27, 68
cosmology 12, 16, 20, 29, 35–36, 46;
  Buddhist 14, 27, 197; Hindu 58;
  ISKCON 3, 63; Jain 75, 91, 93,
  97n37; mythic 71; Vedic 55–56,
  60–61, 65–69
cosmos 3, 36, 71n7, 74, 86, 125, 245
creationism 3, 37, 44–45, 69; Vedic 56,
  58, 63, 65–66,
cyberspace 154, 156, 159, 169, 188, 203

Darwin 32, 36–39, 44–47, 50, 63–65,
  69, 70n3
deities 4, 103, 123, 141, 157, 228; images
  of 158, 162, 164; producing 245;
  worship of 248–49
devotion/devotional 60, 69, 73, 153,
  157–58, 168
diaspora 81, 156, 160, 163–64
dinosaurs 37–38, 41, 52
diseases 123, 126–29, 137, 140–41, 230,
  247; children's 5, 140; types of 142,
  145
disembedding 5, 156, 158–62
disillusionment 54
drugs 124–25, 130, 142, 144, 147
dynamics 172, 246, 251

elites 2, 16, 21, 27, 123, 134
embryo 45, 60, 139, 146
emotions 67, 129, 131, 193
enlightenment 54, 66–67, 191, 194, 196,
  205
empiricism 49, 80
entertainment 3, 74–75, 84–87, 93–97,
  192
epistemology 58, 67, 80, 120, 211–12
esotericism 103, 114, 120
ethics 97n50, 109, 110, 205, 207, 214–21
exorcism 122, 124, 128, 130–31, 133–34,
  252n1

Facebook 173–74, 177–82, 187, 193,
  198, 217
four noble truths 4, 110, 192
fundamentalist 155, 208–9, 222n3

geography 11–17, 24, 27, 75, 76, 171;
  modern 2, 89–92, 94
god posters 158, 162, 164, 180

256 *Index*

globes 2, 11, 16–19, 22
golden age 55, 64, 69
grammar 79, 246
guru 5, 55–59, 69, 157, 162–64, 169

harmony 32, 40, 46–47, 50, 127
herbs 140, 144–47, 148n3
Hindutva 64–66, 164
homogenization 5, 19, 156, 160–61,
    164–65, 187
hostility 41, 54, 69
hybrid 20–21, 24, 191, 199, 227, 234

identity 43, 164, 177, 188, 200, 231;
    Jain 75, 77
image consecration 2, 7, 246, 248–52
intellectuals 6, 16, 66–67, 130, 212,
    216
innovation 111, 153–54, 161, 185, 192,
    199–200
inventions 16, 22, 47, 218

kings 23, 29, 97, 131, 145
knowledge transfer 2, 20, 24

Latour, B. 2, 11–12, 22–24, 26, 29
liberal 65, 69, 70n1, 189, 208
Lopez, D. xi, 14, 28n7, 191
love 4, 35, 42–43, 110, 112, 115, 118n32;
    symbol of 234

magic 44, 55, 135, 139–41, 144, 166;
    efficacy of 247, 252n6
mainstream 60, 79, 110; Hinduism
    164–65; science 50, 65, 78
maps 11, 13, 16–19, 21–23, 27, 91, 240;
    contemporary 74, 95
mathematics 55–56, 58, 65, 79, 96n9,
    100
mediation 158–59, 170, 192, 198, 201,
    239–41
medical texts 4, 122, 125, 129
medicine 34, 125–26, 131–32, 137–38,
    140, 144–47; Hindu 65; religion and
    1, 4, 122; Western 230
military 18, 22, 54, 126, 137
missionaries 11, 14, 16–17, 19, 21, 24
modernism 67, 95, 200, 203; Buddhist
    11–13, 16–17, 20–21, 25, 27, 199;
    Islamic 208
monks 16, 64, 82, 89, 125, 236, 242; and
    missionaries 2, 18, 24–25
monolithic 55, 68
moon 12, 22, 58, 75, 89, 91, 139

nationalism 66–67, 106, 158, 163–65
natural sciences 2, 36, 57, 79, 89, 95n2,
    97n41
new media 5, 21, 171, 173, 187, 189
new religious movements 102, 105–6,
    116–17, 125, 159
Newton 2, 25–27, 46, 79

obscurantism 64, 69
omniscience 19–20, 83, 90–93
orthodoxy 92, 98, 122, 125

pathogens 126–27
performative 6, 206, 212–13, 215, 219,
    221
physics 60, 68, 79–80, 90, 95n2, 105,
    116n10; modern 56, 63, 65–66, 80,
    113; Newtonian 27; Vedic 63
physicians 123, 125–26, 130–32, 134,
    137, 148n3
pilgrimage 78, 95, 98n34, 123, 176; Jain
    sites 74, 76, 82–85, 91, 98n32
planets 2, 20–22, 28, 33, 46; Vedic
    Planetarium 55–56, 63, 69, 71n7,
    97n49
poetry 140, 180, 222n14
poison 5, 126, 131, 138, 140–46, 148n14
politics 123, 134, 166, 214, 221, 222n3
pollution 163, 230, 242n3, 244
possession 4, 122, 124, 126–29, 131, 139;
    beneficial 141; treatment of 146
postmodernism 66–67, 72, 202
preaching 20, 54, 92
printing press 5, 22, 157
prototype 111, 166
providence/providential 2, 32, 35, 50, 54
purity 135, 167, 228

radio 154–55, 165, 216
reconciliation 32, 47, 49–50
recreation 3, 6, 85, 87, 95
reformers 111, 211
religious groups 125, 155, 168, 175
renaissance 74, 215
romantic 31, 35, 46–47, 64, 106

scapulimancy 246, 252n4
scientism 42, 53, 55, 57, 104
scientization 66, 75, 77–78, 80–82, 89,
    92–95, 96n23
scriptures 25, 60, 78–84, 92–95, 96n15;
    Hebrew 51n4; Jain 3, 74, 78–79,
    83–84, 89–90, 94; Vedic 56
secularism 67, 205, 219, 222n11

semiotic triangulation vii, 172
sermon 2, 32, 34–35, 83, 92
social networks 5, 6, 169–75, 177, 179–82, 185
sociotechnical event 7, 246, 248, 250, 252
spiritualism 62, 100, 106, 120
spirituality 62–64, 71n7, 153–54, 156, 197–98, 222n11
standardization 5, 156, 158–61, 164–65
sun 16, 22, 33–34, 74, 78, 111
supernatural 34, 45, 50–51, 58, 70n1, 133
symbols 79, 134, 153, 156, 158, 247, 254

talismans 123, 130, 132n3, 236
tantra/tantric 4, 139, 142, 147
taxonomy 1, 80, 246
television 5–6, 155–56, 158, 163, 216–17, 224
tension 36, 55–56, 81, 124, 126, 207

theology 14, 36, 54, 207; natural 32, 47
therapy 58, 123, 130, 252n3
thermodynamics 37
Twitter 173–74, 181–82, 186–87, 193–94, 217

unnatural 48, 53
Upanishads 2, 32, 51n4, 51n9, 64–65, 253n13

Vedas 56–58, 64–67, 70n1, 137
venom 139, 143, 147, *see* poison
virtues 42, 195–96
vitality 34, 38, 126–27, 138

weapon 41–42, 68, 133; science as 65
worship 58, 137–38, 140–41, 157–58, 164, 247–52; of ancestors 227–28, 230–31, 233–35, 240–41; of the Jina 76, 85–86; of serpents 146; online 160–62, 165n3

eBooks
from Taylor & Francis
Helping you to choose the right eBooks for your Library

Add to your library's digital collection today with Taylor & Francis eBooks. We have over 50,000 eBooks in the Humanities, Social Sciences, Behavioural Sciences, Built Environment and Law, from leading imprints, including Routledge, Focal Press and Psychology Press.

Choose from a range of subject packages or create your own!

Benefits for you
- Free MARC records
- COUNTER-compliant usage statistics
- Flexible purchase and pricing options
- 70% approx of our eBooks are now DRM-free.

Benefits for your user
- Off-site, anytime access via Athens or referring URL
- Print or copy pages or chapters
- Full content search
- Bookmark, highlight and annotate text
- Access to thousands of pages of quality research at the click of a button.

ORDER YOUR FREE INSTITUTIONAL TRIAL TODAY

Free Trials Available

We offer free trials to qualifying academic, corporate and government customers.

eCollections
Choose from 20 different subject eCollections, including:
- Asian Studies
- Economics
- Health Studies
- Law
- Middle East Studies

eFocus
We have 16 cutting-edge interdisciplinary collections, including:
- Development Studies
- The Environment
- Islam
- Korea
- Urban Studies

For more information, pricing enquiries or to order a free trial, please contact your local sales team:

UK/Rest of World: **online.sales@tandf.co.uk**
USA/Canada/Latin America: **e-reference@taylorandfrancis.com**
East/Southeast Asia: **martin.jack@tandf.com.sg**
India: **journalsales@tandfindia.com**

www.tandfebooks.com